SCORES

SCORES!
An Anthology of New Music

**Selection and
Commentary by**
ROGER JOHNSON

SCHIRMER BOOKS
A Division of Macmillan Publishing Co., Inc.
NEW YORK

Collier Macmillan Publishers
LONDON

Schirmer Books
A Division of Macmillan Publishing Co., Inc.
866 Third Avenue, New York, N.Y. 10022

Collier Macmillan Canada, Ltd.

Library of Congress Catalog Card Number: 80–53302

Printed in the United States of America

printing number

1 2 3 4 5 6 7 8 9 10

Library of Congress Cataloging in Publication Data

Main entry under title:

Scores : an anthology of new music.

　"Recent musical compositions selected for their interest, artistic quality, and accessibility to performance ... all readily performable by a wide range of people--musicians and nonmusicians both."
　"Selected bibliography": p.
　Includes index.
　CONTENTS: Exercises, rituals, and meditations. --Music for voices.--Percussion music. [etc.]
　1. Chance compositions. 2. Vocal music. 3. Instrumental music. 4. Electronic music. I. Johnson, Roger Orville.

M1.S44　　　80-53302
ISBN 0-02-871190-4

Contents

v

371494

Preface

This book is an anthology of recent musical compositions selected for their musical interest, artistic quality, and accessibility to performance. Some of the composers represented are among the best known and most influential of our time. Others are not as widely recognized; but each is a serious artist contributing his or her own voice in a unique and personal way. Most of the pieces included can be termed "avant-garde" or "experimental," insofar as these words still have meaning. But, more important, they have been chosen from the widest possible cross-section of innovative, serious music being composed at this time, crossing over all categories, schools, and movements. If only for this reason, it is hoped that this collection will prove a unique and valuable document of the music of our time.

The most important and distinctive feature of this anthology, however, is that the pieces are all readily performable by a wide range of people—musicians and nonmusicians both—and have been collected specifically for this purpose. Most of the pieces are complete; the few excerpts consist of entire sections of easily available published works. None of the pieces were written specifically for this book; none are simplified versions of more complex ones. They are all intended for real performing stiuations, and virtually all have been presented publically, some quite extensively. A number are available in separate published editions or in recordings.

The very fact that collecting such a large body of relatively accessible, serious, and genuine music for nonprofessional performers has even been possible is notable in itself. The only comparable body of work of this sort has been collected in England.[1] The music in *Scores* reflects some of this prior work, but contains a much wider range of pieces.

However, although there is an amazing variety of music here, this book does not attempt to represent a complete and balanced view of all new music. It does recognize and reflect some very interesting and exciting changes in composition and performance which have already had a considerable impact on our culture.

Clearly, there has been a strong move away from the surface and notational complexity that characterized so much music during the 1950s and 1960s. The proverbial pendulum is always swinging, and composers are now involved with more basic pitch and rhythmic material, clearer structures, and a generally less esoteric music.

There are scores here that require no prior musical training at all in order to be performed. Others demand some understanding of musical notation or familiarity with certain instruments. Quite a few have parts which can be learned easily by nonmusicians and then performed along with a few more experienced players. There are pieces here that can be performed almost instantly, and others that, although easy to understand, require some preparation and the development of new skills and sensibilities.

The tremendous diversity of music in this anthology offers the general reader, amateur musician, or other performer (as well as the professional) an exciting insight into contemporary musical practice. It is through the actual performance of this music that one will really come to know it from within. Individuals or small groups at any level of musical experience will find many performable pieces here. A basic familiarity with musical notation will "open up" many other pieces. These scores have an obvious and special value in a wide variety of teaching situations, particularly college and adult-workshop courses in any aspect of contemporary music, composition, experimental theater, modern dance, or "intermedia." A semester or full-year course can readily be built upon this book alone, or in combination with other historical or critical sources.[2]

Teachers of voice, piano, or other instruments, as well as directors of various choral, instrumental, theater, and dance groups should find

---

[1] Both the *Experimental Music Catalogue* and the music for Young Players Series of Universal Edition contain many fine pieces of this type.

[2] Michael Nyman's *Experimental Music* and R. Murray Schafer's *Creative Music Education* (both published by Schirmer Books) are highly recommended as adjunct volumes to this one.

exciting additions to their repertory here. These scores are also very valuable for general music and introductory arts classes on the high school or college level. In fact, this book originated from a smaller collection used for just this purpose at Ramapo College. Students are often presented with music as an entirely passive listening experience, yet musicians all know how immeasurably people's understanding of music is enhanced when they become actively involved in making it themselves. However, the technical barriers to such music-making (notation and instrumental techniques, among others) encountered in so much classical music are not in any way as formidable in many of the pieces here. Through them students can have first-hand experience with basic elements of music—pitch, rhythm, register, timbre, texture, density—with its structures, and with the whole expanding sound world of our time.

This book contains a broad collection of music by living American composers (with some Canadians and British included), yet there are some important parts of the experimental music world not represented here. The wonderful music of Ives, Cowell, Varèse, and Partch falls outside the scope of this book. Fortunately, it is becoming more readily available in print and recording. A number of important living composers are not represented because their music is really performable only by highly trained musicians. Other works which would have been ideal were tied up with various publishers or otherwise unavailable for reprint.[3] New jazz, as well as related work, has not been widely included, since it too requires highly skilled performers and is often not notated in score form. While every attempt was made to contact as many composers as possible in the preparation of this anthology, there are no doubt some pieces which remain undiscovered or overlooked.

It should be noted that many of the composers included here have their performing or petty rights represented by the American Society of Composers, Authors, and Publishers (ASCAP) or by Broadcast Music Inc. (BMI).[4] In the event of a public performance or broadcast of any piece the composer and the proper licensing agent should, out of courtesy, be notified. Even though ASCAP and BMI are supposed to be able to pick up the fact on their own, many public performances and broadcasts in this county go unreported and uncredited, par-

ticularly in educational institutions, where so much new music is presented.

Finally, I should like to thank the many who have provided so much valuable assistance in the preparation of the this book. It is very much a collective product. Each composer was of considerable help in preparing his or her scores, leading me to additional material and providing very valuable advice. Music publishers, too, were extremely generous in allowing works to be reprinted, often against their usual policy. And particular thanks are extended to my wife Louise Egbert and daughter Emma for helping, encouraging, and tolerating me during this period.

R.J.
New York City

---

[3]The music of Lukas Foss, Morton Feldman, La Monte Young, David Behrman, Alcides Lanza, David Tudor, Roger Reynolds, Morton Subotnick, and Charlie Morrow, to mention a few.

[4]ASCAP, One Lincoln Plaza, New York, N.Y. 10023; BMI, 320 West 57th St., New York, N.Y. 10020.

Notes on Using This Book in Classes and Workshops

As noted in the preface, this book has originated from a need for contemporary performance material, collected for inexperienced musicians and liberal arts students. One of its most important and exciting uses will be in educational situations—in schools, colleges, workshops, performing ensembles, introductory and musicianship classes, and courses in new music and "interarts," to cite a few. There has been a growing repertory of new music by many of the most interesting contemporary composers that is fortunately suitable for educational use, even though it was not originally intended—nor has it been widely used yet—as such.

This anthology should be seen as a source book, however, not a method or textbook. The music is grouped by the medium of performance used; no chapter is dependent upon an earlier one. The chapters are meant to be approached not linearly so much as concurrently, according to the needs of a particular class or group. Learning about music through music-making is, of course, central to my own thinking and has been the primary motivation for choosing these particular pieces. There are many ways to use this book and there is music enough to interest and engage just about anyone.

It is important to emphasize the value and necessity of the warm-up, meditation, and chanting exercises and pieces (Chapter 1) in using this book. Performance requires a very special blend of relaxation, intensity, concentration, and centering or focusing of energy. Very experienced performers are so familiar with this state that they can often put themselves into it almost immediately. However, many groups and classes may encounter difficult blocks, and will want to find and explore this kind of consciousness before attempting more elaborate pieces, which often require specialized individual actions. That is the special value of Chapter 1, "Exercises, Rituals, and Meditations." These pieces aid in developing group rapport and in creating an open, expressive environment.

Each group should seek to develop its own warm-up routine based on a combination of physical, vocal, and mental exercises. Although it is placed at the beginning of Chapter 2, "Music for Voices," Kirk Nurock's "Natural Sound" material or similar exercises are a very good way to begin each class. These exercises tend to shake out a lot of tension, and with it some inhibitions and resistance. One could then proceed through Nurock's vocal exercises and on into Chapter 2, or else go back to a chant–meditation piece such as *Meditation Cycle* or *Humming* for a particular focus on the voice and the internal qualities of sound.

The rest of Chapter 1 deals with various forms of internal experience in which the piece is perceived only from within the performance itself and not through listening from outside. Members of a group who take the time to work through the whole chapter to pieces like *en-trances, In the Woods,* or *Evening Ritual* will over several sessions find themselves linked together and attuned to each other in some very meaningful ways.

It seems to me that every group or class will benefit from doing some pieces from Chapters 1, 2, and 3, regardless of its particular focus, resources, or interests. It will be found in most chapters that the pieces in the first half, roughly speaking are relatively accessible and compact. The second half of a chapter tends to have longer and more complex pieces, and usually requires more preparation. Groups of less experienced performers may well want to sample the whole book by choosing a few of the earlier pieces in each chapter, discussing many of the others, and perhaps spending some time in developing one or two of the more complex ones.

Theory or musicianship classes will also find many pieces that are ideal for developing ear-training and performance skills. Some groups may be interdisciplinary and concentrate on those works that can readily be tied in with dance or theater. In fact, Chapter 8 could easily serve as a springboard for a whole semester in music-theater–dance, starting with Eric Salzman's "Notes on Music Theater" and moving off in many directions. Other groups may have a particular combination of voices or instruments, and find a great deal of particular interest in Chapters 5 and 7. Pianists will enjoy Chapter 4, as those interested in electronics will be intrigued with Chapter 6.

Finally, I think all groups will find public performance of these or similar pieces to be a very valuable experience for both themselves and the audience, completing the compositional process by taking music to people.

The music in this book has yet another very important function in serving as a model for or stimulating new compositions. Even without the creation of new pieces, the performance of many works here involves many creative choices to be made either on the spot or after experimentation and reflection. From there it is indeed a short step to vary some of the pieces or, more interesting, create entirely new ones. Teachers or group leaders should enthusiastically encourage original composition—by "nonmusicians" as well as musicians—and perform as many of the pieces as possible. Just as performance draws a person inside a piece of music, composition engages one even more completely through the making of creative choices. Valuable as an educational tool for both composer and performer, it is also a great way to develop a group's repertory of "custom-made" pieces. After all, every group is different, and a piece written this way can take into account the special talents of individuals and a unique sense of a group. Most of the pieces in this book came about originally in response to particular performers or performing situations. These pieces should be worked on, refined, and if possible fulfilled in a public performance.

Obviously, this book presents only a very small sample of the new music available; in this collection I have specifically sought out that that is flexible and more general in application. Groups with more experience or specialized interests may wish to seek out additional material. Publishers are becoming increasingly involved with new music, and the work of at least the better-known composers is quite readily available (see publisher's listing, pp. 343-46). Records are valuable for any group, and a few companies have been devoted to new music (CRI, Opus One, Nonesuch, Mainstream, etc.). A number of smaller labels and private records are available through New Music Distribution Service. The composer biographies (pp. 320 ff.) list recordings of the music of composers in this book. Published and recorded music is of course only a small sample of that which is composed, and with most composer biographies I have given an address through which he or she can be contacted for additional scores, tapes, advice, and information.

Teachers would be well advised to seek out composers whose work they find attractive and engage them to give workshops and performances, or even perhaps write a piece on commission. A very large percentage of these composers are also active in performing their own and other new music, and many are experienced in teaching or workshop seminars. These activities need not be limited to universities; for example, the Ford Foundation's Contemporary Music Project was an extensive program to sponsor composers in the grade and high schools. (R. Murray Schafer's *Creative Music Education*[1] explores his experiences with work of this sort.) The presence of composers can be very catalytic, a fact recognized by many larger universities in their active series of concerts, performances, and lectures. For high schools and small colleges such a program is quite feasible to produce and can be of immense value. This book, then, can also serve as a resource catalogue for those interested in taking interesting and exciting new music beyond the classroom and into the public forum.

[1]New York: Schirmer Books, 1976. His book is highly recommended for anyone involved in music teaching on any level.

Introduction

Much has been written on the diverse and innovative nature of contemporary music. Even a casual glance at the pieces in this collection will reveal an appearance which is strikingly different from traditional, and even early twentieth-century, musical scores. Many of the pieces are simply verbal descriptions or "scripts" for performance rather than notations of the sound itself. Other scores use unusual graphic, musical, or combined notations suited to the particular need of the composer. It will be further noted on closer examination that a majority of the pieces involve some form of indeterminacy, that is, some aspects of the piece have been left to be created by the performers according to certain guidelines, either through prior plan or improvisation. Of course, traditional scores contain such indeterminate elements as dynamics, articulation, tempo, phrasing,and balance which performers have always provided. And improvisation itself has had a long history in music, being considered a particularly high art. C.P.E. Bach, in his obituary to his father, said "How strange, how new, how expressive, how beautiful were his ideas in improvising."[1]

It is an important and distinctive characteristic of a large body of new music that composers leave a wider range of choices up to the performers than ever before, while still providing a basic framework for making them. There are modern scores in which certain important musical details or procedures are given without a fixed linear arrangement or form. Conversely, there are those in which the overall structural design is determined but the actual material is left to the performers' discretion. In some cases the performers relate very intimately to each other and expand or embellish each other's ideas. In others they occupy different, sometimes nonintersecting "musical space" in which they purposely try to avoid obvious cross-influence. And then there are the many combinations of these and other types. Contemporary composers are always exploring different blends of structure and spontaneity in their music.

[1]Hans T. David and Arthur Mendel, *The Bach Reader* (New York: W.W. Norton, 1945), p.223.

There has been considerable misunderstanding with regarding to indeterminacy. Some people feel that composers are in this way abdicating important responsibility or turning over their role to chance. Performers have sometimes interpreted such scores as granting license to play anything they wish, and often have not taken them seriously. It is important to realize that these pieces represent a special sort of creative dialogue between composer and performer in which the two collaborate and share their skills, ideas, and personalities to create a kind of music possible only through this means. Performers, then, should see themselves as co-creators and perform with this attitude in mind. As with any skill, creative improvisation takes time to develop, and performers—both musicians and nonmusicians—must be willing to devote themselves to it in a very open frame of mind.

Other interesting characteristics of new music are reflected herein as well. Many of the composers are involved in seeking new sounds and generally expanding the sound vocabulary of music. Some work with familiar yet normally unnoticed sounds. There is also a growing interest in the creation of new environments for musical performance and in exploring sound in and of new and different spaces. Various meditative and spiritual practices and expanded states of consciousness are explored through sound and sound making. At the same time, traditional tonal elements and compositional techniques are being reexamined and used in some interesting new ways. A number of composers are involved with gradually unfolding compositional processes, patterns, and phase relationships. Overall, influences from the other arts, from the tremendous social and political changes, the whole expanding technology of our time, and from the arts and ideas of other cultures have had a profound effect on music.

These changes in the musical language and music's role in our culture did not happen overnight, of course. The important mainstream composers of the early twentieth century—Debussy, Stravinsky, Schoenberg, Bartók and many more—reflected the breakdown of the older order in music, specifically in the area of tonality, forging the most important elements of the newly emerging musical vocabulary. However, these composers were still very connected to the nineteenth-century tradition, and much of their work is now clearly seen as an extension of that tradition. The more experimental wing of the arts also put down its roots at this time. The Futurists and Dadaists, Busoni, Duchamp, Satie, and others are particularly interesting to us now in the ways in which they broke more dramatically from tradition, drawing upon many other art forms and materials. In this country the music of such major "experimental" figures as Charles Ives, Henry Cowell, Edgard Varèse, Harry Partch, and others is of great importance. It is still being assimilated into the language. One is constantly struck by the sheer power of their originality, particularly when heard in the context of the time in America. Later, the work of John Cage was clearly an important bridge between this earlier experimental tradition and the present generation of composers and other artists from which most of the music collected here has been drawn.

From the early 1950s on, extending well into the 1960s, there was a strong split in the music world. On the one hand were those that took the path coming from Schoenberg and, particularly, Webern. This group, sometimes referred to as the "avant-garde,"[3] brought an increasingly high degree of order and rationality to their music. They sought to create balance and consistent, predictable structure through extending the twelve-tone system to the ordering of all parameters of sound. For them notation became more and more specific, and required ever greater skill and technical refinement from the performer. These structures and systems were not often apparent to the unsophisticated listener (nor were they at times to any listener), so that some of the music tended to sound rather arbitrary and esoteric. After Webern the leading figures in this movement were Oliver Messiaen, Karlheinz Stockhausen, and Pierre Boulez in Europe, and Milton Babbitt, Elliot Carter, Charles Wuorinen, and others in this country.

At the same time there was an alternative tradition which came from the previously mentioned Dadaists and the work of Ives, Cowell, Satie, and others. It became involved with indeterminacy, the

extension of "musical" sound, and open form. These composers, sometimes refered to as "experimental," sought to avoid too much order; they found the elements, events, and chance intersections created spontaneously in performance more vital and exciting than those that could be planned. For them notation became less specific—particularly with regard to pitch—and tended toward graphic and verbal descriptions of the performance itself. Where the "avant-garde" group sought to notate the actual, objective sounds, the "experimentalists" favored descriptions of the performers' actions, materials and attitudes. At the present time, aside from Cage (still a leading figure), there are Morton Feldman, Earle Brown, Christian Wolff, La Monte Young, and Terry Riley and the "Fluxus," "Once," and "Sonic Arts" groups in this country and the "Scratch Orchestra" in England, among many others. It is interesting to note that while the "avant-garde" had largely European roots, the "experimental" movement has been more predominantly American.

It is always convenient to speak of clear dualities or opposite poles—"avant-garde" versus "experimental," or "control" versus "indeterminacy"—and in the more extreme instances this is valid. There is, however, much more involved in understanding the music of the recent past and, certainly, the present. It is better to think of these two directions as tendencies; a composer or a particular piece may favor one or the other or mix both in some way. Such well-known composers as Luciano Berio, Karlheinz Stockhausen, Lukas Foss, and George Crumb achieve much of their vitality from a mixture of chance, improvisational elements within a rather determinate structure. To be sure, this group is usually fairly explicit with the pitch, rhythmic, and timbral elements used in improvisation, and does achieve a relatively consistent sound form one performance to another. Others long associated with the experimental wing—Feldman and Brown in particular—are also now involved with a mixture of very controlled and relatively free elements; their recent music seems to be leaning distinctly toward the former tendency. The younger "modular" composers—Steve Reich, Terry Riley, and Philip Glass being the best known—who were influenced by John Cage, La Monte Young and others, are also very interested on one level in controlled processes and determinate pitch and rhythmic material. Other composers, like Iannis Xenakis, stand somewhat outside this duality—in his case through a very systematic use of random elements.

There are many other ways in which such a duality is becoming of less and less importance. Electronic music, particularly on tape, is a special case since here one is dealing very directly with sound and not

[3]Terminology for the various forms of new music is still very inadequate. "Avant-garde" has come to be used as a very general term to refer to a particular approach to, or aesthetic of, new music. "Serial" is also used to refer specifically to that music directly connected to the extension of the twelve-tone system to other elements of music. The distinction between "avant-garde" and "experimental" (see below) is far from clear either, and it becomes even more foggy as one moves away from the extremes.

performance. Many feel that all music is no more or less than its sound, and that questions of compositional process separate from this sound are meaningless. The kind of liberation of sound that Busoni, Ives, Varèse, or Partch envisioned has become an inspiration to an ever-growing number of composers. There are those who, going even further, have been moving away from the ego-centered, composed music and formality of a traditional concert presentation. For them, function—social, political, personal, curative, or spiritual—is more important than any specific sound structure. Obviously the present time is a very rich, diverse, and fluid one in music and the other arts, as it is in the whole of society. This collection is a sample of some of that diversity and an invitation to explore and share in the act of making a new kind of music.

1 Exercises, Rituals, and Meditations

We will begin with some very special and exciting pieces which explore a particularly intimate, direct, and generative form of music-making. Most are of an internal, meditative quality and use sound and sound making to relax the body, open the senses, and focus the mind. As such, they are not intended for performance in front of an audience; rather they are for individuals and small or large groups in which everyone is an equal participant. Daniel Goode's short commentary which appears below, "Music as Fusion of Mind and Body," together with the introducation to Pauline Oliveros's *Sonic Meditations*, gives many valuable specifics about the methods, purposes, and value of such activities.

In fact, there could be no better introduction to this entire book than *Sonic Meditations,* with its particularly far-ranging exploration of the internal qualities of sound. The pieces which follow it deal with specific kinds of sound or soundmaking. Carole Weber's *Meditation Cycle*, Annea Lockwood's *Humming*, and Bonnie Barnett's △ *Piece,* are focused on breathing and vocal resonance through chanting. Michael Parson's *Mindfulness of Breathing* extends this basic form of chanting to a song with text, the content of which is very germane to the other pieces in this chapter. Daniel Goode's *A Series of 4 Sound Events* introduces various kinds of movement with sound, as well as specific ways for participants to relate to each other and to the environment. The next piece, William Hellermann's *en-trances,* is a progressive series of group participation pieces leading to an extraordinary kind of sonic and personal interaction. David Jones's *Alpha/Beta* explores sound as an abstract language used to express and communicate internal images and perceptions; while there is mention of an audience here, this piece is closer in spirit to the others in this chapter. Richard Hayman's *Arc of Continuous Sound* and Alvin Lucier's *Chambers* deal with specific kinds of sound, the former with a special kind of sound and continuity and the latter with a more diverse type of sonic environment. Kenneth Maue's *In the Woods* moves into an outdoor environment and uses sound for signaling and communication. His *Evening Ritual* follows with a combination of chanting and listening, with one final tone on the gong.

Groups, classes, workshops, and individuals will find that doing these chanting and meditation pieces together with some of the exercises described in "Natural Sound" (Chapter 2) will be invaluable in developing the relaxation, sensitivity to sound, and rapport with oneself and others needed for most of the pieces in this book. An opening warm-up routine developed from this material is therefore highly recommended. (Of course, these pieces are fascinating in themselves, and one may well come back to them often.)

There are pieces in other chapters closely related to these. Clearly, Chapter 2, "Music for Voices," is very directly linked, since it extends and develops vocal sound. Other pieces of interest in this context are:

Chap. 5: *Morning Music II* (Brian Taylor)
Chap. 6: *From the River Archive* (Annea Lockwood)
            Spirit Catchers (Annea Lockwood)
            Gentle Fire and *I Am Sitting in a Room* (Alvin Lucier)
Chap. 7: *Time Goes By* (Karl H. Berger)
            Towards the Capacity of a Room (David Jones)
Chap. 8: *North American Eclipse* (Daniel Lentz)
            Aeolian Partitions (Pauline Oliveros)

Music As Fusion of Mind and Body by Daniel Goode

No matter how many times we are shown or have proved to us that mind and body are really a unity of some kind, there is a persistant intuition and experience of a separation. Though we have found that sex, meditation, drugs, athletics, dance, and communal activities (such as ritual and agriculture) give us moments of that unity—or at least an avenue there—everyday life seems to reinforce the separation again: Either mental life goes on without the body (as in offices) or physical life is engaged in mindlessly. Ultimately it may take religion or "primitive" community or an earth-wide crisis to make a permanent change (assuming for the moment that such a change is desirable).

But there is at least one other place where we may try to look for the unity of mind and body: music. And by music here, I mean the aesthetically radical music that deals exactly with mind and body at the same time because of involvement in basic life processes. Chanting and whilring come most easily to mind. These two activities are done by children spontaneously, by the way, not only by sages and avant-garde artists. Harder to name are the things that get to the root of hearing, seeing, responding to inner and outer events. Hardest is describing the sensations or changes of consciousness that such activities bring about under favorable circumstances. Finally, *describing* by itself will not get us very far. Doing these processes and the pieces dealing with them, then inventing and composing new ones, then personal and group observations to refine the sensibility—this is the only path, and a difficult one. But this music and its aims are as demanding as the traditional music of Western Civilization. Especially hard now, because, I believe, we are forging a new tradition of performed music.

At the same time we are all recipients of the wave of musics from other cultures including the depths of our own found in the indigenous folk musics of Europe and America. This wave has had a profound effect on us. Many of us have now become conscious that one strand of avant-garde music has for several years been trying to re-invent fundamental psycho-musical processes that have been part of some cultures for centuries, even millenia. Never mind that here, though it had to be mentioned. My purpose is to focus on a small part of that avant-garde strand: CHANTING, as a way to mind/body unity, to altered states of consciousness (individual or group). Many people have been involved here. Among musicians with whom I have worked in various kinds of chanting I should mention Pauline Oliveros, Charlie Morrow, and Philip Corner. I have experienced other approaches among musicians as well as dancers, theater people, and those who practice the meditative arts. One piece with which I have been working is the △*Piece* of Bonnie Barnett. It is a good sample of how contemporary musicians are working with ancient and modern ideas, weaving a concern for ritual together with psycho-acoustics and a performed music which breaks down the absolute boundary between professional and non-professional musician . . . .

It should be noted that doing a piece like this is not a short-term project. One does not really know what to expect from it after one or two times through. It is partly that one's perceptions must develop in order to notice the results of the performed processes. Responses must be sifted and savored, compared with other's. Let me mention four phenomena that have come out of my experience with this piece—as guideposts only, perhaps not required necessarily for the piece to work. (1) *Difference tones:* These are extra tones that result from the difference in frequency between two other tones. They occur in somewhat unpredictable acoustic circumstances. A certain level of intensity is usually required to bring them out and they are usually not too far apart in pitch. (2) *Beat tones:* Regular vibrations that occur between two tones that are further apart than a unison and closer than a half-step. (3) *Multi-phonics:* The vocal cords split into two sets of vibrations, usually a high tone and a low tone. Often the group resonances cause or reinforce this phenomenon. (4) *Vowel changes* and other changes in the shape of the mouth. It is best that these phenomena occur spontaneously, not from arduous over-planning. I have chosen the easiest phenomena to analyze. Something should be said about the effect of the physical closeness of the three people doing the piece, the transfer of energy among them, the difference between three people of the same sex and a mixed group doing the piece.

Finally, involvement in music of this kind rests on an unspoken fact: To do these processes is, must be, innately pleasurable to the whole organism. There is no shirking this fact. The new music of participation is pleasurable, as is good dancing, sex, athletics, outdoor work. Our culture has almost succeeded in reducing the pleasure of making music to the obligatory singing of a few Christmas carols, usually for the sake of children. As information pours in from other cultures, we begin to see what we have given up.

Sonic Meditation I – XII   Pauline Oliveros

INTRODUCTION I

Sonic Meditations are intended for group work over a long period of time with regular meetings. No special skills are necessary. Any persons who are willing to commit themselves can participate. The Ensemble to whom these meditations are dedicated has found that non-verbal meetings intensify the results of these meditations and help provide an atmosphere which is conducive to such activity. With continuous work some of the following becomes possible with Sonic Meditations: Heightened states of awareness or expanded consciousness, changes in physiology and psychology from known and unknown tensions to relaxations which gradually become permanent. These changes may represent a tuning of mind and body. The group may develop positive energy which can influence others who are less experienced. Members of the Group may achieve greater awareness and sensitivity to each other. Music is a welcome by-product of this activity.

INTRODUCTION II

Pauline Oliveros has abandoned composition/performance practice as it is usually established today for Sonic Explorations which include everyone who wants to participate. She attempts to erase the subject/object or performer/audience relationship by returning to ancient forms which preclude spectators. She is interested in communication among all forms of life, through Sonic Energy. She is especially interested in the healing power of Sonic Energy and its transmission within groups.

All societies admit the power of music or sound. Attempts to control what is heard in the community are universal. For instance, music in the church has always been limited to particular forms and styles in accordance with the decrees of the Church Fathers. Music in the courts has been controlled through the tastes of patrons. Today Muzak is used to increase or stimulate consumption in merchandising establishments. Sonic Meditations are an attempt to return the control of sound to the indidivual alone, and within groups especially for humanitarian purposes; specifically healing.

Each Sonic Meditation is a special procedure for the following:
1. Actually making sounds
2. Actively imagining sounds
3. Listening to present sounds
4. Remembering sounds

Because of the special procedures involved, most all of the meditations are available to anyone who wishes to participate regardless, or in spite, of musical training. All that is required is a *willing commitment to the given conditions.*

Sound making during the meditations is primarily vocal, sometimes hand clapping or other body sounds, sometimes using sound producing objects and instruments.

Sound imagining is encouraged through the use of various questions designed to trigger auditory fantasy. Individuals are then asked to share what was heard inwardly, with members of the group using any means to describe the experience. Conditions given for listening to present sounds are intended to expand awareness of the auditory environment, both within and without of the individual.

Auditory memory is also encouraged by trigger questions with subsequent sharing of these memories in the group. Some of the meditations involve body movement as well. The term meditation is used simply to mean dwelling with or upon an idea, an object, or lack of object without distraction, or divided attention.

Healing can occur in relation to the above activities when 1) individuals feel the common bond with others through a shared experience. 2) when one's inner experience is made manifest and accepted by others. 3) when one is aware of and in tune with one's surroundings. 4) when one's memories, or values, are integrated with the present and understood by others.

In process a kind of music occurs naturally. Its beauty is not through intention, but is intrinsically the effectiveness of its healing power. This may be felt by the group, and the music relates to the people who make it through participation and sharing, as a stream or river whose waters offer refreshment and cleansing to those who find it.

—I—

Teach Yourself to Fly

Any number of persons sit in a circle facing the center. Illuminate the space with dim blue light. Begin by simply observing your own breathing. Always be an observer. Gradually allow your breathing to become audible. Then gradually introduce your voice. Allow your vocal cords to vibrate in any mode which occurs naturally. Allow the intensity to increase very slowly. Continue as long as possible naturally, and until all others are quiet, always observing your own breath cycle. Variation: Translate voice to an instrument.

—II—

Search for a natural or artificial canyon, forest or deserted municipal quad. Perform *Teach Yourself to Fly* in this space.

—III—

Pacific Tell

Find your place in a darkened indoor space or a deserted out-of-doors area. Mentally form a sound image. Assume that the magnitude of your concentration on, or the vividness of this sound image will cause one or more of the group to receive this sound image by telepathic transmission. Visualize the person to whom you are sending. Rest after your attempted telepathic transmission by becoming mentally blank. When or if a sound image different from your own forms in your mind, assume that you are receiving from some one else, then make that sound image audible. Rest again by becoming mentally blank or return to your own mental sound image. Continue as long as possible or until all others are quiet.

Telepathic Improvisation

To the musicians with varied or like instruments:
Tuning—each musician in turn sits or stands in front of the audience for a few minutes. The audience is asked to observe the musician carefully and try to imagine the sounds of his or her instrument. The audience is instructed to close eyes and attempt to visualize the musician, then send a sound to the musician by hearing it mentally. The musician waits until he or she receives an impression of a sound mentally, then he or she produces the sound. Members of the audience who have successfully "hit the target" raise their hands as feedback to the musician.

After the tuning exercise the musicians distribute themselves throughout the space among the audience members and utilize the following instructions:

> Play only long sustained tones
> Play only when you are actually hearing a pitch, or pitches, mentally
> Assume you are either sending or receiving

If you are sending, try to visualize the person to whom you are sending. If you are receiving, listen for the sound and visualize the sender. The quality and dynamics of the tones you play may be influenced by your feelings, emotional or body senations, or even impressions of colors, which might come from the audience members. Continue until it seems "time" to stop.

To the observers: Try mentally to influence the musicians by wishing for one or more of the following elements: (the musicians are instructed to play only long sustained tones)

A. Focus mentally on a specific pitch. If you are sending, visualize the musician to whom you are sending. If you are receiving, listen for the sound which matches yours. Also visualize the musician.
B. Focus mentally on stopping or starting a sound at a particular time.
C. Focus mentally on loudness or softness of tone production.
D. Focus mentally on the quality of the tone.
E. Focus mentally on an emotional character for the tone.

This meditation is best done in very low illumination, or with eyes closed.

—IV—

Divide into two or more groups. Each group must have a tape recorder and be sound isolated from the other groups. The distance might be small or great, i.e., thousands of miles or light years. Each group then perfroms *Pacific Tell* or *Telepathic Improvisation*, attempting inter group or interstellar telepathic tranmission. A specific time period may be pre-arranged. Each group tape records its own sounds during the telepathic transmission period for later comparison.

Variation: Instead of working in groups each participant works as an isolated soloist.

—V—

Native

Take a walk at night. Walk so silently that the bottoms of your feet become ears.

—VI—

Sonic Rorschach

With a white or random noise generator, flood a darkened room with white noise for thirty minutes or much longer. The band width of the white noise should be as broad as the limits of the audio range. A pre-recorded tape or a mechanical source such as an air compressor may be substituted for the generator, if necessary or desired. All participants should be comfortably seated or lying down for the duration of the meditation. Half way through, introduce one brilliant flash of light or one loud, short pulse. The high intensity flash source could be a photo lamp flash or one pulse of a strobe light. If a sound pulse is substituted for the light flash, it must necessarily be higher amplitude than the white noise.

Variations: a) Find a natural source of white noise such as a waterfall of the ocean and go there for the meditation.
b) If the white noise generator if flat, equalize until the source is apparently flat for the human ear.
c) Do this meditation with a different band width represented in subsequent meditations such as one octave at 5k ro 10khz.

Have you ever heard the sound of an iceberg melting?

Begin this meditation with the greeting meditation (IX). At the designated time for all persons to be present, begin an eight to fifteen minute imperceptible dimming of the house lights down to as dark as possible. When the lights are halfway down begin the flood of white noise at the threshold of audibility. Slowly make an imperceptible crescendo to a pre-determined sound level, safe for human ears. Approximately twenty minutes later introduce one brilliant light flash. After an hour from the beginning has passed, begin projections on the walls of colorful mandalas, patterns resembling the aurora borealis, or simply colors of the spectrum. The light intensity of these projections should be no greater than the threshold of visibility or just noticeable. These may continue for approximately thirty minutes. Thirty minutes before the white noise ends the space should be illuminated by white light slowly over about eight minutes from the threshold of visibility to as brilliant as possible. The brilliance must exceed normal house lighting and approach the intensity of daylight. The end of the light and sound should be sudden and synchronous. Darkness and silence should be maintained for ten minutes or more, then illuminate the space with dim blue light for continued meditation in silence and finally exit of the participants. The duration of this meditation is approximately two to four hours or more. All adjustments of light and sound intensity should be pre-set and preferably voltage controlled in order that all present may participate in the meditation, and that activities extraneous to meditation may be avoided. Participants must be comfortable, either sitting or lying down.

Variation: If multiple speakers are used for the production of white noise, one or two persons per speaker could perform meditation movements such as tai chi in front of the speakers at a distance of two to four feet thus creating sound shadows. The sound shadows could gradually be complemented by visible shadows activated by just noticeable light sources. The duration of this part of the meditation could be approximately thirty to forty minutes and succeed or overlap the just noticebale projected images.

–VII–

Removing the Demon or Getting Your Rocks Off

Sit in a circle with persons facing in and out alternately. If the number in the group is odd, seat the left over person in the center. Each person except the center person has a pair of resonant rocks. Begin the meditation by establishing mentally a tempo as slow as possible. Each person begins independently to strike the rocks together full force maintaining the imagined tempo. When enough energy is present, shout a pre-meditated word. Once selected, the word remains the same. The shout is free of the established tempo, and may occur one or more times during the meditation. The center person is without rocks and selects a word, phrase or sentence to say or intone repeatedly either silently or audibly for the duration of the meditation.

Variations: a) Persons without rocks may surround the circle and follow the same instructions as the center person, independently.

b) Persons may repeat mentally, or actually, one body movement as slowly as possible. One body movement may be simple or very complicated as long as it is continuous and can be repeated exactly as a cycle. Kinetic participants could include the shout or the repeated word, phrase or sentence.

c) Do this meditation in an outdoor environment. Move slowly away from the circle. Move anywhere in the environment but keep in audible contact with at least one other person. Gradually return to the beginning circle.

–VIII–

Environmental Dialogue

Each person finds a place to be, either near to or distant from the others, either indoors or out-of-doors. Begin the meditation by observing your own breathing. As you become aware of sounds fron the environment, gradually begin to reinforce the pitch of the sound source. Reinforce either vocally, mentally or with an instrument. If you lose touch with the source, wait quietly for another. Reinforce means to strengthen or sustain. If the pitch of the sound source is out of your range, then reinforce it mentally.

Environmental Dialogue for the
New Hampshire Festival Orchestra
To Mary and Tom Nee

On Lake Winnepausaukee at sunup or sundown, players of the orchestra are dispersed heterogeneously in small groups in boats all over the lake. Players begin by observing your own breathing. As you become aware of sounds in the environment, gradually begin to reinforce the pitch of the sound source or its resonance. If your become louder than the source, diminuendo until you can hear it again. If the source disappears listen quietly for another. If the source is intermittant your pitch reinforcement may be continuous until the source stops. Aural awareness of the source is necessary at all times even though your reinforcement may be momentarily louder. Reinforcement is distinctly different than imitation. Only strengthen or sustain pitch. Allow the boats to drift unless guidance past obstacles or away from shore becomes necessary.

The Flaming Indian
For Gerald Shapiro and Margot Blum

Tape record a selected environment alone or with a group. Place the microphone carefully in one location. Do the environmental dialogue mentally while you are recording. Reinforce everything your hear mentally. When the meditation is complete, make a translation of the environmental dialogue in the following way: Reinforce the pitches of the recorded sounds with vocal, instrumental, electronic or a combination of these sources. The resulting translation may exist in one or more channels as the translated sounds only or a combination of the translation and original dialogue. A new dialogue is then performed in the same or a different environment with the recorded translation and a soloist or a group, either vocal, instrumental or electronic or any combination. The live dialogue should include the sound of the live environment as well as the recorded translation.

—IX—

The Greeting

Informed persons should begin the greeting at least half-an-hour or more before a scheduled meeting or program.

After you are seated and comfortable, allow a tone to come into mind. Keep returning your attention to this same tone. Everytime a person or persons enter this space, greet them by singing the tone, as you were greeted when you entered this space. Continue this meditation until all are present.

—X—

Sit in a circle with your eyes closed. Begin by observing your own breathing. Gradually form a mental image of one person who is sitting in the circle. Sing a long tone to that person. Then sing the pitch that person is singing. Change your mental image to another person and repeat until your have contacted every person in the circle one or more times.

—XI—

Bowl Gong

Sit in a circle with a Japanese bowl gong in the center. One person, when ready to begin, hands the striker to someone else in the circle. That person strikes the gong. Each person maintains the pitch mentally for as long as possible. If the image is lost, then the person who has lost it, hands the striker to someone else in the circle. This person again activates the gong in order to renew the mental pitch image. Continue as long as possible.

—XII—

One Word

Choose one word. Dwell silently on this word. When you are ready, explore every sound in this work extremely slowly, repeatedly. Gradually, imperceptibly bring the word up to normal speed, then continue until you are repeating the word as fast as possible. Continue at top speed until "it stops."

Meditation Cycle

Carole Weber

This is for everyone to do—you get into yourself and into community with others

The cycle is made up of four elements plus drone

The drone creates an environment which runs 4 hours

Each element is a meditation and is also a preparation for the next

Feel free to get into any or all of the elements of the cycle

First element—getting into the body (a physical exercise)

Purpose: to begin focusing into yourself

Focus your attention on a body part—a hand, knee, foot, whatever

Let that part lead you, pull you into space until you feel yourself stretching

You feel a line of heat, along that stretch. You are warming up the body

When you've stretched as far as you can, slowly transfer your attention to another

part and stretch with that. Move slowly and continuously

If your mind wanders and you discover it has

Bring it back

This is a form of discipline

When you feel you're warmed up, come to sitting—

To begin the second element

Second element—getting into the breath

Focus your attention on your breath

You can put your hands on your back right above your hips and feel air—filling

up, emptying out

Breathing in, breathing out

Bigger, smaller. A cycle, continuous

Image: the earth breathes, it is breathing you in and out

If it moves you to rock back and forth, or side to side, do

Third element—getting into chanting

If your breath wants to focus to the point where it becomes sound: allow it

to happen; you can make a decision to chant

Take time to find each area of vibration sensation

You can move the notes of sounds around until you feel vibration in that area

Feel *o* vibrating in the gut

Feel *oo* vibrating in the solar plexis

Feel *ah* vibrating in the area of the heart

Feel *eh* vibrating in the throat

Feel *ee* vibrating in the area of the third eye

Feel *mm* or *om* vibrating the top of the head

These are nerve centers (*chakras*)

Move the vibration sensation up and down the center line of the body from the gut to the top of the head

You can chant the vowels *a e i o u* and *om*

Om mani padme hom   Alleluya

Fourth element—focusing into an instrument

If you have a sustaining sound instrument or continuous pulsed instrument and now wish to play to the drone or to the activity around you—do

Let everything take its own time

Some notes on the *Meditation Cycle:*

The meditation cycle was compiled out of experiences in California 1970–71 with my first spiritual teacher, Nydfu, and my dance therapist, Joan Englander. Since then it developed and has out of synthesis evolved to a sort of completion of three essential forms: the physical, to bring your focus out of the environment into the body; breathing, to focus from the body into its center through the breath; and chanting, to focus the breath along a center line in vibration and send it out.

It has turned out to be a very beautiful way to move people toward making music. The chanting is always incredible. Has its own character and structure apropos the moment and always brings itself to its own close.

The meditation cycle has been done many times as a four-hour event. The text is put on large posters and hung on the wall. In one event, slides were projected, changing moods with the course of the evening. In another, we used stage lights with gels to illuminate the space, dimming and brightening sunsets and sunrises. It has been done by a group of seven musicians in a concert and done in workshops and teaching sessions.

Humming

Annea Lockwood

Sit in the most comfortable and relaxed position you can find. Close your eyes and let your breathing settle into long, slow cycles. Start humming whenever you wish on the pitch most comfortable for you. Take deep breaths and sustain each note as long as you can with ease, no strain. If the pitch of your note drifts, let it.

Sink into the sound totally let it use your body as a resonator, as a channel for the sound's vibrations and send the sound steadily and strongly out from yourself.

From time to time the whole sound may fade, like a communal breath being taken, and then will begin again naturally.

The humming will end of its own accord. The ending should not be pre-arranged, nor the duration of the experience.

△ Piece
for Kenneth and Pauline

Bonnie Mara Barnett

Three people sit in a △. Locate a comfortable pitch whereby each person can produce a strong, resonant tone.

Focus clearly on the point that is equidistant in the center of the △.   Each one should see that point and reach out and articulate that point with his/her hand.

First send your breath to that point. Then direct pitches toward it. At first all three should send the same pitch (the one determined just after being seated). Movement away from this unison is possible. Sense when to breathe so that the sound is seamless.

The process is one of getting centered, finding your own resonance, and listening.

Through this intense attention directed toward the energy inter-change of the three frequencies at the center of the △ a whole microscopic universe of sonic transformation becomes revealed.

Mindfulness of Breathing

Drone: Michael Parsons

To be sung throughout (wordless) by a few singers beginning before the text and continuing until all have finished the text. Drone singers space their in-breaths so that the sound is continuous.

' means breath in (once only).
Each breath c.15" (10" or so singing, 5" to breathe in.)
Syllables within a breath freely spaced.
Sit in a semicircle. Singers begin one by one, each starting as the previous singer is in the middle of his first breath, after that going through the text at his own rate. (Suggested number of singers: 6 for the text, 4 for the drone).

Text taken from *Visuddhimagga* by Buddhaghosa (interpretations of and commentaries on the teachings of the Buddha, written in Ceylon in the 5th century AD).

A Series of Four Sound Events

Daniel Goode

First Meeting

A preliminary to the 4 events—talk, informal, getting to know one another. My expectations from these events. Hand out instructions for 1st event, "wordless walk." Discussion.

I. Wordless Walk

(1) We collect (wordlessly) on _____ (date) at _____ (time) in _____ (room).
(2) When all are present, we leave in random groups and clusters and walk around campus, now and then stopping, sitting, looking, listening, thinking, feeling, either in groups or alone, without uttering a word or a word-gesture (gesture meant as a substitute for words, e.g.: shaking of head, beckoning, etc.) Some may feel uncomfortable if they cannot respond to questions or comments: one could then carry a card to flash with something on it like "I am on a wordless walk."
(3) At the end of an hour we return to the room which we left and begin to improvise in any manner we choose (e.g. voice, body, objects, instruments, silence, etc.). When each person feels finished, he or she may leave—still without a word.
(4) (optional) Each person writes a short journal entry about his or her experience. These are read at the next meeting, which has already been established in advance.

II. Circles and Sounds

Exercise, meditations, improvisations generated by *Orbits*, a piece for sounds and moving bodies by Daniel Goode.

(1) Walking in circle, accelerating, ritarding; breathing rhythms co-ordinated. Singing one note. Singing two notes, one for speeding up the walk, one for slowing down.
(2) Turning on one's axis:
    during one breath
    during one sound (non-verbal)
    during one word
(3) Turning on floor:finger rotation, elbow and arm; torso, neck & head
    during one breath
    during one sound
    during one word
(4) Duos of vocal or instrumental (acoustic) sound. Eyes closed, each person chooses one note and a regular tempo of their own.
(5) Combining of vocal duets with walking, so that the duet triggers events among the walkers

III. Sound Maps of the Environment

We become dispassionate observers of the aural environment in which we live. For example:

1. One place at various dicrete times of the day or night
2. Large areas covered by the same person or several persons during a specified time length.
3. A sequential plan such as:

times and places A	B	C	D
(9:02)	(9:03)	(9:04)	(9:05)

4. A tape recorder is used simultaneously with any of the above. Comparisions are made between the recorded and remembered environment.
5. Controlled environments: after one place is known fairly well, new sound elements are introduced, and the changes in the whole aural environment are observed.

Notations systems are devised before, during, after any of these; a continuing process of conceptualizing the results is encouraged. At the same time some observation sessions are exempt from this and are for the sheer pleasure for meditation on environmental sound.

IV. Eye Locks

Exercises, meditations, improviations based upon *Stare*, a piece involving choral response triggered the observation of furture staring: the tension and excitement of visual communication.

Stare exercises:

(1) Couple A faces each other, eyes closed. Each person establishes a breathing rhythm. At the point between exhale and inhale, eyes open for that instant. Several couples might do this exercise simultaneously.
(2) Same as #1 but add couple B thus:

   When either of B observes eyes open simultaneously by A, he or she starts a conversation which is answered by the other of couple B. If both ask together, they work it out as one does when such a thing happens in real life. The conservation lasts for only one question and answer, but resumes with another question when triggered again by couple A. Several quartets may do this at the same time.
(3) Couple A as before. The remaining people divide into two choruses placed as B are. When the eye-lock occurs between couple A, the chorus emits a vocal sound according to some pre-arranged plan.

en–trances
for everbody's body doing
(A series of solos and duets leading to a chorus)

william hellermann

dedicated to the *sound out of silent spaces* group and especially its
founder, philip corner, without whom this wouldn't have been

the first en–trance . . . (in)
for everybody's body doing
(a personal and private solo)

. . . not to be listened to

the first *en-trance* to be made by everybody is into their body. . .

upon entering a space to truly *enter* that space
find *your* space within *the* space (a whole *hole*)

. . . at first wander around aimlessly   getting the
feel of things   let your eyes be out of focus
(crossing them a little helps)   and   listen to the
space try to hear into the cracks (creaks?)   try
the space on for size

. . . suddenly you'll know exactly where you fit in

. . . settle down get to know where you're at   make
body contact   roll around a little   *sink in*   get
to know the "best view" from your space (which
direction you like to look out from)

. . . until you feel yourself *here* (not *there*)

once you feel *at home* in your temporary home
moved in   begin to use your voice to move into
yourself (a whole *hole* to move into)

. . . start by singing softly an *ahh* sound in your
middle register on any pitch   just be comfortable

. . . let the sound *swoop* down your back scraping
your spine until it *bottoms* on the lowest note
you can make a   low pulsating sound using almost
no breath force

. . . repeat this over and over again   each time trying
to let the sound go deeper into your abdomen

. . . let each *swoop* last for one full breath with
your low pulsating abdomen note holding out to the
point where you feel yourself *laughing/sobbing*
for the next breath

. . . when you feel ready   begin to *enter* each time
by beginning on your low body note   feel that your
body is in the sound for the sound   and that you
are as *open* as possible (especially your throat)

. . . your will feel your body's body enter the space
of your space and your back begin to come alive
(yourself as a whole *hole*)

the second en–trance . . . (out)
for your body's body doing
(a personal and public solo)

. . . for yourself to hear

the second *en-trance* to be made by everybody is out of their body. . .

when one is centered in their space   with their
body in their body and centered on the sounding of
their body's *root* sound (the lowest sound of
least effort   from which all other sounds come)
the natural urge to *radiate* or expand outward
will be felt (a whole *hole* enlarging)

...the first expansion to make is to add a *forced* breath over or through your *root* sound (as you will discover later this is not in reality a *forced* sound but a first   it will feel that way)

...it will be unstable and you will *slip* back and forth between your breath sound and low body note

...until you feel yourself center on a balance point which will unite the two vibrations into a pleasing *roar* that seems to come more from your chest than your mouth you will begin to feel powerful within yourself

... as you explore this experience and become more centered into it   begin to introduce a pitch into your breath sound

... in the beginning you will become interested in the *effect* of this and find it intellectually interesting   which will interrupt the flow of the previous state   however   continue   always exploring subtle changes in pitch and intensity

... almost magically a sound which feels incredibly right will emerge combining the frequencies of resonance of your body your breath and your pitch of projection

... with time the sound will seem to be coming from a point outside yourself sounding with unexpected force   as your body outside your body

... you are now sounding (sending) yourself as yourself and making an *en-trance* as a whole *wholes* (a whole *"hole"* once removed)

the third en–trance . . . (with)
for another body's body doing
(a personal and private duet)

               . . . for yourself to listen to

the third *en-trance* to be made by everybody is to *let in* to their body. . .

while in an *en-trance*. . .*(out)* state   either from the experience of *the second en-trance* or achieved through some other experience   as soon as you feel consumated in this state and very stable physically move out of your whole *hole* to investigate the whole *holes* around you

. . . again let your eyes be slightly out of focus and your ears very conscious of what's around you until you receive an instinctive awareness of a particular whole *hole* being projected by another

. . . move to that whole *hole* approaching it from behind (do not sneak up on it) focus intently on the back of that person

. . . continue singing one of your three sounds   either the pitch   body   or breath sound (it will be almost impossible to keep more than two of them going as you move)

. . . and place your ear on the back of the other person at a point you sense (receive) as being a special *en-trance* point

. . . you will experience a feeling of enlargement that will be spread through both your bodies   because of the phenomenon of *bone conduction* you will be able to experience the wholeness of their sound almost as they experience it (why our voices sound *strange* to us on a tape recording is because we hear our own voices more through *bone conduction* than through the air)

. . . explore different *en-trance* points

. . . explore the singing of different pitches (sounds) varying the vowels employed and the intensities until a new sense of wholeness is achieved

. . . offer your back to others and share this experience
with a number of other persons   this will begin to
lead to an understanding of your own *wholeness* as
well as an appreciation of theirs (a whole of *holes*)

(and say thanks to dan goode without whom this
en-trance wouldn't be here)

the fourth en–trance . . . (into)
for a body's body pair doing
(a personal and public duet)

                                                      . . . a share to do

the fourth *en-trance* to be made by everybody is to
share the body. . .

the natural extension of hearing is sounding (and
vice-versa) so that the instinctive impulse to
sing into the back one has been hearing into will
arrive (a deeper *whole* to dig)

. . . the experience we are now about to share is based
on the fact that in everybody's back there are a number
of *en-trance* points to be found in the upper area
around the shoulder blades   the way to find these
points is to not exactly look for them   they'll be
received   (the hardest ones to find are your own
which says something about perception   and its joys
it also says something about the difficulty of
scratching your own back)

. . . first   clear your head and once more let your eyes
go slightly out of focus   while regarding intently the
back of someone in front of you   as you begin to
remember   you are interested in finding an *en-trance*
point   and that they are to be found in the upper
part of the back   you'll find one   if you don't
re-clear your head   and begin again (2   3   or more
tries are normal)

. . . if it is your back that is being offered you can
greatly assist in the process by allowing your back
to come alive and radiate its natural   but rare energy
if you have been doing the other *en-trances* this
will be easy (it'll even be hard not to)

. . . when a point is felt   reach out and touch it with
your fingers   rub around gently to precisely fix it
(the hand is not only quicker than the eye it is often
more accurate)   the essential thing is to not reach
out in *hopes* of finding one   this will only lead to
anxiety   and make it impossible to find one   have faith
you'll always know when it is found   it feels good

. . . it is useful to keep in mind that both of you are
locating a mutual point (a joint point)   it will be
both your's and their's and not necessarily the same
for others

. . . once you have found *your en-trance* point lean
forward and place your mouth on it and sing a sound
you sense as the right one   continually adjust this
sound   varying its intensity until you feel a definite
sense of flow taking place

. . . the person being sung into   as they feel the sung
sound spread through their body   can add to the flow
by mentally *sensitizing* their back (you'll love it)

. . . then they should let a vocal sound emerge from
themselves as a *complement* (compliment) to the sound
they are receiving

. . . mutually explore different vocal sounds (different
pitch intervals will have different effects)

. . . mutually explore different *en-trance* points   it
will very often happen that the activation of one
en-trance point will activate another (each point
will have a different spread with some going to the
chest   others to the stomach   others to the arms   and
even some that will appear at the fingertips without
seeming to travel there)

. . . try different body positions (an especially effective one is to have contact between your heads as well as the back)

. . . exchange roles

. . . know that a whole *holes*   has a whole lot of room and that your body's body is more than a body   it's a wholly *hole* body

the fifth en–trance . . . (along)
for everybody's body doing
(a personal and private chorus)

                                                        . . . to be felt not heard

the fifth *en-trance* to be made by everybody is the extension of the body. . .

a wonderful thing to do with your duet is to let it be felt by others (the nature of truly personal acts is that they want to be shared) after all a *whole* is not a *whole* unless it can be *whole*

you can probably think of a lot of ways of doing this but one of the best ways I can think of is to use the fingers

. . . find a sound(s) and an *en-trance* point between yourselves   which activates the fingertips of the person being sung into

. . . re-position yourselves so that the person in front can reach out to touch the fingertips of another pair of *duetters*   who are also   exploring the *fingertip sound*

. . . let this process expand to include all   until a large circle is formed of each duet pair being in *fingertip sound* contact with another

. . . the circle should form so that everyone is facing inward

. . . and then the person in front will be able to sing their sound across the circle making a *web* of connection as well as a line of connection (a wholly whole *hole*)

this will be fun   and very social   enjoy it   you will begin to come out of yourself

. . . trade places (if you want)

. . . let everyone be everywhere

the sixth en–trance . . . (through)
for everybody's body doing
(a personal and public chorus)

                                                        . . . to be gone through

the sixth *en-trance* to be made by everybody is beyond the body through the body. . .

after the whole group has explored their *en-trances* in the form of duets   they will be *prepared* form a chorus (a hole *whole*)

it is only natural that the *singer-into* will want to be being sung into and that the *sung-into* will want to   at the same time be singing into

. . . a group of at least 20 to 30 people will be necessary

. . . they should for a circle with each person sitting with their legs crossed   or side saddle   or spread (whatever is most comfortable) as close to the back of the person in front of them as possible

. . . each person should carefully begin again the process
of locating *en-trance* points by clearing their head
seeing them   and then touching them   before leaning
forward and singing into the point   the points found
now   will most likely be different from the ones
found earlier   especially   after you are being sung
into   (you will not be just   then   and your
perceptions will change)

. . . as everybody is singing into everybody   there will
be a new kind of flow taking place   you will feel
the need to continually make adjustments in your sound
so as to add to the flow   always make these changes
gradually   since any change on your part   in this state
will have distant echoes

. . . everybody's sound will go through everybody

. . . consciously extend yourself   letting your sound
travel as far as your imagination will let it

. . . seek out re-enforcing sounds to expand the flow

. . . if you feel like it   take a *break* once in awhile
and sing into the air   (the experience will be new
but it will still help to re-new it)

. . . once everybody's body is singing in full body
enjoy it   deviating slightly from the sound so as to
continually re-affirm it

. . . after awhile the desire to be alone again will come
accept this feeling and slowly disengage yourself
first sitting up and then gently letting your contribution
to the sound fade away (for some reason   this will
probably happen to everybody as a body)

. . . the whole will be whole

the seventh en–trance . . . (back)
for anybody's body doing
(a private and public chorus)

                                                    . . . to be

the seventh *en-trance* to be made by anybody is
back into the body (after all we're human)

after the body has been gone through   and gone through
there's nowhere to go but to where it came in

. . . laugh   cry   talk   drink and eat a little

. . . sing your words and ideas

. . . be your wholeself that's all anybody wants anyway

(that's the *whole* thing)

what is the ecology of a non'recyclable music?

note:

each *en-trance* may be done as a separate experience
all by itself   but not easily   out of sequence (this
is almost absolutely true for the choral *en-trances*)

the series of *en-trances*   either in whole or in
part   may be used to provide a framework within which
other *meditative-participative* events are experienced

in order to fully achieve the states described for
each *en-trance*   it will almost always be necessary
to undergo the experience more than once   in open
public meetings   this should always be announced so
that nobody has the feeling they have *failed* or are
in some sense *in a lesser state* than others

it would be nice if everybody understood that these
are experiences to take home and *do* with what they
please   but *do*. . .

alpha beta

david jones

alpha

any number of performers assemble within a building, seated apart from each other yet not entirely removed spacially as to affect the total balance of ensemble sounds: select seating at right angles from each other and act independently—make a free choice to interpret an architectural feature of the building or a geometrical object within the structure—concentrate on the form and then slowly produce sounds while your mind moves towards a contemplation of it's internal or external structure, when your mind has fully explored this dimension, continue to play while thinking of the nature of the basic materials from which the selected area or object is manufactured, when this avenue is fully developed, stop playing—still your mind of all thoughts - what significance has the area or object, and what meaning has it for you? after your analysis interpret your reaction in sound until the object no longer has a message for you.

beta

select a face in the audience—it must be someone towards whom you feel an emotional response—if at first you find difficulty in selection or have no reaction continue until you do - having recognized the reason for selection interpret in sound—later try to imagine the personality facets of the selected person and convey these in sound images—continue to play the sound picture of the personality, go beyond the visual physical haracteristics of the object of your attentions—later, isolate the person from their environment and play their true self or your vision of this image—continue your interpretation as long as possible until the person is a reality or until your mind has exhausted possibilities in sound.

Arc of Continuous Sounds

Richard Hayman

Choose a number of continuous sounds

They may be instrumental, electronic or natural phenomena

They may be of a steadily varying or recurring quality

Determine an order of the sounds considering contrast and performance requirements

Begin each sound with an equal and patient time between each one's start

When all have begun, stop each sound in the same order and time, the first being the last heard

Chambers

Alvin Lucier

Collect and make large and small
resonant environments:

Sea Shells	Bottles
Rooms	Cabins
Cisterns	Wells
Tunnels	Bells
Cupped Hands	Capsules
Mouths	Craters
Subway Stations	Empty Missiles
Bowls	Cacti
Shoes	Beds
Hollows	Webs
Caves	Pools
Suitcases	Boats
Ponds	Cones
Stadia	Funnels
Water Spouts	Bones
Bays	Stills
Tombs	Gins
Conduits	Draws
Canyons	Tubes
Boilers	Theatres
Pots	Cars
Ovens	Springs
Barrels	Flumes
Bulbs	Trees
	Others

Find a way to make them sound:

Blowing	Ignoring
Bowing	Talking
Rubbing	Singing
Scraping	Sighing
Tapping	Whistling
Moving	Walking
Fingering	Snapping
Breaking	Cracking
Burning	Snoring
Melting	Boring
Chewing	Praying
Jiggling	Loving
Wearing	Spraying
Swinging	Bowling
Bumping	Channeling
Dropping	Freezing
Orbiting	Squeezing
Creaking	Frying
Caressing	Exploding
Bouncing	Poking
Jerking	Screwing
Flipping	Lowering
Levitating	Shaking
Hating	Impeding
Skimming	Dancing
	Others

Sounds of portable resonant environments such as sea shells and cupped hands may be carried out into streets, countrysides, parks, campuses, or through buildings and houses, until outer limits are reached where minimum audio contact can be maintained by a player with at least one other player.

Sounds of the outer environment encompassed by the players may be heard with reference to the sounds of the portable resonant environments carried by the players. Sounds of determinate pitch in the outer environment may be heard in simple or complex relationships to the pitches of the portable resonant environments. Sounds of indeterminate pitch in the outer environment may be heard to take on the pitch, timbral, dynamic and durational characteristics of the sounds of the portable resonant environment.

Sounds of fixed resonant environments such as cisterns and tunnels may be made portable by means of recordings, radio or telephone transmission and carried into inner or outer environments. When carried into inner environments such as theatres into beds, the sounds of the now-portable resonant environments may either mingle with or take over the sounds of the inner environment. When carried to outer environments such as boilers to parks, the sounds of the now-portable resonant environments may be treated as original portable environments.

Mixtures of these material and procedures may be used.

Increasing and lessening of any characteristics of any sounds may be brought about.

In the Woods

Kenneth Maue

Begin in the morning. Bring some lunch, four large discs of day-glo paper, some thumbtacks, and some tape. Choose a roughly rectangular or circular area of solid woods

Enter the woods at different locations along the periphery. Start walking in any direction. Sometimes move toward specific locations; sometimes just wander here and there; sometimes follow streams or paths; sometimes bushwhack; sometimes just sit.

As you walk around, find places to tack or tape your day-glo discs, in such a way that they can be seen by other players as they walk by. And be on the look-out for other players' discs. When you come across one, take it down, carry it for a while, then put it in a new location for someone else to find.

In the middle of the day, find each other by making noises. Make noise by any available means. Make sound and listen. Move toward sounds you hear. When everyone has gathered together, have lunch. Then set out again, each in a different direction. This time, when you find a disc, take it down and keep it. After the day seems to be ending, make your way to the periphery, and wait to be picked up by a car.

Evening Ritual

Kenneth Maue

Note: This performance consists of three parts. There is no overt demarcation between the individual parts; it is up to each participant to decide for himself/herself when the transitions occur.

Part One: Communal Drone
Drone (sing) long, full-breath notes, maintaining single pitches for long durations. Drone on any pitch you like. Drone on the open-throat vowel *Aaaah* for maximum relaxation. Concentrate on the breathing cycle: make it as regular, deep, and smooth as you can. Consciously relax all muscles of the body; let the breathing cycle become automatic. Drone in a firm, bold voice. (Restrained, quiet droning can tense the vocal muscles.) Listen to the whole sound body—the other droners. Change pitch only when you feel a sense of significance in doing so. End together.

Part Two: Unison Silence
Maintain smooth and relaxed breathing. Listen to the sounds of the environment.

Part Three: Waiting for the Gong
Continue to sit in silence; maintain smooth and relaxed breathing. Wait for the Gong to ask to be sounded. At just the right moment, one player responds to the Gong by striking it once.

2 Music for Voices

The voice of course is the original and most fundamental musical instrument. People of every culture sing and make an extraordinary variety of other sounds with their voices. We all relate very directly to the voice; no instrument can rival it in the variety and flexibility of its sound or in its power to communicate. This chapter presents a wide range of vocal pieces which explore first the nonsinging elements of the voice—speech and other sound—and, second, various types of singing.

SPEECH–SOUND PIECES

The excerpt from Kirk Nurock's "Natural Sound" serves as a perfect introduction to this chapter and offers some very valuable warm-ups and exercises. After the two simple forms, "Passing" and "Rhythm Chant," Nurock's *War and Night* is a more extended piece which develops directly from the exercises and techniques he presents. Robert Ashley's *She Was a Visitor* and Christian Wolff's *You Blew It* explore the sound elements—rather than the meaning or content—of these two respective verbal phrases through repetition and prolongation. They transform the way we hear these common words and in so doing suggest and reveal something interesting in our everyday sound world. Carole Weber's *Breath Pieces* and Barbara Benary's *Solkattu* are based not on words but on various other vocal sounds. The first is a free collection of various sounds made by and related to breathing, while the second uses specific syllables and rhythms of South Indian drumming. These first five pieces are among the most accessible in this book, and are very good for beginning a class or workshop.

While still quite performable, the remaining works are more elaborate and varied, and do require greater preparation. Richmond Browne's *Chortos I* is based on Biblical texts presented in a variety of ways along with other vocal and percussive sounds made by the chorus; it is quite structured and thoroughly specified. On the other hand, J. George Cisneros's *Continental Drift # 7*, which is based on a part of the *Epic of Gilgamesh*, is very freely developed through experimentation by separate groups of performers, and then combined and perfected as a whole. The New Verbal Workshop's *Ante·axis* and *Gothic* are both speech and vocal sound improvisations for a small group based on certain general structures, techniques, and images. Jim Rosenberg's *Intermittence* is a performed poem for four readers and conductor in which various fragmentary lines of poetry are assembled according to instructions and then read from a score like a piece of chamber music. Finally, Timothy Sullivan's *Intermezzo* relates to the works in both this section and the next through its integration of speech sounds and improvised melodic singing.

The following pieces in other chapters use various forms of vocal and speech sounds with other elements, and are therefore closely related to those here:

Chap. 5: *Exitus* (Frank McCarty)
Chap. 6: *I Am Sitting in a Room* (Alvin Lucier)
           Telephone Matrix (Kenneth Maue)
Chap. 6: *King Speech Song* (Daniel Lentz)
Chap. 7: *Object Pieces* (Roger Johnson)
           Minimusic (R. Murray Schafer)
           Night Speech (Nicolas Roussakis)
           Plastic Containers (Carmine Pepe)
Chap. 8: *Phrase* (Eric Salzman)

Natural Sound: An Organic Approach to Music by Kirk Nurock

Music has a wonderful power ... of recalling in a vague and indefinite manner, those strong emotions which were felt during long-past ages, when, as is probable, our early progenitors courted each other by the aid of vocal tones.
Charles Darwin, *The Expression of the Emotions in Man and Animals*

Society operates on the theory that specialization is the key to success, not realizing that specializaton precludes comprehensive thinking.... What nature needed man to be was adaptive in many if not any direction.
R. Buckminster Fuller, *Operating Manual for Spaceship Earth*

In the past, human sounds were categorized as either language or music. Music, the more abstract of the two, can more directly express emotion, which is also abstract and non-literal. But even in music we find myriad structures and stylizations which tend to inhibit naturalness. Instruments, notations, and performance conventions often frustrate the basic expressive impulses and produce a formalized result. Emotional flexibility is limited variously by song forms, precomposed texts and lyrics, and entertainment considerations (arrangements, performance order, use of reliable effects, etc.)

Recent developments in contemporary music and theater have had considerable success in extending freedom of personal expression. Toward this end we have already seen: a reevaluation of what constitutes musical sound; new notations affording performers maximum individual choice within a composed structure; a redefining of the roles of performer, director, composer, conductor, and audience. ... One of the most significant developments in music of our time is the creation of electronically produced sounds. The synthesizer and related computer techniques now make available a vast spectrum of sounds with an incredible capacity for detail and accuracy, far beyond what any live musicians can create. This development (plus the continuing availability of excellent recordings of all types of music) today poses a serious threat to the validity and survival of live performances. Our belief is that live performances will only remain relevant beyond the Electronic Age by fully developing the one thing no machine can duplicate: the ability to communicate spontaneous human emotion.

We are defining "natural sounds" as those sounds made by the human voice and body without the aid of any external instruments or amplification.

Human sounds are more diverse and expressive than their owners suspect. As our vocabulary of sound grows, we will gain a richer expressive range which will be broadening in music as well as all communication. Our task is to develop in each individual the ability to express immediate feelings through the most personal, natural sounds he is capable of creating ....

The process of natural sound is therapeutic as well as musical. One understands oneself by knowing one's sounds. To express oneself in a group in this fashion is to have a deep, open relationship with others. A good performance is one in which the fewest guards and defenses are evident.

What was once valued as:	Will be seen in terms of:
clarity	honesty
originality	personality
facility	self-knowledge
control	direction
flexibility	openness
discipline	spontanaiety

To reserve this experience for people who have training and facility in formal music is a mistake. It can be available to everyone. An audience is a vicarious orchestra, the least rewarding kind. More people will seek involvement in performing groups when they become aware of their natural sound as an alternative to the vocal and instrumental music of the past. Sound will be created proudly and openly without thought of "dilettante" or "professional." It will be a here-and-now experience of music making for the hear/see/feel/pleasure/pain/discovery/growth/release/group-interaction/fun of it. We are all musicians naturally. Music belongs to everyone.

PLANNING OUTLINE FOR WORKSHOPS IN NATURAL SOUND

Natural Sound is a technique designed to develop the creative sound potential innate in us all. No previous training is necessary; however people with musical background will also gain broader perspective from Natural Sound. Neither instruments nor amplification are used—only the sounds of the human voice and body. During one two-hour workshop, participants are taught materials through which to have an expressive, creative experience in sound. Subsequent workshops develop group interaction and performance values.

Environment

Ideally, a Natural Sound workshop should be held in a large, open space with a clean, comfortable floor. No furniture is needed. Lighting should be dim but not dark. There should be fifteen to twenty-five participants. Loose, comfortable clothing should be worn. If recording equipment is available, certain exercises should be recorded and played back after the session (see "Passing," "Rhythm Chant") [below]. A workshop should last two hours.

These have been found to be the most efficient circumstances, producing the most fruitful results. But Natural Sound can be done in any environment, by any number of people. Each situation will create its own experience. . . .

The director of a Natural Sound workshop should have previous expreience in some area of group leading (teaching, Yoga, music, dance, therapy). He should carefully review and practice presenting the materials until he is comfortable with the language. Each director will bring to a group his own style and personality. But, in a general sense, workshops should be led in a relaxed, peaceful tone. Questions or problems should be dealt with in ways which encourage individual freedom and creativity, and are not critical or judgmental. Warm-up exercises should be led patiently and timed carefully, watching the group's responses and progress.

Warm Up

All stand in a large, spread-out circle.

Shaking out:	Loosely and relaxedly, shake whole body: arms, legs, head, neck, face; allow the torso to be especially loose and free.
Stretching:	Stand with a straight spine, shoulders relaxed. Slowly stretch arms forward and upward; finally reach over head to ceiling, raise up on toes (while holding this position, slowly inhale). Exhaling, slowly come down from toes, bend forward from the waist, fold entire torso down, arms hanging loosely, head hanging relaxedly. Gradually come back to upright.
Head/Neck:	(Briefly repeat shaking out. Bring circle in close and all sit on floor) Sit with a straight spine. Let your head drop forward. Rotate it around to R. shoulder, to back, to L. shoulder, to front. Repeat once and reverse direction for two full times.
Face:	(Remove glasses.) Stretch the face wide open (hold), relax. Squeeze the face tightly together (hold), relax. Wiggle the face around in all directions, relax. Use tongue to press out skin of lips and cheeks. (Above may be repeated in varying orders.) Create friction in the palms of hands (by rubbing palms together). Apply warm palms to skin of face and massage skin deeply.
Throat:	First, distinguish between a closed and open throat. The throat is closed while making the sound of a hard g as in "good." Then open to the sound of "ah." All try. Do not attempt to feel the neck externally; rather, sense the internal sensation of the throat opening and closing. Stretch the throat wide open (hold). Relax the throat., letting it gradually come closed. . . tightly closed. Relax the throat, letting it gradually come open. . .open wide (The jaw may remain relaxed throughout; the movement is in the throat only.) Repeat and accelerate the process. Finally, wiggle the throat around in all directions.
Deep Breathing:	Sit at place in circle, in any cross-legged position (or extended legs). Do not block lower abdomen with raised knees. Gradually and slowly inhale into the abdomen, then the chest. (Hold approximately 10 seconds) Exhale slowly from abdomen, then chest (hold air out approximately 5 seconds) Repeat this patiently until all are breathing deeply and relaxedly. Encourage taking more into abdomen, more into chest, filling the torso with more and more air, each time. (Variations: bellows breath, alternate nostril breathing from Hatha Yoga.)

The above exercises may be augmented by other similar shaking, stretching or breathing exercises from Yoga, dance, or theater sources. The emphasis should be on accessible techniques rather than specialized skills or long-range goals. Also, it is best to talk the group through an exercise, explaining each step as it is done. This creates ongoing activity rather than big pauses while explaining the exercise first and executing afterwards . . . .

Vocabulary

Phrases which appear below in quotes are recommended as directions to be used verbatim. Rewordings of these indications can lead to confusion and muddled sound responses.

Registers:

Inhale all together. While group holds breath, say, "Make a sustained sound in your low register." Then make sound immediately and cue the group to join you ("ah" or "oh"). Then repeat same in middle register, high register. "Inhale . . . sustain your lowest possible tone and slowly slide from the bottom of your range to the top." (Begin immediately and cue others to join.) As group reaches top, give a cut-off gesture and say, "Return to normal breathing."

"We have just covered the three basic registers of the voice: low, middle, and high. For the moment, suffice it to say they are where you think they are. We won't define exactly where one ends and the next begins. They simply exist relative to each other: low, middle, and high. There is the additional falsetto register in men only. It is a gentler, softer tone which sits above the high register. [Demonstrate, or have someone demonstrate it first.] All the men inhale . . . falsetto sustain [begin and gesture men to join] . . ."

Further vocabularly may be taught more informally, pausing between items to clarify or answer questions.

Shake:	A fast alternation between any two tones. Try in each register. (Somewhat akin to trill or tremolo in traditional music.)
Slide:	A sustained tone which gradually travels higher or lower (glissando, traditionally).
Flutter:	A series of short tones in rapid succession. Varieties: flutter breath (like a child's "machine gun" imitation), flutter tongue, flutter throat, flutter lips ("brrrrr"). Careful not to confuse the flutter with the shake.
Short tones:	Effective when done by full group as random short tones in all registers.

Simple pieces can now be made by dividing the group in two or three sections, assigning a progression of the above elements, and conducting dynamics (loud and soft).

Breath sounds:

So far, all of the sounds have been voice sounds. Another category is breath sounds which use no voice.

"Simply imitate these sounds as I make them [sustain the following using no voice; listen to make sure no one is adding voice—"z" for "s," etc.]:

S, Sh, F, H, K, P, T (short)

Now improvise and find your own breath sounds. Use your lips, tongue, and cheeks freely." Let group experiment briefly, then fade them out.

Percussion sounds:

"So we've had voice and breath sounds. Another category is percussion sounds."

Label, demonstrate, and have group join the following: tongue clicks, jaw joint clicks (L. and R.), dental clicks (clicking teeth together, lip pops, finger snaps, flesh slaps). Knuckle and bone cracks should be mentioned, but invariably produce uneasiness and should be avoided at first session.

Have group experiment with combining a percussion sound with vocal sound (sustained vocal tone, while slapping cheeks lightly, etc.). Combine two vocal treatments (a shaking slide, etc.).

Emotional sounds:

"So now we've had three categories—vocal, breath, and percussion. We've discussed various treatments—short, sustained, slide, etc. In addition, there are emotional sounds."

Ask group to perform the following (all are to be non-verbal and one at a time:

laugh	cough	shout
giggle	gulp	call
cackle	snort	scream
sigh	crying	whimper
moan	whining	titter
yawn	yelp	plea

Even if none of the above is defined or explained, there will invariably be immediate sound responses to all of the terms. And there will be a remarkable distinction between the sonorities of the various responses.

"So we've just covered a generalized vocabulary of Natural Sounds. Now I'd like to do a Passing." Try not to stop here for questions, or momentum will be lost. The group's energy is probably high and their curiosity is aroused. Proceed to simple forms.

Simple Forms: Passing

A circle, seated or standing. One Person in the group volunteers to lead. He makes a simple sound or short phrase of sounds, and "passes" it to the person to his left. That person imitates it and passes it to his left. This continues around the circle. Each person repeats a given sound until the next one is passed to him by his immediate predecessor. The leader begins a new sound when the previous sound has travelled roughly halfway around the circle. Imitation should be as fast yet as accurate as possible, and the group should be encouraged to "keep the sound moving." The result is a group effort to create a kind of "windmill" of sound. Often, like the old "telephone game," the sound evolves and varies as it travels to the end of the line. Encourage accuracy, but a slight change will actually enhance the windmill effect.

Rhythm Chant

Seated or standing. One person creates a "brief, rhythmic motive" and keeps repeating it. The groups listens carefully, imitates the motive, then improvises on it, always keeping the basic pulse. Encourage the group to listen to he sounds of nearby neighbors and the whole group, and to make little "conversations" with one another by using each other's sounds and sometimes joining together for unison effects. "Let your body get into the rhythm" should be encouraged. Dynamics may be conducted. And Rhythm Chant and Passing may be recorded and heard (preferably *after* the session) to develop an awareness of sound result and performance values.

War and Night
a natural sound piece

Kirk Nurock

Notations

The piece requires 15 voices minimum, 30 maximum. The sections are Men, Men/Women, and Women. They should be distributed as evenly as possible. Cues marked "Slowly Develop" function as a *Rhythm Chant*. "Explo" means to approximate an explosion on the syllable given. B/Pow is pronounced with loose lips, combining "bow" and "pow." "Ind" means entrances are cued individually, down the line ↓ indicates a downbeat. Where no arrow appears, a cue is given and the section simply begins, somewhat together. ♪ indicates a cut-off. ⟨ and ⟩ are traditional cresc. and decresc. Exact durations are not given; they are subject to each conductor's interpretation. Other notations should be self-explanatory, based on a knowledge of the Natural Sound vocabulary. A tape of this piece, performed by 28 voices, can be obtained for reference purposes from Natural Sound Workshop, Inc., 246 Eighth Ave. NYC.

Preliminary Exercise

After doing a full warm-up, have each group member go off into a personal area and "develop a sound or pattern of sound which remind you of an element of nature." No sound should be purely breath or percussion (i.e. there must be some vocal sound.) Listen carefully as the group develops the sounds, and finally call group back and form a circle. As group continues, repeating their sounds, select the 10-12 most colorful and contrasting ones. (The rest are not used in the piece.)

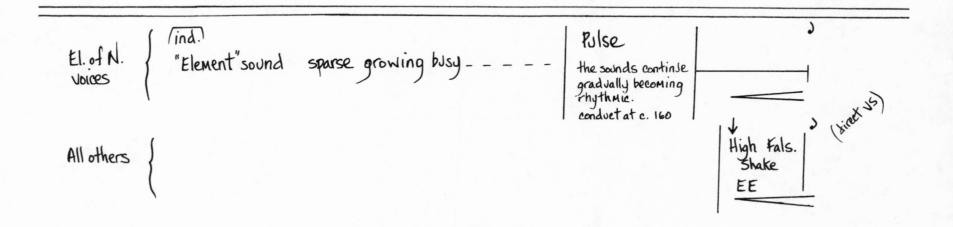

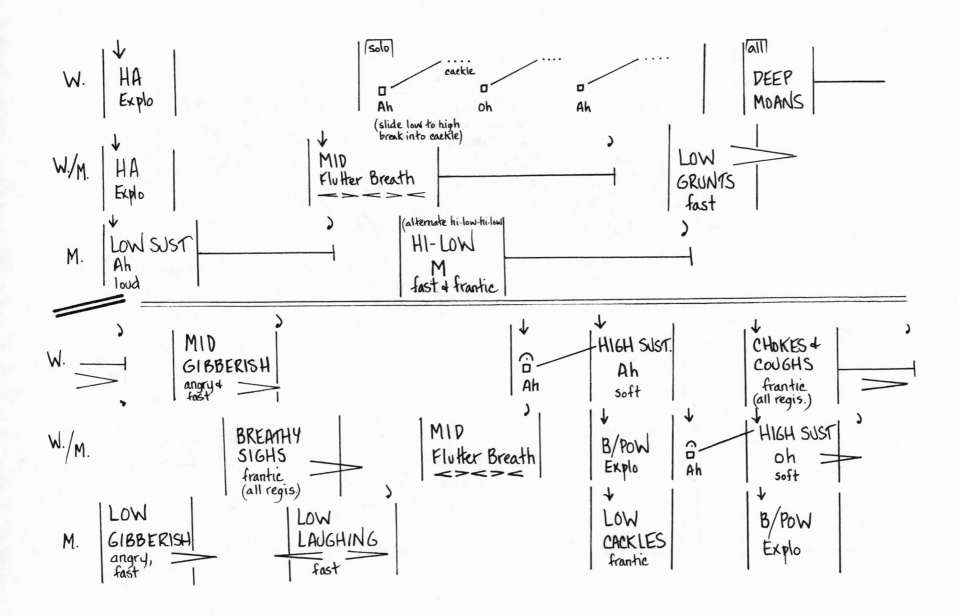

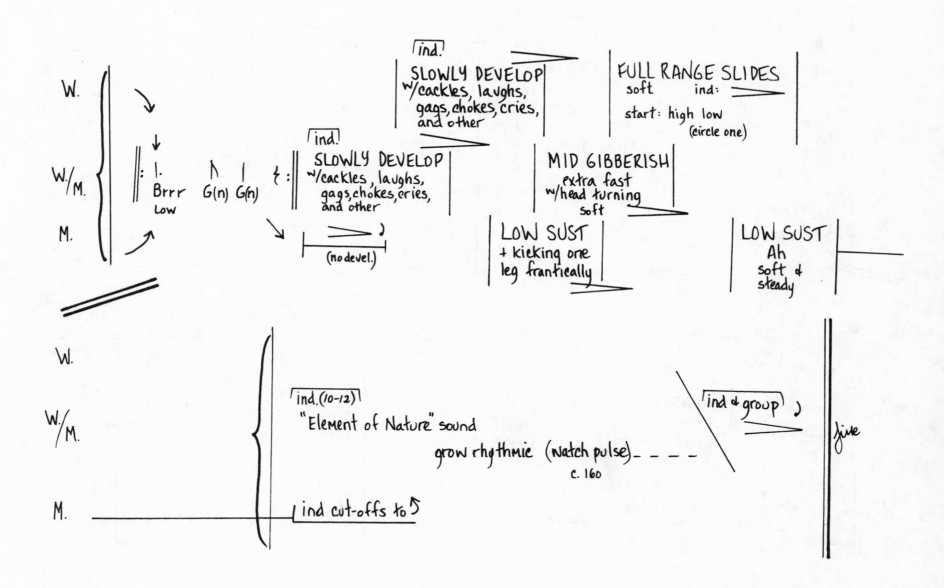

She Was A Visitor

Robert Ashley

Performers

A speaker: repeat the phrase "she was a visitor," periodically and without variation for the duration of the performance. Use a normal tone of voice. This is not the main event.

♩=120

3/4 ... she was a | vi - si - tor | she was a : repeat as often as necessary

Leaders (any number): choose a phoneme of the speaker's phrase and speak that phoneme as quietly as possible simultaneously with its occurrence in the speaker's phrase, letting the speaker's sound mask the beginning of this event. Sustain the sound for one breath. (All of the phonemes can be sustained, except for the *t* sound in *visitor;* this sound remains short, and simply occurs with the speaker's sound.). Do this at your own voice-pitch level. Continue to choose and sustain sounds as long as the speaker keeps repeating the phrase.

(she)	(eve)	(foot)	(sofa)	(zed)	(accou- nt)
sh;	e;	oo;	a;	z;	a;
She......		was.....			a........

(victor)	(ill)	(zed)	(charity)	(tom)	(maker)
v;	i;	z;	i;	t;	er;

visitor...................

Chorus groups (the chorus divided equally among the leaders): sustain the phonemes that are sounded by the group leader. In this, though the group reflects the phoneme choices of the leader, members of the group act as individuals; that is, as each person perceives the leader's choice, he sounds that phoneme at his own voice-pitch level, as quietly as possible, for one breath. (The *t* sound, of *visitor,* may follow at any time soon after it is spoken by the leader.)

Audience: If, when chorus groups are situated among the audience, members of the audience indicate a desire to join in the performance, they should be verbally instructed — during the course of the performance, but briefly and as quietly as possible — individually or in small groups, by members of the chorus. (Group leaders should not stop their activity to make these instructions.)

The Performance

In conventional performance situations arrangements should be such that the group leaders clearly can hear and see the speaker and, in turn, be heard and seen by their chorus groups.

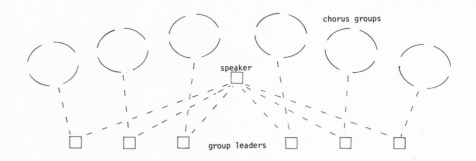

When chorus groups are among the audience, group leaders should hear the speaker, privately, through electronic systems (speaker-microphone to leader-headphones). It should be noted that these conditions contradict the notion of the speaker's sounds masking the beginnings of the sounds made by the group leaders. In fact, the greater the distance between the speaker and the group leader, the more the group leader's sound will tend to anticipate the sound made by the speaker. Thus, the greater the distance, the more quietly the group leader will have to begin his sounds.

When chorus groups are among the audience, the speaker should be alert to those situations where members of the audience are being instructed in order to participate. He should continue speaking until all of these potential participants have had an opportunity to join the chorus.

A group leader may choose a successive phoneme while members of his group are still sounding a previously selected one.

Note: *She was a visitor* may be performed simultaneously with *The Entrance* (p. 000). On that occasion, the two compositions should have approximately the same duration.

You Blew It

Christian Wolff

The letters stand for the sounds, as far as can be managed, which the letters in the above phrase stand for, except that "ou" stands for both "ou" in "you" and the "ew" in "blew".

```
y      ou—b     lou      i      t
t—you      bl      ou       i
it—y      ou      blou
ou—it      y      ou—bl
lou     t—y      ou—b      b      1      ou—i      t—you
ou—blou     it
bl      ou—it
```

Inflections possible at line ends: ? (proper or rhetorical) or (declarative or ironical) or (pleased, displeased or invoking).

Pauses of any lengths are represented by the spaces between letters or combinations of letters.

Durations of sounds may be long (ca. 3 seconds or longer) or free.

Where letters or combinations of letters are connected by a line:

(a) those before the line (e.g. ou—) should be long and those after (—b) are free; then, at the next pair,

(b) those before the line are free and those after long, then

(c) both those before and those after are free.

Thereafter alternate freely between (a), (b) and (c), and occasionally apply one of them to two successive sets of letters or combinations of letters connected by a line.

Each of any number of players may start at any line; repeat any line as often as desired before continuing to another, but do not return to it.

Sing as many of the lines as desired.

When using pitches repeat no pitch on successive vocal articulations.

Breath Pieces

Carole Weber

Notes on the *Breath Pieces*:

The *breath pieces* were part of *people pieces* made to be done by people visiting a little glade in a forest near Art Park, New York.

The idea is that the scores are handed out to people as they gather in the glade. We sit roughly in a circle. One way the piece is done: I say:

I will begin each sound saying what it is (say *bah* with breath). You continue making the sound until you hear me say the next sound. Or: you can make any sound on the page in any order. Listen to yourself and to how long you want to make each sound. Change when you want. Do each sound on the page at least once. Listen to how everyone sounds at once. Make silences too. Listen.

BREATH PIECES

BLOWING YOUR BREATH OUT VERY FAST.... ARUSH....
SAY HAAWAAEEE w/ BREATH

Blowing your breath out very slowly; But loud; But soft.
SAY FOOOOOOO w/ BREATH

Puffing out the cheeks w/ air expel sharply. expel fast hit cheeks

FORMING OH WITH MOUTH SAYING HUH w/ BREATH.

FORMING OO w/ MOUTH SAYING HOO WITH LOTS OF BREATH SAYING HOO w/ LITTLE BREATH for a long time

FORMING EEE w/ MOUTH SAYING HEE w/ BREATH FAST RUSHING SAYING HEE w/ BREATH SLOWLY

SAYING YAA--EE--YOO---- WITH BREATH TAKE A LONG TIME REPEAT

FORMING YEAH w/ MOUTH SAY AEHHH SOFTLY w/ BREATH.

FORMING AHH w/ MOUTH SAYIN HAH w/ BREATH.

SAY HAAAA---HOO--HEE WITH BREATH HAOOEE.

SAYING HEH w/ BREATH

SAYING ...SHEEEEEEE... WITH BREATH SHEEE AH AYEEE

SAYING PA PA PA PA with breath

SASASASA

SAY ...BUHBUH BUH BUH w/breath

SAY S-S-S -S-S -S-S SUCKIN

SUCKING BREATH IN THROUGH THE TEETH

Forming hooo w/ mouth Sucking in breath -through teeth

* Roberta's song to be sung once as breath once as voice (in canon) everybody at their own tempo

Forming shuh w/ mouth Sucking in breath thru teeth

sucking in breath, blowing out breath Hoooo raaa repeat

Sucking in sound HAAWAA EE with teeth
Suck in FOOOOOO; YAA EE YOO; PA PA PAPA; Buh Buh Buh Buh; Sa Sa Sa Sa Sa;

LISTEN TO THE FOREST BREATH SAYING ITS SOUND
Make up your own breath sound try it blowing it out; sucking it in

Suck in Sheeeee; Foooo

SONG ..... ROBERTA GOULD

POPO PO PO PO PO PO PIPA
PAPA   DIPI   PAPA   POPI
PO PI TEE TAA TEE TEE TEE
TAH TAH
TEE TEE PIIPII PAPI
POPO   POPO
PIPI   TEETEE
CACA
          TEE TEE

CACA
      IXTA
          IXTA
              MAL
                  MAL
                      MAMI
MIMI MAMA MOMAH
  MAMI MOMA MAMA
    BABA BABA BABA
      BAB BAB
        AB   AB
          ABABABAB ABAAAAAAAAAAAAA
          AAAAAAAA AAAAAAAAAA

Solkattu

Barbara Benary

In which spoken rhythmic figures are passed around a circle, using syllables taken from South Indian drumming. Gradually the syllable phrases are set to pitches. Other improvisation is added in stages.

Solkattu, meaning literally "bundles of words," is the Tamil name for the spoken recitation of drum strokes.

The players
This piece can be performed by any number of players and a drone instrument which plays only one note.

Preliminaries
Each player makes up a short rhythmic phrase out of solkattu syllables. The phrases should be fairly short and not too difficult to recite. They are made up of these syllables, added together to form a group:

    1 beat: TA   ♪
    2 beats: TAKA or TOM —   (♫ or ♩)
    3 beats: TAKITA or TOM — —   (♫♩ or ♩.)

Some sample phrases that might be made from combinations of the syllables:

A phrase seven beats long could be

    1+2+2+2   or   TA TAKA TOM — TOM —   (♪ ♫ ♩ ♩)

A phrase six beats long could be

    2+1+3   or   TOM — TA TAKITA   (♩ ♪ ♫♩)

A phrase eight beats long might be

    3+2+3   or   TOM — — TAKA TAKITA   (♩. ♫ ♫♩)

Process

The first person begins by speaking his phrase twice. He claps on the downbeat each time. Immediately after, the next person picks up that same phrase and repeats it twice, without losing a beat. He also claps on each downbeat. Then the next person repeats it twice, then the next, until it circles back to the person who started it. He again repeats it twice. Then the next person starts a new phrase and this too passes around the circle repeated twice by each person until it is again spoken by the person who initiated it. Then the next person starts a new phrase. In this way each person introduces a phrase which passes entirely around the circle before the next phrase is introduced.

Whenever a new phrase is introduced, the group waits until they are sure of its length before they begin to clap on the downbeat of each repetition.

Stages of development
1. Phrases are spoken.

2. Phrases are sung. First the drone instrument enters, establishing a tonic pitch. Without breaking the continuous process, players gradually begin to sing the phrases with pitches. Each player repeats his melodic phrase when he repeats the same syllables. However he needn't use the same melody as the player who sang the phrase just before him. Whenever it is not the player's turn to sing a syllable phrase, he should hum or drone the tonic pitch or another harmonious pitch.

3. Chaotic section. One player starts this section by repeating his rhythmic phrase over and over. The player next to him enters doing his own phrase. Then the next enters doing his own, and then the next, until all the players are singing different syllable phrases at the same time, each one clapping on his own downbeat.

4. Resolution. One player joins the player next to him on that player's solkattu phrase (using his own melody, but reciting the same syllables as his neighbor). Then another person joins them on the phrase, using his own melody. Then one by one the others join until all are singing the same syllables at once, though to different melodies.

Chortos   I

Richmond Browne

Commissioned by the Church of Christ, Yale University, New Haven, Connecticut

Notes:

Chortos is the Greek word for grass *(cf. horticulture)*. The Old and New Testament texts use grass as a symbol for something green, living and beautiful which meets some terrible fate—being "blasted," "withered," and smitten."

This piece was written for performance by a chorus of about fifty men in a church service. It may also be done effectively with as few as 25 *mixed* voices, but the solo parts in Section 2 should always be sung by men. (Actions involving less than the total chorus should be assigned during rehearsal.)

If performed in concert, thought should be given to its programming and staging. A dispersal of the chorus on the stage seems to work well.

The piece *is* whatever happens when the instructions are carried out. There are action instructions (what to do, who does it), time instructions (when to act), and attitude instructions (how, and perhaps why, one acts).

The chorus performs the five paragraphs of the text, using one minute for each paragraph, as shown on the following pages. On each of these five sections, detailed instructions are given for creating an improvised minute of performance. Besides speaking and singing, each singer will create sounds by rattling coins or keys and crumpling paper (other than their scores!).

The director may use an electric clock with a large sweep-second hand, placed so that the chorus may see it. Or, he may use his own watch, possibly directing with a circular motion to imitate the sweep of a second hand. In any case, each section is performed within 55 seconds, except the last section which requires the full minute.

The conductor may, after rehearsing with strict timings, use his own discretion to alter the given timings to lengthen some (not all) sound events; the silences should remain at their given durations.

0:

0:00	Begin humming sound.
0:15	Stop. *(Silence.)*
0:16	Ten singers speak one word each, ad lib, during this time.
0:25	Thirty singers speak one word each, ad lib, during this time.
0:35	Every singer speaks one word, ad lib, during this time.
0:45	Every singer speaks five words, ad lib, during this time.
0:55	Stop. *(Silence.)*
1:00	Next page. *(Don't turn now.)*

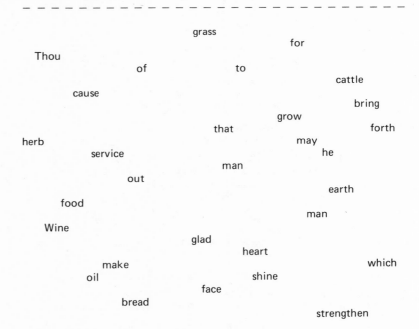

The whole chorus immediately begins humming at 0:00. The humming should be toneless, un-centered, slowly fluctuating in pitch, quiet but dense, and low in the range of each singer.

All starts and stops should occur without emphasis, but with precision.

The time "nodes" at 0:25, 0:35, and 0:45 should not be audible as formal articulations: from 0:16 to 0:55 is a single phrase.

All words should be stated clearly, audibly, and conversationally. Don't act, compete, or call attention to your word. Don't choose your word or your time; let it choose you. There will be a statistical crescendo as more words per second occur; don't change the way you speak, however. Words will (and should) overlap; regular or quasi-metrical patterns should not occur.

1:

1:00	Begin crumpling or rattling paper. *(Now turn page 0:)*
1:15	Stop. *(Silence.)*
1:18	Each singer speaks at least one phrase, ad lib, during this time.
1:45	Stop. Sometime during this ten seconds, each singer crumples his paper once, hard, ad lib, and then drops it. (or just hits the pages of this score against something, once, hard.)
	(Turn page.)
1:55	Silence.
2:00	Next page.

— — — — — — — — — — — — — — — — — —

neither any tree
scorpions of the earth
the third part of trees
the seven angels
the seven trumpets
they were cast upon the earth
only those men
locusts upon the earth
there followed hail and fire
which have not the seal of God
the first angel sounded
it was commanded them
unto them was given power
they should not hurt
all green grass
prepared themselves to sound
the grass of earth
mingled with blood
then there came out of the smoke
in their foreheads
was burnt up
neither any green thing
have power

— — — — — — — — — — — — — — — — — —

Crumple and re-crumple the extra sheet of paper with one hand. Be careful not to make noise with the paper except when indicated. Rattling these pages is acceptable.

Let your eye run over the list of phrases. Sometime between 1:18 and 1:45 simply let yourself speak a phrase (or two or three, but not more). Speak with authority but don't shout; speak with the emotion you feel is appropriate to the phrase. No clowning, no mumbling; neither too fast or too slow.

Don't choose your phrase; let it surprise you; pay no attention to anyone else. Don't wait for a silence; don't be afraid to let silences happen. You will probably not be heard individually except by chance, but both the group sound and the nature of those chance "solos" depend upon every singer's performing the text sincerely and with energy and style, according to the directions. Some phrases may occur more than once; some may not be spoken.

2:

2:00	Begin rattling keys or coins.
2:10	Stop. Three soloists immediately begin to sing as instructed below.
2:27	Begin rattling keys or coins in a crescendo to 2:30 and a decrescendo after it.
2:33	Stop.
2:45	Begin rattling keys or coins. Three soloists stop.
2:55	Stop. *(Silence)*
3:00	Next page. *(Turn page after Ah begins.)*

— — — — — — — — — — — — — — — — — —

I have digged   and DRUNK strange waters,   and with the SOLE of my feet   have I dried up ALL the rivers   of beSIEGed places.

Hast thou not HEARD   long ago how I have done it,   and of ancient TIMES that I have formed it?   now have I BROUGHT it to pass,   that thou shouldest BE to lay waste fenced cities   into RUinous heaps.

Therefore their inhabitants were of SMALL power,   they were disMAYed and confounded;   they were as the grass of the FIELD,   and as the green herb,   as the grass upon the housetops,   and as the CORN blasted   before it can be grown up.

— — — — — — — — — — — — — — — — — —

The three soloists should be a tenor, a baritone, and a bass. They must be confident enough to sing an improvised melodic line, using the spaces in the text as natural points of rest and the capitalized words for vocal melismas. All three begin at the beginning of the text but make no attempt to stay together. Make no attempt to agree as to meter or tuning. Use varied speeds according to the text, but don't rush; soloists do not have to finish the complete text by 2:45. Sing right through the jingling at 2:27 and end naturally as the jingling takes over at 2:45. No stylistic restrictions are intended except that they should sing pitches, not sprechstimme. A free, wide-interval chromatic line is perhaps likely to best fit the mood, which is expressive, mournful, and intense.

3:

3:00   Sing *Ah* continuously.

3:15   Immediately begin to sing the text, ad lib, as described below. Begin very quietly and grow louder . . .

       . . . from 3:30 on, there should be a real crescendo.

3:55   Stop. *(Silence.)*

4:00   Next page. *(Turn page after whistling starts.)*

— —

It is he
that sitteth upon the circle
of the earth,
and the inhabitants thereof
are as grasshoppers;
that stretcheth out the heavens
as a curtain,
and spreadeth them out as a tent
to dwell in:

That bringeth the princes to nothing;
he maketh the judges of the earth
as vanity.

His crowned are as the locusts,
and his captains as the great grasshoppers,
which camp in the hedges in the cold day,
but when the sun ariseth
they flee away,
and their place is not known where they are.

The voice said,
Cry.
And he said,
What shall I cry?

— —

Each singer sings Ah *on a slow improvised glissando, up and down, quite loudly. See the instructions for humming at 0:00 and whistling at 4:00.*

Sing the text to individually improvised melodies, beginning slowly with quiet intensity—accelerating and rising to real anger at the end. Singers may pause individually; the effect should be a melange of sound, with the rising anger in the voices showing through, in the form of a very "hard" sound. Sing out!

If you finish the text (and you should not rush to do so), or even if you have not finished it, by 3:50 you should abandon the text and sing (shout) the word Cry *repeatedly (ad lib) until the cutoff at 3:55.*

4:

4:00   Begin whistling sound.

4:15   Stop whistling. Immediately, starting with your syllable, begin to whisper the text loudly, intensely, and rapidly, ad lib.

4:35   Stop. *(Silence.)*

4:40   Shout your syllable very loudly, once.

4:45   Begin to whistle. Start very low in range and let it rise slowly to your highest pitch, very loud, and hold it.

5:00   Stop.

THE END

— —

Yet I fret not my/self be/cause of e/vil/do/ers,
nei/ther am I en/vi/ous a/gainst
the wor/kers of i/ni/qui/ty.
Yea, they shall not be plant/ed;
yea, they shall not be sown:
yea, their stock shall not take root in the earth:
and Thou shalt al/so blow up/on them,
and they shall wi/ther, and the whirl/wind
shall take them a/way as stub/ble.
Thou car/ri/est them a/way as with a flood;
they are as a sleep; in the morn/ing
they are like the grass which grow/eth up.
For we are con/sumed by Thine an/ger
and by Thy wrath are we troub/led.

— —

The first whistle should be quite loud, and should vary individually in pitch back and forth slowly between approximately F and B; the result will be a strongly beating stream of sound.

In rehearsal, each singer is assigned one syllable by simply "counting-off" the syllables one to a person.

The whispering should be fierce, almost semi-voiced, as fast as possible, though it is not necessary that every singer complete the passage.

The shout must be powerful and organized.

Continental Drift #7
(The Epic of Gilgamesh)

J. George Cisneros

Needed:

—any number of vocal cadres of at least four members.

—one solo reader serving a clocking function to coordinate the cadres.

Operating guidelines for cadres:

—Cadres are encouraged to meet and practice separately.

—A text taken from the original Epic follows. The cadre should familiarize itself with the pronunciation of the entire text.

—Notice that some letters, syllables, and words are marked with a dotted-verticle and cross-barred figure. These forty-six figures give the vocal substance to be used as extended sound material. Through a process agreed to by all members of the cadre, choose any number of these figures.

—Using the group-decided letters, syllables, and words, experiment with various interpretations of the pronunciations.

—Still using a process agreeable to all cadre members (perhaps a new one), decide what can be done with the sound material—pitch, duration, dynamics, repetitions, attacks, silences, etc.—and experiment until all members of the cadre are satisfied.

—Combine results with other cadres.

—Experiment until all members of all cadres are satisfied.

Operating guideline for solo reader:

—Read the text in a soft-spoken manner at a comfortable tempo. Your speed with stops and starts will determine the spacing of the entrances by the cadres.

TEXT:

ER   HEGL   IOSL   AIED   RETB   EETH   ND   UTOS   EERY

USOM   A E T T   EANB   L NW   ENONHA   ED   ID   NA   UREHE

A   WTEYO   O   TEBO   G TH   ARISO   DS   A   DAI   T   THR   I

RTEYU   ORTEB   TH   MENKDUAI   ST * SE   AFDINEMS   T   REHRU

UOEHR   V   RETE   IYD   L   SA   OWIKAD   T H   OREH   ON   YRTA   A

SHTEMU   LNI   I   N   ER   HGOLE   ON   L   BDAE   TE   E

W   MFSI   YREB   OHUO   NA   TPEW   TSRO   ELA   OSUIR

GRH R E H E R HRG RIUSO ALE ORST WEPT AN

OUHO BERY ISFM W E ET EADB L NO ELOGH RE

N I INL UMETHS A ATRY NO HERO H T DAKIWO

AS L DYI ETER V RHEOU URHER T SMENIDFA

ES * TS IAUDKNEM HT BETRO UYERT I RHT T IAD

A SD OSIRA HT G OBET O OYETW A EHREUR AN DI

DE AHNONE WN L BNAE T T E A MOSU YREE

SOTU DN HTEE BTER DEIA LSOI LGHE RE

Ante·axis

a structure for a ten minute improvisation

New Verbal Workshop

Needed

three male and three female voices (speakers)

a stop watch

a small bell

Overall idea

to progress from various kinds of non-sustained sounds to a drone

Sound elements

1. Word fragments—staccato syllables composed of consonant/vowel combinations such as *guh, ti, pah, spk, krrr*

2. Bits of conversations—the subjects limited to events that happened in the past

3. A long silence

4. Rhythmical interjections

5. Any other non-sustained sounds such as laughs, shouts, snorts, cries, clicks

6. A drone

The piece is a concentrated abstract texture within which are mundane and humorous elements. The absolute ordinariness of a conversation, developing into something bizarre, comic or surrealistic, is part of the concept of the non-sustained. This contrasts with the final drone which is sustained, undulating, concerned with tone color, the emphasis being on a uniform texture growing naturally in intensity and then diminishing.

The beginning is very soft, a web of overlapping fragmented sounds. There is no development here. A texture is being made, something rustling, something stirring or growing—a beginning.

One person keeps the stop watch. At three points during the piece, chosen arbitrarily and changing with each performance, the timekeeper makes a pre-arranged gesture which is the signal for all to interrupt whatever they are saying and interject a short rhythmical section. The group decides in advance what sounds will constitute this rhythmic section and the same sounds are used each time, though their pitch and rhythm will vary. The entire group should use the same family of sounds. At the end of the rhythmical interjection each voice returns to whatever he/she was saying previously, as if there had been no interruption. At six minutes the timekeeper sounds a clear sharp note on the bell. Other points in the piece may be cued by the timekeeper as the group wishes.

Somewhere between two and three minutes there is a diminuendo leading to a silence lasting 20 to 40 seconds. It should feel like a long time.

Conversations may arise at any time during the piece except during the drone or during the silence. They should be casual and low-key and concerned with unspecified events in the past—reminiscences, shared experiences. The effect should be of something very commonplace and at the same time mysterious. *(Were you there? Where did you put it? What color was it?)* The conversation begins with a question or statement followed by a response and is limited at first to the two who begin it. After fifteen seconds others may join in. A conversational theme may then be developed, stated and played upon.

The drone begins at approximately seven minutes and continues until the end of the piece. The effect, since it follows a radically different sound texture, should be one of dramatic contrast. The drone should be relaxed at first and swell naturally to a peak at approximately nine minutes and then become gradually softer and more sparse until it ends. The speakers shouldn't be in a hurry to vary it. They should allow themselves to feel its essential vibration, the texture gradually becoming richer and more complex. The uniformity should be one of feeling arrived at together by close listening.

Speakers must realize that they are making a piece of music, so that while they are having conversations and being in some sense casual and everyday, there is still a heightened awareness of creating sound together. Each hears his voice in relation to the other voices and is aware of the overall sound being made—its pitch, volume, density, its mood.

Gothic

an improvisation on primal fears

Needed
six voices, a candle

Form
a progression of three linked duets with accompaniment

How to begin
Each member of the ensemble remembers a primal fear and presents it to the others in a brief statement. The statement may be verbal, non-verbal, a combination of sounds, words, cries. The important thing is that the fear is real—neither exaggerated nor understated. The mood may be expressionistic, dramatic, or narrative. All parody should be avoided.

Some examples of themes that developed when the New Verbal Workshop did the piece:

1. nightmares, especially nightmares remembered from childhood
2. a voice speaking incantations
3. a cry of helplessness and oppression
4. the past rising to the surface and influencing the present
5. unnatural change in a familiar person, place
6. screams of terror

Questions and exercises: Do any of the themes that occur go together? Try them as duets with the other voices providing accompaniment. What progression develops? Are there polarities? e.g.

articulate vs. inarticulate
quiet vs. loud
repetitive vs. disjunct

Find musical equivalents for fear. Find the pulse and pitch, the rhythmic pattern and sound color that expresses someone's fear. Enter into it.

There should be one principal constraint. Whatever is done should be carried to an extreme and sustained fully. For example, if there are screams, they should be as loud as possible and they should go on and on. They should become an end in themselves. The same should apply to any statements. The point is that this piece deals with the kinds of statements that are usually kept in check, if they are made at all. There should be no restraints on expression. On the contrary, the very lack of restraint should be turned into a form of discipline. Excess should be deliberate, so that it recovers the expressiveness which it lost in breaking the normal boundaries of expression.

The piece
The structure that should develop is three duets with accompaniment. The first two voices enter quietly and sparsely. Their themes are separate, but the performers relate in the timbre of their voices and their timing. An accompaniment develops, the whole trying to create the feeling tone and rhythm of the two fears. When the first section seems about to end, the second pair of voices begins a duet, overlapping the end of the first section—the new duet emerging from it, the accompanying voices thinning, hovering between the old themes and the new, until without perceptible transition they are there, in the new material. The second section is more intense than the first, containing perhaps, some non-verbal thematic material. The transition between sections two and three is again feathered. Section three is the most intense of all.

We prepared this piece in a darkened room sitting around a candle. In performance we entered in darkness and the piece began with the lighting of the candle.

The piece can be any length. Ours was 10–15 minutes.

Gothic was collaboratively composed and performed by the New Verbal Workshop. Members were Dale Cockrell, Janet Gilbert, Joan Korb, Herbert Marder, Norma Marder and Richard Wagner.

Intermittence

Jim Rosenberg

Intermittence is a poem for four readers and conductor. The format in performance is that each reader waits for a cue from the conductor, and on receiving a cue recites one stanza. Timing of the cues is thus entirely in the hands of the conductor. It is possible for the conductor to be dispensed with, and the readers to cue themselves, but at a cost of vastly increased rehearsal. The directions below assume a conductor, and that the conductor organizes the performance.

1. Following are 2 pages, each having 8 poems of three six-line stanzas. To prepare the texts for the readers, each page will need to be written out from 1 to 3 times and then cut up into 8 poems. Below the last stanza for each poem is a sequence of numbers indicating which readers are to receive a copy of that poem. (If possible this sequence of numbers should be deleted from the copies the readers actually receive, so that choices which they will make, explained below, are not influenced by the knowledge of whether their stanza is to be also read by someone else.) Each reader should receive 7 poems, and no reader should receive two copies of the same poem.

2. In selecting the readers, a high degree of voice contrast is desirable. There should be two male readers and two female readers. It is desirable that none of the readers have either training or experience in theater.

3. It is suggested that the conductor prepare a large sized mock-up of the schematic, replacing each pair of parentheses by a space large enough to accomodate a copy of any of the stanzas. This will display all of the information needed in a convenient format.

4. Give each reader the appropriate 7 pages of stanzas and a copy of the schematic. (The information contained in the schematic will be conveyed to them by the conductor during the performance, but having a copy of the schematic will give them a chance to see approximately where they are in the piece.) Each reader is to *independently* arrange his/her seven pages in any way desired. The readers should make an attempt to come to some kind of ordering. It

is important that in doing this they not consult each other.

5. When the readers have made their choices they should number their pages, 1 through 7, and on each page label the stanzas down the page as A, B, and C. It is this combination of number and letter which is keyed to the schematic. The conductor's texts should be arranged to match those of the readers, and if a mock-up has been made, as in 3 above, the stanzas should be attached to the mock-up in the appropriate place.

6. *Reading the Schematic.* The schematic is laid out as a sequence of boxes, each box containing parentheses and other symbols, and with either the letter 'S' or a number between boxes. The 'S' and the numbers give timing information, explained below. In what follows, the meaning of each symbol in the schematic will be explained, and then examples will be given. Each box represents an overlay of stanzas, a *pair of parentheses* denoting one stanza. The reader reciting a stanza indicated by a pair of parentheses is given by the large number directly below the left parenthesis, as well as by its position vertically within the box. A *number within parentheses* gives the number of a line (one through six) in the stanza indicated by the parentheses, and indicates that another reader (or readers) will be cued to the beginning of that line. An *equal sign attached to a parenthesis* (i. e. '=(' or ')=') denotes that all other parentheses with equal signs attached, (in the same box), directly above or below the given parenthesis are to occur at the same moment. The *large numbers* at the bottom of the box indicate which reader is to be cued. When two large numbers occur *close together and separated by a comma*, the two readers indicated by these numbers are to be cued simultaneously. (Note their parentheses will have equal signs.) The *small numbers* at the lower right of each box give the numbers of the stanzas indicated in that box, read top pair left-to-right then bottom pair left-to-right, corresponding to the stanzas in order of appearance as indicated by the large numbers.

Examples: The first box on page 1 of the schematic denotes:

(1) Reader 2 begins, reading stanza 1A.

(2) When Reader 2 begins reading line 5 of his/her stanza 1A, Reader 1 begins reading stanza 1A.

The first box on page 2 of the schematic denotes:

(1) Reader 3 begins reading stanza 4A.

(2) Exactly at the point Reader 3 finishes this stanza, Readers 1 and 2 begin simultaneously, Reader 1 reading stanza 5B and reader 2 reading stanza 4B.

(3) When Reader 1 begins reading line 4 of his/her stanza 5B, Reader 4 begins reading stanza 4B.

7. *Timing Information*

(1) When a reader or pair of readers is to begin at the point another reader finishes, the second reader or pair or readers should come in exactly as though simply continuing the first reader's stanza. I.e. the amount of space between the end of the last line of the first reader's stanza and the beginning of the second reader's (or pair of readers') stanza(s) should equal the amount of space the first reader is leaving between lines in his/her stanzas. The readers and conductor should strive for precise timing in this kind of cue.

(2) The letter 'S' between boxes denotes a *short silence*. Its exact length is determined in real time by the conductor:

(a) leaving an amount of time equal to the time the last reader to be heard was leaving between lines within a stanza; *then*

(b) repeating silently the last line of the last stanza heard, unless this line is exceptionally short, in which case the conductor should repeat silently one of the longer lines of the last stanza to be heard.

(3) A number between boxes denotes a silence whose length is determined by the conductor counting the indicated number of beats. The rhythm of these beats should be even and may be determined by the conductor in real time according to what seems to be a natural tempo, roughly within the limits of one beat every 1 to 1.5 seconds. A silence of 8 beats should be clearly distinct from a silence determined by the 'S' method.

8. *Manner of reciting the stanzas.* The lines should be read in a clear non-dramatic way, the words mostly presenting themselves. Avoid exaggerated inflections. The following guidelines for intonation are important:

(1) The voice should not fall greatly except in response to a punctuation mark. For those lines with no punctuation, the pitch contour should be even, or slightly rising. It is especially important to pay attention to the line endings. If there is no period at the end of the line, read as though more is to follow, almost as if the ending of the line has been cut off (without, however, actually "clipping" any of the speech sounds.) Some of the lines are not syntactical, but try to arrive at an even natural intonation.

(2) The intonation in response to a punctuation mark should be the same as it would normally be in grammatical speech, even though that mark may not be in the place where it ought to be syntactically. It is more important that the pitch contour for a line with no punctuation be *clearly distinct* from the pitch contour for a line ending in a period than that either pitch contour fit a prescribed pattern. If a period or comma falls in the middle of a line, a pause for that mark should be very brief, *significantly shorter* than the pause between lines of a stanza.

There should be a short pause between the lines of a stanza, slightly longer than a normal pause between sentences, but not so long that the reading seems to lag. They should fit naturally with the rhythm of the line, and will probably be about the length of a longer syllable. When a reader is reading simultaneously with another reader, each reader should keep to his/her own sense of the rhythm of the stanza, as if the other reader were not there. The conductor should point out during rehearsal if anyone is reading too fast, too slowly, or too unevenly with respect to the others, so that a gradual equilibrium of rhythm is achieved, but the readers should not overtly attempt to synchronize themselves in real time. If it should happen that two readers are reading the same stanza simultaneously, they should absolutely *not* attempt to read in unison. A slight disparity in timing, preserving minor inaccuracies of each reader, is desirable.

The readers should try not to be tardy in following a cue, though absolutely precise timing is generally not necessary. In those cases where a reader is cued at the beginning of a line of another reader, (indicated in the schematic by a number between parentheses), the two need not begin actually simultaneously. Careful timing is important in these instances:

(a) when readers are cued to the ending of another stanza.

(b) a cue after a silence determined by an 'S' in the schematic.

(c) when two readers enter simultaneously. It is suggested that each reader who has a simultaneous entrance with another reader mark such a stanza with an asterisk, so as not to be surprised by the other reader and to be able to come in after the cue very precisely.

1 Slight flashes, disparate	1 Center two sections with the head
2 Stone especially smooth	2 Crawling out. Canvas pounds
3 Location ship it down.	3 Up with its own notch
4 Magnified the bottom	4 Stepping flowers.
5 Darting and then habitual shadow.	5 Rescinded order of folding.
6 Seen bending	6 The one will carry extra

1 Star engage not know that name.
2 Two the cluster squinting
3 Predictable from enter the tail
4 Colored streak.
5 Better after midnight.
6 Reference direction

1 Shape exchange the newer
2 Passing variation. The higher end
3 Speed the gap is shrinking.
4 Behind.
5 To the third but might get on
6 Consistently advantage

1 A reason comes of melting
2 The signpost tending carry off.
3 Mask shouting
4 Natural point because it cross
5 Speed. Continuous wearing.
6 Several white, beyond view

1 Rushing and measured the head
2 Other direction. Just as smooth
3 Narrow the sign have been counting
4 Uphill begins again.
5 The straight as by exposed if shoulder
6 A foot, even one branch

1 In spite of it no stationary appearance.
2 Theory over shimmer.
3 Name the former story. In mythology
4 The ones appear as grouping.
5 Singled out
6 Season as it dip straight down

1 Are the single posts
2 Two sweep crossing.
3 Longer for it getting over.
4 Same green background
5 Crossing need the screen.
6 Elevated neighborhoods

1 Piled above it.
2 Gently and repeating diamond
3 Rings
4 Distorted. Front range of trees
5 Facing lower part.
6 Walked entirely around

1 Seclude.
2 The string as each by pace
3 Hanging moss.
4 Popular song an step unavoidable
5 Descent and then the knees.
6 Equally busy

1 Red pair alternating
2 Shoulder. No dark outline
3 Cast it diminishes their brightness.
4 Time not expect a shadow
5 Slowly loss. The bank
6 Require a sudden headlight

1 Number of advance.
2 Fraction then the mandatory
3 Planning.
4 Right the one arriving.
5 Broad outlines of direction
6 45.

1,2

1,2

---

1 Relative blue.
2 Older streak and if several a crossed wisp
3 Moving.
4 An arrangement, gap in the bank
5 Structured altitude of the billow
6 Resist interpret that shape.

1 Dashed white.
2 Speed, the radio cannot
3 Chain of three. The hairpin
4 At roof between which call a dome
5 Cap.
6 Posted limit

1 Moving gaps.. A halo
2 White the speed and pass in front.
3 Mostly silver
4 Waiting if clear circle
5 Travel for the sudden breaking out.
6 Famous shadows

1 Examine older. Many frame
2 Missing as if trees.
3 Fewly narrow when the flat
4 Layout. Demographic sectioning
5 Body of water and the pull
6 Ascending

1 Heavy row direction then advance.
2 Surround in still see it.
3 Two notes designed the largest distance
4 Points of moisture
5 Nothing of the inward once arrived
6 Reflection of sound.

1 Acquire the main juncture
2 Hardly refuse
3 Nothing turn.
4 Town the gateway self proclaim
5 Immediate dryness.
6 Presuming on the meal

1 Hidden by explained the seeing angle.
2 Speed one hour earlier each
3 Position in the amount the dark.
4 Closer gravity
5 Where it hopes to float.
6 Regular precess

1 Spire. Identify in sprawling
2 Nuclear research.
3 Largest from when bay straight line
4 Curious shape.
5 Popular known now sitting outside.
6 Aircraft eye level

1 Intermittence.
2 Muffled. It mix the hour then is clear
3 The sudden difficulty glare.
4 Correlation with the wind
5 Having seen to the hill
6 A residual heat. Unprepared

1 Sign of always on the same
2 Supposedly the largest project
3 Switch.
4 Slightly down the right green
5 Exit 1. Familiar
6 One more valley

1 Intense, cast the road appear very white
2 Lamp and nothing present
3 Pull to the shadow.
4 Brighter than for not having been accustomed.
5 Diminish seen the way stars
6 Dominating object. The face

1 Notorious avenue.
2 Some intend in fabrication
3 The stand in shows if other paper.
4 Mostly covered
5 Seldom louder the open door.
6 Drifting groups

1,2,3

1,2,4

1,3,4

2

1 Boxes. Raising the dirt
2 Only several colors.
3 Tall the one cluster away.
4 Variety each a method
5 Package of seeds
6 The several not in rows

1 Glass sides, hanging
2 Interrupted by turn of the head.
3 Pecking
4 In twice of the time gathering.
5 Direction of the scatter.
6 Gradually spilled

1 Occasional the roof
2 Circled out. Crawling
3 The group if then the dish.
4 The one who puts it out.
5 A pigeon
6 Small grassy

2

1 Between and the eyes.
2 If surrounding but far enough.
3 Hanging
4 But no new distinctness. A tree
5 And out completely block the shed
6 Remain fixed

1 A means by dispersal.
2 Knowledge that the train
3 And bounce downward.
4 More which is it then to see
5 Of dim outline.
6 Not the sense or silhouette, straining

1 If arriving and see it move
2 Small progression
3 A mark means meadows and a post.
4 Silver as the front.
5 Small line, dark the ground level
6 Knowing to approach cooler. Taken

2,3,4

1 Seldom longer drift.
2 Eyes as quickly motion
3 Curvature the trailing feathers
4 Memorized if backwards causes no alarm.
5 Waiting longer no sudden dive.
6 At rest proceed beyond the next

1 Blotted streak
2 Fist inside behind the neck.
3 Purple from the sun does not move.
4 Blinked, shifting then the more intense
5 Nothing really has that color.
6 Again to back for blue

1 Lately seen in pairs.
2 Replace the handled for exception
3 If by knowing they are out
4 Thinner.
5 Almost more than perching
6 Only one. The mother

3

1 Ceramic positions
2 Not by writing.
3 Small contain that might get lost
4 Row of books. The support
5 In left notes.
6 Varieties of ink

1 Buckets of they more than heavy
2 Hammer tail one broken
3 Rust inside to get the cord.
4 Painted over, small compartments
5 Straw destroy if finding tape.
6 Many glue

1 Oldest letter
2 Light become the corner.
3 Table no travelling
4 Clamp together.
5 Roll. The extra sheets
6 Too stained

3

1 Semblance of the back it blue.
2 Clearly first one
3 Duration of flash. Mating
4 Continue even though dead.
5 Not the whole abdomen
6 While rising

1 Three at even once.
2 Nearness if it makes the turn the head
3 Seldom on the porch, under
4 Not enough watch over distance.
5 Version of brightness
6 Coordinate attention

1 First behind the house
2 Still if dusk up and silhouette
3 Large body.
4 Number of flashes. To the west
5 Few for resting on the blade.
6 Walking the fields, continually farther out

3,4

1 Scattered parallel.
2 Color light come on itself.
3 Essential near square
4 There the brightest. Main avenue
5 Up the general glare.
6 Specifically recognize the sign

1 Infer helicopter. Flashing
2 At level down below
3 District.
4 Two in brightest where they meet.
5 Off the sides in houses then by extra colored
6 Blocked

1 Several banks.
2 Under lighthouse
3 Sweep the distant going off.
4 Both sides of the bridge.
5 Following, though mostly
6 String yellow

3,4

1 Quilting, to be seen
2 Number of windows.
3 The seen internal compartment no horizon
4 Dipped and only blue
5 Turning angle then restored.
6 Chosen side.

1 Of the those large enough
2 Many will identify the highway.
3 Personal landmark.
4 Seeming much too far
5 Wide and nothing of the industrial
6 Closer view

1 The extent of the river. Outside
2 Particular poles.
3 Feeling then the gear
4 Straight line
5 Sudden in appearance asphalt
6 Impact only once. The reverse

4

1 Access freshness the rocks
2 No new circulation.
3 Cooler the pointed then the back
4 Narrows with barely elevation
5 Of gone out.
6 Dressing while still dark

1 Small enough to see as if bent
2 Run up the composition
3 Standing.
4 They appear before the cracks.
5 Carried up the brushing full face
6 Newest preparation

1 Curling by from someone else.
2 Still as if early cluster
3 Serenade. The twice
4 Never as the hearing carry upward
5 Failing to worry over losing traction.
6 Below and stirring

4

INTERMITTENCE by Jim Rosenberg   Schematic

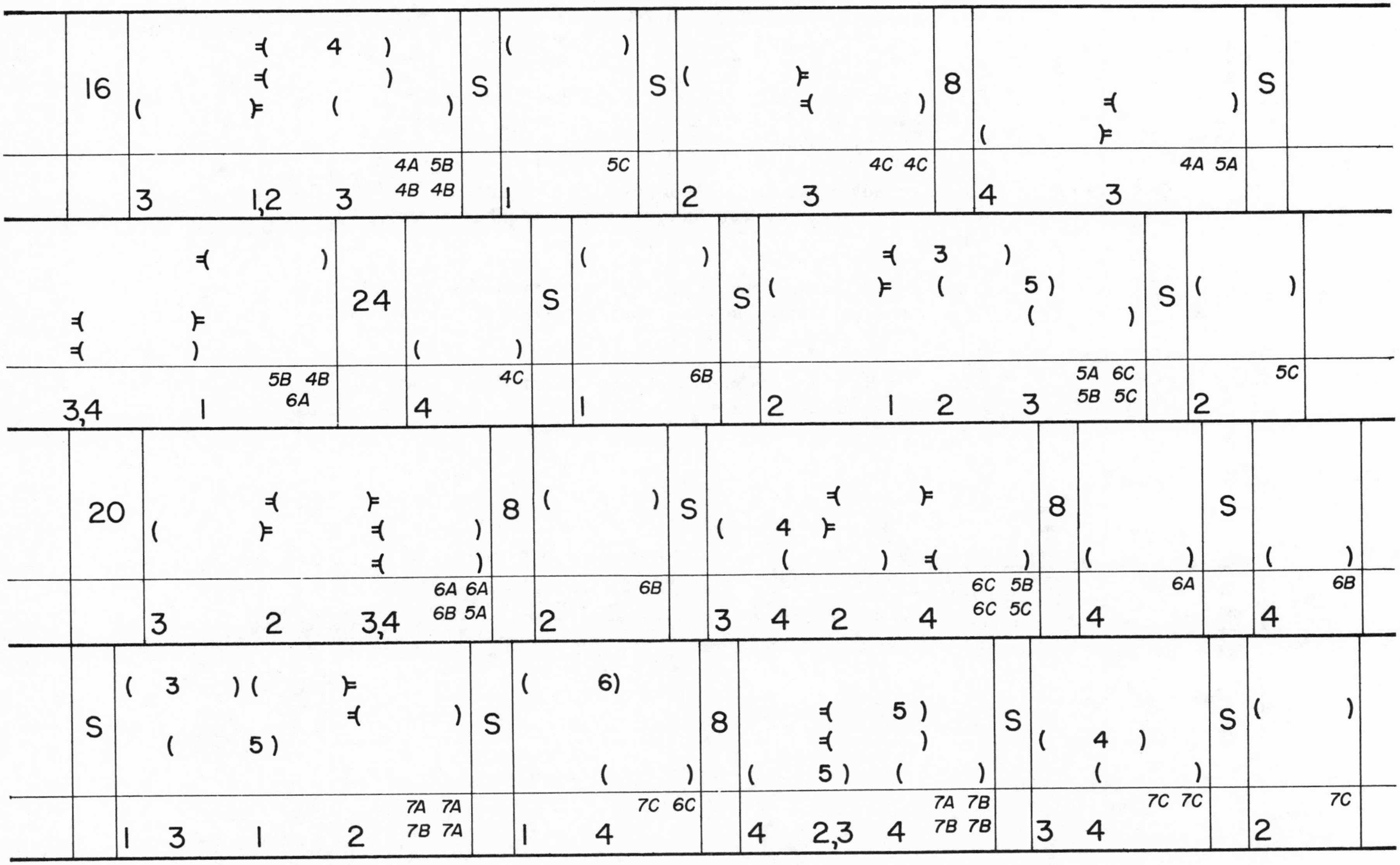

Intermezzo

Timothy Sullivan

A vocal piece for a group of five to about fifteen people. Performers sing improvised melody lines in a smooth madrigal style, and speak isolated words.

The piece requires a leader, two or more soloists, and a chorus divided into two groups (leader and soloists are members of the chorus).

Words to be sung on a sustained pitch are underlined with a straight line, words to be sung melodically are underlined with a wavy line, and spoken words are not underlined.

The text, which consists mainly of words which begin with "in-", appears in heavy letters.

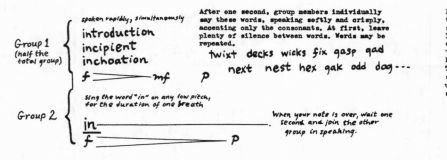

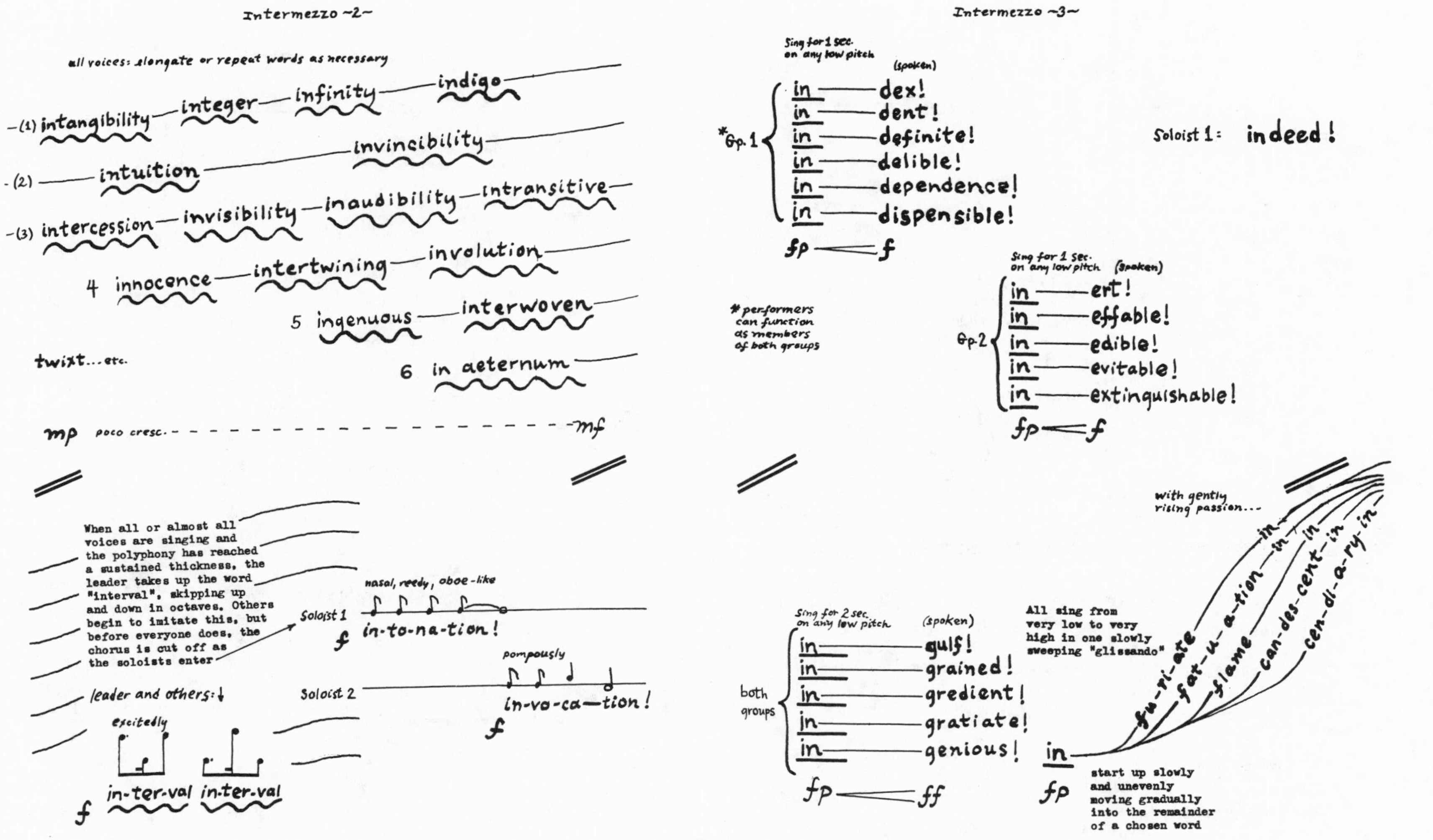

Intermezzo ~2~

all voices: elongate or repeat words as necessary

-(1) intangibility — integer — infinity — indigo

-(2) — intuition — invincibility

-(3) intercession — invisibility — inaudibility — intransitive

4 innocence — intertwining — involution

5 ingenuous — interwoven

twixt...etc.

mp   poco cresc. - - - - - - - - - - - — mf

When all or almost all voices are singing and the polyphony has reached a sustained thickness, the leader takes up the word "interval", skipping up and down in octaves. Others begin to imitate this, but before everyone does, the chorus is cut off as the soloists enter

leader and others: ↓

excitedly

f   in-ter-val   in-ter-val

nasal, reedy, oboe-like

Soloist 1   in-to-na-tion!   f

pompously

Soloist 2   in-vo-ca—tion!   f

Intermezzo ~3~

Sing for 1 sec. on any low pitch   (spoken)

*Gp.1 {
in ——— dex!
in ——— dent!
in ——— definite!
in ——— delible!
in ——— dependence!
in ——— dispensible!
}
fp ——— f

Soloist 1:   indeed!

performers can function as members of both groups

Sing for 1 sec. on any low pitch   (spoken)

Gp-2 {
in ——— ert!
in ——— effable!
in ——— edible!
in ——— evitable!
in ——— extinguishable!
}
fp ——— f

Sing for 2 sec. on any low pitch   (spoken)

both groups {
in ——— gulf!
in ——— grained!
in ——— gredient!
in ——— gratiate!
in ——— genious!
}
fp ——— ff

with gently rising passion...

in — fu-ri-ate — in — fat-u-a-tion — in — flame — in — can-des-cent — in — cen-di-a-ry — in —

in   fp

start up slowly and unevenly moving gradually into the remainder of a chosen word

All sing from very low to very high in one slowly sweeping "glissando"

Intermezzo ~4~

one, two or three voices hold a high note, staggering breathing if possible

(in)

at the top of the gliss., most of the voices execute a short quick fall.

Soloist 1: **instantly!** f

Soloist 2: intermission! intervention! f

informally incidentally, mp

All others:

{
involuntary!
   intoxicate!
investigation!
   inventory!
invigorating!
   invariably!
innoculation!
   infallible!
indigenous!
   incinerator!
}
f

---

the two or three voices continue to hold the high note

All others {

intervention!
involuntary! in toto! incite
intoxicate!
investigation! incisive inclination! inflate
inventory!
invigorating! India, Indiana! inhale
invariably!
innoculation! interlarded interview! Inca
infallible! inherent inheritance! inboard
indigenous!
incinerator! integral intake

ff   diminuendo - - - - - - - - - - - mf - -

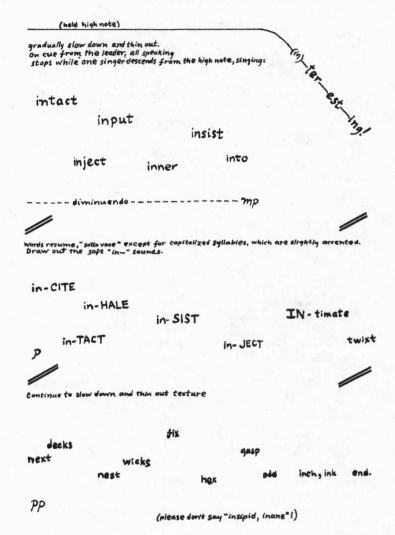

Intermezzo ~5~

(held high note)

gradually slow down and thin out.
On cue from the leader, all speaking
stops while one singer descends from the high note, singing:

(in) -ter -est -ing!

intact

input

insist

inject inner into

- - - - diminuendo - - - - - - - - - - - mp

Words resume, "sotto voce" except for capitalized syllables, which are slightly accented.
Draw out the soft "in-" sounds.

in-CITE

in-HALE

in-SIST IN-timate

in-TACT in-JECT twixt

p

Continue to slow down and thin out texture

fix

decks gasp

next wicks

nest hex add inch, ink end.

PP

(please don't say "insipid, inane"!)

SUNG VOCAL MUSIC, CHORAL
AND ENSEMBLE

The music in this section uses various forms of traditional singing. A series of relatively simple choral pieces, chants, and rounds is followed by several pieces for solo voice. The section also introduces the use of conventional musical notation, but of the sort which is still very accessible to anyone, with perhaps a little coaching.

Kenneth Maue's *Becoming Chant* and Barbara Benary's *Moon Cat Chant* and *Singing Braid* are all very closely related, and involve repetitive patterns and various regular permutations of pitch and rhythmic material. The two pieces by Alvin Curran—*Processional* and *Rounds*—are also closely related to each other in their use of repetitive material and rounds, and may actually be performed as one piece. They make simple use of instruments or hand clapping, yet are still predominantly vocal. The works by James Tenney are self-explanatory and very accessible. Meredith Monk's *Change* uses simple material but with a striking modulation in the vocal timbre from an open, straight tone to a very nasal quality. Dennis Riely's *What Is a Kiss?* and Noel Da Costa's *Five/Seven are rounds*—the latter more elaborate in texture—and use more complex rhythms and twelve-tone pitch series. As such they are certainly more difficult to sing, and may necessitate instrumental doubling for some groups during rehearsal.

Other choral music, which follows very directly from this section, is found in Chapter 7.

Becoming Chant

Kenneth Maue

This is a metric chant for any number of people.

Introduction
The poem is recited on a single recitation pitch by a single singer.

The chant:
Each line is five beats is length. This rhythm is established and kept
by a pair of finger cymbals:

The group chants the text in strict and continuous rhythm. All can use
the same pitch, or else they may divide into octaves and fifths.

The moving line:
Lines of the text which are underlined have a moving part. Half the
chanters should remain on their chanting pitch. The other half move
from their chant pitch up a scale and back again:

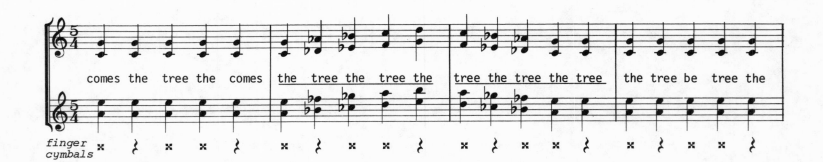

The seed becomes the tree
The tree becomes the wood
The wood becomes the house
The house becomes the home
The home becomes the past
The past becomes the gem
The gem becomes the gift
The gift becomes the seed
Amen, amen

The seed be seed the

seed be comes be seed

be comes the comes be

comes the tree the comes

the tree the tree the

tree the tree the tree

the tree be tree the

tree be comes be tree

be comes the comes be

comes the wood the comes

the wood the wood the

wood the wood the wood

the wood be wood the

wood be comes be wood

be comes the comes be

comes the house the comes

the house the house the

house the house the house

the house be house the

house be comes be house

be comes the comes be

comes the home the comes

the home the home the

home the home the home

the home be home the

home be comes be home

be comes the comes be

comes the past the comes

the past the past the

past the past the past

the past be past the

past be comes be past

be comes the comes be

comes the gem the comes

the gem the gem the

gem the gem the gem

the gem be gem the

gem be comes be gem

be comes the comes be

comes the gift the comes

the gift the gift the

gift the gift the gift

the gift be gift the

gift be comes be gift

be comes the comes be

comes the seed the comes

the seed a seed the

seed a men a seed

a men a men a

men a men a men

Moon Cat Chant

Barbara Benary

This chant is derived from a permutation process used as an aid to memorization in ancient Vedic chant. The pattern is called Ghana Vikrti:

1–2–2–1–1–2–3–3–2–1–1–2–2

Words followed by a dash (–) are two beats long.
Words without a dash are one beat long.
The score is chanted in strict meter reading across the columns, left to right.
At the end of each section, allow a pause of five seconds or more. Then continue on at the same tempo as before.

The irregular groupings within a line can be highlighted by striking finger cymbals at the beginning of each:

We come– come– we we come– to to come– we (etc)

⌘   ⌘   ⌘   ⌘

The chant can be performed in unison, in octaves, or in parallel motion at any interval. Long words (followed by dash) are chanted at a single pitch. Short words (no dash) are a half step lower. A favorite arrangement of mine is two parts chanting parallel at the interval of a major third, thus:

Ghana   Vikrti

We come –	come– we	we come – to	to come – we	we come – to
Come – to	to come –	come – to the	the to come –	come – to the
To the	the to	to the house –	house – the to	to the house –
The house –	house– the	the house – of	of house – the	the house – of
House – of	of house –	house – of the	the of house –	house – of the
Of the	the of	of the moon –	moon – the of	of the moon –
The moon –	moon – the	the moon – the	the moon – the	the moon – the
Moon – the	the moon –	moon – the moon –	moon – the moon –	moon – the moon –
The moon –	moon – the	the moon – cat –	cat – moon – the	the moon – cat –
Moon – cat –	cat – moon –	moon – cat – is	is cat – moon –	moon – cat – is
Cat – is	is cat –	cat – is still –	still – is cat –	cat – is still –
Is still –	still – is	is still – and	and still – is	is still – and
Still – and	and still –	still – and far –	far – and still –	still – and far –
And far –	far – and	and far – clouds –	clouds – far – and	and far – clouds –
Far – clouds –	clouds – far	far – clouds – greet	greet clouds – far –	far – clouds – greet
Clouds – greet	greet clouds –	clouds – greet us	us greet clouds –	clouds – greet us
greet us	us greet	greet us and	and us greet	greet us and
us and	and us	us and say –	say – and us	us and say –
and say –	say – and	and say – no	no say – and	and say – no
say – no	no say –	say – no more –	more – no say –	say – no more –

Singing Braid

Barbara Benary

This piece is to be performed by three singers, or by a larger group (up to nine) divided into three sections. Each of the three uses a chime, bell or woodblock to keep their rhythmic place.

Basic rhythmic pattern

The three singers make an interlocking pattern by alternating two notes in time. Each is rhythmically "off" by an eighth note from the others, thus-

There is no overall downbeat. Each singer should hear his own part as being on the beat, and the others as offbeat in relation to him. Use an open "a" or "la" syllable.

The melodic sequence

Beginning with the percussion instruments, the three singers establish the rhythmic interlock. Then, one at a time, their vocal parts are added. All begin with the first two pitches. From there, the singers very slowly go through a series of pitches by changing one note at a time. One can think of the sequence as linear or cyclic. I prefer cyclic. The performance can consist of as many cycles as the players desire.

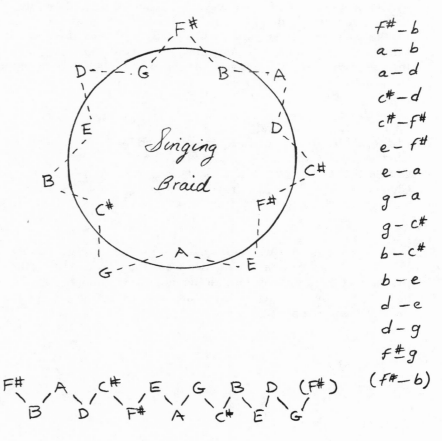

Changing the pitches

After the initial combination of notes has been heard for some time, the players begin to change notes, one person at a time. The changes should proceed in a leisurely way. If a group of more than three is singing, they are divided into three rhythmic parts; however persons on the same rhythmic part do not need to change their pitches simultaneously. In fact, the more they "spread out" the richer will be the melodic texture. Pitches may be sung in any octave convenient to the voices.

Begin..F # and B
Change F # to A ....result A and B
Change B to D................................ result A and D
Change A to C #.......................... result C # and D
Change D to F # ....result C # and F #
etc.

Each player proceeds around the cycle of pitches at this own speed. When reaching the initial two pitches again, the players who get there first stay at those pitches until all the other have gone through their changes and have caught up. When all are again on the initial notes, the piece may end or another cycle may begin.

Elaboration of the basic braid

Instrumental parts may be added to elaborate successive cycles. For instance, the vocal parts might be doubled by xylophone, marimba, vibes or the like. These instruments might also improvise repeated fragments built on the pitches being sounded at the moment in the basic braid. Slow and ornate obligato might be improvised on bamboo flutes, or else wind or string instruments might pick out individual tones from the matrix and sustain them.

Very slow alterations of volume and tempo might be introduced—for instance, slowing down as players approach the end of a cycle of pitches.

Ending

After the singers have all arrived at the opening two pitches for the final time, they drop out, one by one. But the bells or chimes that mark their rhythmic place are allowed to continue on a while longer before stopping.

Processional

Alvin Curran

Instructions

The performers enter the performing-space one by one clapping to the above rhythm in unison. After everyone has entered the space the soloist begins singing and Version I ° is sung by all. When Version I ° has been performed several times individual singers may move on to Version II ° or the whole chorus may begin Version II ° on a signal. After several repeats the performers may introduce variations into the basic structure. When the basic structure is no longer recognizable the soloist begins clapping or drumming

$$(\textit{♩}=132) \quad \textbf{\textit{fff}}$$

which is picked by everyone (the singing ceases) and is performed until near exhaustion, stopped all together and suddenly by a signal from the soloist. A long pause should follow, long enough to gain total silence in the room. The silence should be maintained as long as possible and then another music should begin. (e.g. the drone of *Rounds* might be effective here).

The vocal sounds of Version I° should at first be vowels only to which w, wh and m sounds may be added *gradually*, by Version II° n, and d, b, t, p may be *slowly* introduced, finally any other consonants. "Real words" are to be avoided where possible. The singing may be recorded and later played back against itself. Let the audience come in but not take over.

Rounds

Alvin Curran

The three steps in performing each strophe are:

1. Sing the first four notes and words in their given order. Always sing each note long and loud and as "in tune" as possible. Pause only to breathe in between notes.

2. Sing the same four notes in any order 1-3 times. Brief pauses may be taken between notes.

3. Again, sing the first four notes as given and add the final note, which should be held for as long as possible.

Mode of Performance

For 3-10 voices: One singer begins the first strophe alone. The second singer enters just after the first has sung the word "cloud." The third enters just after the second has sung "cloud" and so on. After a singer has sung all the strophes he joins the drone singing one or alternately all of notes in the final chord at the end of the seventh strophe. These may be sung at will. At any time after the last singer joins the drone, the performance may end.

For 10 or more voices: The singers should divide themselves in small equal numbered groups. One singer of each group shall act as well as conductor of that group. Group entrances are staggered as described above. Steps nos. 1 and 3 are to be sung in unison; Step no. 2 may be performed in unison according to an agreed plan, or left to the individual singers to interpret, until signalled by their conductor to go on to no. 3. The performance ends as described above.

The Drone

The drone consists of a small number of any wind, string, percussion or electronic instruments playing sustained or plucked tones with long pauses between attacks, on the interval of a perfect fifth which is selected as the tonality for the performance. The notes of this interval may be played in any order, separately or together. Occassionally other notes from the vocal part may be played as well. The Drone should begin before the voices enter. The tonality here is given as g-c, and is transposable to any other convenient tonality.

Means of performance other than this one are to be encouraged.

A Rose Is a Rose Is a Round
for Philip Corner

James Tenney

What is a Kiss?

Dennis Riley

Words by Robert Herrick

Once or twice _unisono_; then, as a round; repeat _ad lib._

Hey When I Sing These 4 Songs Hey Look What Happens
for Mixed Chorus

James Tenney
1971

"Hey When I Sing" version from the Seneca by Jerome Rothenberg and Richard Johnny John from Jerome Rothenberg (ed.), *Shaking the Pumpkin*, Anchor Books, 1972. Copyright © 1972 by Jerome Rothenberg. Used by permission.

Note: Tenors and basses sing each line through twice; sopranos and altos join in the second time only.

Change
for Four Voices

Meredith Monk

Voice I enters singing a round, clear tone with a vowel between "ah" and "uh" (a soft "ah") and remains singing this phrase throughout the piece. After four or five repetitions of Voice I, Voice II enters singing the same round, clear tone with the same vowel as Voice I. Voice II sings line A a few times, then B a few times, then back to A a few times, then on the C a few times and back to A and finally to D a few times. At this point Voice II may freely select lines but should end the piece on line D. Voice III and Voice IV come in together after about four phrases of Voice II. They then freely drop out and re-enter several times to the end.

After all four voices have entered, they begin a process of changing the vocal timbre to an increasingly nasal sound. It gradually and imperceptably modulates to an *extremely* rough, nasal, creaking, tremolo "eee" sound. As an image, it is as if the voice ages so that the last quality is that of a very old person.

Recording: *Key;* (Lovely Music LML-1051).
Copyright © 1969 by Meredith Monk. Used by permission.

Five/Seven

Noel G. Da Costa

☆ May also be played by 2 instruments in range --- [ex. ob./Cello; Trpt./tb.]

SOLO VOCAL MUSIC

These works for solo voice demand greater vocal skill and performing experience than earlier ones in this chapter. They are offered here as a small sample of a much larger repertory which is among the most interesting and exciting in recent music. They are all very personal to the composer–performers and come from each one's own special skills and psyche. Charlemagne Palestine's six songs are exciting vocal, visual, and physical performance pieces by a composer who combines many of the traditional and more recent art forms (music, visual arts, theater, "video"). Joan La Barbara's *Hear What I Feel* describes the performer's preparation an hour before the performance and sets up a situation in which the performer reacts to unknown objects that are touched but not seen. The only specific control given here by the composer is that the actual performance be ten minutes long. Other than that it is the performer that creates all the sounds and the structure of the piece, each time from a new physical situation. Bill Beckley's *Songs* are delightful miniatures which are quite visual yet clearly performable. Many were conceived for gallery performance in conjunction with photographs and sculpture, to which they are closely related. Since they are all for different voices and the last two for four solo singers, it would be interesting to have them performed together, in any order, using the four voices soprano, alto, tenor, and bass. Christian Wolff's *Song* and *Double Song* are both very open scores to be created by the performers. While both feature solo singers, they do use various simple forms of accompaniment. Malcolm Goldstein's *Yosha's Morning Song* is based on transcriptions of a child's morning singing, and as such involves quite a few unusual vocal sounds and qualities. It is important that it be sung in a simple, direct, and completely undramatic manner. The two sections from Meredith Monk's *Our Lady of Late* are part of a work which extends the voice in an extraordinary variety of ways. It is a piece which comes from her particular vocal abilities and is, to a considerable extent, a personal work. The first section, "Knee," is rather straightforward in notation but uses a very special nasal sound. "Slide" is much more graphic and improvisational, exploring as it does rapid and extreme shifts in register. Jana Haimsohn's chant-like *I Ain't Listen,* a personal piece as well, is also an extraordinary exploration of the voice, in this case through rhythmic development of a wide variety of consonant and vowel sounds coming from language.

Other works for solo voice or ensemble with other instruments are:

Chap. 1:   *Humming* (Anneal Lockwood)
   Mindfulness of Breathing (Michael Parsons)
   W Piece (Bonnie Barnett)
Chap. 6:   *The Duke of York* (Alvin Lucier)
   Solo for Voice 43 (John Cage)
   Narrative Song and *Stereo Song* (Laurie Anderson)
   King Speech Song (Daniel Lentz)
Chap. 7:   *Object Pieces* (Roger Johnson)
   Minimusic (R. Murray Schafer)
   Olson III (Terry Riley)
   The Great Learning (Cornelius Cardew)
   Time Goes By and *The Smile That You Send Out* (Karl Berger)
   "Fairy Song" (Richard Peaslee)
   Tom Thumb (Stephen Mayer)
Chap. 8:   *North American Eclipse* (Daniel Lentz)

Overtone Study for Voice (1970)

Charlemagne Palestine

Sing a sustained *ah* on one pitch, holding your breath as long as possible. While maintaining the same pitch begin exploring all the possible fluid changes of shape your mouth, tongue and lips can create. *Ah - ay - ee - aw - oh - oo* : use this simple vowel study to begin. At the start move fluidly from one vowel to another. Listen to what happens over the sustained pitch. Soon you will begin to hear higher sounds above your singing pitch. These are overtones. Soon you will begin to bring out certain overtones easily by singing a specific mouth shape on the fundamental. Arpeggios are possible by moving the mouth quickly from shape to shape. These are your raw materials for this study. Many versions are possible ranging from few minutes to a few hours. Begin simply, becomming more complex later on. For best results sing this study in a reverberant room. It will help accentuate the overtones.

Overtone Study with Cigarette (1970)

Charlemagne Palestine

Same approach as in previous study except with a lit cigarette in mouth. Sing overtones until cigarette reaches lips and becomes too painful to continue.

This study is about endurance as well as sound. For that reason an unfiltered cigarette is more challenging.

Singing Against the Floor (1973)

Charlemagne Palestine

To begin, kneel down on your knees—clasp your two hands together—let your body sway from side to side—begin to sing a sustained tone on one pitch. Gradually let the swaying get faster and faster until finally you let yourself fall down on your right side—singing all the while not changing pitch, breathing as naturally as you can—letting the movement punctuate the internal rhythm of the sound. Slowly get back on your knees and repeat movement again and again—eventually getting faster and faster—leaving out finally the preliminary swaying—becoming simply: falling - getting up - falling - getting up - falling etc. - singing one sustained pitch all the while until you are out of breath. After your final fall, remain lying on the floor until your strength returns. The more stamina you have, the longer the version. This is a study in sound, motion and endurance.

Singing Against the Wall (1974)

Charlemagne Palestine

Same basic process as in previous study. Kneel on your knees near a wall. Begin singing a sustained tone on one pitch. Sway side to side slowly at first, gradually picking up speed, soon slamming your right shoulder against the wall as hard as you can, singing all the while. Repeat again and again, getting faster and faster until pain and exhaustion force you to stop. Remain in a repose position hugging the wall with your shoulder until you regain your strength.

Singing Against the Face (1975)

Charlemagne Palestine

This work may be performed sitting, standing or on one's knees. Begin by singing a sustained tone on one pitch. Gradually begin swaying your body front to back, front to back from the waist up—eventually awaying faster and faster, singing all the while. Then slap your left cheek with your left hand as hard as you can. Then your right cheek with your right hand - again and again, slowly at first, picking up speed until pain and exhaustion force you to stop. Remain in repose until you regain your strength. The longer you endure, the better.

Singing on the Run (1972)

Charlemagne Palestine

Begin singing on one tone as in Overtone Study (1970). Slowly begin to walk and sing - gradually picking up speed to a fast walk, eventually breaking into a run, singing all the while. Keep running until you are out of breath. Stop wherever you are and catch your breath. Then begin again as many times as you can. Each time singing the same sustained note. The more endured, the better.

Hear What I Feel
for solo vocalist with assistant

Joan La Barbara

...Vocal sounds produced as immediate reaction/response to touching objects not known to the performer who has prepared by spending an hour in isolation with visual and tactile sensory deprivation.
...

Materials needed for performance:

6 small clear-glass dishes
1 small table
1 short stool or chair
1 water dish and clean-up cloth
masking tape and tissue
modeling clay
microphone and amplification system

Performance Diagram

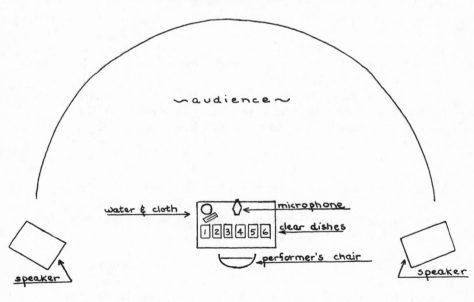

Preparation:

The performer sets the six glass dishes in a row, holding them in place with pieces of modeling clay which is removable and reuseable and will not harm wood surface of table. It is important that the dishes be stationary so that the performer need not worry when executing the piece in the "blind" condition about dishes spilling or breaking.

Closing the eyes, the performer should feel the edge of the table and the position of the first dish (see diagram), making sure that the reach is a comfortable one. Then the performer should use the hands and feel the row of dishes to get an idea of the length of the row.

A water dish and cloth are placed in the upper left corner of the table. The water dish should also be made stationary with a piece of clay and water placed in it at the time of set-up.

The person gathering the materials (the assistant) for the dishes should remember that those materials will inspire the sounds, so the textures should be as varied as possible. My only stipulations are that the items do not crawl and will not injure the performer.

Set up a microphone and amplification system so that the sounds made by the performer can be picked up over the distance range of the table. The performer's voice must be amplified so that small sounds will be audible to the audience.

Performance:

One hour before concert time the performer goes to an area other than the performance space, places tissue (paper, cotton, etc. so that the tape does not pull off eyelashes and the adhesive on tape does not get into eyes) on closed eyelids and tapes the eyelids shut. (At least three pieces of tape are necessary for each eye, taping across the eyelid out to the side, down to the cheek, and to the center side of nose.) The performer then finds a comfortable position to sit in and relaxes, leaving hands open and palms up. Hands can rest on performer's legs or side of chair but fingers and palm side of hand must not touch anything for the duration of the hour.

The performer should be conscious of all thoughts that occur during the hour. It is not a period for meditation or organized thinking. The mind should be relaxed and thoughts should flow to the differences between this state of experience and day-to-day mental meanderings. Special attention should be paid to changes in hearing and perception of sound and other events.

When the assistant comes to take the performer to the concert space he/she should not touch the performer's hands. The assistant can guide verbally, give right or left direction signals, indicate obstructions quietly and should guide the performer by touching the arm or back until the performer is seated comfortable at the prepared table.

During the time the performer spent in isolation, the assistant placed the gathered items in the arranged dishes, placing each item in a separate dish and taking care not to let items overlap. Mixed items of a similar nature are permissable in the same dish if it is the intention of the assistant. Items should not become mixed by mistake or carelessness.

To begin, the performer settles him/herself and waits until feeling relaxed enough to let the sound reactions flow in an uninhibited manner. Using one hand (whichever hand is most comfortable for the individual) locate the first dish (far left in row, as indicated). The back of the hand can be used to find the left edge of the table but the fingers should encounter the substance in the first dish as the first tactile sensation experienced since the piece began.

The performer responds vocally to inner feeling resulting from touching the materials. Simply open the mouth and release the sound completely. It will shape itself. The most meaningful sounds are the ones most freely produced.

The performer proceeds from left to right through the series of dishes, responding to each substance and spending as much time as needed with each substance to completely investigate the substance and his/her reaction to it.

After responding to the substance in the last dish the performer cleans the fingers with the water and clean-up cloth, then removes the eye tapes. At this point the performer may look at the dishes, learning the nature of the substances that inspired the sounds.

The piece is finished at this point of discovery.

Approximate duration: one hour and ten minutes.
   (one hour isolation experience, ten minutes with audience)

Excerpts from program notes:

"*Hear What I Feel* is a search for new sounds. During a series of concerts with poets and writers I discovered some unusual sounds by reacting emotionally to the words and letting the emotion rather than the intellect direct the sound. Continuing my experiments in finding new ways to inspire unorthodox sounds, I decided to delve into the area of psychology and place myself in an extraordinary situation. The visual sense is one of my strongest senses and therefore one of my strongest needs. Perhaps because I'm near-sighted I've always been very aware of what I'm able to see — and how my perceptions of objects differ when aided by corrective lenses. I chose to block that sense, depriving myself of visual stimulation and/or information in order to heighten the reactions of my other senses. For concert situations I spend one hour in isolation with my eyes taped shut, also denying my hands any sensation other than that of air and dust. I prefer to spend that hour in a space outside the concert room in order to include the discovery of new surroundings as part of the piece's sound and to experience the shock of suddenly bringing the solitary state of mind, created by being along with one's own thoughts, into a space occupied by other people and respond to this without the advantage of visual information. The piece involves vocalizing my immediate responses to touching a variety of unknown substances, chosen by persons other than myself. I do not know what the materials are until the end of the experiment when I remove the tape from my eyes."

There are more notes on *Hear What I Feel* . . . thoughts leading up to the performance, thoughts during the conceptual stage of the piece, thoughts that occurred during performances, reminiscences and musings after performances;

The piece reveals itself to me and others reveal their reactions.

The material included here should suffice to describe the piece, its formative process and lenghty analysis, its performance possibilities and results.

It is always different.

Songs

Bill Beckley

"in" (sung to a nightingale)

iiiiiiiiiiiiiiiiiiiiiiiiiiiiiiiiiiiiiiiiiiiiiiiiiiiiiiiiiiiiiiiiiiiiiiiiiiiiiiiiiiiiiiiiiiin

"are" (sung to a cardinal)

aaaaaaaaaaaaaaaaaaaaaaaaaaaaaaaaaaaaaaaaaaaaaaaaaaaaaaaaaaaaaaaaaaaaaaaaare

song for a sliding board (sung in its entirety while standing
                          at top of slide)
"are"

aaaa   a a a a   a   a   a   a   a   a ahrre   a a a a a a aaahrre

song for a chin-up

"are"

pp
Tenor
a a a a a a a a a a a a a a a a a a r e

song for a pole vaulter

"are"

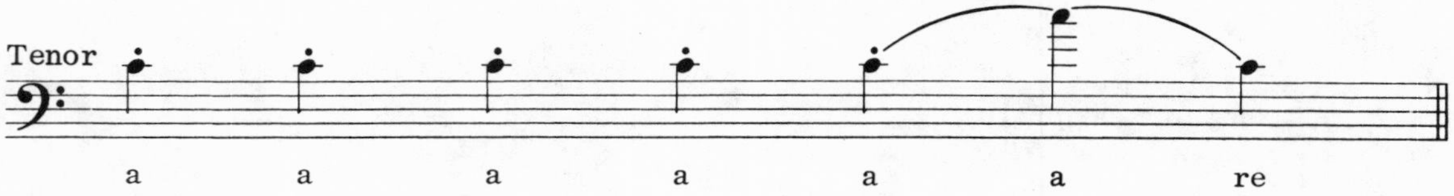
Tenor
a a a a a a re

"or" (sung to a condor)

Tenor
slur
oooooooooooooooooooooooorooooooooooooooooooooooooooroooooooooooooooooooooooor

song for a push-up

"are"

Baritone
pp
a a a a a a a a a a a a a a a a a r e

song for a hurdler

"are"

Baritone
a a a a re

"is" (past and present)

a quartet

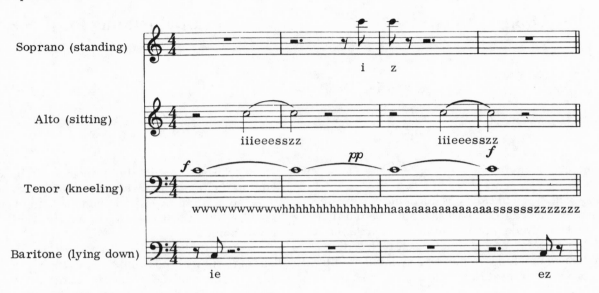

"is" (past and present) var. 1

Song

Christian Wolff

One singer, any number accompanying.

The singer should choose a name he likes. If it is the name of someone you yourself know, then use the full first name. If not, use the first, middle (if usual) and surname. Make one sound on each syllable of the name or for each letter or combination of letters not exceeding a syllable in length; and once make three sounds on a syllable or letter or combination of letters. Do not repeat the name more than once, if that.

The accompaniment should be made up of chords of at least five sounds (one sound may sustain through from one chord to another, but not through more than two subsequent chords). Once use four sounds for a chord. Play each chord simultaneously with a sound of the singer. If there is only one name, the singer should at some point make one of his sounds without accompaniment; if more than one, two sounds without accompaniment.

Double Song for JRN & CMAW

Christian Wolff

No more beer: sing lightly or speak with lilt (something like a sigh without the final downward fall) each word, beginning with the first repeated as often as desired, then the second as often as desired, then likewise the third, all in approximately the rhythm of your respiration.

Fee fie fo fum: at the same time, in the same way, but only on every second or third or sixth or seventh breath. At least two singers, in any case a more or less equal number doing each of the texts, each singer using the rhythm(s) of his own breathing.

Optional accompaniment: no more than one for every five singing (one may accompany fewer than five) independently playing continuous melodies (not necessarily characterised outstandingly by pitch, having four or more alterations of sound, generally quiet) at any time, with any amount of pause between them, but always beginning together with one of the singer's sounds.

Yosha's Morning Song

Malcolm Goldstein

For solo voice, singing.

To be sung simply. The moment of each sound alive with the immediacy of discovery; awakening to the possibilities of the voice, sounding (varieties of tonal qualities of syllables, the registers of the voice, the energy of dynamics and articulation). *Not* to be sung in a theatrical or dramatic manner by intention.

Each line is about 30 seconds; each line consists of graphic-melodic contour and "text" to be sung:

Graphic notation:

Pitch (melodic) contour; proportional space on page indicates duration (including blank space for silence). Double vertical lines (//) indicate a very long silence; thickness of contour line indicates loudness or intensity. There are occasional suggestions of intervals (3rds, 4ths, etc.) within the melodic contour.

Syllables:

"text" or sounding quality of melodic curve with occasional additional information for the manner of singing the syllables.

Other sounds:

"Sneeze," "cough," etc. in as natural a manner as possible.

This piece may be performed with *Yosha's Morning Song Extended* which is included in Chapter V.

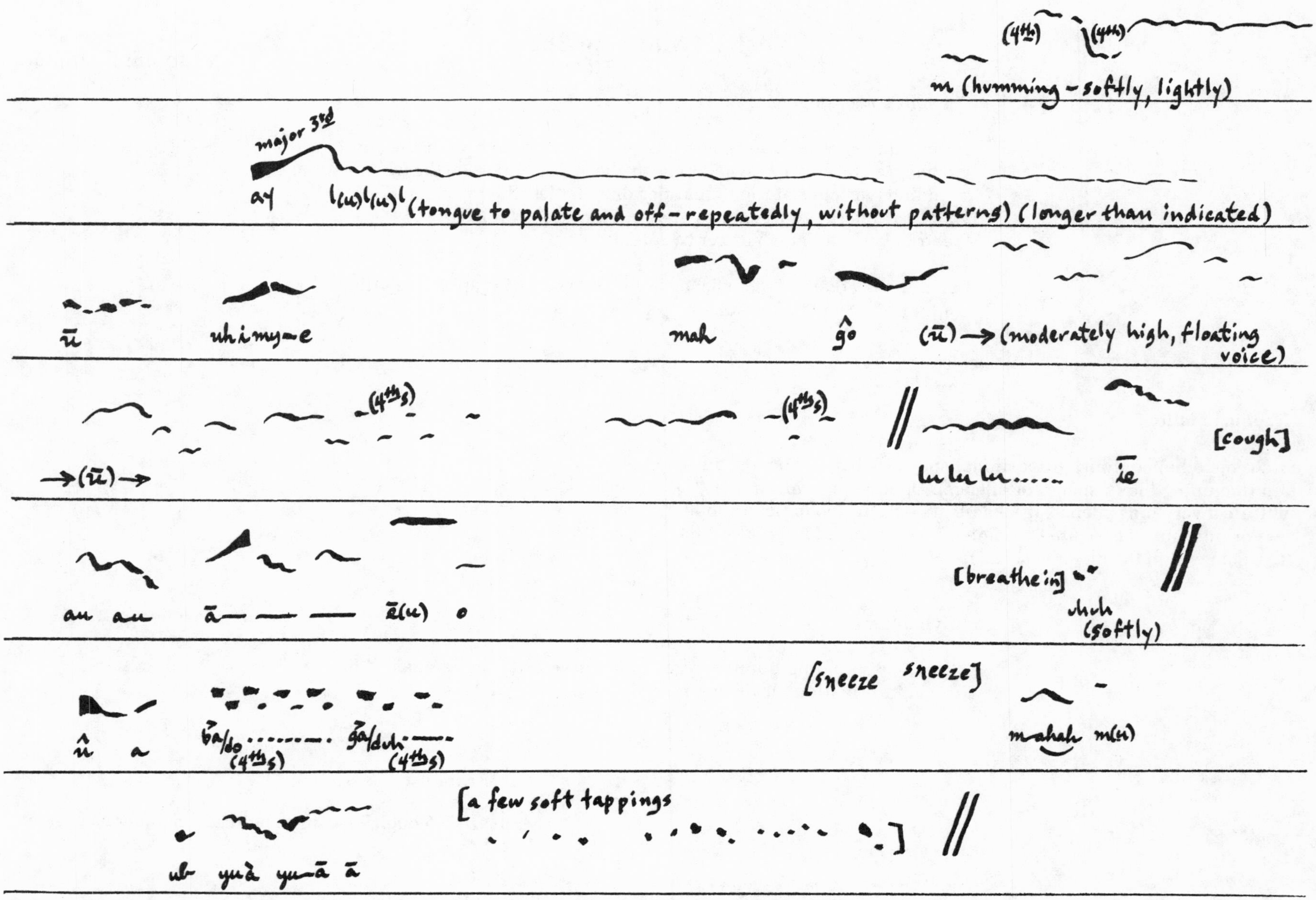

(4th) (4th)

m (humming – softly, lightly)

major 3rd

ay   l(u)l(u)l (tongue to palate and off – repeatedly, without patterns) (longer than indicated)

ū   uhimy–e   mah   ĝo   (ū) → (moderately high, floating voice)

–(4ths)   –(4ths)

→(ū)→   lu lu lu......   īe   [cough]

au au   ā — —   ē(u) o   [breathe in]   uhuh (softly)

[sneeze sneeze]

û a   ba/do........ (4ths)   ga/duhi—— (4ths)   mahah m(u)

uh yuà yu–ā ā   [a few soft tappings   . ʹ . •   • • • •..... • •.] //

yâ (tight voice, growl) la (tongue moving in mouth) myau

l   üh ––––––– yoh ū   ga–ul a   ga–ul a yeah

yashe mul ah buh l b l   al   ū yu   uh   da bū

lu grâ (hard voice) gra [laugh] [talk] [laugh] da-bu da   bu yeah   le le le le (breath in sounding ū) le leh

üh lele chuh   mah   l ah ūh duh .... ūh .... ahuh uh...

(4ths) (uh) →   (4ths) (uh) →   uh oh   ae ay hye üh oh

nuh (drone, low and soft, undulating — for about 2 minutes, with silences occasionally)   //

m ––––– a è (moderately low pitch) (beautiful pitch!)   [deep breathing in]

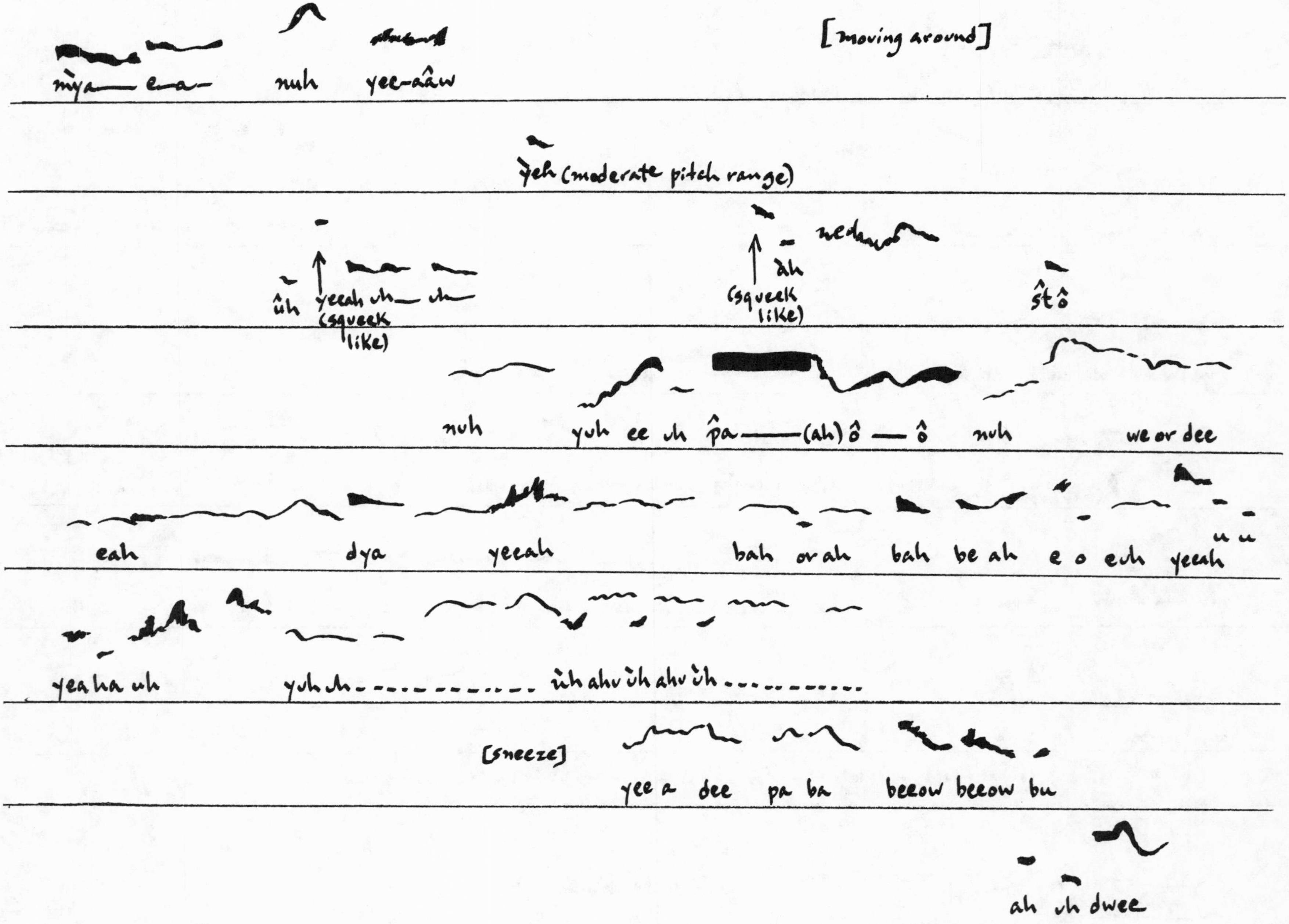

[moving around]

mya— e-a—   nuh   yee-aâw

yeh (moderate pitch range)

ûh   yeeah uh— uh   ah   ŝt ô
(squeek   (squeek
like)   like)

nuh   yuh ee uh p̂a——(ah) ô — ô   nuh   we or dee

eah   dya   yeeah   bah or ah   bah be ah   e o euh   yeeah uu

yea ha uh   yuh uh- - - - - - - - - - ûh ahu ûh ahu ûh - - - - - - - - - - -

[sneeze]

yee a dee   pa ba   beeow beeow bu

ah uh dwee

"Knee" and "Slide" from Our Lady of Late

Meredith Monk

Our Lady of Late is a composition for a soprano voice and a wine glass filled with water. The entire work, which runs an hour, is divided into 16 shorter sections. Each section deals with a particular vocal quality or setting. Our Lady of Late is a vocal meditation exploring the full spectrum of the female voice including elements of pitch, color, texture, timbre, rhythm, harmony, range, emotion, character and movement.

The range of the vocal part is from D below middle C to high C# (two octaves above middle C). The glass is played by wetting the index finger and rubbing it around the rim of the glass, producing a drone during much of the entire piece. The drone changes pitch five times during the course of the piece, which is achieved by drinking a particular amount of water from the glass.

Our Lady of Late was first presented as a tape score for dancer/choreographer William Dunas' dance work, Our Lady of Late, on May 1, 1972. It has since been performed live in many places in the United States and Europe.

Performance Notes on the Two Excerpts

Knee: The voice quality is very nasal, ragged, high and rough. The voice slides into the notes, and there are slight pitch changes within the notes. The syllable "ni" is generally sustained with the attacks coming within the phrases or notes.

Slide: The voice slides from the flat, non-vibrato, clear, very high head tone down through the glottal break to the low chest voice. The voice simply touches the top note but does not hit it squarely or stay on it before the slide. The pitches are approximate since the voice does not "sing" a particular note for any length of time. The voice glides in circles, spirals and peaks. Sometimes the figure is in the high head voice, sometimes at the break in the middle. Towards the end of the section there are more percussive impulses and shorter attacks. The speed of the slides varies from slow to very fast as indicated.

Since these two sections are presented out of context from the rest of the work, it is suggested that they be performed as exercises or experiments rather than as finished concert pieces.

Recording: Our Lady of Late, Minona Records MN 1001

Knee

Slide

I Ain't Listen

Jana Haimsohn

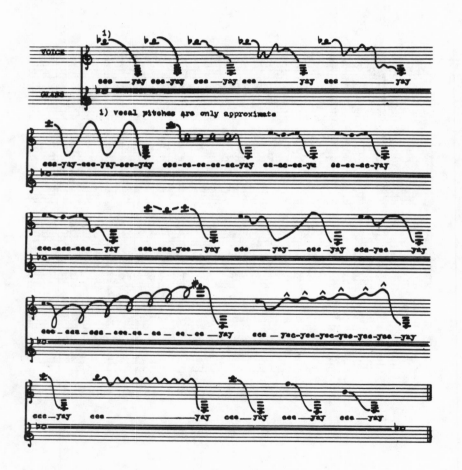

For solo voice, preferably performed amplified with microphone. The pitches used are relative; begin at a low comfortable pitch, sound resonating in throat. Language phrases are all done with a Spanish accent.

The first part of the piece is much like a chant. The flavor depends on the performer's ability to move freely through the material, being able to play with emphasis on accented syllables and variations of volume, attack and articulation. Maintain a full, rich tone even in the low register. Explore the improvisational sections fully, playing with speed, accent, rhythm and harmonics. Syllables may vary from those suggested.

At the end of the improvisation, after going through all the pitches, repeat Part I and end with a very brief improvisation, as in Part II, either bringing the volume down to finish or cutting off abruptly.

I AIN'T LISTEN

Jana Haimsohn

Repeat
Part I

$\mathcal{3}$ Percussion Music

While song is the extension of the voice and of speech, music also results from our hands, our body, and our instruments. Percussion instruments are certainly among the most basic and accessible to the performer, at least at first. The development of percussion, highly refined in some cultures, has been a relatively recent event in Western music; it remains one of the most fertile areas for exploration. The music in this chapter reveals a great interest among the composers in rhythm and rhythmic manipulations and permutations of patterns, also an important aspect of new music. Many of these scores are ideally suited for the development of strong rhythmic sense and skill, and will thus be of great benefit to the less experienced musician.[1]

Christian Wolff's *Stones* and *Sticks* are good starting points for the free exploration of percussion sound and having some fun as well. Philip Glass's *1 + 1* allows a solo performer freedom to develop rhythmic patterns from two basic units according to various simple additive procedures. An excellent exercise in itself, it is also an interesting illustration of an important procedure in all of Glass's more extended music. *Clapping Music* has a similar role in Steve Reich's music by illustrating, on a fairly simple scale, the idea of a phase pattern—that is, gradually moving one part ahead of the other, fixed one until at last they return full circle in phase. Along with Richard Hayman's somewhat similar piece *Crystal*, it is a fascinating exercise and performance piece. Both require considerably more concentration to perform than it might seem. Kenneth Maue's *Convergence #1* is also somewhat related, being based on some interesting interlock-

ing patterns derived from a sequence of random numbers. Daniel Goode's *Bell-Rows* and Michael Nyman's *Bell Set No. 1* share an interest in a common timbre as well as in permutation and expansion. The latter piece is particularly good for a larger number of performers using additional instruments. Harold Budd's *Lirio* and James Tenney's *Maximusic* are short descriptive solo percussion scores, while Carter Thomas's *Instant Cash* might be considered something of a theater piece. Beth Anderson's *Valid for Life* and Edwin London's *Roll* are each involved with sustained percussion sound and a variety of timbres. They are very visual scores as well, the latter carrying out a rather extended pun. William Hellermann's *to the last drop* is also a particularly visual score—almost a cartoon—though one in which performers react to the visual image and are influenced by it quite differently than with a conventional score. Dennis Anderson's *Gamelan* is a more complex percussion score, reflecting an interest in the Indonesian orchestra; it will demand some practice from even those with greater musical experience.

There are many other pieces herein for percussion in combination with other instruments or voices: Most of the music in the first part of Chapter 5 makes use of percussion. Works such as *In the Aeolian Mode, 30's, Les Moutons de Panurge,* and *Daydream* from the second part of Chapter 5 also specify percussion instruments. Several pieces in Chapter 6 reflect an interest in rhythm, such as Phased Loops, Pendulum Music, and "Knocking Piece II" (from *4 Do-It-Yourself Pieces*). Many scores in Chapters 7 and 8 make use of percussion instruments in a great variety of ways.

[1]For actual rhythm studies and drills the reader is referred to Hindemith's classic *Elementary Training for Musicians* (London: Schott, 1946).

Stones

Christian Wolff

Make sounds with stones, draw sounds out of stones, using a number of sizes and kinds (and colours); for the most part discretely; sometimes in rapid sequences. For the most part striking stones with stones, but also stones on other surfaces (inside the open head of a drum, for instance) or other than struck (bowed, for instance, or amplified). Do not break anything.

Sticks

Christian Wolff

Make sounds with sticks of various kinds, one stick alone, several together, on other instruments, sustained as well as short. Don't mutilate trees or shrubbery; don't break anything other than the sticks; avoid outright fires unless they serve a practical purpose.

You can begin when you have not heard a sound from a stick for a while; two or three can begin together. You may end when your sticks or one of them are broken small enough that a handful of the pieces in your hands cupped over each other are not, if shaken and unamplified, audible beyond your immediate vicinity. Or hum continuously on a low note; having started proceed with other sounds simultaneously (but not necessarily continuously); when you can hum no longer, continue with other sounds, then stop. With several players either only one should do this or two or two pairs together (on different notes) and any number individually.

You can also do without sticks but play the sounds and feelings you imagine a performance with sticks would have.

1 + 1

Philip Glass

Any table top is amplified by means of a contact mike, amplifier and speaker.

The player performs 1 + 1 by tapping the table top with his fingers or knuckles.

The following two rhythmic units are the building blocks of 1 + 1:

1 + 1 is realized by combining the above two units in continuous, regular arithmetic progressions.

Examples of some simple combinations are:

The tempo is fast. The length is determined by the player.

Clapping Music
For Two Performers

Steve Reich

The performance begins and ends with both performers in unison at bar 1. The number of repeats of each bar may be fixed, or performers may move from one bar to the next whenever they feel it is appropriate. In the latter case, they should try to keep the number of repeats of each bar roughly the same. Since the first performer's part does not change, it is up to the second performer to move from one bar to the next. The second performer should try to keep his downbeat where it is written, i.e. on the first beat of each measure (not on the first beat of the group of three claps), so that his downbeat always falls on a new beat of his unchanging pattern.

The choice of a particular clapping sound, i.e., with cupped or flat hands, is left up to the performers. Whichever timbre is chosen, both performers should try to get the same one so that their two parts will blend to produce one overall resulting pattern. The clapping may be amplified.

Crystal

For Percussion Instruments

Richard Hayman

A pattern to be repeated by each part is formed from the rhythmic modes:

TROCHEE

IAMB

DACTYL

ANAPAEST

SPONDEE

TRIBRACH

The number of parts determines how often each mode is repeated before continuing to the next. The dactyl, anapaest and spondee being twice the lengths of trochee, iamb and tribrach are repeated half the times. Odd numbers set the pattern by the even number one larger. Thus for 3 or 4 parts the pattern would be:

For 7 or 8 parts each mode would be repeated twice the above.

A lead part begins the pattern followed by a second after as many units of ♩. as parts. Each part follows similarly repeating the pattern. A single solo tribrach by the trailing part signals the reentry of the lead part. The lead may be always the same or may rotate to all parts. All follow in turn after one less unit than before. After there is one unit of distance between each part there is a rest of one unit of ♩. and the pattern is repeated by all parts in unison. Without pause a lead part begins again followed after one unit by all parts in turn. As before, parts begin and follow, the units of distance increasing until the original distance is reached, the trailing voice's solo tribrachs ending.

A short form for 2 parts uses a pattern and distance based on 4. The lead part reentry is on the last tribrach of the second to prevent overlapping. End just before the unison described above.

Convergence #1

Kenneth Maue

One player reads a stream of numbers within the range 6-12, randomly sequenced, at a steady tempo. Other players play the spoken numbers. Beginning on a unique spoken number, each player makes a sound, then counts the same number of spoken-number pulses as the spoken number on which he began, then sounds again, counts again, sounds again, etc. Example: in the following stream of numbers, a player sounds on the underlined numbers: [the first 8 is randomly chosen]

<u>8</u> 12 11 8 7 10 10 6 <u>12</u> 7 10 9 6 8 11 10 <u>12</u> 12
9 7 6 7 10 8 10 8 7 <u>10</u> 11 9 11 6 <u>12</u> 10 6 <u>9</u> 8 10 12 6 <u>9</u> 11 7 8 etc.

For sounds, use percussion instruments of long decay. For practice, players can go through a series like the one above in unison. Then for performance, they begin on successive spoken numbers and proceed until they converge into unison. The whole process can be repeated any number of times. The reader can vary the tempo of his number reading in any way, so long as changes are made within the other players' capacity to change tempos without losing their places.

Bell Set No.1

Michael Nyman

For at least four performers playing any combination of pitched or non-pitch highly resonant metal percussion instruments.

Any performance must use all four rhythmic structures, which are played simultaneously, one part per performer.

Each note of each 3, 4, 5 and 6-note group must be assigned to its own instrument which plays only that note throughout.

Instruments may be assigned in families (e.g. the 4-note rhythm may be played on cymbals of different sizes, the 5-note on gongs, etc.) or as mixed groups.

Dynamic — each note to be struck as firmly as possible with hardest suitable sticks.

Tempo — anything from ♪ = c. 100 to ♪ / c. 200 (Methods, inaudible to the listener, may have to be devised to ensure that all players maintain this constant pulse.

Players all begin together and end together, either after a predetermined duration or after each player has reached his/her last figure (preferable the latter).

Each rhythm is to be repeated over and over before moving without a break to the next. Where there are more than four players and one or more of the parts has to be "doubled", no attempt at synchronisation between these identical parts should be made.

Alternative versions are possible for keyboard and plucked instruments that have strong attack and long decay — such as piano, electric and acoustic guitar, vibraphone, harp, etc.

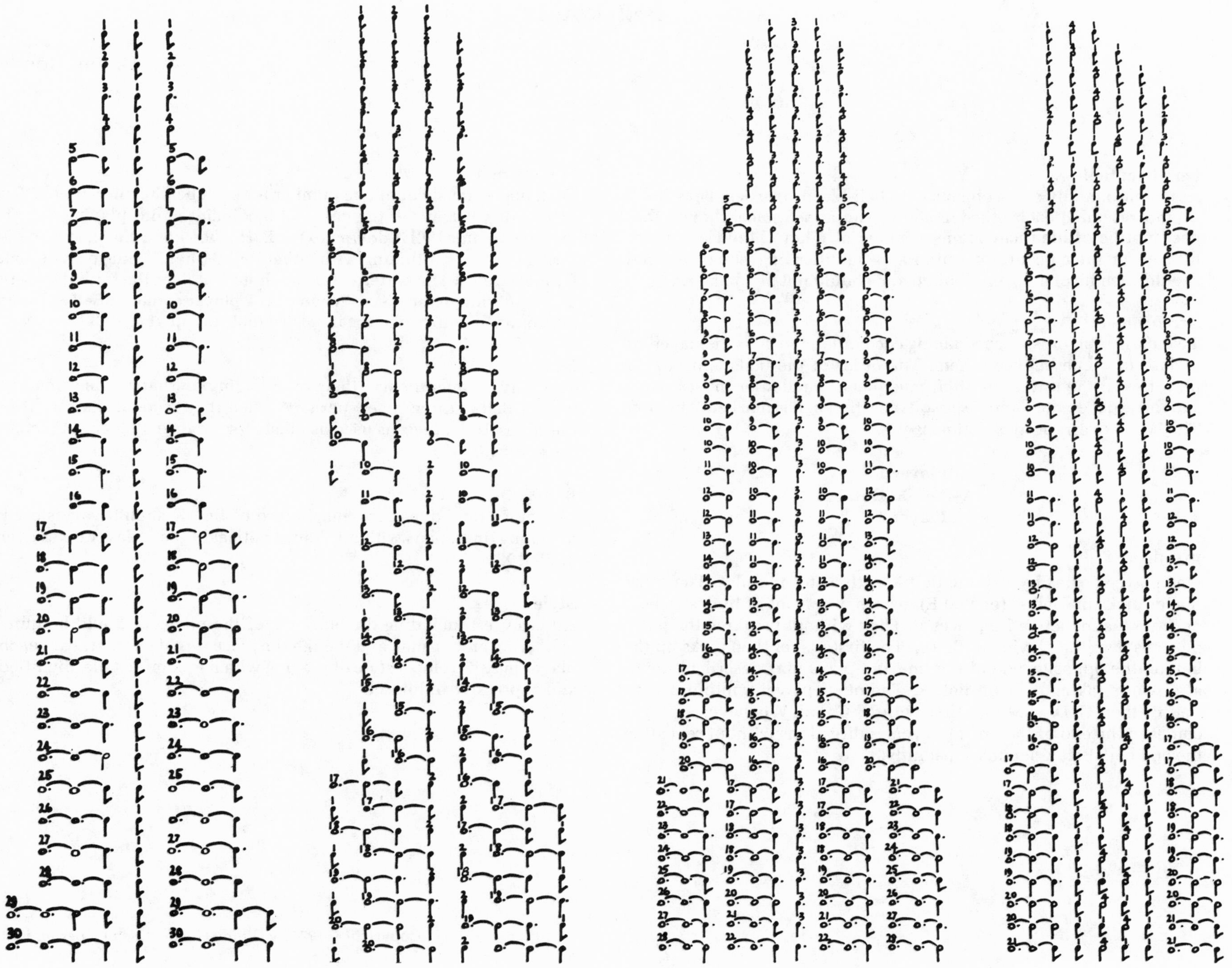

Bell–Rows

Daniel Goode

Family of Bells

Assemble a family of six objects with bell-like properties. These bells should resemble each other in sound and appearance, though they need not be of identical shape or material. They should be chosen mainly for their beauty of sound and qualities of resonance. They should each be of a different pitch and should not be too heavy.

Arrangement

Two players sit cross-legged facing each other, the bells displayed on a cloth in a line between them. The order of the bells is up to the players, but the lowest in pitch must be suspended or must rest on supports that do not damp its resonance (that bell is marked X below). The bells are arranged as follows:

Player 1
A–B–C–X–D–E
Player 2

Playing

One player begins by striking Bell X with a steady pulse. The other player picks up Bell A (or Bell E), brings it in front of him, strikes it once with a mallet and replaces it. Then without breaking the pulse he takes over the playing of Bell X. The first player then picks up the bell on the opposite side of the line and plays it as described for A, afterwards taking over on Bell X. The other player continues with Bell B (then C, D, etc.), the first with D, C, etc. Whenever a player comes to the end of the line he reverses directions without repeating the end bell. Bell X sounds constantly.

Moving Bell A

Each player must count one number for each bell he plays up to 5 (go to 1 again). Whenever the count of 5 coincides with playing Bell A, that player puts Bell A down next to E. He then has a choice, when his turn comes, of continuing with either Bell B (then C, etc.) *or* with Bell E (then D, etc.). The pattern of these choices creates the formal variety and repetition in the piece. When next a player comes to Bell A on his 5th count, he will replace it in its original spot next to Bell B.

Ending

The players must devise their own ending: perhaps when one has moved Bell A three times; perhaps when they recognize a repeat in the series. If the piece is used as music for a dance, that could dictate the ending.

Bell X

The pulse rate, dynamics and timbre of Bell X should vary slowly over long time spans with no change noticeable as a player takes over on Bell X.

Style

All gestures, including the entrance of the players, should be quite deliberate and formal, and though the piece is undemonstrative, each player may develop a style of playing which is comfortable, dignified and expressive of himself.

Lirio

Under a blue light, roll very softly on a large gong for a long duration.

Harold Budd

Guadalajara : 24 : viii : 71

MAXIMUSIC
for Max Neuhaus

James Tenney

MAXIMUSIC

for Max Neuhaus

(1) Soft roll on large cymbal; constant, resonant, very long.

(2) Sudden loud, fast improvisation on all the other (percussion) instruments except the tam—tam(s)—especially (but not only) non-sustaining ones; constant texture; continue until nearly exhausted from the physical effort, but not as long as (1); end with tam—tam(s) (not used until now)— just one blow, as loud as possible.

(3) Same as (1), but now inaudible until all the other sounds have faded; continue ad lib but not as long as (1) or (2), then let the cymbal fade out by itself.

James Tenney
6/16/65

Instant Cash
for Larry Stern

Carter Thomas

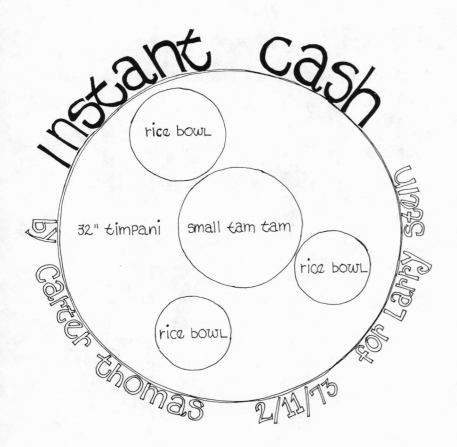

<u>instructions</u>
cash needed : 17 Pennies
              12 nickels
               9 dimes
              10 Quarters
               5 half dollars
               2 silver dollars

1) use 32" timpani, 3 different sized rice bowls, 1 small tam tam or Gong.

2) Player strikes timpani with hands, or sticks of his choice.

3) Player continues to depress Pedal at whatever rate he Pleases.

4) while doing this, the Player should drop coins <u>one at a time</u> (any order of coins) into a rice bowl or tam tam of his choice and improvise freely.

5) anytime after all the coins are dropped, the Piece may end.

Valid for Life

Beth Anderson

Trio for two large matching strung things (such as piano or harp)
and one set of large membranophones.

All instruments are played with huge velvet beaters the performers make themselves.

Play a long, soft, full, round roll on the strings and membranes.
Variations in the roll are derived from the changes in typeface.
Several performances may be layered in the studio and mixed
live with the performers. All performances should be delicately
amplified.

Minimum duration is 10 minutes.
Maximum duration is free.

beth anderson

Roll
for 3 to 12 players

Edwin London

Members of the Percussion Family meet quite often before, during, and after concerts for the benign purpose of breaking bread and otherwise refreshing themselves. This piece is for them.

Three Proposals for Disposition of Personae During Performance

1. The stand-up buffet
2. The sit-around table
3. For a larger group, a re-creation of the *Last Supper,* wherein the Director is betrayed by one of His Disciples.

(Choose one of the above mentioned proposals, or in similar spirit, fabricate an analogous situation, keeping within the nature of the goings on.)

Each member of the group brings one type of roll to the proceeding, to present to colleagues.

Some Possibilities

Onion Roll
Hamburger Bun
English Muffin
Croissant
Popover
Kreplach
Bismarck Roll
Pork Roll
Piano Roll
Jelly Roll
Hot Cross Bun
Bran Muffin
Parker House Roll
Scone
Ravioli
Bagel
Tootsie Roll
Bank Roll
Poppyseed Roll
Cinnamon Bun
Corn Bread Muffin
Brioche
Gem
Won Ton
Kaiser Roll
Clam Juice Roll
Argyol

There will be opportunities for the players to eat the rolls in the context of a performance. To assist digestion (roll-aid) it is suggested that players manufacture sonic roll correlates which 'represent' the physical and metaphysical shapes of the received gift ridbits. Other salutory uses ought to be found for inedible items such as Bank Roll, Piano Roll, and Argyrol.

Remember: To Play Roll is to Play a Role

(For smaller ensembles it may become necessary for some players to perform more than one role, though this solution is not recommended for dieting persons. However, one must not underestimate the psychodramatic potential.)

There are four classifications of instruments participating in Roll:

a. Glass; b. Skin; c. Metal; d. Wood.

Twelve differently tuned specimens of each category, one each per role, are called for. These instruments can be rolled by a variegated series of beaters, including snare drum sticks, brushes, felt sticks, assorted mallets (aforethought), and sundry other devices dreamed up for any given occasion.

A fifth sounding category is necessary. It is marked off in the score by brackets— (*Stones*)—stones for rolling. Marbles are certainly qualified and convenient (perhaps shaken when placed inside pots or plates), but this suggestion need not rule out choices arrived at for other compelling reasons.

A duration for *Roll* is predetermined by the Director and/or a Host ("I will fetch a morsel of bread, and comfort ye your hearts; after that ye shall pass on.") This will permit players to regulate their actions in time, thereby leading to an amicable coordination of intent. For example, the stave marked 9/9 in the score will have that percussionist stretch the role throughout the total agreed-on duration; he (she, it) will only be able to eat (and drink) prior to or after completing the task. The 8-1/9 player would play his part twice—first in the proportion of 8/9 of the total agreed-on duration, then repeated in 1/9 of the total. This player can refresh himself prior to, in between the two repetitions, and after his appointed rounds. Similarly the 4-3 2/9 player does his part three times and has an additional refection option thereby. Although it seems that it will be easiest to perform the composition in durations related to multiples of nine, this should not discourage anyone from making computations of time. ("Haste makes waste, but he who hesitates is lost.")

There is a series (the Roll Series) of twelve definitions of the word *Roll* listed on the back of this page. These are to be assigned to each participant to guide him in a metasomatic alteration of the material in the given musical mix. Too, there are twelve literary quotations, also to be distributed, one per celebrant, to facilitate a harmonious nomographic course of events.

The Director, in any case, is to present an orderly procedure for a well-regulated meal. The Betrayer's role ("if there need be one" says the once born soul) is to confute order and to disrupt the Director's program to procedure—though in a very subtle and saintly manner. His identity must not be blatantly revealed; it should be apparent only to the perspicacious observer.

On the score itself, each player is provided with six or seven synonyms for the word *Roll*. These are to be utilized as performing directions in the manner of common practice terms, such as allegro, moderato, appassionato, etc.
The sonic resultant envisioned by the composer is of a finely textured, quasi steady-state, somewhat complex roll of finite duration, to be experienced in a communal setting ere the cock crows.

As to the final crescendo, stage lighting may be used to underline this pre-dawn happening.

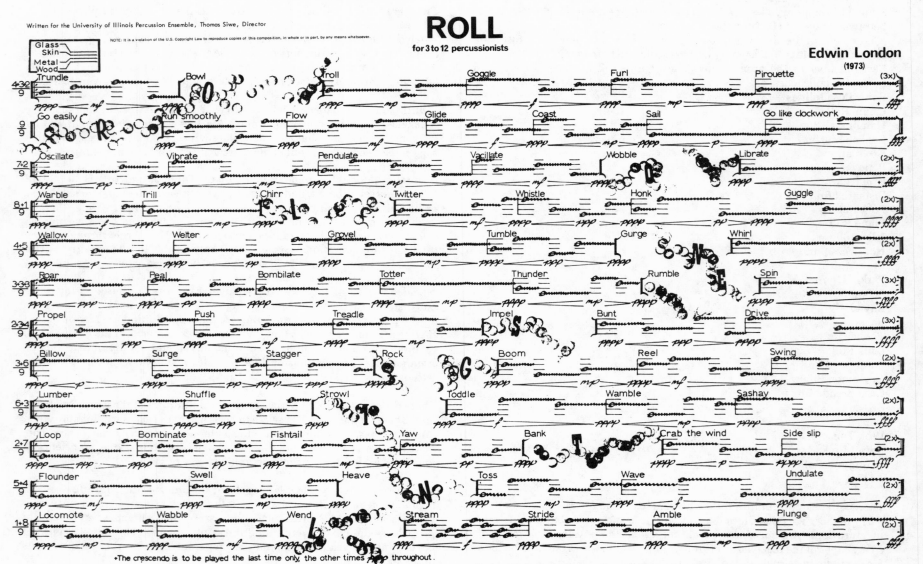

ROLLS SERIES I –definitions

1. ROLL. . .a rapid and uniform pulse produced by alternate strokes of drum sticks. This phenomenon is perceived by the ears as being a continuous sound.

2. ROLL. . .a small loaf of bread; more properly speaking, to be one which has been rolled over or doubled before baking.

3. ROLL. . .a scroll which lists names used to ascertain whether one or another of a set of persons is present.

4. ROLL. . .a piece of parchment which is written upon or is intended to contain writing and is convenient to handle or carry when rolled up.

5. ROLL. . .a small quantity of tobacco leaves rolled up into a cylindrical mass.

6. ROLL. . .a round cushion or pad of hair or other material, forming part of a woman's head-dress.

7. ROLL. . .an instrument used for crushing clods.

8. ROLL. . .a loud, continuous, reverberating peal of thunder.

9. ROLL. . .to move or impel an object forward on a surface by making it turn over and over.

10. ROLL. . .to pronounce or sound with a trill.

11. ROLL. . .to turn the eyes in different directions with a kind of circular motion.

12. ROLL. . .to perform a periodical revolution.

ROLL—The character which one undertakes or assumes with reference to the part played by a person in society, life or drama.

ROLLS SERIES II–quotations

1. "Happy King, Whose Name The Brightest shines in all the rolls of fame."
—Alexander Pope

2. "Whoso diggeth a pit shall fall therein: and he that rolleth a stone, it will return upon him."   —Proverbs XXVI: 27

3. "I hear the roll of the ages."   —Tennyson

4. "Moverover the Lord said unto me, Take thee a great roll, and write in it with a man's pen concerning the Maher-shalal-hash-baz."   —Isaiah VIII:1

5. "I came home rolling resentments in my mind and framing schemes of revenge."   —Swift

6. "Jesus the same night in which he was betrayed took bread."
Corinthians I 11:23

7. "The organ rumbled and rolled as if the church had got the colic."
—Dickens

8. "Now when the even was come, he sat down with the twelve. And as they did eat, he said, Verily I say unto you, that one of you shall betray me."
—Matthew 26:18

9. "Deep woes roll forward like a gentle flood."   —Shakespeare

10. "Roll me over, Yankee soldier."   —Marlene

11. "Eyes which rowle towards all, weep not but sweat."   —Donne

12. "And when I looked, behold, an hand was sent unto me; and lo, a roll of a book was therein; And he spread it before me; and it was written within and without: and there was written therein lamentations, and mourning, and woe. Moreover he said unto me, Son of man, eat that thou findest; eat this roll and go speak unto the house of Israel. So I opened my mouth and he caused me to eat that roll. And he said unto me, Son of man, cause thy belly to eat, and fill thy bowels with this roll that I give thee. Then I did eat it; and it was in my mouth as honey for sweetness."   —Ezekiel 2:9–10, 3:1–3

to the last drop
from <u>visible musics</u>

(an eye score)

William Hellermann

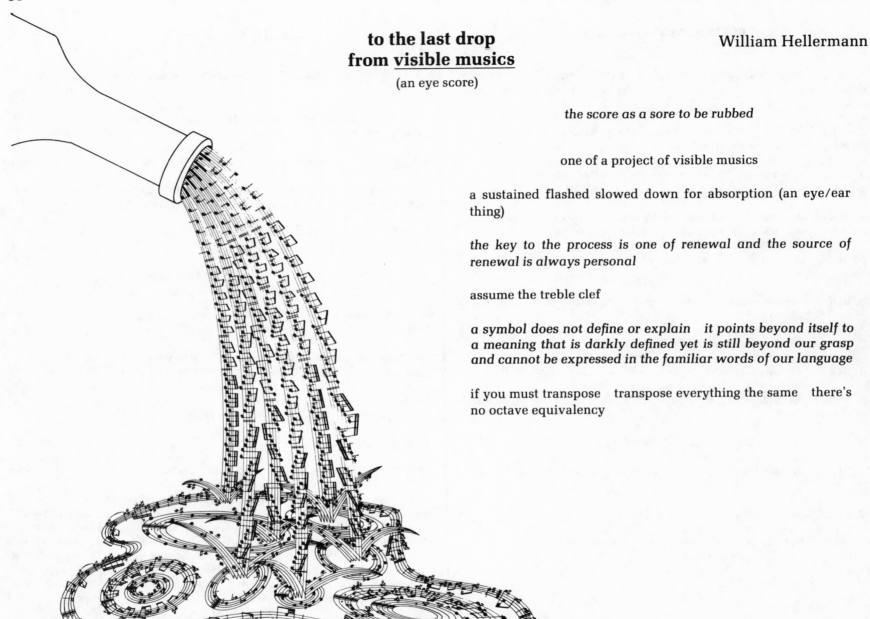

the score as a sore to be rubbed

one of a project of visible musics

a sustained flashed slowed down for absorption (an eye/ear thing)

the key to the process is one of renewal and the source of renewal is always personal

assume the treble clef

a symbol does not define or explain   it points beyond itself to a meaning that is darkly defined yet is still beyond our grasp and cannot be expressed in the familiar words of our language

if you must transpose   transpose everything the same   there's no octave equivalency *syntax is the heart of devination—to locate the function of a thing in the structure of the process*

let it flow (of course) and get a lot of water in there (i love the sound of pouring water (glug-glug)) a tape perhaps

transformation is the peeling away of the irrelevent—a matter of time

open with the *pouring* it can be a canon   always repeat (the "double lines" indicate optional repeats within the flow)   for example   one player enters doing the first "bar" then the second on the second stave   etc   gradually moving down   always repeating   or   all enter together as a group *glug* repeating each "bar" a number of times

a gesture is a deliberate act   which is undertaken for the power which comes from making a decision

next is the *splash* event   quick and out of measured time

sounds are there to distinguish the silence

then the *puddle* events with each player moving to the *puddle* of his pour (and splash)   directly   do these by playing over and over the first three notes   then adding the fourth note   then the fifth   etc   until all the notes in the *puddle* are being played and   then remove the first note then the second   etc

hell is false repetition   monotony is constant variation

go on to your next *puddle* spreading out in the same fashion as before   and then to the final *outside puddle* event   with everybody at different points   internally repeating the indicated groups and moving on as they feel it   flow away (out) in this fashion

there are no connections   only relations   the only relation is difference

i like the idea of using tuned bottles   marimbas or vibraphones would work too

killing time to let sound live

the point is to use your imagination   only read *from*   don't read *into*   the thing as itself   not depicted elaboration is always confusing   simple direct things coming from your personal experience   triggered by the score *image* will always be real and understood

if music is only music   it's not music (it's a kind of muzak)

all quotes from my notebooks some mine   some paraphrases   and some other's I don't know who—my apologies

Gamelan

Dennis Anderson
1975

Instructions

This piece is for solo marimba and percussion ensemble. All players begin on circle corresponding to their number. Soloist waits for Player 1 to finish his circle. Each player in the ensemble plays his circle and moves around the big circle to the next circle. Accompaniment dynamics should not reach above *mf*. Upward stems indicate right hand — all of these notes are ♭. Downward stems indicate left hand — all of these notes are ♮. Soloist repeats measures 221 to 230 until the entire ensemble is in unison on that section. As soon as measure 221 is played in unison, the ensemble moves on to the end. Marimba dynamics are to be added at the discretion of the soloist. All strong beats should be accented. [The four ensemble parts are reproduced on pp. 101–104.]

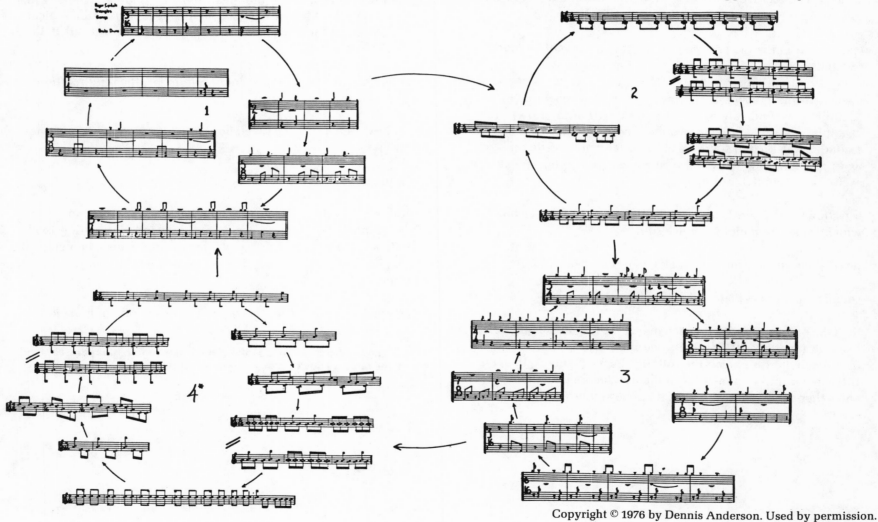

MARIMBA:

INSTRUCTIONS

PLAYER 1- Gong, Chimes (with hard yarn mallets)
          and finger cymbals
PLAYER 2- 3 Brake Drums, Vibes (no pedaling),
          Triangle - Xylo may substitue for Vibes
PLAYER 3- Gong, Triangle, Xylophone
PLAYER 4- 3 Brake Drums, Finger Cymbal, Vibes

   Each player begins in
the circle that corresponds to
his number (ie. Player #1 in
circle # 1) and plays the
events of that circle. Then
the players move to their
next circle and play that.
On mallet circles, stems that
go up are ♭'s, and are to be
played with the right hand.
Stems going down are ♮, and
are played with the L.H.
As each player finishes
all the circles, he plays
the event in the box,
Synchronizing with
the Soloist (one at a
time). When this event
is performed in unison,
the soloist and ensemble
play the box one more
time (in unison) to the end.

✱ Circle 4 should be
performed twice before
continuing on to circle 1.

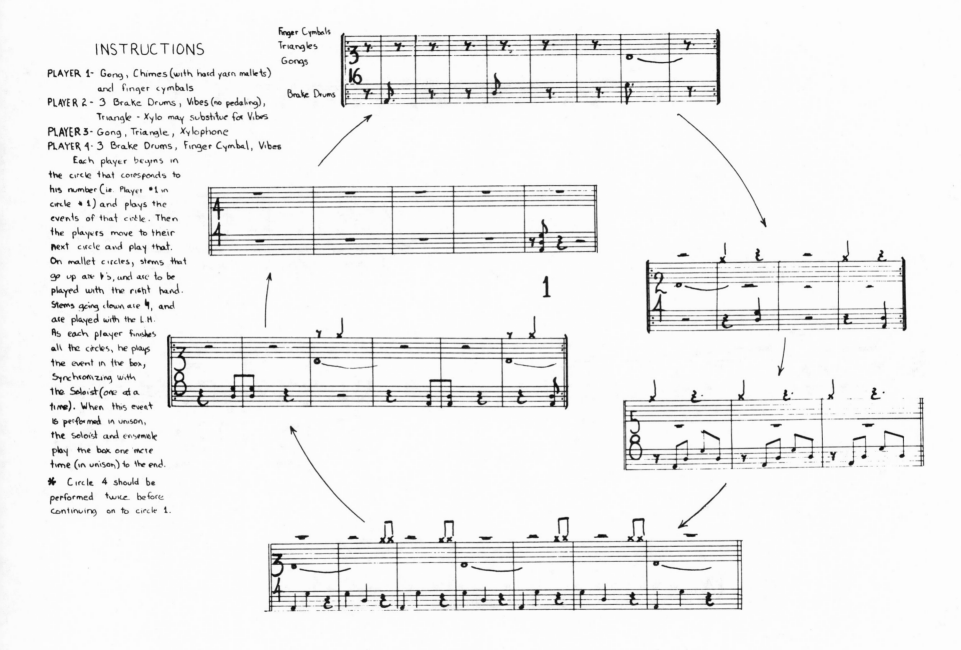

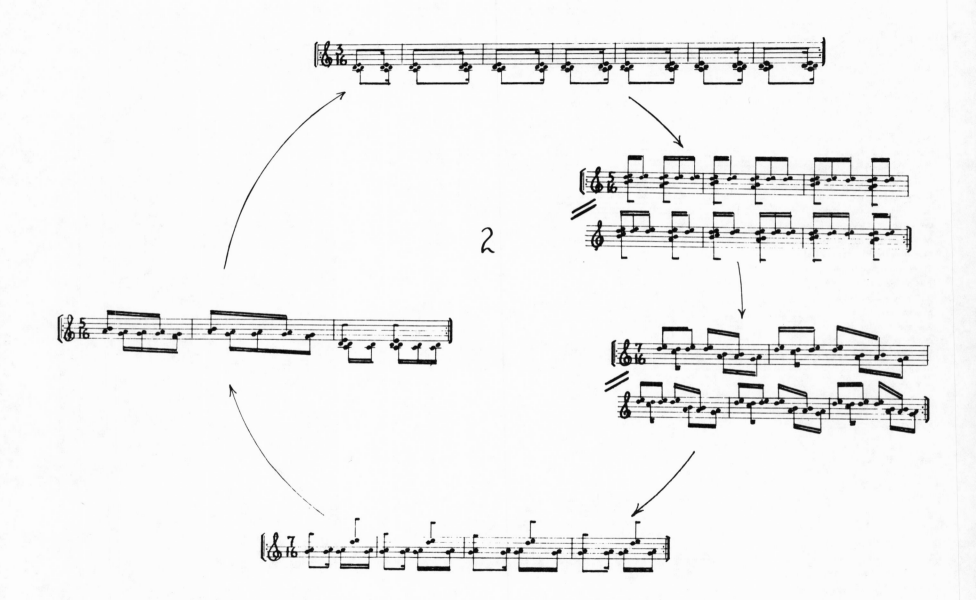

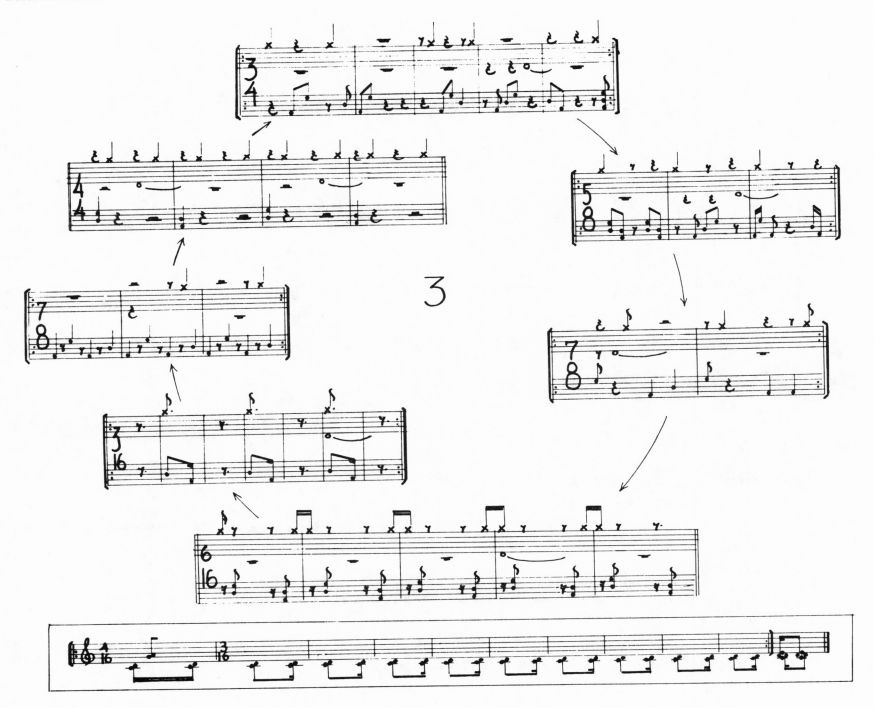

4 *Piano Music*

The keyboard works included here are extremely varied in musical idiom, notation, degree of indeterminacy, and level of difficulty. Most require some familiarity with the piano and music notation, and some degree of playing technique.

Tom Johnson's *Doodling* is certainly performable by anyone; it is interesting in that it is specifically intended only for use by a solitary player, not for an audience. Charlemagne Palestine's two pieces are based exclusively on specific sonorities and rhythms, giving the performer only general directions on how they are to be presented. The Marion Brown and Meredith Monk works use fairly traditional tonal elements—though in some unusual ways—and both contain sections of contrasting improvisation. The George Crumb piece is fascinating in its use of several layers of sound material, one of which is a dream-like quote from Chopin. Tui St. George Tucker's work, *Little Pieces for Quartertone Piano*, is quite unique in that it is played by one player on two pianos tuned a quarter-tone apart; it thus explores the interesting world of microtones in a still quite accessible way. The works by Dick Higgins and Robert Ashley involve a considerable degree of improvisation in performance; the Borishansky piece presents various forms of humor and "theater."

Among the ensemble works Otto Luening's *The Bells of Bellagio* is ideally suited for players of different degrees of proficiency, since the second and particularly the third parts are very slow-moving and easy to play. Jim Fox's *Maybe Once or Twice* and Michael Parsons' *Rhythm Studies* are somewhat similar "modular" pieces developing from short motives, which are gradually changed over a very level, almost static "surface." With some careful listening and attention to detail they are both quite practical. Charles Capro's *Crabcar Phase* is rather more complex, and requires considerable concentration on the part of the players. Very similar in concept to Reich's *Clapping Music*, it uses a much longer and more varied basic phrase, a pitch sequence that is moved out of phase while the underlying rhythm remains constant. George Cacioppo's *Cassiopeia* is perhaps the most complex piece here; it allows considerable freedom in realization. The score is a unique "landscape" of very specific pitch, timbral, and dynamic information together with very subjective visual material intended to stimulate the performers' imaginations on many levels.

Many other pieces in this book make use of piano, electric piano, prepared piano, or organ and are recommended for further study and performance. Those specifically for keyboard with other instruments or voices include:

Chap. 2: *Five/Seven* (Noel Da Costa)
Chap. 5: *Five Easy Pieces* (T.J. Anderson)
         In the Aeolian Mode (James Tenney)
         30's (Jon Gibson)
         F# Section in D Major Prelude of Chopin (Philip Corner)
         Daydream (William Albright)
Chap. 6: *Tower of Power* (Beth Anderson)
Chap. 7: *"Fairy Song"* (Richard Peaslee)
         Tom Thumb (Stephen Mayer)
         Here and There (Stuart Smith)
Chap. 8: *Dragoon* (David Cope)
         Aeolian Partitions (Pauline Oliveros)

Doodling

Tom Johnson

Begin some very soft doodling with your right hand in the upper part of the keyboard. Continue the doodling as you read. Do not let your playing distract you from your reading, and do not let your reading distract you from your playing. The two must accompany each other. Now, without stopping the right-hand doodling, play a loud low note with your left hand, and sustain it for a moment. Continue the doodling and, whenever you feel the time is right, play another loud bass note. Do not wait too long between the loud low notes, but do not play them too close together either. Try not to worry about when you should or should not play another loud low note. If you become too involved with thinking about that, you will not be able to carry out your other tasks as well. Your attention should always be about equally divided between the three things: the reading, the right-hand doodling and the loud low notes.

Of course, you are quite limited in what you are permitted to play at the moment, and the music might become tedious after a while to someone who was only listening. But that is immaterial since these are *Private Pieces,* and are only for your own entertainment. The piece will not be tedious to you since it is not easy to do three things at once. The only way you can do all three well is by dividing your attention equally between them, so that you never ignore one of them. If you forget about the doodling, it will not sound the way you want it to sound. If you forget about the loud low notes, there will be a long awkward gap in the music. If you forget about the reading, you may miss some instruction or idea.

After another paragraph, you will be asked to play something else, but in the meantime continue playing and reading as you have been. If you find that you have been paying more attention to one of your tasks than to the other two, try to balance your attention more equally. Although no more instructions are necessary at the moment, the text is continuing in order to give you time to achieve a sense of balance between the three things, so that they seem to accompany one another. You have three more sentences in which to try to achieve this balance before going on to a new section of the piece. Now only two sentences, including this one, remain before the paragraph will end and you will be asked to do something else. This is the last sentence of this part of the piece.

Now stop playing, but continue reading. At some point during this paragraph, play a single note and sustain it. It may be loud or soft, high or low, black or white, but it must be a single note, and must be played only once. You may choose to play it early in the paragraph, or you may wish to play it toward the end of the paragraph. Perhaps you will want to read more of the text before making your decision. You must, however, remain within the limits of the paragraph. So if you have not played your note by this time, you must do so soon, as the paragraph is almost finished. You may wish to pause a moment before proceeding to the next paragraph, which will be quite demanding.

Resume the doodling with your right hand, as you did in the beginning of the piece, but this time let it gradually become more energetic. For a while it can be played by the right hand only, and should sound as it did at the beginning, but soon it should become faster. As it accelerates, you will probably want to use the left hand too, so that you can play more and more notes in less and less time. As the doodling becomes faster, you should also let it move into a wider range. By now the doodling should be noticeably more energetic than when you began this section. Do not let it increase too quickly, however, as there is still quite a ways to go before it reaches a peak. Gradually begin to use more and more of the keyboard and let the intensity increase until it is quite furious. Do not let the tension subside, even for a moment, and continue building until you are playing as wildly as you can. You may play anything necessary to maintain the high energy level. By now you should be playing as loud and fast as you can. You will perhaps find it more difficult to concentrate on the text now than when you were not playing so vigorously, but try to read the text as carefully as you have been, without making any sacrifices in your playing. Continue playing as wildly as you can, and look for ways that will enable you to play even more wildly. Do not be afraid to make booming or crashing sounds, if they will fit in with what you are already doing. When you find yourself running out of ideas or energy and want to end the piece, play one enormous crash and stop. Then listen for a moment to the silence.

Sonority A vs. Sonority B (1968)

Charlemagne Palestine

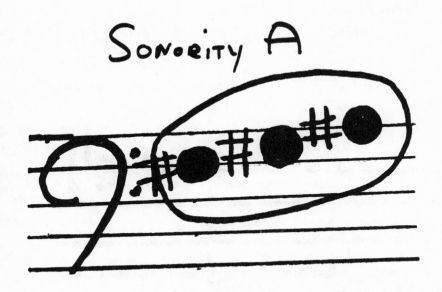

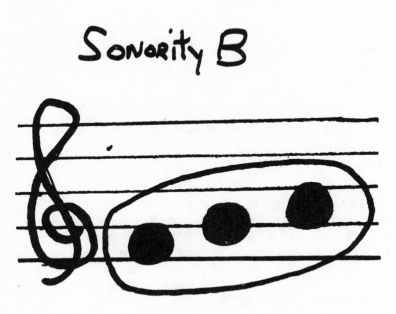

Notes

Keep sustain pedal down during entire work.

First play Sonority A with all three notes simultaneously, with the left hand, with ♪ = 238 in a pattern of continuous eighth notes for approximately five minutes: A A A A A A A A etc. for five minutes. During this time let the natural momentum of your body decide whether the tempo speeds up, remains the same or slows down. After five minutes let the sonority die away naturally. Wait a moment in complete silence. Now repeat the same procedure using Sonority B, all three notes simultaneously with the right hand at ♪ = 238: B B B B B B etc. for five minutes. Again let the momentum change naturally with your body. After five minutes let the sonority die away and wait again a moment in silence. Finally play Sonorities A and B in alternating pattern at ♪ = 238: A B A B A B A B A B A B A B A B etc. for ten minutes, again following natural body momentum. Let both sonorities die away and the work is completed. Dynamics and touch are up to the pianist, naturalness being preferred to contrivity throughout.

A Major Seventh (1973)
In The Rhythm Three Against Two

Charlemagne Palestine

Keep the sustain pedal down during this entire work.

First play the interval of a major seventh (G + F♯) simultaneously, introducing it to the ears. Allow it to die away completely and wait a few moments in silence. Now play the interval again in the rhythm three against two at a relatively fast tempo of your choice for approximately ten minutes — three in the left hand, two in the right. Soon your hands will probably speed up and slow down by themselves — let them. After ten minutes, keep playing without pause but add first the lower G, then the higher F♯ to the interval as doublings. Continue now for another five minutes, then stop abruptly and let the sounds die away completely. Throughout let changes of momentum, dynamics and touch happen by themselves, the player becoming merely a servant for the interaction between interval, the keyboard and the body — allow them full reign.

Sweet Earth Flying

Marion Brown

FINE

The title of this composition was taken from a poem written by Jean Toomer. It was written for improvisation. Like my other composition, *Afternoon Of A Georgia Faun*, it is a sound structure that gives my impression of something ineffably connected with Georgia, my home. It has been recorded by Muhal Richard Abrams and Paul Bley, and can be heard on IMPULSE Records AS-9275.

Sunday Come Down
for Piano

Marion Brown

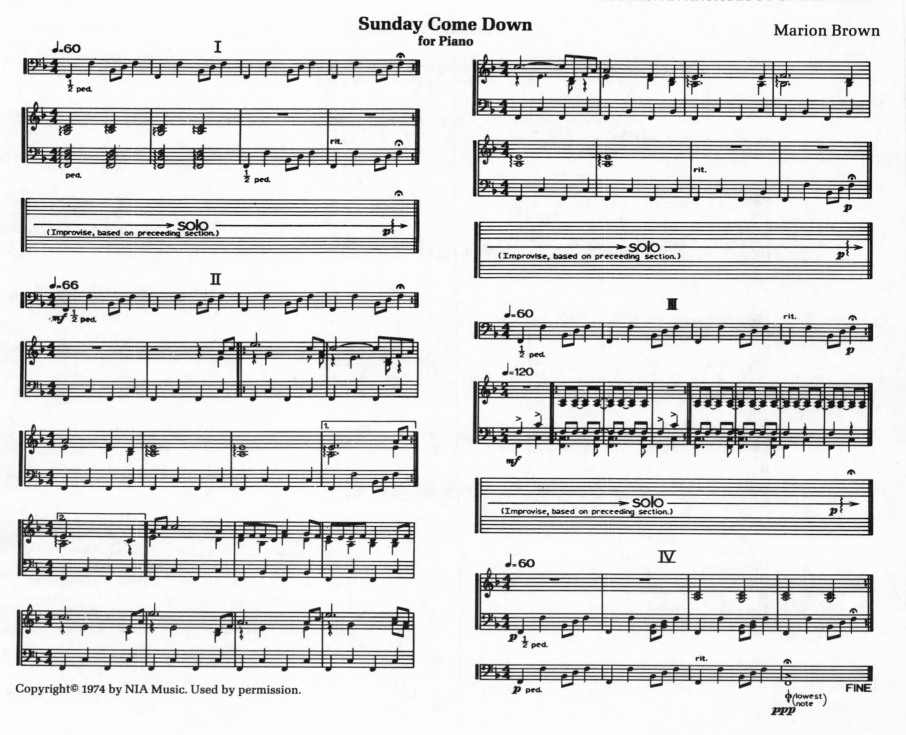

Paris

Meredith Monk

(1) Improvise a very rough, ragged phrase, keeping the fingers constantly moving and the hand rotating at the wrist from normal playing position completely around to the back.

Dream Images (Love–Death Music)
from Makrokosmos, Volume I

George Crumb

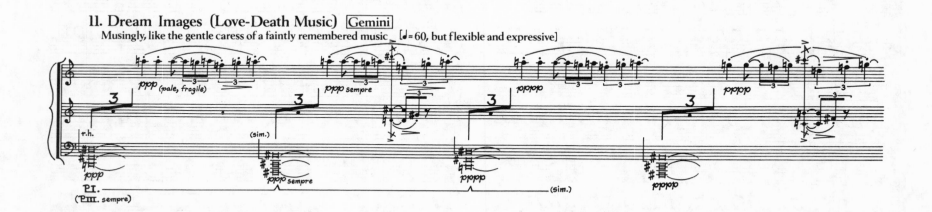

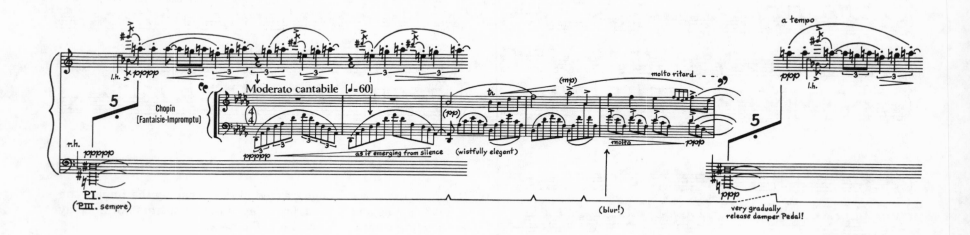

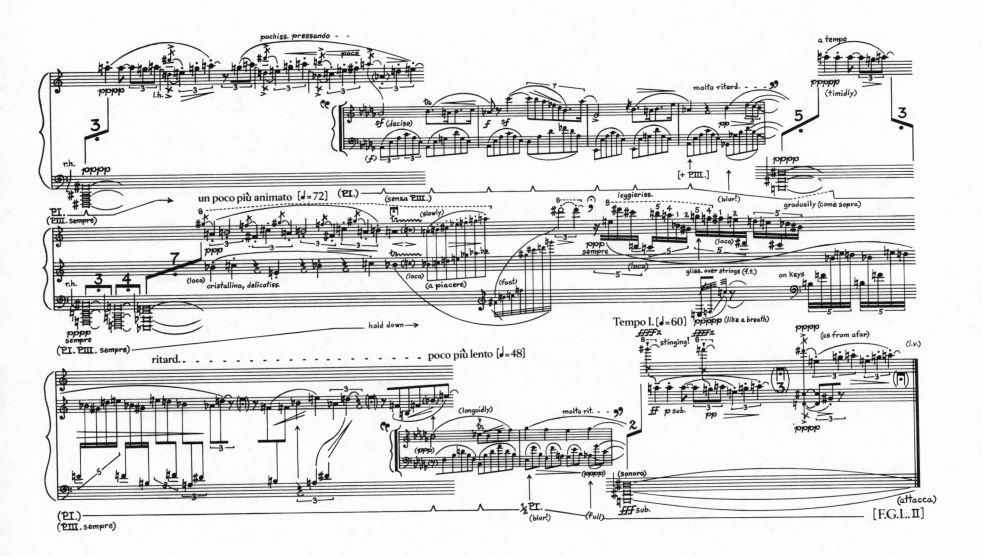

Little Pieces for Quartertone Piano

Tui St. George Tucker

Place two pianos with keyboards at right angles. Tune the piano on the player's left to standard tuning (A = 440) and the piano on the player's right a quartertone down. The player plays one piano with his left hand and the other with his right hand. To make the damper pedal reachable on the right piano, place a board (mine is 36″ x 2″ x 3/4″) on it; attach with rubber band or string. Play tones with a down-pointing arrowhead V over them on the right piano. Chords enclosed in a large down-pointing arrowhead V should also be played on the right piano.

Litany Piano Pieces

Dick Higgins

#1–Litany Piano Piece for Emmett Williams

Tempo: very moderate.
Volume: mezzo-piano to piano.
Material: in the right hand play only the four note chord composed of a bass, the fourth, fifth and octave above that. The left hand plays only three note chords consisting of a bass, and the fifth and tenth above it. Play *Only* on white keys, and round off to the closest white key.

Rhythm: play in common time only (4/4), with quarter notes which can be grouped occasially into triplets, and with occasional syncopations between the right and left hands.

Interpretation: play off close groupings of intervalic descents and ascents against large ones, or very large ones. Frequently use contrary or parallel motion between the hands for extended passages. Work for a very calm, even texture. Once in a great while allow the chords to cluster into or to cross over each other. Make no attempt to avoid melody.

Pedal: either use only or never use *una corda-* don't shift this within a performance. Use the damper only to even out large intervalic movements.

Duration: either carry on for a predetermined number of minutes or, preferable, let the duration be fixed by a simultaneous performance of Emmett Williams' *Litany and Responses.*

#2–Litany Piano Piece No. 2
for Emmett Williams

A pianist selects a chord to be played with his right hand, and a different chord for his left. He selects a characteristic dynamic and tempo for the performance. He works out the movements and relationships of the two chords in any diatonic scale or other gamut; the two hands may each be working in a different scale, mode or gamut, but they do not change within any one performance.

He plays in the dark and as long as desired.

(*Variation*; drop the single scale, mode or gamut and let these shift according to some consistent pattern, as, for instance, with the "melodic" minor scale).

#3–Litany No. 3
for Any Two Keyboard Instruments
(or one instrument and its recorded image)

1. Two of any keyboard instruments are needed, or one instrument and its recorded image. Two performers are needed, or one performer and his recorded image.

2. Each performer follows the general movement of traditional four-part composition and voice-leading, but with these qualifications:

a. Chords emphasizing the major triad are avoided for the most part, and where these occur they are used only as passing tones and on unstressed beats.

b. Whenever a performer notices that he has suggested a tonal center, he moves to a surprise modulation from that center.

c. A movement is emphasized among unrelated or unresolved relationships among chords based on minor triads and major seconds.

3. Each performer ignores the other (or his image) completely with respect to what he is doing.

4. The meter is *mostly* common time (4/4), though this may shift for variety and use brief passages in other meters. The volume is loud throughout. The speed is moderate to slow. The duration is flexible.

5. Before performing this piece the performer should listen to a sample performance made or taped by the composer, and then improve upon it.

#4–Litany No. 4 for Piano

1. Litany No. 4 is like *Litany No. 3* except that it is always played on pianos and uses different sorts of materials (see item **2**, below).

2. The right hand uses only octaves *followed* by the fourths and fifths between them, in eighth notes (octave-second-octave-second-octave-second). The left hand uses any white notes with the fifth and tenth over a fundamental.

3. Movement may be parallel, opposite or oblique, modal or diatonic in effect, using related or unrelated movements rhythmically. The volume is mezzopiano throughout. The implications and controls from *Litany #1* may be applied.

#5–Litany No. 5

1. *Litany No. 5* is like *Litany No. 3* except that the two instruments (or the instrument and its recorded image) need not be a keyboard instrument (though they may be) but could also be a tuned, struck instrument and/or a plucked stringed instrument. Sample combinations: organ and harp, two harpsichords, celesta and glockenspiel, live and taped carillon, piano and guitar, etc.

2. The material for both hands is any huge, arpeggiated or occasionally unarpeggiated chord or tone cluster, white-note-only or mixed white and black, with or without gaps and holes in their midst. The volume is as soft as feasible on the instrument such that both instruments can be heard: occasional intrusions of maximum volume are used, but these do not last long.

3. All other factors are as per *Litany No. 3*.

Three Pieces for Piano Solo

Elliot Borishansky

Continuum

a. on the ledge of the piano keyboard cover.
b. in the air 4 inches above ledge

Trial Run

Piano Music

The Machine

Instructions

The piano is completely closed when the performer enters. There is no piano chair. A block of wood has already been placed in the sounding board area. The keyboard cover remains shut.

The performer enters carrying a tool box. He soon presses the sostenuto pedal. This turns the machine on and off. His foot should be ca. 3 inches from the pedal so that there is that added percussive effect when it strikes. (♩ = pedal)

All playing is done by a second pianist offstage who does not exist for the audience since the music he plays is the sound of the machine.

B. At this point the performer walks over and raises the lid all the way. He peers in and scratches his head. His back is to the audience. He walks around the piano so that he faces the audience. He opens the tool box and takes out a rasp and files on the block of wood already in the sounding board area.

We are now at C. When C is completed the performer returns to the sounding board area, takes a brace and bit and proceeds to bore into the block of wood. Offstage, the pianist simulates the sound of splintering wood. One method is to crack a walnut with a screw-type nutcracker.
Fragment D is performed. Back at the sounding board area, the performer takes out a hammer and screwdriver, making sure that these tools are seen by the audience. He crawls under the piano on his back. His feet are facing the audience. He bangs with his hammer in the manner indicated at E but extended. A metallic sound should be produced. He then takes the screwdriver and as he turns it, a horrendous creaking sound should be produced offstage.

Fragment F is begun. Once the Alberti bass has established the fact that the machine is in order again the performer may pack up his tools, lower the lid and walk offstage in the direction away from the pianist all to the tune of the Alberti bass. The performer forgets to turn the machine off and only when he remembers and returns to press the pedal does the music stop. The performer walks off.

The Machine

The Entrance

for Two–Manual Electric Organ

Robert Ashley

for Larry Leitch

Make 36 equal stacks of pennies. The stacks should be big enough to activate any key on either manual. Make 18 stacks heads-up and 18 stacks tails-up.

Begin by placing one "heads" stack on any key; then, place a "tails" stack on the corresponding key of the other manual.

thereafter. . .

1. Place a stack of either denomination immediately next to or among (on the manual with) the stacks of the opposite denomination, producing a display in which all of the "heads" or all of the "tails", but one — the most recently placed stack — are on one manual, while the most recently placed "heads" stack or "tails" stack is on the other manual.

2. Then, one at a time move the stacks that were on the keyboard (previously) to their respectively opposite manuals, producing a display in which all of the "heads" are on the one manual and all of the "tails" are on the other manual.

3. Continue in this manner (Repeating 1 and 2 alternately) until all of the stacks are on the keyboards in a uniform display.

4. Remove any single stack, taking from that stack one penny, which will represent that stack thereafter. Invert that penny so that its denomination is opposite that of the stack it represents and place it on the key from which the stack was removed, producing a display in which all of the "heads" or all of the "tails", but one, are on one manual, while all of the stacks or pennies of the opposite denomination are on the other manual.

5. Then, one at a time move all of the stacks or pennies, except the most recently placed one, to their respectively opposite manuals, producing a display in which all of the "heads" are on one manual and all of the "tails" are on the other manual.

6. Continue in this manner (repeating 4 and 5 alternately) until all of the stacks have been replaced by single pennies in a uniform display.

If a stack is spilled, it should be reassembled before proceeding.

Eight Solutions Out of a Numberless Variety

1.   Assemble an audience and perform the work as though the idea of the composition and the audience's expectations were the same.

2.   Eliminate the fact of the audience, but retain the notion of a performance.

3.   Allow the audience more freely to determine its relationship to the performance and retain the notion of a performance. (David Tudor)

4.   Eliminate the notion of a performance, but allow for the possibility of a body of observers who may or may not consider themselves to be an audience.

5.   Retain the notion of the composition as work performed, but eliminate the notion of the performance:

a) record the performance without regard to the possibility of its reproduction;
b) record the performance under the strict limitations imposed by the requirements of reproduction (e.g., having defined that the reproduction will last twenty-two minutes, train yourself to accomplish the work of performing the composition within that time).

6.   Eliminate the notion of a performance and eliminate the fact of the audience. (George Brecht)

7.   Allow for observers whose role is undefined, as in Item 4, and retain the notion of a performance, but eliminate the act of performing:

   a)   perform the work in a place remote from possible observers and without regard for the possibility of reproduction for those observers;

   b)   perform the work in a place remote from possible observers, but allow for the possibility of immediate reproduction in a place that is open to observers.

8.   Allow for observers whose role is undefined, as in Item 4, and retain the notion of the composition as work performed, but eliminate the notion of a performance and eliminate the act of performing.

ENSEMBLE MUSIC
Part I of **The Bells of Bellagio**
for 2 or 3 Players at 1, 2 or 3 Pianos
For John and Charlotte Marshall

Otto Luening

As the title indicates, the piece should sound like bells; every note should be accented and the damper pedal should be held down throughout the entire piece. It should be interresting for the players to figure out the different canonic combinations of these pieces for themselves.*

There are four obvious ways in which the piece can be performed: parts one and two alone; parts one and three alone; parts two and three alone (in this version, take the tempo a little faster)—all these played on one piano;

finally, all three parts together at one, two, three or more pianos. The players should also find other ways to perform the piece. For piano ensemble groups, simply have more than one player on each part, as long as each part has the same number of players. This might be a particularly useful device in group piano teaching.

When the hands cross, make room for your partner; on unisons, decide who will play the note.

I. Hail!

OTTO LUENING

Maybe Once or Twice
for 2 Pianos

Jim Fox

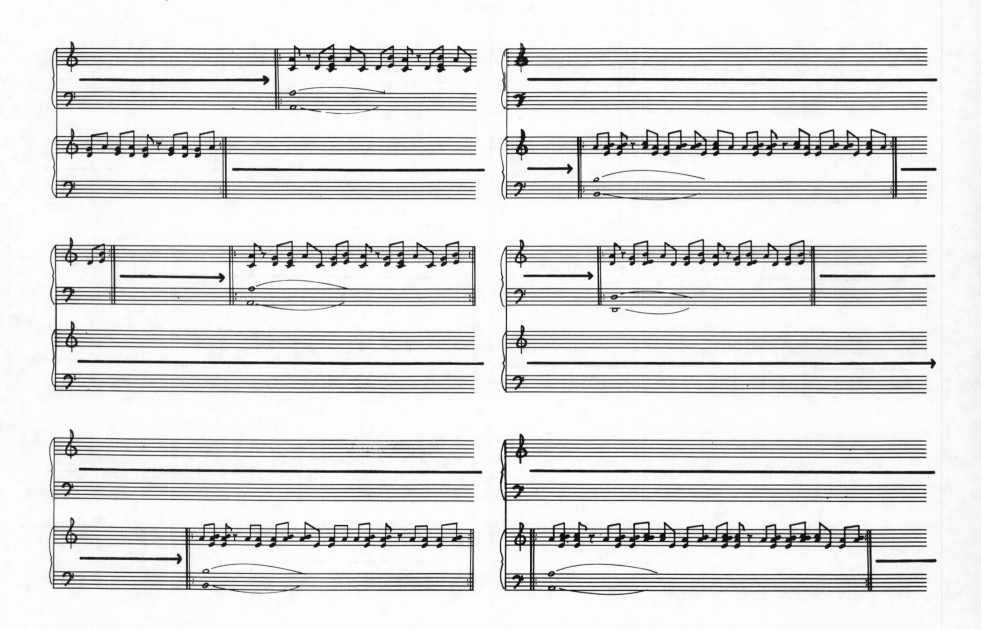

1979

Rhythm Studies I & II
for two pianos

Michael Parsons

Each figure is repeated over and over. Pianist 1 begins playing figure 1, and Pianist 2 enters soon after, beginning figure 1 on a different beat. After a number of repetitions Pianist 1 changes to figure 2 while Pianist 2 continues playing figure 1. Then Pianist 2 moves on to figure 2 (beginning it on a different beat from Pianist 1) . . . . . . etc. Do not pause between figures. Move through the piece in this way, playing alternately the same figure and adjacent figures and when on the same figure avoid unisons.

Crabcar Phase
for Two Pianos

Charles Capro

Begin at 1. and proceed playing each line up to and through 10. In line 10 the first Ab is absent and all the notes have been moved ahead one position, although the rhythm is the same. This phasing process is continued with each note moving ahead one position on each repeat. When the two pianos are again in phase (unison) pick it up at line 9, and regress by playing lines 8 through 1. It is suggested that the player of Piano II memorize the sequence of notes as an aid to performance.

PIANO II

135

Begin at 1. and proceed playing each line up to and including line 9.
Then this last line is repeated many times while Piano II moves out of
phase with it. When both players are again together, play this line
once completely and regress by playing lines 8 through 1. Piano I has
the option of playing this piece in any register provided the contour is
unchanged and the choice of register is adhered to for the entire piece.

Cassiopeia

George Cacciopo (1962)

Lettered symbols with number subscripts represent pitch.

White pitch symbols are played as harmonics.

Number subscript refers to octave register:

> The lowest tones on the piano are A_0, Bb_0, and $B\natural_0$. The next tone, C_1, is the beginning of the first octave register. Succeeding C's mark the beginning of the remaining registers. All other tones are numbered according to the 'C' immediately preceding them. C_4 is middle-C. C_8 is the highest tone on the keyboard.

Undefined Sound Paths: paths with unlettered pitch symbols

> Actual pitch may or may not be supplied by the performer. The spatial interval between unlettered and lettered pitch symbols suggests a range of pitch choices.

Accidentals are placed above the number subscript.

Loudness is proportional to size of pitch symbol.

Time Values:

> a) may be proportional to the linear space between pitch symbols
> b) may be developed spontaneously and variably during performance

Convex paths indicate retardation; concave indicate acceleration.

Four Networks: Fields of intersecting sound paths

Ellipse of Irregular Lines: Visual Fantasy . . . Eye/ear link . . . Sound tracer

> A stimulus involving the psychology of visual perception. Any reaction may or may not involve translation into aural experience. If translation occurs, the performer submits original interpolations: other sound events, visual events, theater . . . .

Island-Form Symbols

> More psychology. To be treated with the same options as the Ellipse. Some penetrate networks; others are isolated.

Dotted Line

> A semi-boundary. Suggests parenthetical or separate treatment of the area embraced. (Another room? . . . Faster, slower? . . . Later? . . . New instrument? . . .)

Each of the four networks consists of a number of pitch-defined paths of sound. The paths are superimposed upon one another and intersect at various points. The piece may begin or end with any of the networks or fantasy forms. The performance may involve a single network, or any part of it, all of the networks, or any part of them, with or without fantasy elements. No performance, however, may be based solely on the Ellipse or other fantasy forms. Any pitch within a path can serve as the initial sound. Sounds other than those at ends of sound paths may move in either direction, playing and/or repeating sounds in any order. Where paths intersect, there is a choice of direction. Any new path may also be played in whole or in part, with sounds occurring in any order. Closed circuits may be developed by making use of the intersection and superimposition of sound paths. This configuration may be repeated any number of times as originally determined, or with permutations. Exit is by way of the most available intersection, or by orbital jump to any other sound path, network, or fantasy form. Sound paths may also be performed directly, ignoring intersections. With this decision all the contents of the path must be played. Any order may be pursued, and the entire figure may be repeated or permuted ad libitum. After completion, other structures may be developed by way of intersection or orbital jump. Sounds along any route may also be played simultaneously. Paths and intersections are numerous enough to insure widespread movement. Decisions may sometimes lead to previously played material, even previously developed configurations. The performer may vary or permute the recurrence freely, or simply ignore it. The piece can end anywhere in any structure either by spontaneous decision during performance, or upon completion of a previously arranged time-limit.

Note: Networks that appear to converge into the Ellipse can also be seen as passing behind it. Perceived in this manner, paths between the two networks can be interpreted as continuities.

Any number of performers and pianos may be involved in performance.

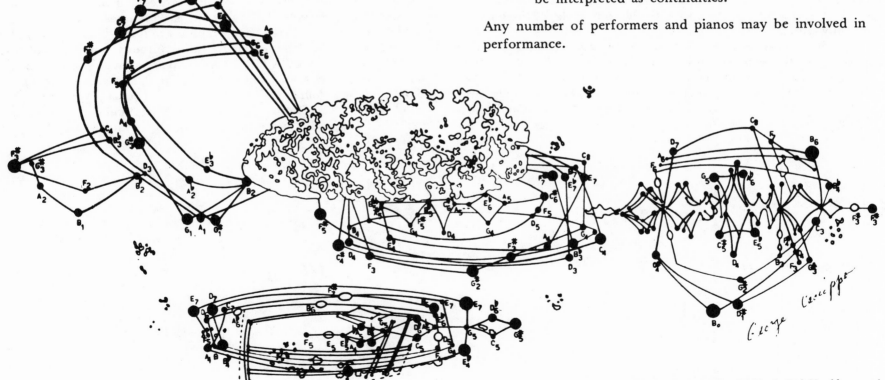

5 Music for Instruments

VERBAL AND GRAPHIC SCORES

These are among the most open and flexible scores in this book, although not necessarily the easiest to perform. The notations here present situations, general guidelines, and structures, but allow—in fact rely upon—the performers to provide many of the pitch, rhythmic, timbral, dynamic, and other details in performance. Unlike traditionally notated pieces, these are primarily concerned not with pitch and rhythm but more with character and quality of sound. Performers here must remember that they are very important co-creators, and must play as imaginatively as possible for these pieces to really work.

The first scores are verbal descriptions of sound or of activity resulting in (among other things) sound. The pieces by James Tenney are quite specific while those of Christian Wolff, Philip Corner, Frederic Rzewski, David Jones, and Barney Childs are more general and allow for quite a range of interpretation. Malcolm Goldstein's *Yosha's Morning Song Extended* is, as the title suggests, an in-strumental interpolation of various sounds and phrases suggested by te original vocal version in Chapter 2, *Yosha's Morning Song*. It may be used separately or with the original song. All of these pieces specify various details, fundamental sound materials, or situations, allowing the overall structure to develop differently from them each time. By contrast, Brian Taylor's *Morning Music II* gives the basic structure—based on the idea of simultaneous, highly contrasted sound layers—but allows the performers freedom to interpret and express this structure. Jeffrey Levine's *Parentheses* and Robert Ashley's *Quartet* are both visual, graphic scores in which a variety of symbols are to be interpreted by the performers according to in-structions. Jerry Troxell's *Elegy* is a graphic score with some specific notation for a jazz soloist and ensemble. Frank McCarty's *Exitus for Band* combines elements of vocal breath sound but as played through wind instruments. These last two pieces in particular would make exciting additions to the repertory of a variety of larger ensembles.

Swell Piece
for Alison Knowles

James Tenney

Swell Piece

for Alison Knowles

To be performed by any number of instruments beyond three, and lasting any length of time previously agreed upon.

Each performer plays one long tone after another (actual durations and pitches free and independent).

Each tone begins as softly as possible, builds up to maximum intensity, then fades away again into (individual) silence.

Within each tone, as little change of pitch or timbre as possible, in spite of the intensity changes.

James Tenney
12/67

Swell Piece No. 2
Swell Piece No. 3

James Tenney

SWELL PIECE NO. 2 (for any five or more different sustaining instruments):

for Pauline Oliveros

Each performer plays A-440, beginning as softly as possible, building up to maximum intensity, then fading away again into (individual) silence. This process is repeated by each performer in a way that is rhythmically independent of any other performer, until a previously agreed-upon length of time has elapsed. Within each tone, as little change of pitch or timbre as possible.

SWELL PIECE NO. 3 (for any eight or more different sustaining instruments):

with respect to LaMonte Young and his COMPOSITION 1960, No. 7

Divide the instruments into two approximately equal-numbered groups, primarily on the basis of a treble-bass distinction. The higher-pitched group plays the F-sharp a tritone above middle C, the lower-pitched group the B a fifth below. Play as in Swell Piece No. 2, but "for a long time".

James Tenney
March, 1971

Groundspace or Large Groundspace

Christian Wolff

1. Make single sounds, occasionally very long; very soft to mf. Play melodies or flourishes of about 4 notes or changes of sound (or changes of aspects of a sound), of about 3, 8, 25 notes or changes. Allow spaces between playing, at least so that you may every now and again get a sense of the space in which you are playing, and at least once so that there is a point when no one appears to be playing.
2. Instruments or sound sources that carry well start in a middle distance of the space and then move off and away.
3. Instruments or sound sources that must be immobile can also use amplification and loudspeakers apart from themselves and possibly movable.
4. Instruments or sound sources that do not carry far start in the middle distance and approach potential listeners.
5. At some time a player may seek out another player and play a duet with him.

(Examples of (2): brass instruments, motors (at no more than medium loudness; if greater loudness inevitable, start at a remoter place and move still further away); of (3): piano, if there is no vehicle to move it or the terrain is bad; of (4): doublebass, electrically powered sound source with a weak battery.) For various instruments and sound sources one will have to determine how well, in the circumstances, they carry, at no more than medium loudness. Borderline cases could move in directions other than those indicated for (2) and (4), e.g. on the pattern of a fan, for the most part away from the centre (several centres are possible). Movement and making sounds may coincide but neither should make the other obviously awkward or difficult, except very occasionally.

Each player should take the limits of the space to be wherever he is sometimes audible, at whatever loudness, to one other person and where he can sometimes hear one other person. If these limits are passed, he may consider the piece finished.

Looking North

Christian Wolff

Think of, imagine, devise, a pulse, any you choose, of any design. When you hear a sound or see a movement or smell a smell or feel any sensation not seeming to emanate from yourself, whose location in time you can sense, and its occurrence coincides, at some point, with your pulse, make your pulse evident:
in some degree; for any duration.
(a)   Express all coincidences.
(b)   Express only every tenth one.
(c)   Forget your pulse and play as closely as you can to every second, fifth, twentieth and single expression of pulse of one other player (this can be repeated as in a loop).
(d)   Play a very long, generally low pitched and quiet melody without particular reference to a pulse (once only).
(e)   At any point stop.
(f)   At any point stop, think of another pulse, and proceed as above.
Or: think of, imagine, devise, any number of pulses. . .and so on, as above.

Pit Music

Christian Wolff

"A pit is dug [or discovered] to serve as a resonance cavity or sound bowl, and close to it a wand [or other flexible material] is stuck into the ground [or otherwise set firm] with a string tied to its free end. The other end of the string is knotted into a piece of bark or similar material, which is placed over the pit like a lid over a pot and is weighted down [or otherwise secured] by a ring of stones or earth. The wand and lid are then adjusted to create sufficient tension to keep the string taut. In playing, the musician's [musicians'] interest in melody asserts [may assert] itself."

From Prose Collection. Copyright © 1973 by Christian Wolff. Used by permission.

Play

Christian Wolff

Play, make sounds, in short bursts, clear in outline for the most part; quiet; two or three times moves towards as loud as possible, but as soon as you cannot hear yourself or another player stop directly. Allow various spaces between playing (2, 5 seconds, indefinite); sometimes overlap events. One, two, three, four or five times play a long sound of complex or sequence of sounds. Sometimes play independently, sometimes by coordinating; with other players (when they start or stop or while they play or when they move) or a player should play (start or, with long sounds start and stop or just stop) at a signal (or within 2 or 5 seconds of a signal) over which he has no control (does not know when it will come). At some point or throughout use electricity.

From Prose Collection. Copyright © 1973 by Christian Wolff. Used by permission.

Fanfare*   Philip Corner

*or another kind of musical function.
(ideas in mind: "background," "furniture," "decor" music; outdoor Protest; "Miserere;" March; Orgy; Scherzo (really funny); Meditation.

Form this as a process
starting from raw lump of unprogrammed sound-matter
made
out of progressive definitions:

l.   spirit

2.   materials

3.   relationships

4.   form

Clarifications will come from progress as possibilities arise and are explored, are rejected, developed, refined. After these four main areas have been considered, decisions are to be made for performance, as to limits, as to controls, as to freedoms. As to duration.

A process for generating and structuring a freely conscious performance.

These things are specified as an opening of a way to play, for whoever may—they may!—play their own music. A starting place, let them carry, from these words, ideas, their own, as far as they might. It is theirs; no credit need be given. Only if there is a result which stays closely within, has muchly depended on, this script—should acknowledgement be (graciously) offered.

Melodic and Rhythmic units, appropriate ones, played around. Some abstracted from their positions in the literature, fragmented and developed. A method of systematic work: locate, notate, a large number of these. Their use in the performance could be as pre-planned and comprehensive as felt to be desirable. An unpredictable cuing scene might make use of visual projections, making the patterns seen by the audience.

A lively improvisation arises from quick response to perceived patterns. In rehearsal, the difficulties are pushed against, polishing new techniques which, even should they never appear, enlarge the range of possibilities. The performance itself moves between a free complexity and rather tight moments of virtuosity.

Exercises: Pass sound from one to the other. . .
/ link by keeping a common characteristic.
/ or within a constant time-area.

Send a rhythmic element around in a circle. Pick up the speed.

Settle into a rhythmic groove, stay together on it, awhile.

It may be desirable to fix in advance the general outlines of the formal design. Certainly, it should be a part of the practicing, to pick up on changes and carry the flow in a coherent way.

As a simple plan, this was agreed on:

Open with a real sense, a presenting of, the character—favor long tones, built-up sonorities.

Move into a strongly rhythmic pattern, piling up on the repeating motive brought in by any instrument. Stay with it. Close brilliantly. Go up in a blaze of glory!

—Clearly, such a schema is infinitely extensible, a kind of rondo in which successive "couplets" utilize a new motivic element. The section or sections in between can also be differentiated to any degree—by color, intensity, inner speed, density, and such factors. Even by the specification of harmonic-aggregates, even single pitches or intervals, which can be pre-decided, picked up spontaneously, or cued by visual means.

In this manner, any number of non-identical repetitions may be (like at least a half dozen on our first day) created and recreated.

three activities within a space

david jones

a string player:

create extended and detached durations of a single note or of an aggregate ... filligree textures on the level of audibility... later introduce and terminate with dyads, high register harmonics, microtones and a single extended glassandi; all these are to be of extended duration, longer than the opening, i.e. as long as is physically possible ... limited range of intensity towards inaudibility, mute on throughout ... move from a sigh to a whisper.

a percussionist:

select a sound producing object of metal with a vibrant point of attack and a relatively long decay ... commence the performance ... listen attentively to the resonance and play only when the sound will add to the environment or change the conditions created by another player ... feel free to move within the performance area.

a wind player:

hum a sharpened accidental of low register *sfz*, repeat any number of times then play a contrasting pitch/timbre ... repeat these two activities ... alternate the order over extending periods of silence ... retain the intensity and concentration of the opening attacks throughout the performance.

Variation on a Theme of Harold Budd

Barney Childs

Any number of string players, 4-20.

Decide ahead of time about how long the performance is to be. One player should be agreed upon as the one to give the start and stop cues. Just before beginning, untune each string randomly, either up or down; do not check what pitches you have achieved. Put on the mute.

During the piece you will play single long tones. Each tone may be as long as you please but must not be shorter than five seconds. Always play in the dynamic range p-ppp. Do not try for a precise pre-decided pitch; place stopping finger on fingerboard in the part of the instrument's range you want the pitch to sound. Since the strings are "out of tune," you won't be able to guess ahead of time anyway. Pitches once begun must be maintained except in the case of microtonal alteration, and this is to be done extremely slowly, by a gradual very slow one-way rocking of the stopping finger; roll on the ball of the finger. Don't slide the stopping finger, or pick it up and move it, to make these alterations, which may occur at any time you wish during the playing of a tone but no closer together than twenty seconds. You may use both artificial and natural harmonics if and when you wish. All tones are *arco*.

Each tone ends a silence: that is, be silent as long as you feel you wish to be, in terms of what *you* are playing, before playing a tone. Each tone, therefore, should end a personal silence which you have allowed to continue as long as you can: the beginning of a tone must feel necessary, unavoidable, to end your own particular silence. Whether other people are playing or not doesn't matter; they are, after all, involved in *their* own personal silences. Ignore them, both in selection of pitch and in when you play.

Deep Springs
6.50 PM 6 April 1969
only three clouds are yet lighted

Sound Pool Notes

Frederic Rzewski

The *Sound Pool* is a free improvisation session whose limits are undefined. It is left open at both ends and in the middle. Any sound might be part of the music, depending on how you hear it.

Bring your own sound, and add it to the pool when you feel the moment is right. Don't take anybody else's instrument away from him. Make both sounds and silences. The more people playing, the less there is for each individual to do. If everybody plays all the time, the result may be boring or unpleasant. On the contrary, a general silence can be interesting.

Loud instruments (drums, electric guitars) should be set up in a place where they don't dominate utterly. The space belongs to everybody. Loud instruments should accompany softer ones (flutes, harmonicas); that is, they should be played softly enough so that the softer sounds can be heard occasionally.

Three kinds of activity:
   1. Silence: listening to, and reflecting on the sounds around you; thinking about what you are going to do.
   2. Accompaniment: providing a background, or support, for a sound made by somebody else; any sound over which someone could play a solo.
   3. Solo: a prominent or leading sound; a thematic statement. Let every player at some time play a solo, or have the possibility of doing so.

Let each soloist play a theme, or a variation on a theme. Solos meant to be heard by many people should be played from a prominent position.

Form groups: move around, find someone with whom you can play together, and play a duet. Let there be a group in the center, several others in the periphery and any number of individuals, listening or playing, either standing apart, or occasionally joining with one or another group, or co-ordinating the action of two or more groups.

If somebody is playing something you don't like, stop what you are doing and listen to him for a while, and then try playing with him. If somebody seems to be playing too loudly, try to find another location in the room where you can hear better. If somebody plays very loudly for a long time, to the general irritation of many people—Tubby the Tuba—indicate to him in some way that he is taking up too much space. Avoid, however, telling other people to stop.

If you are a strong musician, mostly do accompanying work, that is, help weaker players to sound better. Seek out areas where the music is flagging, and organize groups. Be a timekeeper: provide a basic pulse, without drowning out the others. Let the stronger players circulate among the various groups, rather than congregating in one place. Let them stop from time to time and check out the general ensemble, and consider how to establish unifying links among the single groups.

Play long sounds and short ones, soft as well as loud; discover new ways of playing, other than those you are used to, and influence other people to play in different ways. Sometimes imitate what another person is doing, and sometimes play in sharp contrast (for example: against a long sustained sound, make short, spaced, percussive attacks and visa versa). Sing; use hands and feet; play the room; make sounds by scraping, scratching, and striking on floor walls, and furniture taking care not to damage anything.

Find your own theme and improvise on it. Improvise on somebody else's theme, combine the two.

Most of the time accompany somebody else, in a way that will make him want to accompany you. Occasionally play for yourself alone, without regard for whatever else is happening.

In this agglomeration of individuals, it is not important to be together all the time, to do the same things at the same time; just as there is no reason why everybody should have to work from 9 to 5. We may be able to achieve our purpose (good music) more efficiently by avoiding such uniformity, by "letting a hundred flowers bloom."

Morning Music II
for Five Players

Brian Taylor

A long piece appearing as an unchanging landscape; but with constant variety. The four types of sounds are always present: *Transforming, Constant, Repeating,* and *Scattered.* Each of the five players begins with one of these types of sounds (see below for schedule) and stays with it for at least 10 minutes. Then all players shift to another sound *each;* maintaining the "same" overall sound landscape. This goes on until all have played every one of the types of sounds. The beginning and end may be staggered, or players may choose to enter and exit all at the same time.

Transforming: continually changing from one sound to another, in *slow* evolution. The score for scattered sounds may be used as a stimulus, or may not. The sound may disappear and re-appear altogether, but only *gradually* into and out of the silences.

Constant: One sound-quality, as unchanging as possible, going on for designated time non-stop.

Repeating: One sound or group of sounds, followed by a period of silence. This pulse (of sound and silence) is repeated over and over. It may be sped up or slowed down slightly as needed.

Scattered: Simply go from one sound to the next, in any order, with a period of silence between each. Silence lengths may be from 1/4 second to 30 seconds; explore all durations. Sounds may be repeated or omitted as needed. Keep in mind that two people will be playing scattered sounds at once; response and interaction is therefore possible as a pair, or possible with others in the group.

Interaction is actually possible, probable, and preferable in any one of the sound categories.

Schedule for players

player	10´	20´	30´	40´	50´
1 Constant	transforming	scattered	repeating	scattered	
2. repeating	scattered	constant	transforming	scattered	
3 scattered	constant	transforming	scattered	repeating	
4 transforming	scattered	repeating	scattered	constant	
5 scattered	repeating	scattered	constant	transforming	

These are approximate times—switches between one and the next type of sound must be immediate, with no hesitation. 10 minutes for each is a minimum, the piece may be longer. If a shortened version is desired, play only the first 10' (or 20', or 30' mm, etc.). . .of the above schedule.

Scattered Sounds

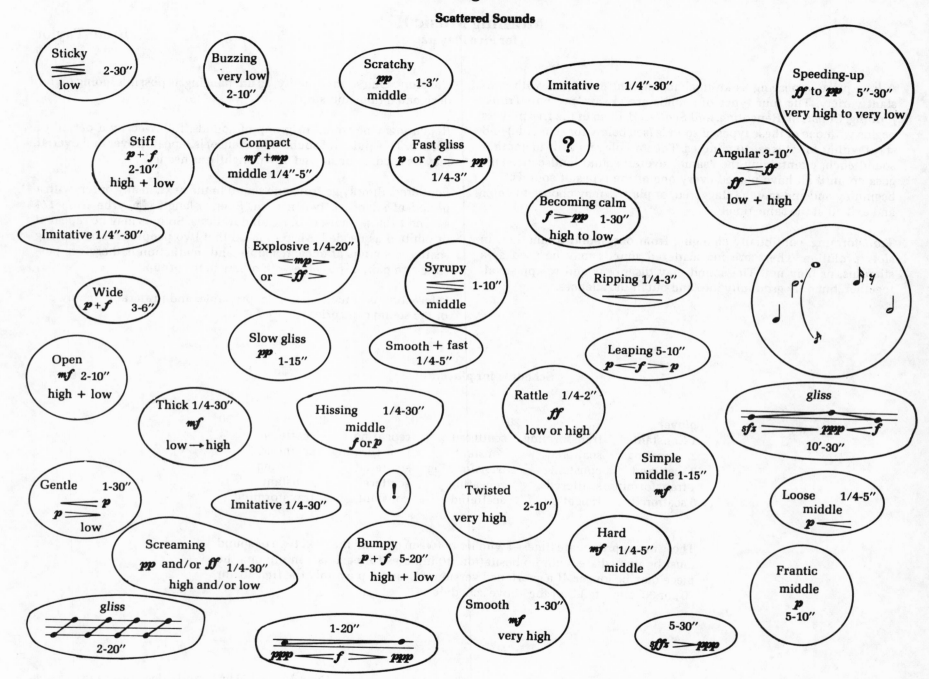

Yosha's Morning Song Extended

Malcolm Goldstein

To be performed with a singer performing *Yosha's Morning Song*, preferably a small ensemble, perhaps a trio.

Or to be performed as an instrumental chamber ensemble (trio up to a maximum of an octet—not too thick a sound so that all can hear one another).

The score consists of two pages:

1. A page of nineteen sounds and phrases. The material is to be played by an instrumentalist (any timbre and possibly one instrumentalist playing several timbres or instruments, if desired). Indications in brackets are for instruments like guitar, piano, etc. where some adjustments are necessary to realize the sound. The tempo of each event is variable, as is often the pitch, registration, loudness, timbre, etc. (except where specifically indicated). Tempo is dependent upon time limitations of the moment (see below) and the expressive dynamic of the ensemble.

2. A page of a labyrinth/map indicating:

    In boxes, the number of sound events to take place within the time (number of seconds) indicated above or along side the box. In performing the number of sound events as indicated in the box what should occur is a *collage* of various sound events one after another, *with no silence between* each sound event, so as to create a larger phrase/texture. The total duration indicated should be filled with this phrase/structure so that the duration of each sound event, as well as its proportion in the newly created phrase/structures, is always (probably) different—as necessitated by the moment of realization.

    Numbers, or lines, between boxes, indicate seconds of silence between sound events.

    In addition, some boxed events have additional instructions which might indicate specific choice of events, or the way in which variable events should be realized.

    "Sustained" means a choice of a single thing such as "low sustained note . . . " "deeply breathing in" "bending a pitch" "high register (squeaky)" etc.

    Double boxes mean repeat the same sound event in each successive double box.

The manner of realization:
Starting anywhere in the labyrinth, follow the path in any direction (without immediate backtracking or pacing back and forth), trying to explore the whole terrain eventually and keeping ears open to the whereabouts of others. If performed with *Yosha's Morning Song* (see the end of Chapter II), the instrumantalists should begin first, allowing the singer the silent duration as indicated on the first line of the vocal score, and then stopping *with* the final sound of the song. If performed as an instrumental piece, the duration is open, to be determined by the performers, though probably no less than ten minutes.

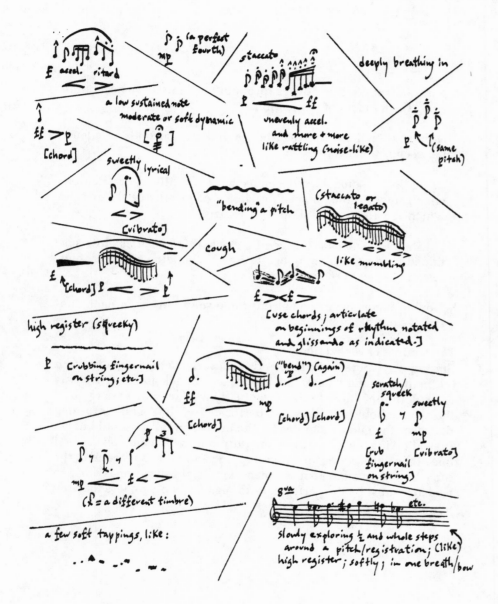

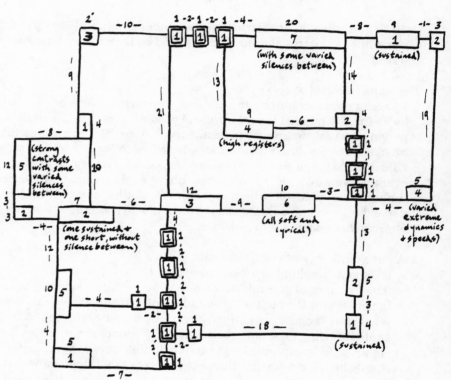

Parentheses
Plan of Performance for Any String Instrument

Jeffrey Levine

PARENTHESES is a plan for performance by any string instrument. It can be played as a solo performance or, as many as 8 different performances can be played simultaneously.

There are 49 events, each with 4 characteristics and as many as 4 modifiers of those characteristics. Every performance begins in any upper left corner of the piece and continues either from left to right, horizontally, proceeding to the next line, or from top to bottom, vertically, proceeding to the next column. The performance is finished when all 49 events have been played (by each performer).

Each sign refers to a specific characteristic or modifier (of a characteristic) of the event in which it appears. REGARDLESS OF THE DIRECTION IN WHICH THE PIECE IS READ, IT IS ALWAYS THE POSITION OF THE SIGN IN THE SQUARE WHICH DETERMINES THE CHARACTERISTIC OR MODIFIER TO WHICH IT REFERS.

The 4 large signs in the corners of each square determine the main characteristics of the event.

Upper left = duration
Upper right = dynamic
Lower left = left hand position
Lower right = right hand activity

The (as many as) 4 smaller signs in the middle of each square are possible modifiers of the main characteristics. Each one refers only to that sign in the corner to which its position in the middle is analogous.

The signs in the middle of the sides of each square refer to the length of the pause between 2 successive events. Only that sign in the middle of the side shared with the following square (according to the direction in which the piece is being read) is relevant. At the end of a line or column the sign in the same position as that of the preceding square is used.

Parentheses surrounding any sign are applied only when they appear in the same direction as that in which the piece is being read. The characteristic or modifier in parentheses MUST either be used as it is, or be replaced by or used in combination with the characteristic or modifier in the corresponding position of the preceding and/or following event.

DURATION is the length (in time) or each event exclusive of the pause or fermata.
DYNAMIC is not absolute; rather it is the general dynamic character of the event.
LEFT HAND POSITION refers to the generally accepted positions on the string

instruments. There are 7 positions, each one determined by the first finger which must rest on the notes of the diatonic major scale of which the highest open string is the fifth. The position may also include neighbouring half positions. The performer plays on all the strings between the position (of the event) and the bridge, but never between the position and the nut.

RIGHT HAND ACTIVITY is the mode of sound emission as determined by the appropriate sign.

MODIFIERS (the smaller, centrally located signs) can be applied within the duration of the event in which they appear, but not necessarily for the entire duration of the event. They may also be omitted, except when they are enclosed in parentheses.

Fermatas and pauses can be either relative to the length of the preceding event, or of constant duration for the entire performance.

NOTES

As short as possible - as short, in time, as it is necessary to play the event as it is determined by its characteristics and modifiers.

Outside material - any means of sounding the instrument except the bow or the hand (for example: kettle-drum's stick, wood or felt; aluminium or glass rod; rubber ball; etc.).

Number of notes - possible combination of long to short, and many to few (notes) within the duration of the event. Number of notes is the modifier of DURATION, and, therefore, can be used in the same manner as the other modifiers. Trill - as fast as possible, periodic, with as small an interval as possible (i. e. microtonal). Semi-trill - an interrupted aperiodic trill of varying speeds and intervals.

Accents, sforzandos, crescendos and diminuendos are always within the general dynamic character.

Glissandos are always within the limit determined by left hand position. Tremolos, when used with col legno battuto, arco staccato, pizzicato, or "outside material" can mean ribattuto.

Any tuning of the strings is acceptable.

Open strings may be used sparingly.

Only different versions may be performed simultaneuously.

It is possible to perform PARENTHESES using combinations of live and pre-recorded performances.

Como (Italy)
September 1970
Duration 10' ca.

↓ Nessuna pausa *No pause*	↓ Pausa breve *Short pause*	⊡ Fermata breve *Short fermata*	⊙ Fermata *Fermata*	❋ Note esplicative *See notes*

	DURATA *DURATION*	DINAMICA *DYNAMIC*	Posizioni della mano sinistra *Left hand position*	Attivita' della mano destra *Right hand activity*
+	❋ Piu' breve possibile *As short as possible*	ff	7	❋ Altro materiale *Outside material*
⊞	3″	f	6	Col legno tratto *Col legno tratto*
☐	4″	mf	5	Col legno battuto *Col legno battuto*
■	7″	mp	4	Pizz.(e pizz. alla Bartok) *Pizz.(and snap pizz.)*
⊕	12″	p	3	Arco staccato *Arco staccato*
⊖	20″	pp	2	Arco portato *Arco portato*
●	28″	ppp	1	Arco legato *Arco legato*
	QUANTITA' di NOTE *NUMBER of NOTES*	MODIFICHE *MODIFIER*	MODIFICHE *MODIFIER*	MODIFICHE *MODIFIER*
+	Poche: brevi *Few short*	Accenti *Accents*	❋ Trilli *Trills*	Note doppie *Double stops*
⊞	Molte: brevi *Many short*	Sforzando *Sforzandos*	Semi—trilli *Semi-trills*	❋ Tremoli di note doppie *Double stop tremolo*
☐	Molte: brevi Poche: lunghe *Many short Few long*	Accenti e sforzando *Accents and sforzandos*	Glissando: note reali *Glissandos real notes*	Sul ponticello *Sul ponticello*
■	Poche: lunghe *Few long*	Crescendo *Crescendos*	Glissando: armonici *Glissandos harmonics*	Sul tasto *Sul tasto*
⊕	Lunghe e brevi uguali *Equal long and short*	Diminuendo *Diminuendos*	Armonici reali e artificiali *Harmonics real and artificial*	Tremolo *Tremolo*
○	Molte: lunghe Poche: brevi *Many long Few short*	✕	Vibrato molto ampio,aperiodico *Very wide vibrato,aperiodic*	❋ Tremolo sul ponticello *Sul pont. tremolo*
●	Molte: lunghe Molte: brevi *Many long Many short*	◇	Non vibrato *Non vibrato*	Tremolo sul tasto *Sul tasto tremolo*
.	Il doppio o la meta'della durata data. *Double or half of given duration*	Il doppio o la meta' della dinamica data. *Double or half of given dynamic*	Effetti ad libitum (toccare,sfregare,tirare la corda—ronzii ecc.) *Any effect (touch string, pull string over finger board, buzz, etc.)*	Attivita' ad libitum (battere sullo strumento,suonare sui diversi punti o lati del pont. o della cordiera,ecc.) *Any activity (hit instrument, play on other side of bridge or tailpiece, etc.)*

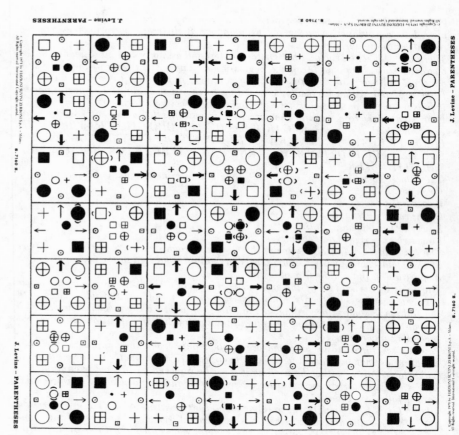

Quartet
for Any Number of Wind or String Instruments

INSTRUCTIONS

	Tone	voice sound, any pitch, **added to** an ordinary tone (Wind players will sing into their instruments while playing; string players will hum while playing.)
(V)	**Duration**	very long, one full breath or full bow
	Change	voice only; up or down, as gradually as possible, over any range
	Spacing	as short as possible

	Tone	any kind of noise, except vocal or instrumental
(N)	**Duration**	the natural duration of the noise; continuous-type noises can have any duration
	Spacing	as short as possible

	Tone	silence
•	**Duration**	one full breath at a natural pace, not "held" or suspended
	Spacing	no time interval

SCORE

The score represents a program of sound-actions, **not** a time-schedule of events. Each action will have its own duration, according to the instructions below. The time interval between successive actions (sounds) is included in the meaning of the note-symbols. Read the score left-to-right, top to bottom, in the conventional manner.

NOTATION

All sounds are to be played very softly (*pp*).

Symbols for notes produced on an instrument represent any pitch of the player's choice. Other dimensions of the notes are as follows:

	Tone	the manner of producing the sound
	Duration	the length of the note itself
	Change	the inflection of pitch during the sound
	Spacing	the time interval between the note indicated and the note that follows it.

	Tone	ordinary
●	**Duration**	very short (dying away very quickly), but not staccato
	Change	none
	Spacing	any interval that is possible without using a new breath

	Tone	ordinary
○	**Duration**	very long; one full breath or full bow
	Change	up or down, as gradually as possible, over a range of two half-steps
	Spacing	as short as possible

	Tone	vibrato, very wide and slow (exaggerated)
(≡)	**Duration**	very long; one full breath or full bow
	Change	none
	Spacing	as short as possible

When any symbol is followed by a breath mark, the breath begins immediately after the note.

PROCEDURE

All players use the same score (or copies).

Individual players begin whenever they are ready.

Start on any breath mark (•).

Perform the program of actions in a continuous manner, beginning again at the top as many times as necessary.

The performance ends when the last player has stopped playing.

OPTIONS

Once during the performance a player may "think through" a sequence of up to four sounds, as if to play, but remain silent.

Once during the performance a player may interrupt his own program of actions to imitate (as closely as possible) the actions and sounds of any player of an instrument different from his own.

Whenever no other instrumentalist is playing (tones or noises), a performer may "think through" any succession of symbols and remain silent. However, as soon as any playing-sound is made, the performer must resume playing.

During the instrumental performance a chorus (or other instrumentalists) may read aloud from any variety of texts—as quietly as possible.

If actors or dancers are used, they should be seated among the players, as though asleep.

Elegy
for Jazz Ensemble and Soloist

Jerry Troxell

Performance Notes

- The work may be performed with 7 to 19 players.

- Any instrument except the bass or percussion may be given the solo part.

- Pitches and sounds for the solo line are to be decided upon by the soloist, however the dynamics and line contours given are to be carefully followed.

- The single line on which the solo part is written represents a comfortable, low pitch in the solo instrument's range. The single line in the accompaniment represents a mid-point in the range of the like-instrument group.

- The graphic portions are to be realized with musical sounds that the group deems appropriate for the given visual representations.

- ⊓ denotes a pause of indefinite length, $\overset{2}{⊓}$ a pause of definite length (seconds).

- ↘ denotes a bending of pitch downward, ↗ a bending upward.

- ⟶ means that a sound continues to the next line or page.

page 1

Duration of
this page
ca. 60 seconds

ELEGY

for Jazz Ensemble and Soloist
by Jerry Troxell

A

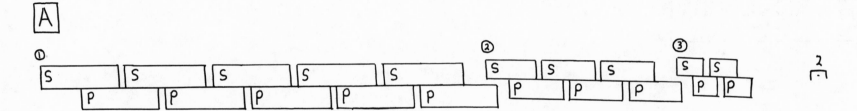

① The soloist plays five long sounds in succession with the percussionist responding to each one after it begins.

② Three of the sounds and responses are repeated but with moderate durations.

③ Two of the sounds and responses are played but with short durations

page 2

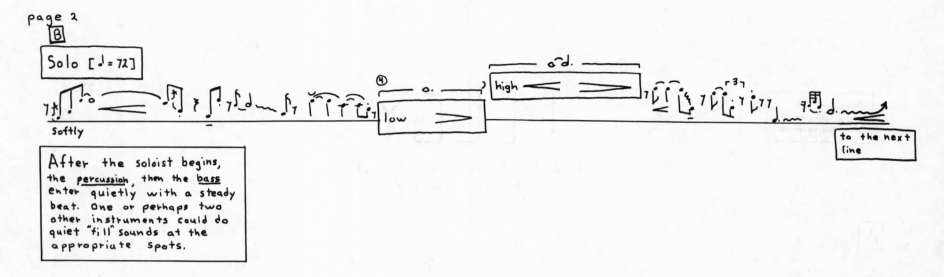

Solo [♩=72]

Softly

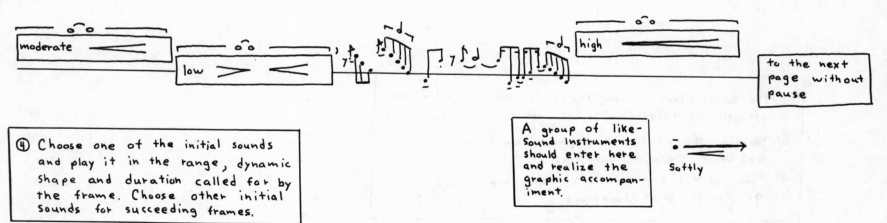

After the soloist begins, the _percussion_, then the _bass_ enter quietly with a steady beat. One or perhaps two other instruments could do quiet "fill" sounds at the appropriate spots.

④ Choose one of the initial sounds and play it in the range, dynamic shape and duration called for by the frame. Choose other initial sounds for succeeding frames.

A group of like-sound instruments should enter here and realize the graphic accompaniment.

Softly

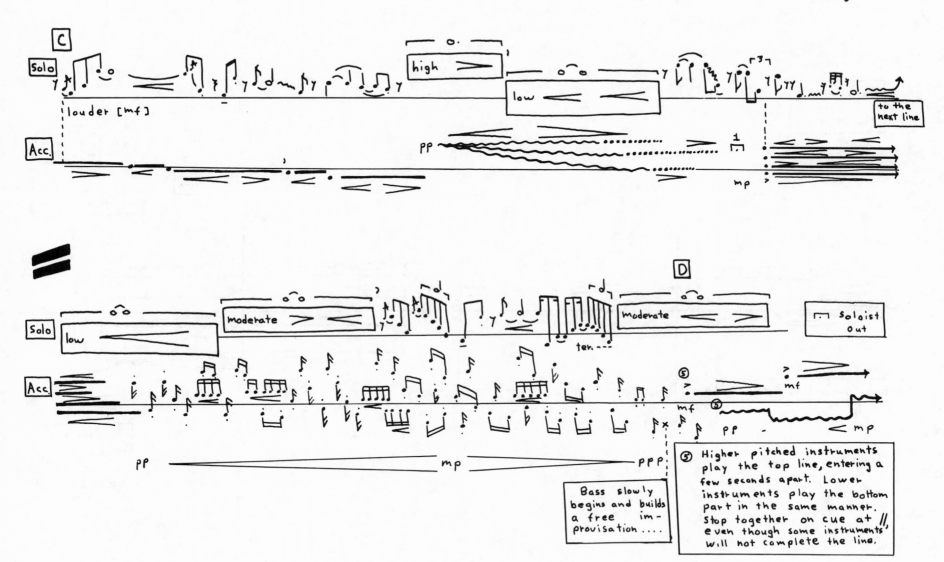

Bass slowly begins and builds a free improvisation....

⑤ Higher pitched instruments play the top line, entering a few seconds apart. Lower instruments play the bottom part in the same manner. Stop together on cue at **//**, even though some instruments will not complete the line.

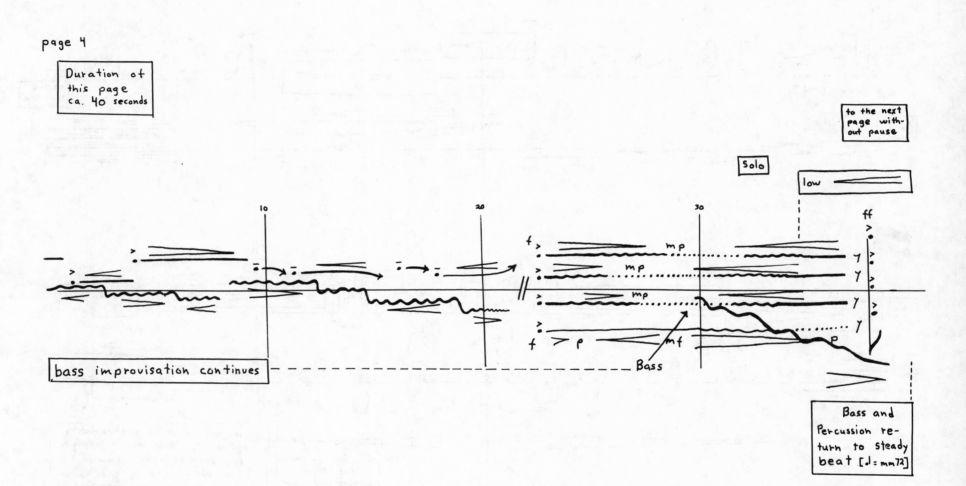

page 4

Duration of
this page
ca. 40 seconds

to the next
page with-
out pause

Solo

low

bass improvisation continues

Bass

Bass and
Percussion re-
turn to steady
beat [♩=mm 72]

page 5

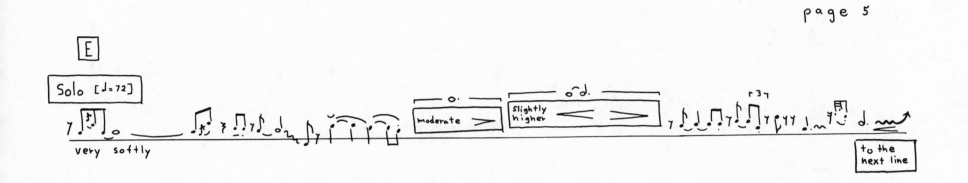

page 6

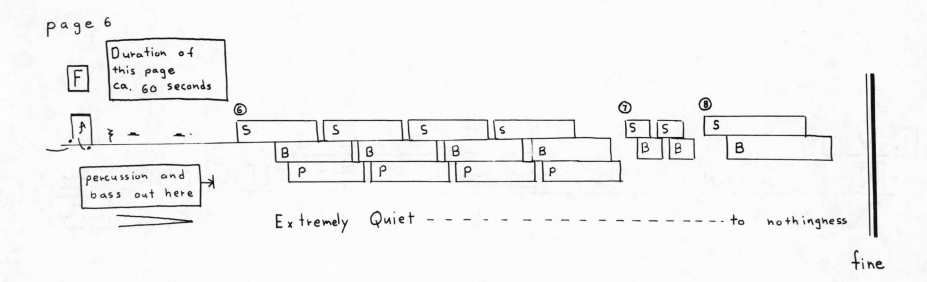

Duration of
this page
ca. 60 seconds

F

percussion and
bass out here

Extremely Quiet — — — — — — — — — — — — — — — — — to nothingness

fine

⑥   The soloist restates 4 of the initial 5
     long sounds with the bass and
     percussion responding to each one
     after it begins.

⑦   Two of the sounds are repeated
     in short duration and with only
     the bass responding

⑧   The last of the initial sounds is
     played in a long duration with
     only the bass response

Excerpt from Exitus for Band
for Larry Livingston

Frank McCarty

—FOR LARRY LIVINGSTON—

Exitus is a linguistic composition for Band or Wind Ensemble, in which vocal sounds are processed through wind instruments.

The minimum instrumentation required is five performers for each of parts 1-4, and four percussionists. The suggested distribution may be altered to accomplish equal balance.

Woodwinds

1 - Piccolos, Flutes, Oboes, Bassoons, Alto + Bass Clarinets, Saxophones.

2 - Bb Clarinets.

Brass

3 - Trumpets, Horns.

4 - Trombones, Baritones, Tubas.

Percussion

5 -
1. Sus. Cym., tambourine, bongos.
2. Gong, sandpaper blocks, tomtom.
3. Snare Drum.
4. Bass Drum.

To these may be added timpani, triangle, woodblock, and other non-keyboard instruments, to be used in the free sections after [G] and at [I].

If possible, the four groups should be homogeneously distributed around the conductor, with associated percussionists directly behind each section.

Vocal sounds should be made through the instruments with the lips up to, covering, or encircling the tube opening or mouthpiece. Pronunciation should be very distinct. Breathing must be staggered in long, connected sections.

Specific words are notated linguistically while single vocal sounds use phonetic symbols.

Consonants: H = un-voiced air-sound. K = cat. P = pat. S = sat. ʃ = sheet. T = to. ð = the. W = voiced air-sound combined with whistle.

Vowels: i = beat. I = bit. ε = bet. ɑ = bought. ʌ = but. ʊ = boot.

Curved lines over vowel changes indicate dipthong-like glides.

Symbols in succession are performed as connected sounds. = sSS

Hyphenated symbols are rhythmically separated. T-T-T-T

Pitch is of no notational concern in this work. However, it is acceptable if accidental instrumental sounds result from certain embouchure-like vowel formations.

Dynamic Content is expressed by the vertical axis: the larger, the louder.

Durations are expressed proportionally on the horizontal axis within fixed meters and tempi.

Graphic Notation is employed in sections marked divisi, to illustrate the overall textures made up of individual, indeterminate contributions.

∴ = individual Key, mechanism, or instrument-body sounds.

⌒ = connected (passage-like) Key, mechanism, or instrument-body sounds.

δ δ = velar clicks made in back-side of mouth. Not tongue-clucks.

x x = hand pops on pipe or mouthpiece of instrument, using palm of hand.

⋇ = final sound: all performers remove instruments from lips but continue "ssss", on cue, velar click, and hand-pop. fff.

•••● = percussion pulses: size indicates amplitude and accent—the larger, the louder.

.... = vocal fry (lion's breath): single pulses from relaxed vocal cords.

Brass mouthpieces will not jam if turned after inserting. Turn back to remove.

EXITUS for BAND
by Frank McCarty

♩=60

* Single-reed insts. remove mouthpieces, double-reeds remove reeds.

** Clarinets remove mouthpieces.

† ¹Sus. Cym. (soft), ²Gong (soft), ³Snare (brushes), ⁴B.D. (brushes).

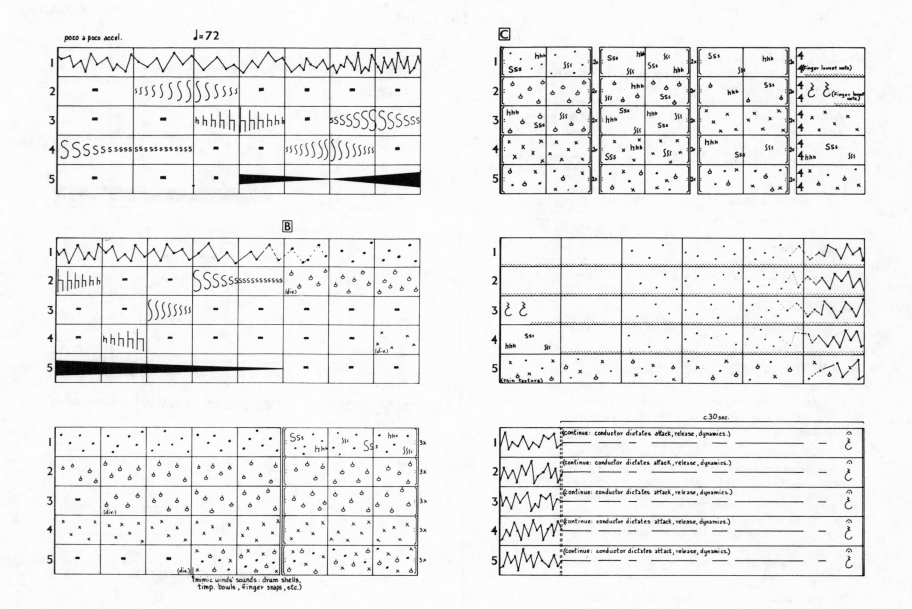

PITCH—NOTATED SCORES

The pieces in this section are more specifically notated than the preceding, particularly with regard to pitch. Most retain some form of indeterminacy and improvisation, but—in contrast to the graphic scores—tend to give the performers particular pitch and rhythmic material with which to work, while leaving a rather open form. Basic familiarity with musical notation and fundamental instrumental skills are therefore required for most pieces. However, quite a few are accessible to young or amateur musicians, and almost all have parts that can be easily learned by nonmusicians.

We begin with several works by James Tenney which were originally designed as postcards. They are each miniatures with a specific content and structure, focusing on some single element—a note, chord, sound, or texture. T.J. Anderson's *Five Easy Pieces,* miniatures as well, are traditionally notated but allow for some substitutions in instrumentation (percussion for Jew's harp and possibly a clarinet for the violin). Michael Parsons' *Piece for Guitars* is in a more open form; the playing technique is well within the grasp of most players of this currently popular instrument. James Tenney's *For 12 Strings (Rising)* may be hard for some to perform without substitution, but for any string section, class, or workshop it will be a very accessible and interesting sound-and-texture piece. Tenney's *In the Aeolian Mode* and Jon Gilson's *30's* provide basic harmonic and rhythmic material from which to build loosely structured improvisational pieces; they are particularly well suited to larger ensembles.

Quite similar to these, Philip Corner's *The F# Section in the Middle of the D Major Prelude of Chopin . . . as a Revelation* is essentially a "process' that can be applied to any collection of notes. It explores the various voices and sound layers in a single measure of Chopin, revealing after many repeats interesting tangents, sub-melodies, resulting patterns, and other psychoacoustic phenomena. Frederic Rzewski's *Les Moutons de Panurge* has material performable by both musicians and nonmusicians, and is a very intense and forceful piece.

The final works in the chapter are all more extended and varied concert pieces, and require somewhat more instrumental skill. The combinations of instruments are quite diverse; most of the pieces are very flexible. David Koblitz's *Rigor Vitus* is for three of any instrument. His *Harmonica Monday* is a fascinating sound piece for multiple harmonicas and a solo cello; the solo part is not even absolutely necessary. Richmond Browne's *Reri Velocitatem* ("to reckon velocity") can be performed by any three instruments capable of controlling pitch and dynamics. William Albright's *Daydream* is like the Tenney and Gibson pieces in that it provides basic material but is quite flexible as regards structure and instrumentation. Aurelio de la Vega's *The Infinite Square* is arranged in such a way as to allow the performers to follow the grid of notes and patterns in any direction. Earle brown's *Module 1* is a beautiful chordal piece for chamber orchestra in which the rate of movement is controlled by the conductor. In a workshop or class it could be done without the composer's specific instrumentation although in any public performance that should of course be respected.

Koan   James Tenney

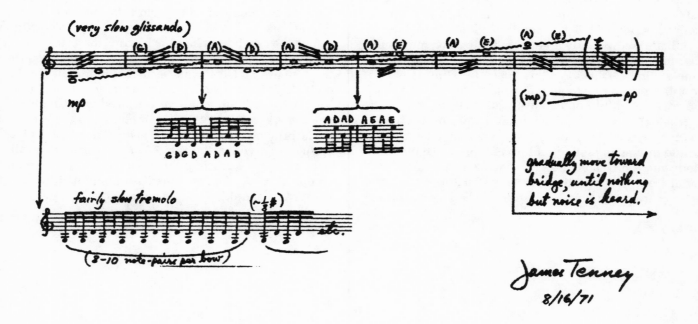

From *Postal Pieces 1954-71*. Copyright© 1971 by James Tenney. Produced by Marie McRoy at the California Institute of the Arts. Used by permission.

Cellogram James Tenney

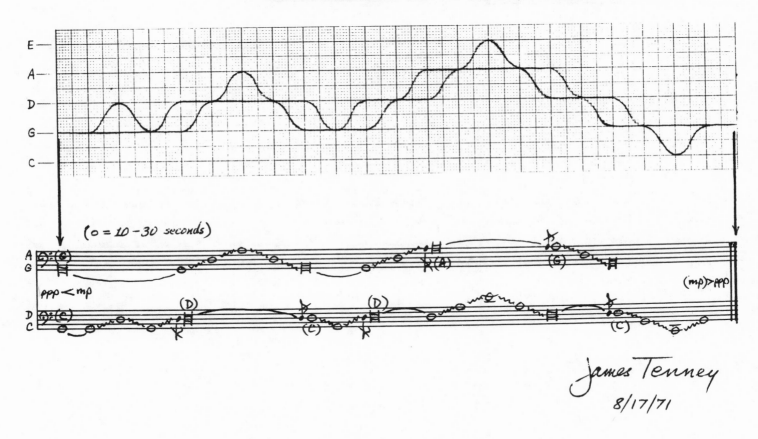

Beast

James Tenney

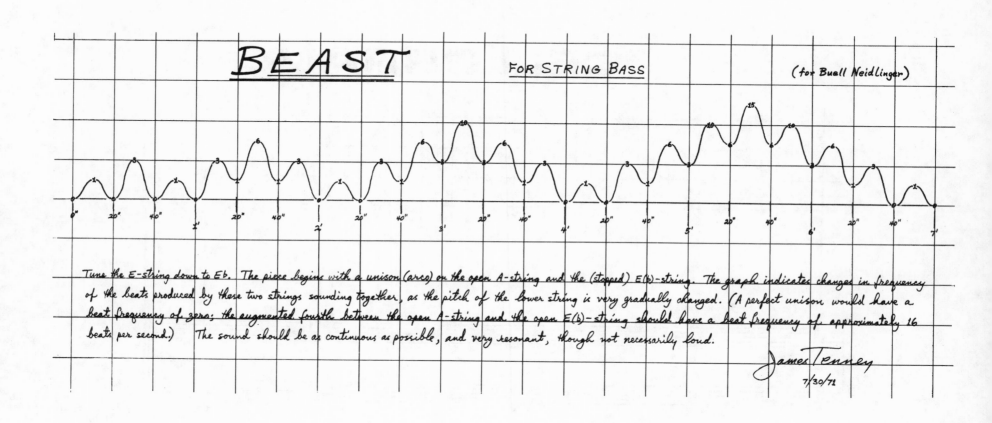

Tune the E-string down to Eb. The piece begins with a unison (arco) on the open A-string and the (stopped) E(b)-string. The graph indicates changes in frequency of the beats produced by these two strings sounding together, as the pitch of the lower string is very gradually changed. (A perfect unison would have a beat frequency of zero; the augmented fourth between the open A-string and the open E(b)-string should have a beat frequency of approximately 16 beats per second.) The sound should be as continuous as possible, and very resonant, though not necessarily loud.

James Tenney
7/30/71

August Harp

James Tenney

A U G U S T   H A R P

for Susan Allen

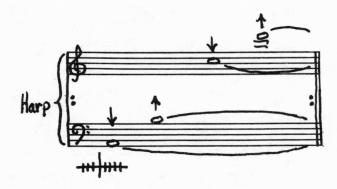

Let the tempo be determined by,
and synchronous with the breath
(↓ = exhalation, ↑ = inhalation)

Play this figure four
times with each pedal-
combination. After
every fourth repetition,
improvise a new pedal-
change for one or more
of these four strings.
Try not to repeat a
pedal-combination already
used. Continue as long
as any variation still
seems possible.

James Tenney

8/17/71

Five Easy Pieces
for Violin, Piano and Jews Harp

T.J. Anderson

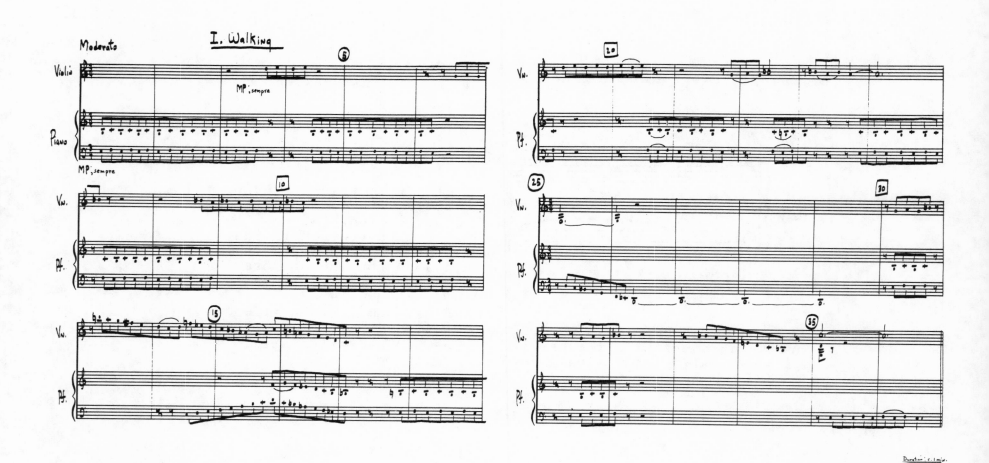

IV. Rain

1. Improvise filigree as fast as possible
   in an uneven manner.

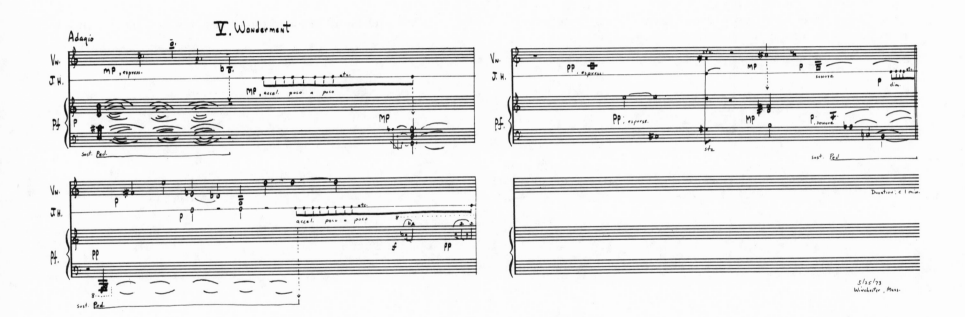

Piece for guitars no. 1
(any number of players)

Michael Parsons

Players sit spaced well apart, not in a group. Begin one by one.

Part 1: each player takes each of the 11 2-beat phrases and plays it over and over alternating the 2 beats regularly (number of repetitions freely chosen). Choose a *different* tempo from any other being played at the time: keep exactly to the chosen tempo for each phrase. Play each phrase in this way once only—play them in any order—between phrases, pause for any length of time (judge it according to the context).

Part 2: each player plays each of the 7 chords once only in any order, with pauses of any length between them. Go on to part 2 any time after finishing part 1 (i.e. without waiting for other players to finish part 1).

Allow each chord to sound for 1-2 seconds, then damp strings.

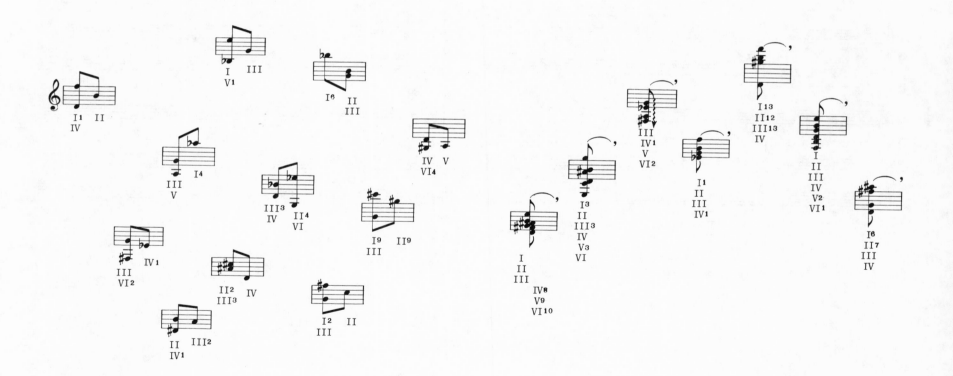

For 12 Strings (Rising)

James Tenney

(Notes measure 4 should be repeated 100 to 200 times, yielding a total duration of about 7 to 13 minutes)

In the Aeolian Mode

James Tenney

for the California New Music Ensemble

for prepared piano, marimba, vibraphone, flute and alto voice (the ensemble may be augmented by harp, clarinet, muted violin or viola, and/or other similarly gentle instrumental timbres).

Each player improvises a continuous melodic line on these pitches (always beginning on A, and using the G and F as neighboring tones only)—legato, mp, mostly in eighth-notes at about mm = 180, with all players synchronous on the eighth's. Let a performance begin with the prepared piano, the other players entering freely. Occasionally any player may drop out for a short time, but this is to be preceded by a "cadence" consisting of a sequence of different A's (in any octave), at any higher multiple of the eighth-note unit.

The pianist should prepare the following strings in such a way that the aggregates produced each contain a prominent pitch at the octave. The damper-pedal should be held down throughout the performance.

The vibraphone pedal should be held down, with motor *off*.

Soft mallets should be used for both vibraphone and marimba.

The performance may be of any duration, but the longer the better. The end will be signalled by the pianist playing (for the first time) his lowest A, thus:

The other players then play their own "cadences", sustaining the last note until a cut-off cued by the pianist.

30'S

Jon Gibson

For any number of performers.

Each performer has two pitches, timbres, chords or sonorities.

Percussion instruments, such as drums, cymbals, wood blocks and marimbas play the score as written—that is, rhythmically, or at times just the first quaver of a tied grouping (the notes marked with X) may be played.

Sustaining instruments, such as organs and winds, also play as written, or may play the notes of a particular tied grouping as one note. For instance in section six the grouping may be played as dotted minims (𝅗𝅥.) instead of six separated quavers ♪♪♪♪♪♪ . In addition with keyboard instruments each hand may play a chord rather than a single pitch, and more than one performer may play at one keyboard.

If chords are used their notes should be chosen with discretion. Octaves, perfect fifths and fourths should predominate. Dissonant relationships become irritating to the ears very quickly in this piece so that a generally sonorous, consonant sound, utilizing voicings within a particular scale or tonality, is recommended. Here is one possible sustained low keyboard part. (These notes can be repeated in other relationships in a higher part by another performer on the same keyboard):

All performers start at **one** (not necessarily all at once) and repeat it until they wish to go on to **two, three,** etc., successively down the page.

Sections should not be changed by everyone at once. One performer can still be on **one** while other performers are on **two, three, five, six** and even **thirty.**

However it is necessary to stay together in the sense that everyone must always play the last two beats (the semiquaver figure) at the same time at all times.

As the piece progresses it is possible to skip sections or go back to previous sections and replay them, bearing in mind, however, that in general the various juxtapositions should be repeated enough times to be reasonably heard and appreciated.

Proceed at a leisurely pace, taking your time with each section. The piece can last for any length of time from twenty minutes to an hour or so—perhaps longer.

When all performers have reached **thirty** and repeated it to their satisfaction, the piece should end abruptly (on cue) at the thirty second beat of the cycle (the semiquaver figure).

Explore other ways of performing the piece.

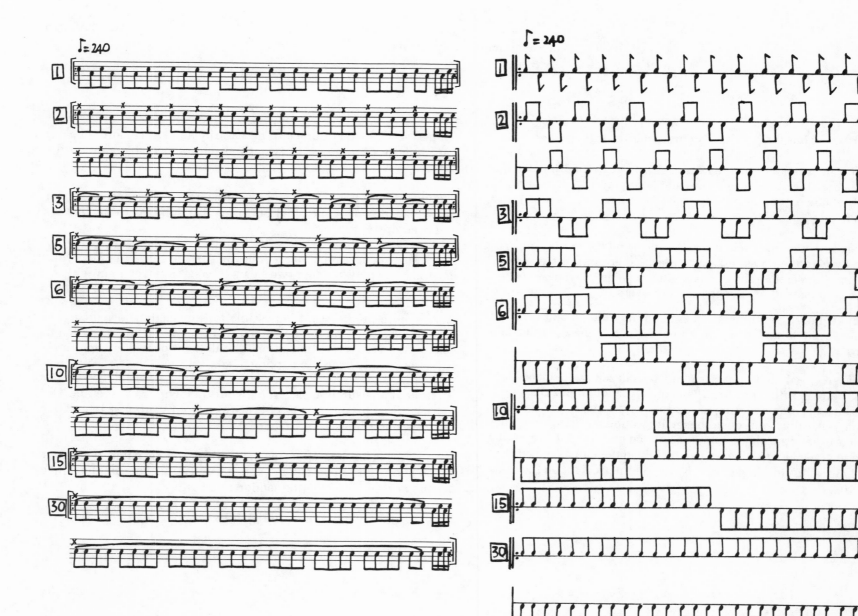

The F# Section in the Middle of the D Major Prelude of Chopin . . . As a Revelation

Philip Corner

A piano solo or piece for piano with one or more added instruments.

The piano starts the piece playing the repeated measures (measures 14 through 16 of the *Prelude*) over and over throughout the piece.

Play very softly and not too fast, pedaling as indicated without emphasizing any voice.

After a while the upper voice (1) is brought out either by accenting, if piano solo, or doubling with another instrument, as illustrated below.

1. Quite loud and brilliant; continue; stop suddenly.

It continues by bringing out or doubling each successive voice (2,3,4,5).

2. Bring out once, then fade back. Continue until well established.

3. Bring in after 2. Once in, continue with occasional pauses.

4. Start very softly and build very gradually.

5. Start and end at a moderate level, louder in between.

After each voice is brought out it eventually blends back into the continuing soft repeated bar—to continue in the mind until the next entrance.

While it was the original intent to bring out the voices in descending order, this is not a fixed necessity.

Once a voice has been in, it may sound again (through accenting by the piano or doubling by another instrument) combining with the more recently entered ones and thus giving times of two, or even three voices together. It is also good (with a larger ensemble) to invent additional extra parts derived from the original (6,7,8,9,10).

The piano ends the piece using this cadence phrase (11):

11. Piano cadence figure.

As an extension of the piece, it is possible to create a "Prelude to the Prelude": This may start with a long tone or repeated long tones derived from the starting pitches. It may happen with all of the tones, forming a sustained F# major chord.

This chord, which is similar to the piano cadence phrase, may be brought back at the end, but very softly.

This defines a process which should work well with any succession of chords when arranged to give a broken pattern which suggests clearly delineated voices, each having its distinct rhythmic placement.

Les Moutons de Panurge

for Frans Brüggen

**For any number of musicians playing melodz instruments
and any number of nonmusicians playing anything**

Frederic Rzewski

Musicians

all in strict unison; octave doubling allowed if there are at least 2 instruments in each octave.

Instructions: Read from left to right, playing the notes as follows: 1, 1-2, 1-2-3, 1-2-3-4, etc. When you have reached note 65, play the whole melody once again and then begin subtracting notes from the beginning: 2 through 65, 3 through 65, 4 through 65 . . . 62-63-64-65, 63-64-65, 64-65-, 65. Hold the last note until everybody has reached it, then begin an improvisation using any instruments.

In the melody above, never stop or falter, always play loud. Stay together as long as you can, but if you get lost, stay lost. Do not try to find your way back to the fold. Continue to follow the rules strictly.

Nonmusicians

are invited to make sound, any sound, preferably very loud, and if possible are provided with percussive or other instruments. The nonmusicians have a *leader,* whom they may follow or not, and who begins the music thus:

As soon as the pulse has been established, any variations are possible. Suggested theme for nonmusicians: "The left hand doesn't know what the right is doing."

Rigor Vitus
(to be played by three or more of the same instrument)

David Koblitz

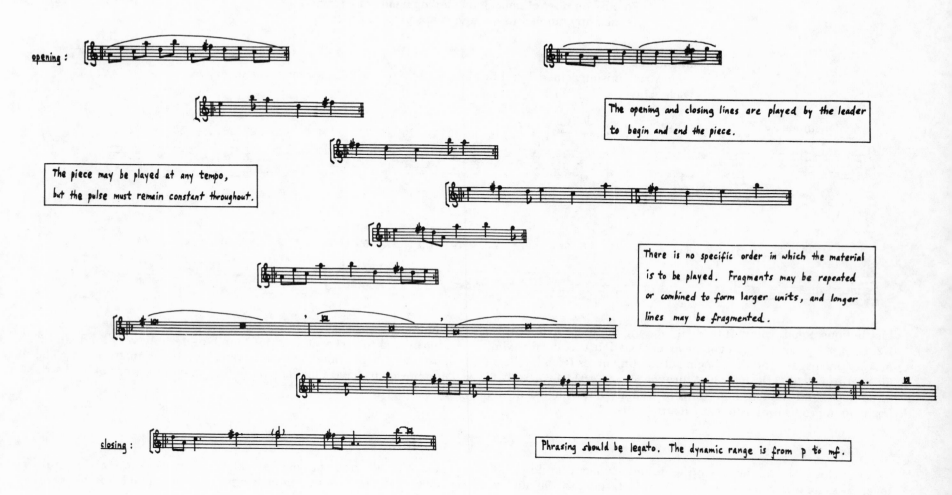

The opening and closing lines are played by the leader to begin and end the piece.

The piece may be played at any tempo, but the pulse must remain constant throughout.

There is no specific order in which the material is to be played. Fragments may be repeated or combined to form larger units, and longer lines may be fragmented.

Phrasing should be legato. The dynamic range is from p to mf.

May 1973

Harmonica Monday Part II

David Koblitz

Note: Harmonica parts are limited to pitches produced by "blowing": i.e. the notes of the major trial of whatever key the harmonica is in. A pure, vibratoless tone is desired.

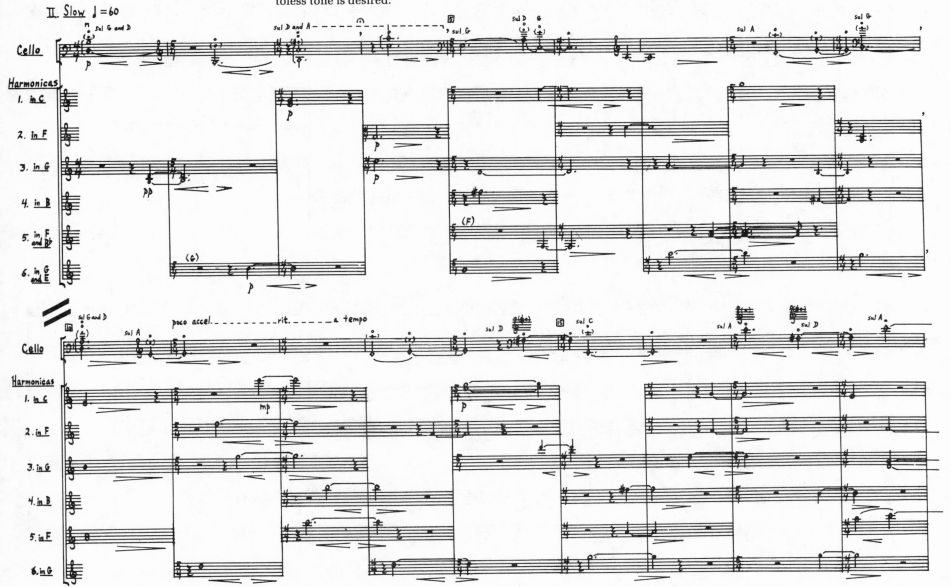

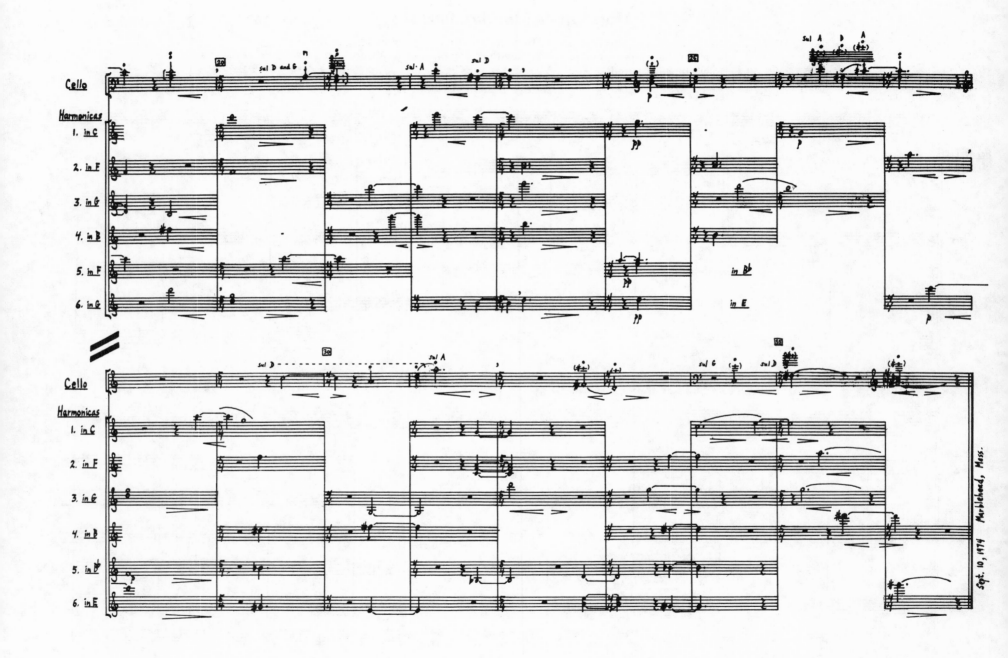

Reri Velocitatem

Richmond Browne

The piece may be performed with any combination of three instruments, provided only that each instrument permits the player sufficient control over the sound after attack to enable him to make the indicated dynamic fluctuations. The player reads the music in the common clef (or clefs) of his instrument.

Form. Each player begins by choosing, at random, a page of music to play first. No two players should begin with the same page. Each player plays the five pages in order. He then repeats the page on which he began. The act of playing each page coincides in time with the action of the other players playing their respective pages. Thus the performance consists of *six* "movements", each a trio. Between movements players pause.

Speed. The speed of each movement is a function of the time allotted to it. The shortest time feasible for a performance of any given movement is probably on the order of 12 to 15 seconds; the longest is probably 50 to 60 seconds. The players may estimate these durations, or may employ a clock in performance. (The use of a "conductor" leads to a more precise timing. The conductor is responsible for providing some visible motion—circular or quaternary, expressive of the allotted time—so that the 1/4, 1/2, and 3/4 markings may be noted by the players and their estimation of velocity regulated. The motions of the conductor should *not* be interpreted as beats. A movement has no "seams" and no climax.)

Notation. The notation is a visual symbol of the sound required. A horizontal line indicates the existence of sound at the given pitch. The vertical width of the line indicates relative volume. A dot is a short note. A large dot is a *loud* short note. Legato exists only when a vertical line connects two horizontal pitch symbols. Legato should be instantaneous and without nuance, except when some mode of attack is specifically indicated. Players should observe carefully all indications of attack, crescendo, accent, etc. but may alter notes which exceed the range of their instrument. Stylization (tremolo, pizzicato, flutter-tongue) at the player's discretion is recommended.

Time is indicated on the horizontal plane. The length of a given note is to be estimated by the player, who should attempt to move his eye along the line at a steady pace without keeping a beat or attempting to construe any exact proportions between the various lengths of pitch symbols. The speed at which the eye moves (and the sound unfolds) is

determined by the amount of time available to the movement according to the plan used.

One suggested plan of movement times:

I.	25/30 seconds
II.	12/15 seconds
III.	50/60 seconds
IV.	12/15 seconds
V.	50/60 seconds
VI.	25/30 seconds

3

Daydream

for three keyboard players and sustaining instrument or ensemble

William Albright

Players I., II., and III: select from the following (duplications permitted)

      vibraphone
      marimba
      chimes
      celesta
      piano
      electric piano
      . . . . . . more exotic instruments such as cloud chamber bowls or steel drums may also be possible
      . . . . . . all mallet instruments should be played with softest possible mallets

Player IV: sustaining instrument such as:

      pipe organ (one or more 8′ flutes)
      electronic organ
      harmonium
      glass harmonica
      synthesizer
      accordian
      . . . . . . if a sustaining instrument is not feasible, the part may be played tremolando by any of the first group of instruments
      . . . . . . also possible would be an ensemble such as female chorus, strings or wind group

All parts may be doubled or trebled. Players should be as widely separated as possible. *Sempre* pedal unless otherwise indicated.

The intent is to obtain as lush a blend of sounds as possible: a glutinous, inseperable web. Slight differences in tuning may create unusual acoustic effects: sounds that appear to contract and expand in space (phase-shifting). The effect might also be likened to that of a glass harmonica.

Barlines indicate points of synchronization. Players should use their ears to guide the pacing of events; expressive liberties, within certain confines, are encouraged.

DAYDREAM

William Albright (1975)

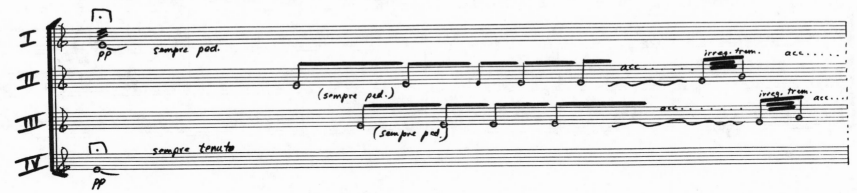

Pacing of events is ad lib, but very slow

*in configurations of more than two notes, distribution of the tremolo is ad lib.

The Infinite Square

for any number of instruments
Commissioned by Gloria Morris

Aurelio de la Vega

Duration: Indeterminate
Play in groups of any number of instruments concentrically or ex-
centrically in any direction.

Module 1   Earle Brown

DIRECTIONS FOR PERFORMANCE

MODULE I and MODULE II are to be considered as two separate scores which may be performed independently, simultaneously, or either one of them may be performed simultaneously with MODULE III or with any future MODULE that may be added to this series of works. Any *two* of MODULES I, II or III will not exceed the instrumentation of a normal large orchestra. There must be a conductor for each MODULE being performed.

There are 4 pages of score for each of MODULES I and II. Each page has either 4 or 5 chords; the chords may be played in any sequence and each may be held for as long as the conductor wishes, at any constant or variable loudness.

Each conductor of each MODULE must have an indicator with a moveable arrow which will inform the musicians of the *page* (1, 2, 3, 4)· from which he will choose chords ... (each *page* of the score corresponds to a horizontal *line* of notes on each instrumental part). The indicator and the arrow will be supplied with the instrumental parts.

From any of the pages, the precise *chord* which the conductor has chosen is indicated to the musicians by the fingers of his *left* hand. The left hand indication is to be a preparation preceding the down-beat given by the right hand for the moment of attack. The size and speed of the down-beat must give the loudness and character of attack which is desired.

ALL CHORDS ARE "FERMATA" (⌢): TO BE HELD BY THE MUSICIANS UNTIL SPECIFICALLY CUT OFF BY THE CONDUCTOR. (Wind instruments are to breathe when necessary and comfortable and to re-sound the note for as long as the chord is held by the conductor.)

The score is written in "C" concert.

Parts are transposed where necessary.

In most cases the notes for *two* instruments are on *each* part. Of the two instruments, the one for whom that part is intended is circled and the note to be played is indicated either by a tick (✓), or by an abbreviation (ob. = oboe), or the note is consistently either the top or bottom note of two:

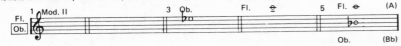

(MODULE II: oboe part; first line corresponding to 1st page of the score. Oboe has notes in only chords 3 and 5.)

Each chord on pages 2 and 3 of the score of both MODULES utilize *all* the instruments scored for that MODULE: i.e. no two or more of the chords on those pages can be sounded simultaneously in any one MODULE. Any change from chord to chord will involve *all* of the conductor's players.

On pages 1 and 4 of both MODULES, the first *four* chords may be combined and overlapped in any sequence and combination: i.e. they are four small chords which, when played simultaneously, *add up* to the full instrumentation of that MODULE.

Chords number 5 on pages 1 and 4 of both MODULES utilize the *full* instrumentation of that MODULE.

In regard to forming and conducting relationships between the two Modules:—

Chord number 5 of page 1 of MODULE I is intervallically the same as the *summation* of chords 1 to 4 of MODULE II, but are orchestrated differently. Chords 1 to 4 of MODULE II sounded simultaneously with chord 5 of MODULE I will produce an intervallic unison between the two MODULES, in a contrasting colour distribution.

The same is true between chords 1 to 4 of MODULE I and chord 5 of MODULE II.

The same condition exists on page 4 of both MODULES except that the orchestration of the intervals between the two MODULES is as exactly alike as the two instrumentations allow.

Although the two MODULES *may* be performed separately it is requested that they be performed *together* if at all possible. (As more MODULES are written and become available it will be insisted that they be performed in any combinations of two or more).

DO NOT PHYSICALLY SEPARATE THE TWO GROUPS : seat the musicians normally but distribute the parts so that alternate chairs have materials for alternate conductors .... the two groups are to be uniformly intermixed on the stage. (This allows any *one* chord of any one MODULE to sound from the total stage-space and eliminates the distraction of visual and/or sonic competition, which is not the intention in the work).

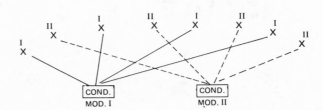

NO PLAYERS MUST BE TOO FAR TO THE RIGHT OR LEFT OF THE CONDUCTORS BECAUSE THEY MUST HAVE A CLEAR SIGHT-LINE TO THE INDICATOR AND ARROW ON THE FRONT OF EACH PODIUM.

The indicator and arrow should be mounted over the top of a music stand placed just in front of the podium which the score is on: (they will consist of large numbers facing the orchestra, and a movable arrow within comfortable reach of the conductor and in full view of all musicians).

Extract from letter to Toru Takemitsu relative to rehearsal and performance:

("Orchestral Space"; Tokyo 1968;conducted by Ozawa und Akiyama.)

ALL CHORDS ARE TO BE HELD (FERMATA) AS LONG AS THE CONDUCTORS WISH.

THE LOUDNESS CAN BE VARIED IN ANY WAY ... from chord to chord and during any one chord.

Rehearse moving from chord to chord (any one on the page to any other) so that there is no break between the chords .... unless the conductor *wants* a period of silence to intervene.

I PREFER that both conductors conduct chords from the same pages at roughly the same time ... i.e. both conductors on pages 1, then pages 2, then 3, then 4 etc .... BUT THE CHANGES OF PAGE NEED NOT BE SYCHRONIZED EXACTLY: i.e. one conductor makes the change from page 1 to page 2 before or after the other conductor changes .... during the page changes there will be an overlapping for some moments but statistically there is more time for possible overlapping when the conductors are on the same pages than when they are on different pages.

In Paris we (Carvalho and I) did pages 1 to 4 in sequence and then ended by doing pages I for the second time. You two conductors can play the 4 pages in any sequence you like but after deciding the sequence you both must do the same sequence at roughly the same times (as described above). If you wish, you can do the 4 pages in your sequence and then do any one or more pages for the second time. The general "tempo" of pages, however, should not allow you to do more than 5 or 6 pages in *approximately 12 to 15 minutes of performance time*. It should not be less than 10 minutes. The maximum length should be determined (roughly) by your feelings of the extension of intensity that you feel possible between the materials, the musicians, and two of you as conductors.

When you are on the pages together you can conduct the chords on those pages in any sequence (left hand signals to orchestra) any number of times, for any amount of time.

LET ALL OF THIS BE VERY LOOSE AND NATURAL AND INTUITIVE, BUT WITH AWARENESS OF THE TOTALITY AT EVERY MOMENT.

I would like it to be relatively *slow moving-transforming* and *quite static* with independent and simultaneous rising and falling of intensity (loudness). It can be a *very gentle* and also a *very powerful* sound. It should have a tremendous feeling of intensity ... never very dramatic but *dramatically simple* and *intense.*

MODULE I

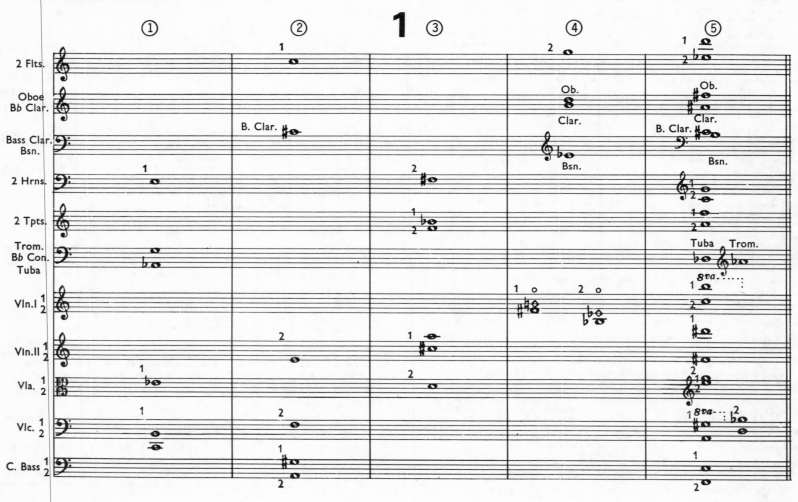

MODULE I

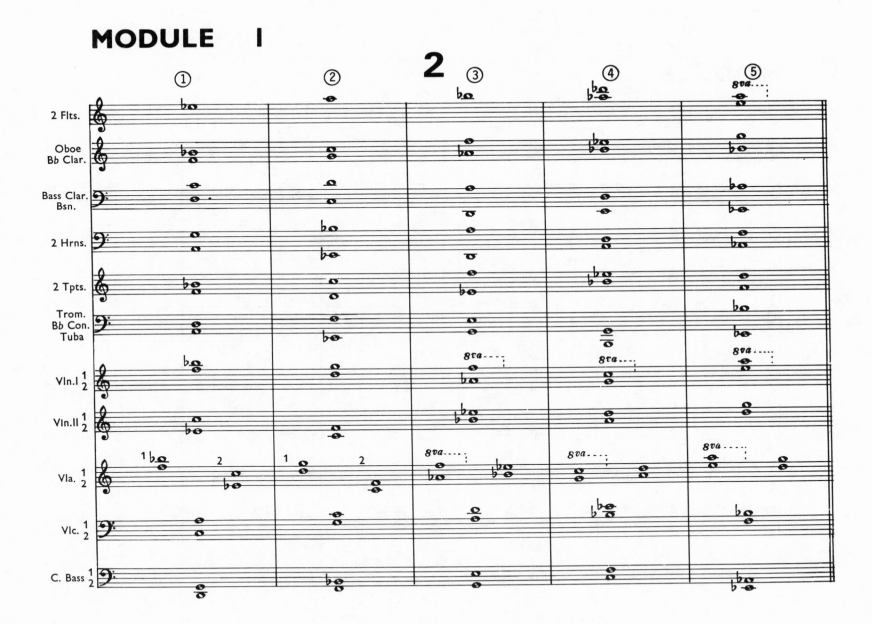

MODULE I

3

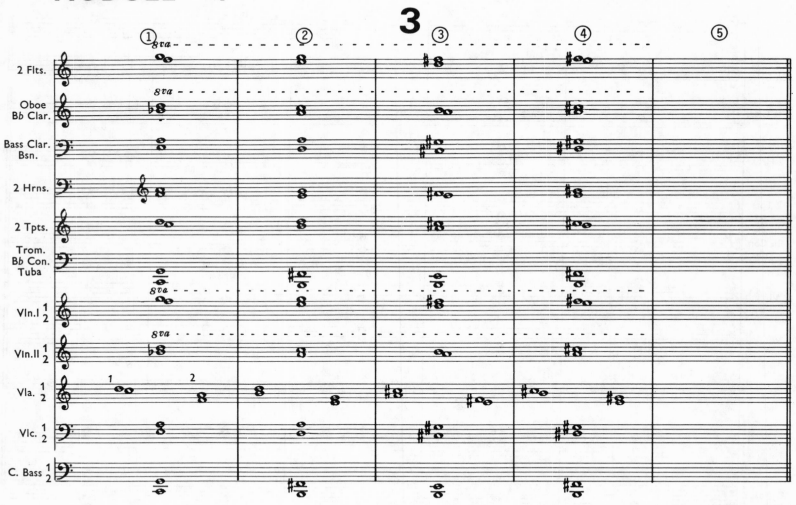

MODULE I

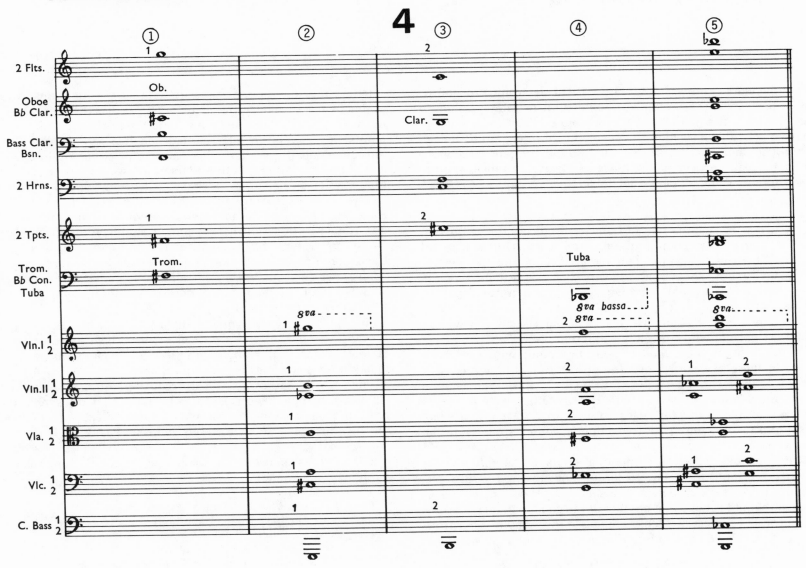

6 Electronic Music

All of the works in this chapter make use of electronic procedures in some form, from very simple amplification to rather elaborate sound synthesis and modification. Since the early 1950s composers have been actively engaged in the development of electronic music, first through modification of recorded sound on tape and more recently through an ever wider range of electronic music synthesizers, computers, and other special devices.

TAPE PIECES

There are at least three types of electronic pieces: those created directly on tape, those combining tape and live performance, and those in which the electronic elements are realized in live performance (usually somewhat differently with each performance). Works of the first type do not usually involve a score, and therefore most are not suitable for this book. The few tape pieces included here are of a very open and non-specific nature which suggests many varied realizations, each of which is really a different piece.

Anyone with the most modest recording equipment can make versions of these pieces, and even go on to original tape pieces. A series of sounds can be recorded using only a simple cassette recorder. Much more can be done with one or, better, two reel-to-reel recorders since they allow for easier editing, varied speeds, tape echo, reversal of direction, and, with two, copying sound from one to the other machine. The addition of electronic sound-generating and modifying devices (either in individual units or combined in a synthesizer), a multi-track tape recorder, and mixing facilities expands the composer's resources considerably. Those interested in tape music should get one of a number of the good manuals or books available on the subject and look into one of the many fine electronic-music studios located in colleges, universities, and in most cities.

PERFORMED ELECTRONIC MUSIC

The particular advantage to the musician working with tape pieces is that one is dealing with sound as directly as possible and not with some form of notation, necessarily imprecise, which must be interpreted by others. The trade-off, of course, is that the sound is recorded, with all the distortion and limitations of tape and playback equipment. A mixture of recorded and live sound can be a very attractive one; it is explored here in such pieces as Alvin Lucier's "*I Am Sitting in a Room*," Beth Anderson's *Tower of Power*, John Cage's *Solo for Voice 43*, Laurie Anderson's *Narrative Song*, Ben Johnston's "Casta" and "Recipe" (in *4 Do-It-Yourself Pieces*) and Daniel Lentz's *King Speech Song*. The other works involve various forms of live electronic amplification, generation, or modification of sound. Steve Reich's *Pendulum Music* uses feedback from swinging microphones, Cage's *Solo for Voice 23* amplifies the sound of a chess game and Anderson's *Duet for Volin and Door Jamb* amplifies the percussive sounds created by the bow in a door jamb. Her drawing of the Electronic bowed instrument suggests using a tape head on the violin, which is played by strips of tape that replace the hair on a number of bows. Carl Michaelson's *Game* gives, first, instructions to build a simple ring modulator, and then a piece for two flutes using it. Daniel Goode's *Faust Crosses the Raritan Somewhere in West Africa* and Alvin Lucier's *The Duke of York* require the use of a synthesizer. There are also two pieces using the telephone, a work synchronizing film, and sound. Gordon Mumma's *Three Electronic Pieces* use, among other things, television sets and laser beams.

Other works using amplification, tape, or other forms of electronic modification include:

Chap. 2: *Hear What I Feel* (Joan La Barbara)
          I Ain't Listen (Jana Haimsohn)
Chap. 3: *I + 1* (Philip Glass)
Chap. 7: *Here and There* (Stuart Smith)
          Towards the Capacity of a Room (David Jones)
Chap. 8: *Roma* (Larry Austin)
          Gloria Patri (Phil Winsor)
          Aeolian Partitions (Pauline Oliveros)

From the River Archive

Annea Lockwood

Find a brook or fast flowing river in as isolated a place as you can reach. Placing the microphone(s) near the surface at a spot where the water is creating a richly textured sound, make a tape recording at least a half-hour long. Note the name of the river, the place and date.

Play the tape back on a cassette recorder, in some public place, for one person at a time, (using headphones). Turn the listener's head very gently from side to side, tilted towards one shoulder, then towards the other as he or she is listening. Suggest that the listener closes his or her eyes to listen. Tell each other personal experiences with rivers/brooks/etc; dreams involving them; memories.

*   *   *   *

Find a place at which a river is passing through rocks or over logs, gently (i.e. not white water).

Search out every layer of the sounds the water is making until you can hear the whole intricate texture, until the river is flowing through your body.

Stay there from sunrise to night, or from sunset until dawn.

*   *   *   *

Choose a place where the river cascades through falls, over a weir, through a gorge or canyon, so that the sound approaches white noise.

Stay there all day, letting the sound change you and aware of those changes.

*   *   *   *

Phased Loops

Daniel Goode

Phased Loops are short tape loops, each recorded against itself at a minutely different speed. Each loop piece is complete when it has gone a whole cycle of in-and-out-of-phase with itself.

Electronic Book

Daniel Goode

The Electronic Book is made by covering the erase head of a tape recorder, then recording on a tape loop the sounds of our present surroundings. What is recorded on the loop gradually disappears with each contact of the record head and is replaced by new sounds, those in turn disappear and are replaced. . . . The result of this constant process is fed into another tape recorder and stored as a record of the process and of the progress of the day as heard by the microphone.

Tape Terrains (1967–68)

Charlemagne Palestine

A sustained electronic sonority of slowly changing timbre is recorded on audio tape previously recorded on a few times and allowed to deteriorate with age causing the chemical coating on the tape to become irregular in its dispersion. The result is a solid state sound whose external rhythmic activity is determined by the terrain of the audio tape—a kind of sonorous relief map on hilly tape terrain.

Gentle Fire

Collect, on tape, examples of ambient sound events such as those made by

Screeching brakes	Falling trees	Slamming drawers
Chattering guests	Breaking windows	Digesting food
Warring gangs	Shattering glass	Melting snow
Rioting prisoners	Gnashing teeth	Whirring blades
Stalling motors	Spraining ankles	Scolding maids
Colliding meteors	Stretching muscles	Scalding kettles
Creating politicians	Snapping vertebrae	Steeping tea
Orating politicians	Flooding rivers	Cracking ice
Arguing lawyers	Erupting volcanoes	Clicking dice
Heating kilns	Gushing wells	Splitting diamonds
Shooting rifles	Flaming burners	Limping legs
Coughing engines	Spinning wheels	Draining dregs
Droning turbines	Reaming rotors	Frying eggs
Squealing tires	Crumbling cakes	Marching bands
Manouvering tanks	Snorting hogs	Swelling glands
Drilling squads	Tolling bells	Sizzling steaks
Buzzing saws	Rasping coughs	Crashing boors
Landing jets	Gnawing rats	Embarking tours
Drilling rigs	Scratching claws	Drying lakes
Dripping faucets	Fracturing bones	Rising bread
Knocking radiators	Stampeding herds	Dying ponds
Dragging tailpipes	Laughing hyenas	Drooping fronds
Hawking newsboys	Scraping forks	Hardening arteries
Squeaking shoes	Sinking boats	Clogging drains
Tapping canes	Horns in fogs	Eroding cliffs
Wailing sirens	Freezing bogs	Boring drills
Spurting blood	Ringing phones	Spilling oil
Roaring trains	Slipping cogs	Sliding hills
Hissing cats	Fraying cables	Driving piles
Rattling snakes	Groaning tables	Turning stiles
Raging fires	Popping corn	Hammering jacks
Snarling dogs	Skidding bikes	Belching furnaces
Collapsing mines	Howling mikes	Stomping boots
Bursting bombs	Humming choirs	Splintering bats
Burning houses	Closing banks	Sputtering fats
Sinking ships	Rolling logs	Roaring crowds
Nagging wives	Bawling brats	Moaning victims
Snoring husbands	Creaking doors	Clanking chains
Braking trucks	Rotting tombs	Pelting hail
Crashing planes	Stabbing knives	Springing traps
Diving bombers	Heaving seas	Ringing alarms
Ripping fabric	Slipping discs	
Tearing paper		

Using an electronic music synthesizer or any equivalent configuration of electronic components, process these examples in such a way that they become transformed into what could be perceived as sound events of different origin such as those made by

Ocean waves	Snapping twigs	Swishing tails
Wind in trees	Crunching snow	Hammering nails
Flowing streams	Chewing beavers	Opening jails
Boiling tea	Swimming tuna	Laying rails
Cooing doves	Sounding dolphins	Emptying pails
Droning bees	Spouting whales	Stacking bales
Jumping fish	Blowing gales	Wiring speakers
Walking spiders	Popping corn	Frying eggs
Crawling babies	Tooting horns	Making beds
Purring cats	Neighing horses	Painting reds
Crying loons	Baaing sheep	Buttering muffins
Hooting owls	Mooing cows	Erasing errors
Laying hens	Blowing breezes	Assuaging terrors
Snapping turtles	Drifting sands	Stopping bottles
Swaying palms	Rising bread	Screwing corks
Barking dogs	Pitching hay	Entering ports
Cracking ice	Sucking pigs	Swaying dancers
Falling rain	Billowing sails	Healing cancers
Squeaking shoes	Jingling coins	Cheering teams
Buzzing saws	Straining loins	Jumping beans
Hatching eggs	Draining pipes	Splitting jeans
Bouncing balls	Murmuring pines	Waving queens
Passing ships	Humming birds	Scuttling crabs
Rocking boats	Lofting passes	Honking geese
Squirting clams	Escaping gasses	Winding tape
Clicking stones	Flowing gowns	Hanging crepe
Croaking frogs	Combing tresses	Smacking lips
Warbling birds	Dragging carts	Bumping hips
Howling wolves	Playing parts	Creaking ships
Cackling geese	Ascending balloons	Clapping hands
Running water	Laughing girls	Marching bands
Perking coffee	Frowing clowns	Rattling bones
Whooping cranes	Running boys	Hewing beams
Thumping rabbitts	Chanting braves	Rubbing towels
Cawing crows	Blooming flowers	Turning cogs
Scolding squirrels	Mowing lawns	Nibbling mice
Clattering hoofbeats	Nuzzling fawns	Passing floats
Flapping wings	Sprouting chives	Weaving strands
Burning embers	Quaking aspen	Watering hoses
Crackling fire	Spinning tops	Easing throttles
Whistling kettles	Wringing mops	

For example, snarling dogs become crunching snow, crashing planes, laughing girls and manouvering tanks, ocean waves.

Record these transformations on tape in any sequence on any number of channels, using any manner of mixing, overlapping or fading, taking care only that the process of change from each original sound event to its final state of transformation is slowly, gradually and clearly heard.

Deploying microphones in remote places, bring about these transformations in real time by the human manipulation of the synthesizer or with the help of self-governing control systems.

Based on these procedures and experiences, design for your personal use and store in your mind an imaginary synthesizer with which, when used in conjunction with blocking, masking and pattern recognition techniques, you can willfully bring about such transformations at any time in any place without the help of external equipment.

LIVE ELECTRONIC MUSIC

Spirit–Catchers
Annea Lockwood

4 microphones each mixed out to an individual loudspeaker through a separate channel. Loudspeakers arranged each in a corner of the room facing in.

Four people have each been asked to bring with them an object which they have had for many years—an object such as one would never throw away in a move—something which seems to have attached to itself something of its owner's self or history, a spirit-catcher. (Shamanistic term for an object, e.g. a stone, in which ally spirits are stored or exorcised spirits held.)

Choose people who have feelings somewhat like these about objects and are easily articulate in a performance situation.

Four chairs or cushions are arranged N S E W, in front of each is a microphone on a stand. Each performer chooses a chair, and seating him/herself with the object between his/her hands, begins to remember aloud all its associations, all the events connected with it, gradually uncovering all the accessible layers of feelings and memory accumulated around the object.

The four people are talking to themselves, thinking aloud, introverted and should aim to become oblivious of everything but the memory process, oblivious of audience, amplification, the other speakers. Remembering has an ebb and flow to it, a shifting momentum which is the focus of this piece. Words come slowly, spaced out, until an image has crystalized, when the voice changes, is charged with energy, and the pace of the talking increases and the density of imagery with it.

The person mixing brings up amplification for each speaker successively, in the consistent order, N.W.S.E.N.W.S.E. Cross fade from speaker to speaker. Overlaps should not go beyond a minute—not aiming for simultaneous multiple voices, just for smooth transitions from one speaker to the next. Spend at least 3 minutes with each speaker each time. Amplification levels high enough for audience to hear easily, but no higher.

The duration of Spirit-catchers is open. Each speaker simply stops talking when no more memories/images come to mind. When the last speaker has ended, the piece is ended.

I am sitting in a room

Alvin Lucier

Necessary equipment:

    1 microphone
    2 tape recorders
    amplifier
    1 loudspeaker

Choose a room the musical qualities of which you would like to evoke.

Attach the microphone to the input of tape recorder #1.

To the output of tape recorder #2 attach the amplifier and loudspeaker.

Use the following text or any other text of any length:

> "I am sitting in a room different from the one you are in now.
> I am recording the sound of my speaking voice and I am going to play it back into the room again and again until the resonant frequencies of the room reinforce themselves so that any semblance of my speech, with perhaps the exception of rhythm, is destroyed.
> What you will hear, then, are the natural resonant frequencies of the room articulated by speech.
> I regard this activity not so much as a demonstration of a physical fact, but more as a way to smooth out any irregularities my speech might have."

Record your voice on tape through the microphone attached to tape recorder #1.

Rewind the tape to its beginning, transfer it to tape recorder #2, play it back into the room through the loudspeaker and record a second generation of the original recorded statement through the microphone attached to tape recorder #1.

Rewind the second generation to its beginning and splice it onto the end of the original recorded statement on tape recorder #2.

Play the second generation only back into the room through the loudspeaker and record a third generation of the original recorded statement through the microphone attached to tape recorder #1.

Continue this process through many generations.

All the generations spliced together in chronological order make a tape composition the length of which is determined by the length of the original statement and the number of generations recorded.

Make versions in which one recorded statement is recycled through many rooms.

Make versions using one or more speakers of different languages in different rooms.

Make versions in which, for each generation, the microphone is moved to different parts of the room or rooms.

Make versions that can be performed in real time.

The Duke of York
for voice and synthesizer

Alvin Lucier

Two persons design a musical performance in which one of them, the synthesist, uses an electronic music synthesizer of equivalent configuration of electronic equipment to alter the vocal identity of the other, the vocalist, who selects and orders any number of songs, speeches, arias, passages from books, films, television, poems or plays or any other vocal utterances including those of non-human intelligences, in ways determined by his or her relationship to the synthesist and the particular purpose of the performance.

Performances may be used to strengthen personal ties, make friends with strangers or uncover clues to hidden families and past identities.

In strengthening personal ties, one, with the help of the other, selects examples that either or both have known and remembered since childhood, arranging them in the order of their emergence in their awarenesses. In making friends with strangers, the vocalist selects examples that the synthesist might have known and remembered, based on assumptions as to race, color, date and place of birth, manner of speech, dress, hair style or any other outward sign, arranging them in the order that they might have emerged in the synthesist's awareness. In uncovering clues to hidden families and past identities, vocal examples of any kind may be arranged in any order or in temporal or geographical clusters. Examples may be taken from letters, diaries, memoirs, musical works of biographies of real or fictitious persons.

The vocalist sings, speaks or utters the examples to the synthesist through a microphone and amplifier system. He or she may read from script or score, memorize or listen through headphones to a record player or tape recorder upon which are stored the examples in their chosen order. Separations between examples are determined either by the legnth of time it takes to change each record or by the natural spaces that are formed by turning pages, splicing or collecting and recording examples.

The vocalist learns to mimic recorded examples as perfectly as he or she can, without interpretation or improvization, in order to partake of and communicate to the synthesist as fully as possible the vocal identity of the recording artist represented by each example. All aspects of the sound images including those produced by recording techniques and other special effects should be regarded by both performers as much a part of the remembered or imagined identities as such vocal considerations as inflection, articulation, timbre, breath control, projection or vibrato. During those parts of examples in which the recording artists rest or where it is impossible to follow, the vocalist either imitates the accompanying parts or leaves gaps. Whole examples, not parts of examples, should be used.

In cases of vocal identities for which there are no recorded examples, the vocalist tries to imitate the vocal identities as he or she imagines them to be.

The synthesist alters the vocal examples as they arrive from the vocalist, trying to make them sound as much as possible like the originals as he or she remembers or imagines them to be. Any disparities that arise between either performer's remembrance of original examples, their imitation, re-recording or cover versions should be regarded as inherent discontinuities in space or time. In uncovering clues to hidden families or past identities, the synthesist composes a set of examples designed to sketch biographies of persons other than those sketched by the vocalist. The separate sets of examples are then performed simultaneously.

Within each example, the synthesist makes one or more alterations of any aspect of sound including pitch, timbre, range, envelope, vibrato or amount of echo. Alterations, once made, may not be lessened but may be incerased from example to example to produce a continually changing composite vocal identity made up of many layers of partial identities.

In performances involving more than two persons, the synthesizers may be played separately or linked together.

Sounds made by the synthesizer itself should be considered its attempt to establish continuity or to express its inability to cope with the situation.

Faust Crosses the Raritan Somewhere in West Africa. . .

Daniel Goode

--- a performance piece for synthesizer

Take a familiar tune, a march or anthem, for example:

"On the Banks of the Old Raritan"

Tune the sequencer to the beginning notes of the tune, as many as there are places to the sequencer. (This may take some clever shaping of the melody to fit the rhythmic grid of the sequencer.) Thus, for a 10-place sequencer, we have:

While the sequence is repeating (live), re-tune the *first* sequencer note to the 11th note of the tune (or the number plus one of the total sequencer places.) *Take your time. . .* and let the stages of re-tuning provide variations on that note as it comes around in sequence. Make use of microtonal and sliding effects, overshoot and finally land on the new pitch, ornament it. Then, in a like manner, tune the second sequencer note to the 12th note of the tune; the third to the 13th and so on to the end of the tune, re-tuning the entire sequencer step by step as many times as necessary; ending when all places of the sequencer have been tuned to the last note of the piece. (A chart of these changes for each dial of the sequencer is useful.) Some microtonal differences in this final unison are part of the sound of the piece. Let it go on this way for a while as a "coda."

A suitable wave-shape and envelope should be chosen. Changes in timbre, envelope, and volume may by used during the piece, but should always be gradual and subtle.

Pendulum Music

for Microphones, Amplifiers, Speakers and Performers

Steve Reich

Three, four or more microphones are suspended from the ceiling or from microphone boom stands by their cables so that they all hang the same distance from the floor and are all free to swing with a pendular motion. Each microphone's cable is plugged into an amplifier with is connected to a loudspeaker. Each microphone hangs a few inches directly above or next to its speaker.

Before the performance each amplifier is turned up just to the point where feedback occurs when a mike swings directly over or next to its speaker, but no feedback occurs as the mike swings to either side. This level on each amplifier is then marked for future reference and all amplifiers are turned down.

The performance begins with performers taking each mike, pulling it back like a swing, and then holding them while another performer turns up the amplifiers to their pre-marked levels. Performers then release all the microphones in unison. Thus, a series of feedback pulses is heard which will either be all in unison or not depending on the gradually changing phase relations of the different mike pendulums.

Performers then sit down to watch and listen to the process along with the audience.

The piece is ended sometime shortly after all mikes have come to rest and are feeding back a continuous tone by performers pulling out the power cords of the amplifiers.

Tower of Power

for Linda Collins

Beth Anderson

Hold as many keys and pedals down as possible, using only your body. At as loud an amplitude as possible, using both your ears and equipment to decide. For a minimum of five minutes, using your self and your audience to decide. Changing timbers a minimum of five times, without letting any notes up. Avoiding any sharp contrasts, allowing your organ to dictate the possibilities.

Four rehersals of the piece are to be taped and played back in exact syncronization with the performance through four speakers placed symmetrically around the church, taking into consideration the origination of the organ sound. All should blend.

Prepare your
spirit   mind   ears   body   family,   but   avoid   any
discussion of sound

Three Electronic Pieces

Gordon Mumma

1. Crosshatch for Lowell Cross

Three color television receivers of the same
  model
each receiving a different color video
  transmission
from the outside world
are connected together
with the following arrangement:
the red intensity information from receiver A
is applied to the red beam of receiver B,
likewise B to C, and C to A,
the blue intensity information from receiver
  A
is applied to the blue beam of receiver C,
likewise B to A, and C to B.
Appropriate extensions of this scheme
are applicable to interconnections of any
of the nine electron beams.

San Francisco

2. Foreskin   *for B.L.*

The outputs of two current-limiting power
  supplies
are connected to a nude, seated dancer
with surface or subcutaneous electrodes
in an appropriate arrangement to the tongue,
foreskin or glans, clitoris, labial folds, ear
  lobes,
mammary nipples, anal sphincter, and soles
  of the feet,

with current limiting adjusted to establish a
  spectrum
between the thresholds of mild discomfort
and below the threat of cardiac trauma,
employing either automatic or
assisted manual random operation of the
  current limiters
within the established spectrum,
present facing a live audience for twenty-one
  minutes.

New York City

3. Stovepipe   *for Richard Nelson*

An ensemble of low-power lasers
each with a deflection system producing a
  horizontal scan
adjusted in length to the diameter
of a corresponding mirror-surfaced, gravity-
  balanced stovepipe damper
in an ensemble of operating chimney
  stovepipes
is arranged such that the vertical deflections
of the horizontal scans
are reflected by the undulating dampers
onto various surfaces
within a commodius enclosed space,
dimly illuminated with winter afternoon
  light
and comfortably accessible to the public.

Harwich, Cape Cod

Solo for Voice 23
0' 00" No. 2
Theatre with Electronics (Irrelevant)

John Cage

Directions

On a playing area (e.g. table, chessboard) equipped with contact microphones (four channels preferably, speakers around the audience, highest volume without feedback)

Play a game with another person (e.g. chess, dominoes) or others (e.g. scrabble, bridge).

From *Song Books (Solos for Voice 3-92)* by John Cage. Copyright © 1970 by Henmar Press, Inc. Reprint permission granted by the publisher.

Solo for Voice 43
Theatre with Electronics (Relevant)

John Cage

Directions

Improvise a melody using the following text by Erik Satie (four times) recording it meanwhile. Let the first time be approximately 17 seconds, the second 49 seconds, the third 52 seconds, and the last 53 seconds (total duration: approximately two minutes and fifty-one seconds). Play back the recording and then sing it recording it a second time. Then play both recordings simlutaneously.

From *Song Books (Solos for Voice 3-92)* by John Cage. Copyright © 1970 by Henmar Press Inc. Reprint permission granted by the publisher.

et TOUT CELA M'est adveNU

PAr LA FautE DE La musIQUE .

et tOut CeLA M'Est adveNU PAR

LA FAUTE DE la musique .

et tout cela m'est advenU Par la

FAUE DE LA MUSIque.

et tout cela m'est ADVenu par la faute de la musique.

Narrative Song for Voice and Audio Tape

Laurie Anderson

(The following story is told over the audio tape of sounds which accumulate into the basic rhythm track for the song *Is Anybody Home?*)

I live by the Hudson River and a lot of boats go by. They glide by so quickly—on the other side of the river—camouflaged against the Jersey shore. Sometimes it's hard to tell which is moving—the boats or the shoreline—and it seems like all of Manhattan has has come unanchored and is slowly drifting out to sea.

I've spent a lot of time trying to film the boats, so I set up a camera near the window.

...and every time I hear a horn, I run to the window, but I usually miss them. It's the kind of timing, the kind of synching, that's been getting into the songs I've been writing lately. Like walking upstairs in the dark when you think there's one more step than there actually is ...

...and your foot comes pounding down with nothing underneath ... or like the piano we got a few months ago ... only a few keys on it work so we put it out in the hallway near the door and when people come in, they kind of rake their hands over the keyboard and play the few notes that work. It's sort of a doorbell now.

I was trying to work on a song for a performance, but all the sounds around were so distracting, it was hard to concentrate. My mother called and said, "Why don't you come out here to write your song? It's real quiet, we've just put all new carpets down." When I got there, I noticed that the new carpets were so thick that none of the doors closed. The only door that still worked was the door to the parrot's room. It was a swinging door and every time someone came through, the door whacked into the parrot's cage and the parrot screamed and the scream filled the whole house through all the half-open doors ... and this is the song I finally wrote.

(The above makes up the basic track, which continues into a song scored for violin and voice.)

Stereo Song for Steven Weed

a song for two microphones and two speakers on opposite sides of a small room

Laurie Anderson

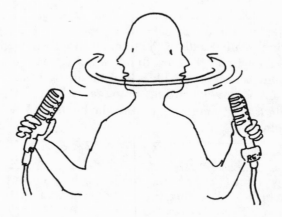

(every few words, the head is turned)

Steven Weed wrote in his book that the FBI asked him to come in and answer a few questions. He said it didn't look like an interrogation room at all—there were no bright lights.

But he said they were very clever. There was an agent on his right and an agent on his left and they alternated questions so that he had to keep turning his head in order to answer them. He said that after a few hours of doing this, he realized he's been shaking his head the whole time and that no matter what answer he'd given—yes, or no, or I don't know—the answer had always looked the same: no.

This song is scored for violin and voice, imitating each other and rapidly changing microphones.

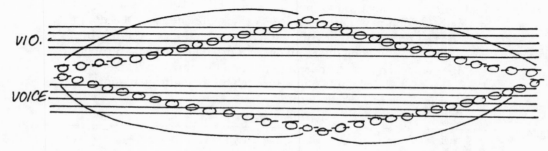

Duet for Violin and Door Jamb

Laurie Anderson

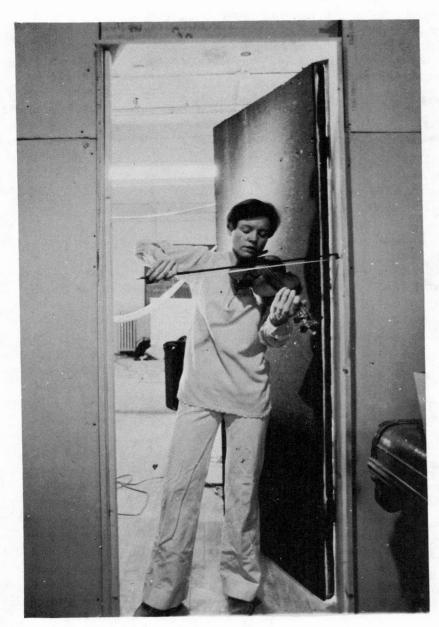

This piece is performed on the threshold of a door between two rooms. Contact microphones are placed on the jambs. As the bow knocks back and forth, limited by the width of the door, the percussive sound is amplified and fed through speakers in one of the rooms. The speakers for the (electric) violin are located in the other room, making it a duet for the adjoining rooms, as well. The tonal is mixed live with the percussive by kicking the door open and shut.

Film/Songs in 24/24 Time

Laurie Anderson

Film/Songs were composed in an attempt to equalize sound and picture—to do away with the idea of the subservient "sound track." The effect is this: you are watching a film which suddenly begins to flicker (frames are blackened or whited out). This is made doubly perceptible because the sound also starts to flutter . . . .

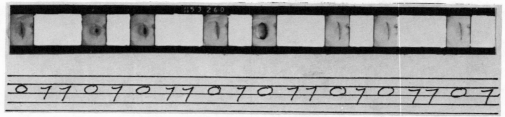

Natural dark-to-light rhythms (the opening and closing of a door) are expressed in increasing and decreasing volume.

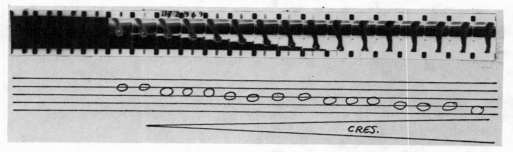

Or, for example, slight movements are expressed in oscillating tones, which move quickly, twenty-four frames representing only one second.

The color sections of *Film/Songs* have the advantage of requiring no camera. Rhythmic patterns are painted directly on the film, paralleling the spoken or sound/music text.

Game
for Two Flutes and Ring Modulator

Carl Michaelson

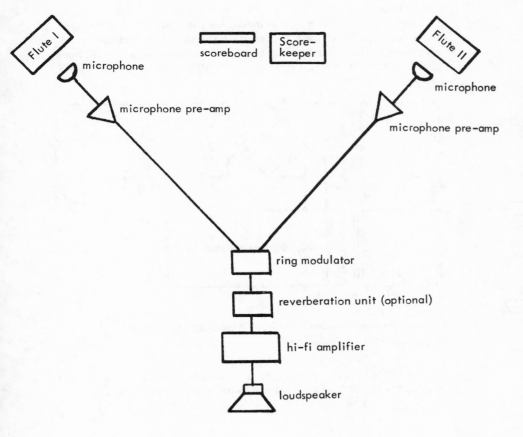

GAME is a musical event, combining both competition and improvisation. Each performance creates a new series of variations upon the given theme. This is made possible by following the rules of the game and by the interaction of the two flutes with a ring modulator (see cover diagram). The ring modulator, into which the outputs of both flutes are fed, remains silent if either Flute I or Flute II plays alone. However, when the two flutes are sounding simultaneously, the ring modulator produces a phantom third voice. The players, while adhering to the sequence of pitches as written, will compete by alternately attempting to stimulate this third voice, thus both "scoring" and producing a new variation during the attempt.

First the ring modulator is turned on. Flutes I and II each choose a part (e.g. Flute I plays A, Flute II, B). The piece is then played through as written. After this, the game begins.

Each flutist prepares to play the same part again. However, this time (and during the whole competition) while every note in parts A and B *must be played*, adhering to the written sequence of pitches, the time values and vertical aspects are ignored.

The player of the B part is in the scoring, agressive position. *Each note B plays scores a point*: he scores a point for himself every time he plays simultaneously with A, thus making the ring modulator sound; he scores a point for A whenever he plays a note which fails to "catch" A, and the ring modulator remains silent. The player of the A part is in the position of a baseball pitcher, throwing out his notes which B attempts to "hit". Therefore, A should play his notes as staccato and unexpectedly as possible. False starts, histrionic gestures and all attempts to distract the B player are to be encouraged. Because B has only half as many notes as A, he may let A play several notes without attempting to catch him (thus scoring no points for anyone); however, since B *must* play all the notes in his part, he will lose a point to A for each unplayed note once A has finished his own sequence.

Once all the notes in both A and B have been played, the players change parts. Thus each player has a chance to score in the agressive B position, and one inning is completed. The game may last as many innings as desired.

Keeping score is best done by two people. One person keeps his eyes glued on whoever is playing the B part. Every time B plays a note, the scorekeeper should point at whichever player scores the point (B if the modulator sounds, A if it doesn't). Another person should keep a running tally which can be entered on the scoreboard after each half-inning. Since there are eleven notes in the B part, the total number of points scored by both players in each half-inning will be eleven.

GAME
For Two Flutes and Ring Modulator   Carl Michaelson

The ring modulator is a device which has two inputs and one output. The output consists of the sum and the difference of all frequencies fed into it. It is traditionally used with a sine wave oscillator connected to one of the inputs, and the audio material to be modulated connected to the other input. In this case, no oscillator is needed since the flutes are modulating each other. Should a ring modulator not be available, one can easily be built, using four germanium diodes (type 1N60 or HEP R9135), and three UTC A-15 transformers connected as shown.

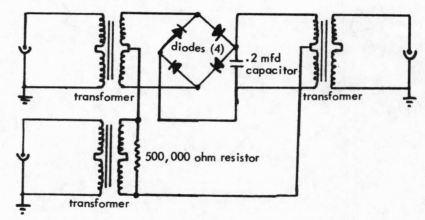

Anyone with even a rudimentary knowledge of electronics will find the unit easy to construct.

4 Do-It-Yourself Pieces

I. Casta ★   Ben Johnston
for Norma Marder

Choose a position on stage where you will record, another, elevated, where you will type (recorded, with mike for voice and contact-mike for typewriter), a third, spotlighted, where you will perform, accompanied by tapes of yourself which are recorded earlier in the performance. A fourth position should be chosen for a recording technician who has three tape recorders, four speakers, three tape loops, mixers, and microphones. Earphones should be provided for you and for the technician during the recording of the loops.

A sample schematic for this kind of setup is here provided:

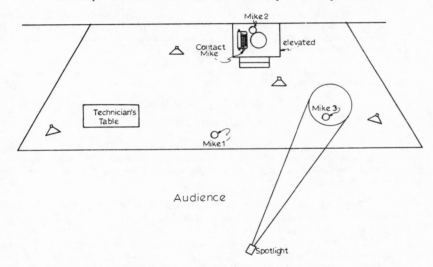

Prepare four segments of 45 seconds each of noises of all kinds you make instrumentally and/or vocally. At least one third of the sounds should be vocal. A significant number should be scatological. Write down a list of these sounds such that from it you could identify each sound. Prepare a sequence of at least twenty-five excerpts ranging from very brief to a phrase or two in length, selected from standard repertory works you can perform. A significant number should be virtuosic.

The sequence of events is as follows:

★ SUBSTITUTE HERE YOUR FIRST NAME. IF THE NAME SUGGESTS ANY PARTICULAR PIECE OF PERFORMING MATERIAL, USE THAT IN THE PREPARATION OF THIS PIECE.

∗(1) Record on a loop the first 45-second segment;

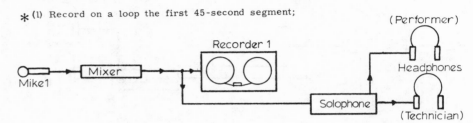

(2) Record on a second loop the second 45-second segment mixed with the first;

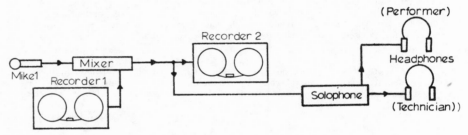

(3) Record on a third loop the third 45-second segment mixed with the mixtures of the first and second;

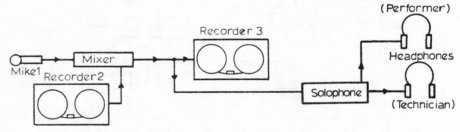

(4) Record on the first loop the fourth 45-second segment mixed with the mixture of the first, second and third.

∗ Schematics by George Ritscher. Used by permission.

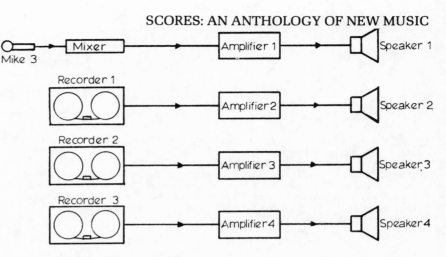

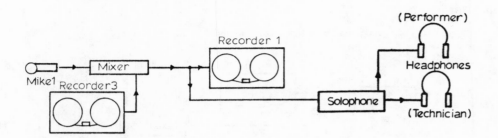

During this sequence, repeat the last sound of each segment over and over like a broken record until the next segment is set to record. After the fourth segment, go to the typewriter as you repeat this final sound. Then type out on file cards twenty-five of the sounds you have been performing, using the list you have prepared. While you type, hum, whistle and otherwise travesty the repertory excerpts you are going to perform next.

While this is going on, amplified through one of the speakers, the recording engineer should record 45 seconds of it on the second loop. He should also take out one second of the third loop and splice it into the fourth.

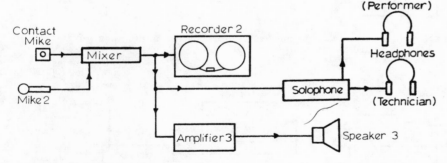

Next, as the loops are started in playback, one by one, proceed to the spotlight area, shuffling the file cards as you go. On arrival, perform the repertory excerpts, one by one. After each, perform what is on the top file card and then throw the card into the audience. When you reach the end, throw away your score also.

All during this section, the recording engineer should build the volume of the loops gradually until the last 45 seconds drowns you out completely. He then escorts you, still performing, from the stage. On the first curtain call he turns off the sound.

Timing must be tight and fast-paced. The piece must last no longer than ten minutes.

II. Recide for a ★
for Katherine Lity

Record 15 minutes of outdoor sounds at a place and at a time when sound is intermittent and somewhat varied. Do not alter this sound recording in any way except when balancing the loudness levels in performance.

Record also (preferably the same) 15 minutes of indoor sounds at a place or places in a house (not including kitchen, utility room, or bathroom) where sound is intermittent and somewhat varied. Electric machinery sounds should not be allowed to predominate. (Heavy housecleaning without loud or continuous electric appliances might well supply a suitable amount and variety of sound.) Do not alter this sound recording in any way except when balancing the loudness levels in performance: at that time this recording should be made to predominate slightly over the first-mentioned one, with which it is to be played simultaneously.

At a time of day when activity is neither very active nor very sparse, station yourself near the door of a commercial establishment such as a grocery store, department store, or a drug store. With a stopwatch time (and write down) for 15 minutes when people enter and exit. This sequence of durations will determine the timing of your actions on stage. (With each new duration, change activity.)

★ SUBSTITUTE HERE YOUR PERFORMING SPECIALTY (e.g. RECIPE FOR A DANCER, RECIPE FOR A BASSIST, RECIPE FOR A SOPRANO, RECIPE FOR A MIME, RECIPE FOR AN ACTOR, ETC.)

Design a stage set which is as much like your own bedroom as possible, unless your room is too cramped for practising your performing. If it is, modify the design to permit such movement as is necessary. The room should be completely furnished with real objects.

Write down on separate small pieces of paper a number of actions you typically perform in your bedroom, which is equal to approximately 2/3 of the number of durations in the timing sequence previously written down. The remaining 1/3, completing that number of actions your timing sequence requires, should be sequences of repertory performance, which you could practise in your room. Put these pieces of paper, folded, into a large container and draw them out one by one without looking at them. This list will determine the sequence of actions you perform on-stage. Assign to each its corresponding duration, using your timing sequence.

When you perform your actions on stage, simultaneously play back the two 15-minute recordings of indoor and outdoor sounds.

Manner of performance, lighting, dress should be totally naturalistic. At the end of the 15 minutes, go out of the room. The performance should be rehearsed carefully, timings kept precise and natural.

III. Conference: A Telephone Happening
a conference call for telephonists
for John Cage

Get the telephone numbers of a number of people who are reachable (wherever they may be) by telephone. The number of people shall be equal to the number of a hexagram of I CHING obtained by tossing coins. Assign to each a topic of conversation (e.g. politics, sex, religion, gossip, science, etc.). Toss coins again, once for each participant to determine from the text and commentaries of each hexagram his topic of conversation. At an agreed upon time place a conference call to all of these people.

Each person shall prepare for the conference by collecting a number of quotations pertinent to his topic, each containing no less than 64 words. The number of quotations each participant has shall be equal to the number of a hexagram of I CHING obtained by tossing coins. Something of their overall character can be inferred from the text and commentaries of this hexagram. These quotations should be written down, each on a separate slip of paper, to be put into a hat and drawn out one by one to be read at the time of the conference.

On the occasion of the conference call, each participant, as he draws out a quotation to read, tosses coins successively to determine by I CHING the number of words of it he will read. The order in which participants speak is determined informally, conversationally, politely. When each participant has read all of his quotations, he says "Good-bye," but remains on the line until all are finished. When the initiator of the conference notices from the goodbyes that all participants have finished, he thanks them and says, "Good-bye," terminating the conference.

IV. Knocking Piece II
for Jack McKenzie

Take X (various sizes of) "super-balls" and Y (could equal X or not) membrane and wood surfaces (each sounding surface with electronic amplification via contact or other microphones) and using Z (any number) of players, bounce them according to the instructions for timing and loudness given below. Each successive sound of each player should have a contrasting timbre. Loudness can be controlled by (1) nature of vibrating surface and efficiency of resonator; (2) size of ball; (3) height from which ball is dropped; (4) individual amplification control for each player. There must be over-all amplification and band-pass filter controls, after the final mix, these to be controlled by a technician, according to the sectional levels of dynamic indicated by his "score." All preparations are to be visible to the audience.

Take 2 times Z decks (two contrasting decks for each performer) of ordinary playing cards, each including one joker (53 cards per deck). Each card will call for its face value (A, 2, 3...JQK equals 1, 2, 3...11, 12, 13) in seconds. Joker calls for 0 seconds. Suits determine loudness:

♣ = very soft;   ◇ = soft;   ♡ = loud;   ♠ = very loud.

Before each performance make an uneven cut of one of the decks. Replace each of the cards in the thinner pile of the cut with its exact equivalent from the contrasting deck and shuffle the mixed deck at least three times. Place the mixed deck face down, and on cue to begin playing, turn up the cards one by one thus determining the duration and loudness of each event. The cards of the contrasting deck (the thin cut) indicate silences. The joker means: without interrupting the duration sequence indicated by the cards before and after it, superimpose any loud, incongruous noise.

The technician makes his "score" using a deck of cards, without joker. Before each performance he cuts the cards several times. On the first cut, the numerical value of the card indicates the number of sections into which he will divide the performance. The length of sections may be freely decided by him, but the sum total must equal 364 seconds, or six minutes, four seconds. He must cut again, once for each section. The number he gets will determine the dynamic character of each section, according to the following table:

A - erratically varying loudness
2 - very soft, decrescendo
3 - very soft
4 - very soft, crescendo
5 - soft, decrescendo
6 - soft
7 - soft, crescendo
8 - loud, decrescendo
9 - loud
10 - loud, crescendo
J - very loud, decrescendo
Q - very loud
K - very loud, crescendo

The suit will determine the filtering according to the following correspondences:

 = no filtering;   = low band pass;

 = high band pass;   = erratically varying filtering.

The technician gives the cue to begin.

Telephone Matrix

Kenneth Maue

An information matrix in which a group of players generates sentences out of single words through one-to-one telephone communication.

Each player sits by a telephone. In the beginning, each player has a list of all the other telephone numbers in the matrix, without identification of the numbers with their respective operators.

Each player has a memory bank, consisting of a piece of paper on which he can write information (words) that has been input or transferred within the matrix. A unit of information in the memory bank consists of either a common English word or a sequence of words that constitutes a part of a common English sentence, syntactically correct.

At any time during the matrix, a player may enter a single-word unit of information into the matrix by thinking up a word and transferring it to another player. Players should be careful to input words of all parts of speech. A transmission consists of calling one of the other numbers, speaking the unit of information clearly, and hanging up; No self-identification or other communication is permitted. If a player makes a transmission attempt and is thwarted by a busy signal, he must then attempt to transmit the information to another number. If the call is answered, the information is transmitted. If this attempt results in a second busy signal, the player who has attempted the two unsuccessful transmissions must strike the unit of information permanently out of the matrix.

To prevent excessive loss of information from the matrix, each player should stay off the telephone for sufficient durations, to allow transmission attempts to reach him successfully.

At any time during the performance, a player may join two units of information already in his memory bank end-to-end if the resulting unit of information constitutes part of a common English sentence.

Fused units of information can be transmitted to other players, just as single-word units of information can be transmitted, subject to the same double-busy signal cancellation rule.

When a player, through fusing units of information in his memory bank, arrives at a syntactically complete English sentence, he may continue to operate in the matrix for as long as he likes, and may continue to add words or groups of words to this sentence to make it more elaborate. But at any time after completing a sentence, a player is free to suspend operations in the matrix, by not making any more transmission attempts and by not answering the telephone at all. A given player, getting a no-answer response from another telephone, knows that that player has suspended operations, and should not call that number again. A transmission attempt that results in a no-answer response does not count toward the cancellation of the unit of information, as in the case of a busy signal.

In the end, one player will become aware that he is the only player remaining in the active operations in the matrix. There is no way, at that point, that this player can complete his sentence. Therefore, the whole matrix is terminated. This remaining player announces the termination to the other players by giving a call to each of them, this time letting the phone ring just once and hanging up. At this time, all the players go to a common location and compare the results of their activities.

Note: In the event that a player receives a call from a player outside the matrix, he minimizes the length of the call, perhaps by offering to return the call later, and also asks that person to contribute one word to the matrix. The player receiving such a word may transmit it to another player, but may not fuse it with something already in his memory bank.

King Speech Song

for soloist / thirteen cascading echoes

Daniel Lentz

Performance Notes

The *King Speech Song* is comprised of a set of 13 individual pieces, each intricately inter-related to the others both musically and textually. Only the first piece is heard alone. All of the others are heard (and performed) in conjunction and in synchronization with all of those preceding them. After all 13 are performed, they form the complete composition (see RESULT in the score), which is a setting of texts from speeches of Martin Luther King — plus one line, the last, from the Old Testament of the Bible, a phrase that was often repeated in various forms by individuals through-out history, including the 16th century reformer, Martin Luther. The music is not scored (nor heard) in the "normal" left-right manner of most music. For example, the first piece (or "source"), "I see fear glowing," is performed by the Soloist in "real-time," and is then heard as an echo 13 times in precise synchronization with the following 12 pieces, or sources. Each piece is titled according to the particular new textual formation it introduces into the overall scheme. These are:

No. 1)	I see fear glowing	No. 8)	The missed land
No. 2)	I see glory coming	No. 9)	We must stand & hope
No. 3)	I've seen the fearing man	No. 10)	I've been the top
No. 4)	We hope	No. 11)	Two more shall die
No. 5)	I dream	No. 12)	I have a dream today
No. 6)	I've overseen the land fearing man be	No. 13)	We shall die
No. 7) ·	Let's drink more		

After the Soloist completes the performance of the 13th piece, he/she then listens (with the audience) to the RESULT which, by then has cascaded into the complete musical speech.

Of equal importance to the text is the music, or notes. All of the notes seen in the score are derived from 2 crystal wine glasses which are struck (or rubbed) at precisely the same moment as the word particles are spoken or sung. The 23 different pitches (over two octaves) seen in the RESULT are caused by the activity of the Soloist who drinks from the glasses in order to change the pitch of each glass (and the constant return of each piece as a long echo).

* *The two glasses should be made of very fine crystal. The first, or larger one should be a goblet of the 'Burgundy' type with a capacity of approximately 18 ounces, and the second a goblet of the 'Claret' type with a capacity of approximately 14 ounces. The larger glass (No. 1) should have a pitch—when empty—of F-natural, the first space of the treble clef. The smaller glass (No. 2) should have a pitch of E-flat, the fourth space of the treble clef. No. 1 must have 12 levels clearly marked on its bowl. When the glass is nearly full it should be on level 1 which is an octave below the pitch when the glass is empty (level 12). The level and pitch change as the Soloist drinks from the glass—to the next level. The 12 levels and consequent pitches are as follows:

Glass No. 1 sounds an octave below the written pitch in the score (pages 1–5).

Glass No. 2 should have 11 levels marked on its bowl. The 11 levels and consequent pitches are as follows:

Glass No. 2 sounds as written in the score.

In order for the glasses to produce the pitches written in the score, they are struck with a mallet or the rim of the bowl is rubbed with the index finger. The mallet should have one end made of felt and the other of cork. The glasses are struck with the felt end of the mallet except when the note is white when it is struck with the cork end.

When a word particle (or phoneme) is spoken it should be done so in a voice uniform to the other spoken particles. When a particle is sung the note should be the same as that of the resonating glass. Although it

is not too important which octave the singing voice uses, it should be consistent and follow the melodic line as written in the score's RE-SULT. This means that the voice might be an octave lower (or even higher if the Soloist is a high-voiced female) than the glass on some particles and unison on others.

The dynamic level of the glasses and voice should always be *mf/f*, except when marked otherwise. The method of attack must be han-dled with extreme care if the resulting text and music is to become comprehensible. In particles ending in soft consonances (such as "n") or vowels the shape should be as follows:

$$\textit{sfz} \mathrel{=\!\!=\!\!=} \textbf{\textit{p}} \mathrel{=\!\!=\!\!=} \text{(niente)}$$

The effect is one of the voice and glass ringing through, like a piano with the sustaining pedal depressed after a note is struck. Other particles will have to be articulated with the exact time values in-dicated in the score, especially those ending with hard consonances (such as "t").

* *Note: More important than the actual pitch of the empty glasses are the relative pitches between the two glasses. For example, Glass No. 1 could also have a pitch — when empty — of E-natural. If this is the case, No. 2 should then have a pitch of D-natural. If the glasses to be used have different pitches when empty from those indicated here, simply transpose the entire score in the direction necessary. (Voice range might also be a consideration in the choice of the performance glasses.)

Whenever possible the glass should be allowed to resonate until all its sound has stopped — the exception being when a note is incom-patible with the new key entered on page 3 and back again from page 5 to 1. Sometimes there will not be sufficient time since the Soloist will have to drink to the next level quickly. If this occurs in any place other than on the phrase "Let us eat and drink" (where the glass can be leaned while it is still resonating), the glass resonance should be stopped before the glass is leaned and subsequently drunk from.

Note: Do not articulate those word particles which appear within parentheses. These are included as pronunciation guides only.

The liquid used in the glasses must be red wine. A young and light Beaujolais is probably the best wine for this piece because it will not so easily 'gag' the performer as a heavier Burgundy or Claret might. The Soloist should open the wine in full view of the listeners. He/She then fills the glasses to the first level marked on each. After the glasses are properly tuned, the piece begins. It is to be expected that the Soloist could become quite inebriated during the course of the performance. For this reason, great care must be taken in these details.

Note: There should be a one beat pause after each piece; that is, before an additional piece begins.

Both glass(es) and voice must be amplified. Ideally, two high quality condenser microphones would be used. The loudspeaker(s) used must not be within sight of the listeners. It should be as if the Soloist's sounds and echoes are coming from the natural acoustic of the performance space.

The System:

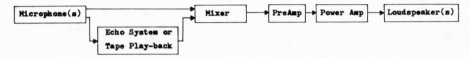

If the facility to produce the 13 cascading echoes in the formation (and timings) required is not available to the performer, he/she should produce a tape (a 16-track studio would simplify this procedure; it can then be mixed down to a quad, stereo, or mono result) which can be used in a performance. Either way, the end-result should be the same. If the echo system is used for the performance, an electric light metronome (or strobe) will be required for exact tempo and synchronization. Its pulse must not be visible to the listeners. There are 100 notes and 92 different speech particles that make up the RESULT of the score, and these must all be synched in their relative and precise positions in order for the text and music to be intelligible.

A stand for the glasses will be needed. It should be covered with cloth or foam to prevent noise from entering the echo system. . . as the glasses are placed on it.

Drink away from the microphone(s) as this too will introduce unwanted noise.

If possible, the piece should be memorized. This will help prevent the break-up of the visual line between the performer and the listener.

The lighting should be simply — (preferably) a single soft spot.

After the Soloist completes the performance of the 13th piece, he/she stands back and listens to the final result of all 13 pieces echoing for the last time.

Score Symbols.

♩ = Glass No. 1 (struck, rubbed, spoken or sung with simultaneously)
♦ = Glass No. 2
𝅗𝅥 or 𝆒 = Glass is struck with the cork end of the mallet
⁓ = Glass rim is rubbed to produce the indicated pitch
, = Drink from glass to next level marked on it
② = Example glass level for No. 1
⑨ = Example glass level for No. 2

⬆ or ⬇ = Lean glass in direction of the arrow

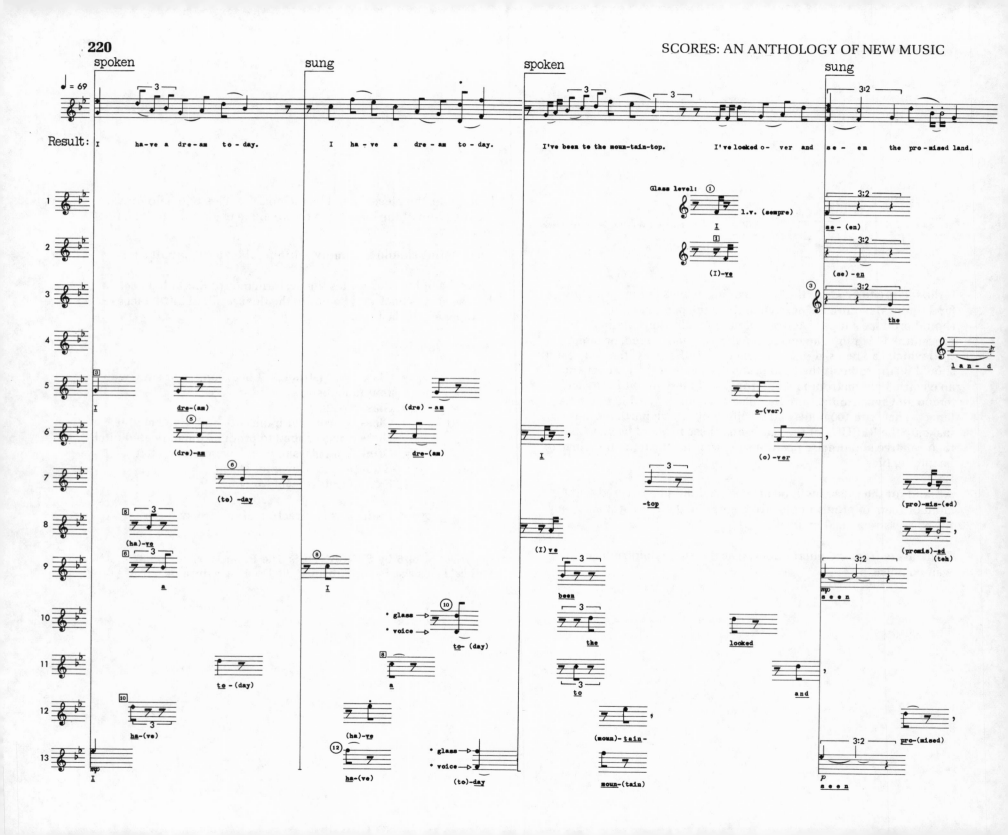

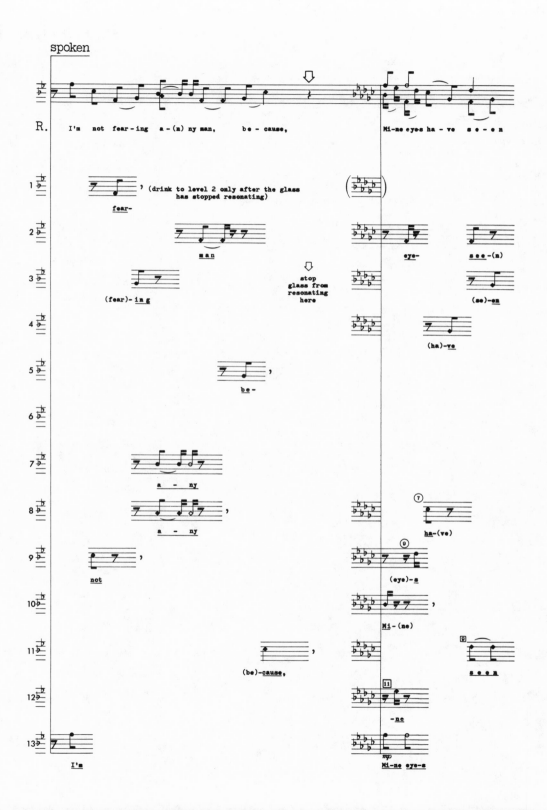

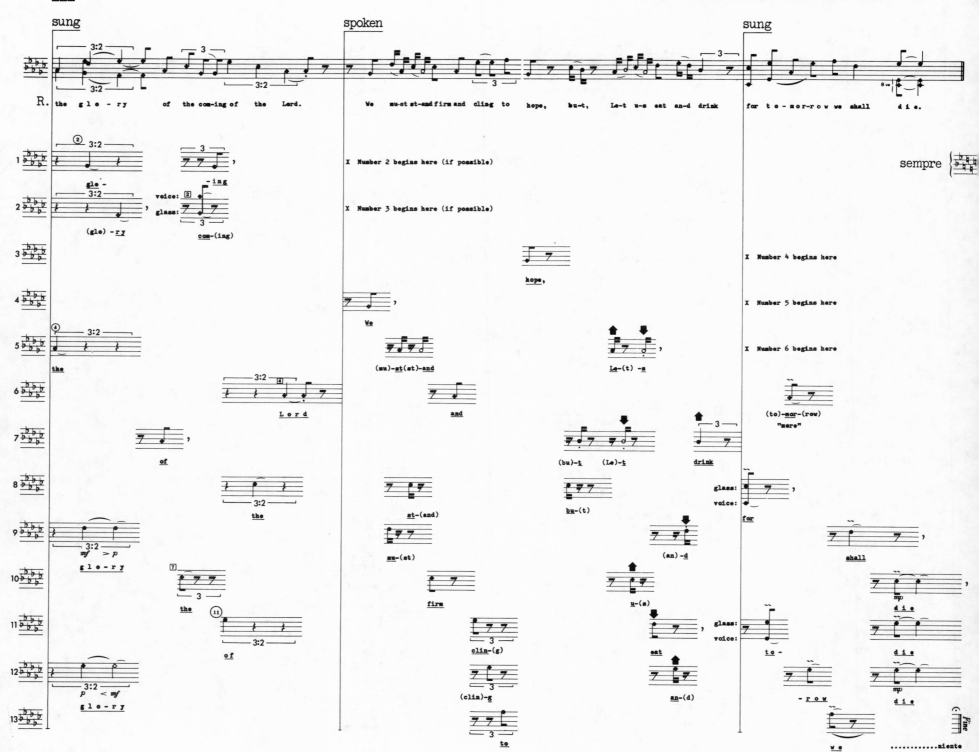

7 Music for Mixed Ensembles

Chapter 7 includes some extended works for voices, instruments, and electronic devices in various combinations. My own *Object Pieces* and R. Murray Schafer's *Minimusic* are both for any handy combination of voices and instruments, and are quite flexible and open. They are closely related to the graphic and verbal scores in Chapter 5, although they both use some specific pitch notation. Terry Riley's *Olson III* (which has not hitherto been generally available in this country) is closely related in style to his well-known *In C;* unlike that piece it has voices and words. "Paragraph 2" of Cornelius Cardew's *The Great Learning,* the text of which is from the Confucian classic of that name, combines voices and drums in a more flexible and varied manner. Nicolas Roussakis's *Night Speech* and Carmine Pepe's *Plastic Containers* both follow directly from some of the vocal techniques introduced here at the beginning of Chapter 2,

and, although using instruments, are still predominantly vocal. The works here of Karl Berger, Richard Peaslee, and Stephen Mayer combine voices and instruments somewhat more traditionally. Each derives much of its basic material from popular, vernacular music and will for that reason be of particular interest to many. D. B. Rama's *Pavali* is directly based on the "expressive mode" *(a raga)* and time cycle *(tala)* of South Indian music. While originally intended for Indian instruments, it is performable by Western substitutes or a singer. Stuart Smith's *Here and There* and Daivd Jones's *Toward the Capacity of a Room* are both graphic, verbal scores that follow practises described in Chapter 5, and add electronic elements. The former uses the night-time sounds of a short-wave radio as an instrument, while the latter explores the specific resonance of a room and an intimate relationship with the audience.

Object Pieces

Roger Johnson

Notes on a process

Object Pieces, like physical objects themselves, do not change significantly but simply exist in a more-or-less static state for a certain period of time. In the extreme an *Object Piece* would be entirely constant in all respects such as an electronic drone, pulse or repeated pattern of events. This concept is, however, broadened here to include pieces in which one or more prominent element (pitch, rhythm, register, volume, etc.) is constant while allowing for some degree of change among other elements. Most important is that the pieces explore and project the idea of static state. The pieces may be very complex, requiring considerable time for the listener to fully perceive the complete texture and really understand the static nature of the piece. Pieces may also be very basic, simple and direct.

The pieces given are only suggestions, and no attempt has been made to set this idea into any fixed form. Performers are encouraged to create variations on the pieces and to work out entirely new treatments of the basic idea. Any combination of voices and/or instruments may be used—one performer or a large number. They may be rehearsed and highly refined, improvised at the moment or made into tape pieces. The length of time is determined by the performers based on the material and the performing situation. Some cue for ending should be arranged so that the pieces simply stop and do not fade or dissolve. Larger forms may be created by stringing together a series of pieces or by some pattern of alternation between two, three or more pieces. As with the pieces themselves, no attempt at progression between pieces should be attempted. Each piece should always be clearly distinct from the others.

The following are several examples of object pieces which are interesting in themselves and further illustrate some of the possibilities within this general idea. It should be understood that these pieces belong solely to the performers who make them.

1. Spontaneous Object Piece

For any number of performers singing and/or playing anything. Without prior consultation each performer decides upon a sequence of some musical event or events. At a given moment each performer executes the chosen pattern without change until all agree to stop.

Variations:
Agree ahead of time on some specific characteristics or limits to the sounds produced.

Performers may wear earplugs so as not to be influenced by each other. They may also play from different places and mix their sound electronically. In these cases a tape of the result would be interesting and valuable to all.

2. Pulse Piece

For any sustaining instruments, percussion instruments with resonance or voices. Performers set a very slow regular pulse (one beat every 10 to 20 seconds might be good). The speed should depend upon the resonance and decay time of the instruments and the room. Each performer makes some sound, or remains silent, on each beat. Variation in these sounds is possible, but it should not be too extreme. If a wider variety of sounds is desired each performer should establish some repeated pattern of several sounds. Each beat should be of similar volume, or there should be some pattern to the volume changes.

Variations:
Replace the slow steady pulse with a simple repeated pattern of slow varied rhythms.

Performers may choose dry, crisp instruments and increase to basic tempo considerably.

Players may wear masks or play in the dark to eliminate eye contact and try to feel the beats together.

3. Register Piece

Choose a very extreme high or low register or a narrow middle registral band and develop relatively static material or material with some repeated pattern of change to express the register.

Variation:
Choose two, three or even more discrete registers to be played simultaneously. Performers may remain on one or create patterns which pass among these registers.

4. Long Tone Piece

Play very long, soft, sustained tones which start at a moderate volume and gradually fade. Decide upon other fixed elements such as timbre, register, absolute length of the various tones, specific pitches, etc.

5. Rhythm Piece

Each performer chooses or is assigned a rhythm to be performed on an instrument, by clapping or vocally. The resulting polyrhythmic texture is then maintained as long as it is interesting.

6. Pitch Piece

Decide upon a particular pitch, interval, chord or pattern of pitch changes as the basis for the piece. Each performer may have one unique pitch or all may create patterns which share the pitches. Some instruments or voices may sustain pitches while others play active patterns of pitches.

Variations:

Choose a fragment of an existing piece or several simultaneous fragments from the same or different pieces to be played over and over by one or more performers and serve as the basis of the pitch and rhythmic material for other performers to work from. See Philip Corner's *F# Section* for a specific example of this idea.

Select a four note chord, one note for each performer. Begin singing or playing until a perfect blending of volume, timbre and sonority is achieved. At this point the piece begins and may run as long as desired or once attained be remembered or made into a tape loop.

7. Tone Cluster Piece

Select a particular twelve note tone cluster and work out ways in which each performer will create it in time. Several suggestions follow and many more can be easily devised:

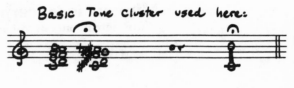

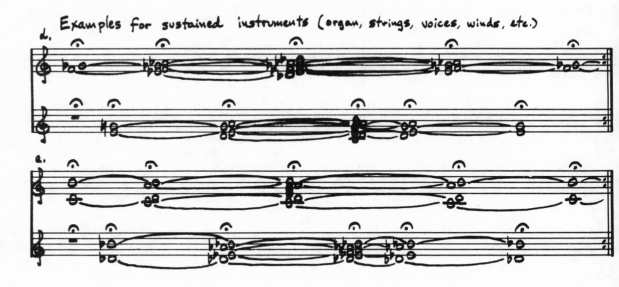

Minimusic (excerpts)
for instruments or voices

R. Murray Schafer

DIRECTIONS FOR PERFORMANCE

Each page of the score should be cut along the dotted lines.

1. All performers begin in box 1 though their entries should be staggered.

2. Performers may proceed in any of the directions indicated by arrows. Any number of pages may be turned (forward or backward) but having arrived at a box the player must perform it.

3. The numbers in circles refer to approximate durations in seconds. When underlined the numbers in circles refer to **exact** durations in seconds.

4. Any number of instrumentalists (or singers) may perform, but the group must be small enough that each performer can hear each of the other performers clearly.

5. As will become apparent, MINIMUSIC is primarily an exercise in improvisation and ear training. During rehearsals it has been found desirable to stop periodically to check if each player can identify accurately the box being performed by each of the other players. They must learn to listen to each other that closely.

6. The piece ends when one by one the performers lay down their instruments. Then turn to the final page for concluding instructions.

7. Whenever the word "play" occurs singers should substitute "sing". They may produce a variety of suitable vowel and consonantal sounds *ad libitum*.

8. Whenever one performer arrives at Box 18 (Paul Klee's "Twittering Machine") all players immediately jump to that box and perform it also. Then all players move out in different directions from there.

9. There may be pauses between the boxes ranging from ½ second to 6 seconds — or longer if necessary. Above all, avoid "jamming" the piece by producing incoherent textures. For instance, if a player has a soft effect let him wait until the loud sounds have ceased — and so forth.

10. The following symbols are used to indicate intervals:

−2	minor second	+2	major second
−3	minor third	+3	major third
P4	perfect fourth	P5	perfect fifth

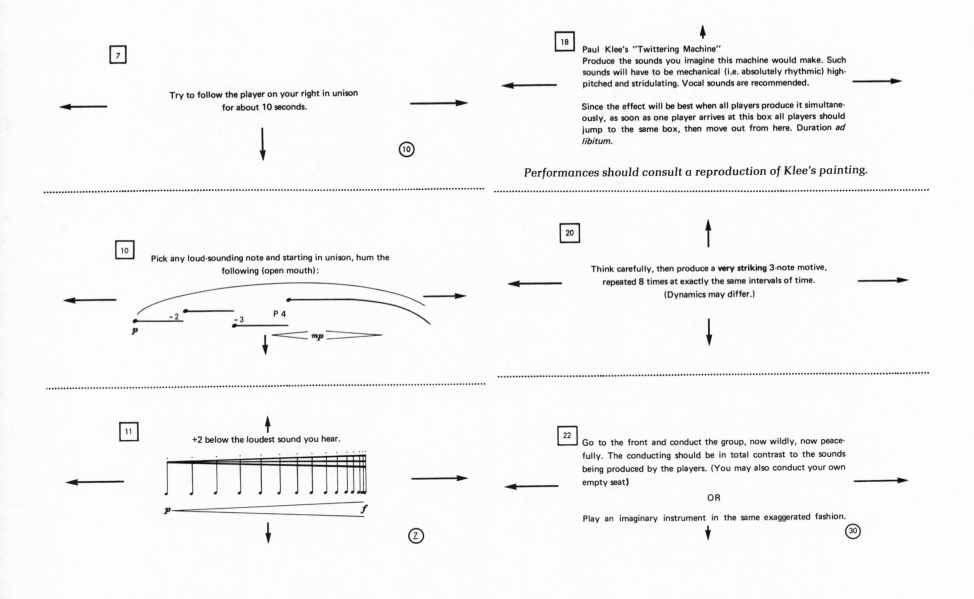

7

Try to follow the player on your right in unison
for about 10 seconds.

18 Paul Klee's "Twittering Machine"
Produce the sounds you imagine this machine would make. Such
sounds will have to be mechanical (i.e. absolutely rhythmic) high-
pitched and stridulating. Vocal sounds are recommended.

Since the effect will be best when all players produce it simultaneously, as soon as one player arrives at this box all players should
jump to the same box, then move out from here. Duration *ad
libitum.*

Performances should consult a reproduction of Klee's painting.

10 Pick any loud-sounding note and starting in unison, hum the
following (open mouth):

- 2   - 3   P 4

p   *mp*

20

Think carefully, then produce a **very striking** 3-note motive,
repeated 8 times at exactly the same intervals of time.
(Dynamics may differ.)

11 +2 below the loudest sound you hear.

p   *f*

22 Go to the front and conduct the group, now wildly, now peace-
fully. The conducting should be in total contrast to the sounds
being produced by the players. (You may also conduct your own
empty seat)

OR

Play an imaginary instrument in the same exaggerated fashion.

23

Play two lines of a hymn or a hymn-like tune.

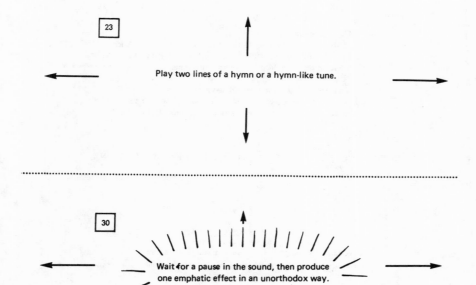

30

Wait for a pause in the sound, then produce
one emphatic effect in an unorthodox way.

31

Any lowish note.

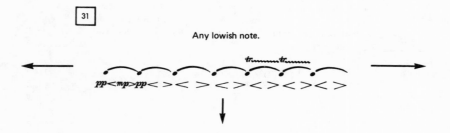

When they wish to end the piece the players lay
down their instruments one by one. Then they
speak the following, very deliberately, one word to
each performer.

THIS

IS

THE

END

AUGUST

19

69

(A low, dominant-seventh chord)

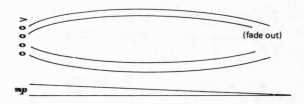

(fade out)

Olson III

Terry Riley

Performance Instructions:
For any number of voices and/or instruments.

Tempo is free, although not too slow, and all note values are equal.

Where a chorus is used, it is best to divide into groups of four to six singers who perform together as one unit. In this way a better balance is achieved and the performers can stagger their breathing.

Octave transpositions may be made, but the contour of each phrase should be as written.

The piece may be performed with each performer or group of singers starting at the beginning, although not necessarily together, and moving to each new phrase without pause after an indeterminate number of repeats. Performers should not attempt to remain together. The piece ends when the last performer has finished the last phrase.

Alternatively, each performer may start anywhere in the piece and proceed in order, as described above, through the phrases, returning to 1 after 30, and stopping just before whatever phrase was used to start.

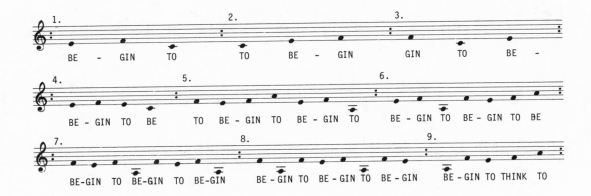

The Great Learning, Paragraph 2

Cornelius Cardew

A Performance

A number of groups are formed each consisting of the following: one drummer, one lead singer and a number of supporting singers. These groups take up positions as widely separated as possible, and each group functions autonomously, as follows: The drummer starts with the rhythm of his choice. When this rhythm is established the lead singer sings through the notes of the first bar as described above, each entry coinciding with the initial stroke or rest of the rhythm. The supporting singers do the same, getting the notes from the leader and entering on each note as soon as possible after the leader. Their function is to support and amplify the leader's voice so that it is not placed under undue strain. The leader must be careful not to sing a new note until all his supporters have finished the preceding one. When all singers are finished with the last note of a bar the leader makes a sign to the drummer who is then free (at his leisure) to select a second rhythm and establish that. He should not leave a gap between the two rhythms. So the cycle proceeds, each drummer going through the 26 rhythms in any order and all singers singing all the phrases in the order given, sticking by their respective leaders.

The final rhythms of all the drummers (i.e., each one's 26th rhythm, probably all different) should be played in the same tempo. To achieve this a position visible to all drummers is pre-selected, and the first drummer to complete his 25th rhythm walks over to this position to play his 26th. Then, as the other drummers reach their final rhythms, they take their tempo from him.

One of the singers may start and stop the proceedings from the same position. Start the piece cleanly: all drummers enter with their chosen rhythms simultaneously on the chosen singer's beat. End it raggedly. (It's probably best if the lead singer of the first drummer to reach his final rhythm does this.) At any time after all drummers have achieved the same tempo or when it appears that this is unlikely to occur, the singer may signal the end, whereupon all drummers complete the rhythmic pattern they are in the middle of and stop. (Don't end on the next downbeat !)

This performance is not the only possible one; circumstances may encourage the devising of others (i.e., all members of the chorus could both drum and sing).

Performance Instructions:

Singing

The notes written as semibreves (whole notes) are sung very strongly and held for the length of one very long breath. The words written vertically over a note are distributed freely along that one very long breath. Sing these notes in the written order making shorter pauses between notes and longer pauses at barlines. The text is sung through five times. If a note is out of range transpose it up or down an octave. The commencement of each sung note should coincide with the initial stroke or rest of the accompanying rhythm.

Drumming

Each drum rhythm is repeated over and over like a tape loop for the duration of one bar of the vocal part. The 26 rhythms fall into 11 groups: 2 pentads, 1 tetrad, 4 pairs and 4 uniques. The words in front of the rhythms are a mnemonic based on this grouping. Like the vocal phrases, the drum rhythms are to be played strong and energetic throughout. Unlike the vocal phrases, they may be played in any order, and the selection of a tempo for each one is up to the individual drummers. The rhythms should be memorized.

Night Speech
Excerpts

Nicolas Roussakis

INSTRUMENTS

Player A

1. Pail of water and rubber hose (approx. 2 ft. long) *
2. Sandpaper (fine) and block of wood.
3. Large sheet of paper (thin)
4. High Shell Wind-Chimes
5. Very High Brass Wind-Chimes
6. High Bamboo Wind-Chimes
7. High Gong
   a. soft mallet
   b. metal object

* Players A and B may share one pail of water.

Player B

1. Pail of water and rubber hose (approx. 2 ft. long) *
2. Sandpaper (coarse) and block of wood
3. Large sheet of paper (thick)
4. Low Shell Wind-Chimes
5. High Brass Wind-Chimes
6. Low Bamboo Wind-Chimes
7. Low Gong
   a. soft mallet
   b. wood object

NOTES

1. The chorus is voiceless between MM. 3–61 and MM. 93–End; it is voiced only from M. 63 to M. 91.
2. Each member of the chorus should be equipped with a harmonica or a circular chromatic pitch pipe; if harmonicas are used, they

TABLE OF SOUNDS TO BE PRODUCED BY THE CHORUS **

	Non-voiced		Voiced
IPA symbol	Example of a word in which the sound occurs	IPA symbol	Example of a word in which the sound occurs
u *	t<u>oo</u>l [tul]	j	<u>y</u>et [jɛt]
o *	n<u>o</u>tation [noˈteɪʃən]	3	ca<u>s</u>ual [ˈkæʒʊəl]
a *	f<u>a</u>ther [ˈfaːðɚ]	z	<u>z</u>est [zɛst]
e *	v<u>a</u>cation [veˈkeɪʃən]	ð	<u>th</u>is [ðɪs]
i *	s<u>ee</u>d [sid]	v	<u>v</u>ain [veɪn]
ç	German: ni<u>ch</u>t [nɪçt]	b	<u>b</u>e [bi]
ʃ	<u>sh</u>e [ʃi]	d	<u>d</u>o [du]
s	<u>s</u>ee [si]	g	<u>g</u>et [gɛt]
θ	<u>th</u>ing [θiŋ]		
f	<u>f</u>ace [feɪs]		
p	<u>p</u>eel [pil]		
t	<u>t</u>ea [ti]		
k	<u>k</u>ing [kɪŋ]		

* Non-voiced in <u>Night Speech</u>!

** The symbols used are those of the International Phonetic Alphabet [IPA].

<u>NOTES</u> [continued]

2. [cont.] should be in as many different keys as possible, so as to produce an evenly balanced tone-cluster.

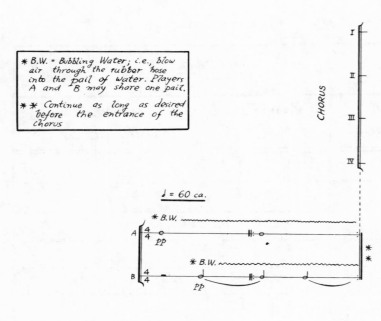

✻ B.W. = *Bubbling Water*; i.e., *blow air through the rubber hose into the pail of water. Players A and B may share one pail.*

✻✻ *Continue as long as desired before the entrance of the chorus*

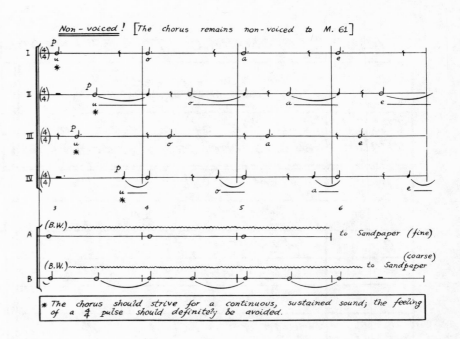

Non-voiced! [The chorus remains non-voiced to M. 61]

✻ *The chorus should strive for a continuous, sustained sound; the feeling of a 4/4 pulse should definitely be avoided.*

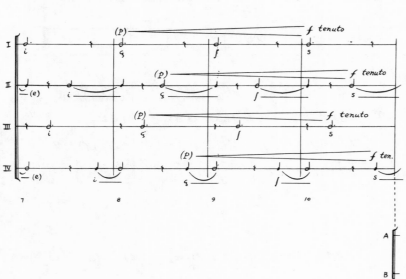

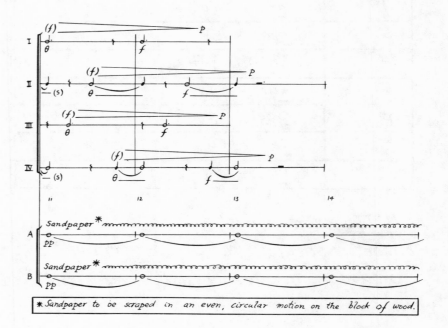

✻ *Sandpaper to be scraped in an even, circular motion on the block of wood.*

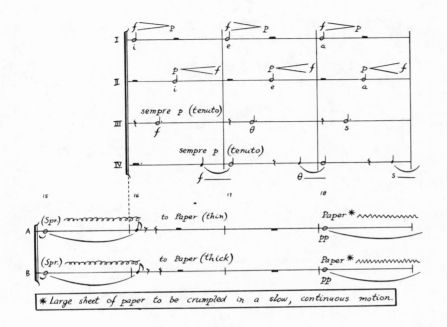

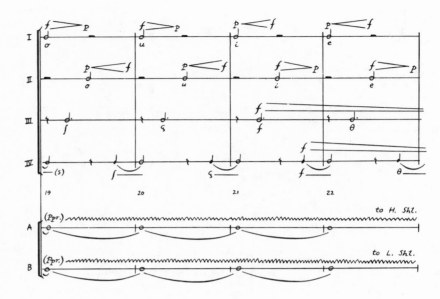

✱ *Large sheet of paper to be crumpled in a slow, continuous motion.*

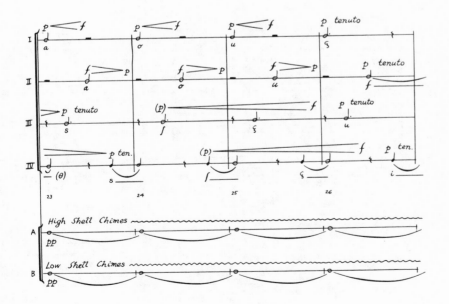

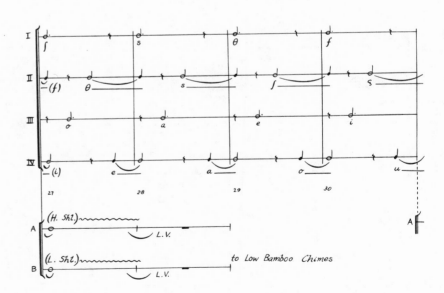

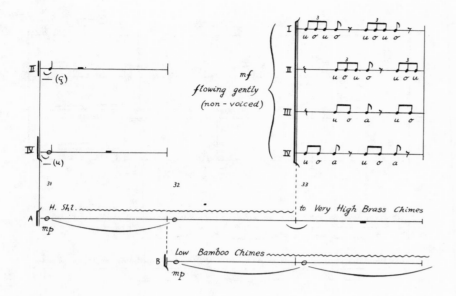

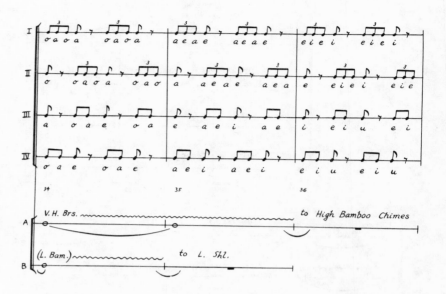

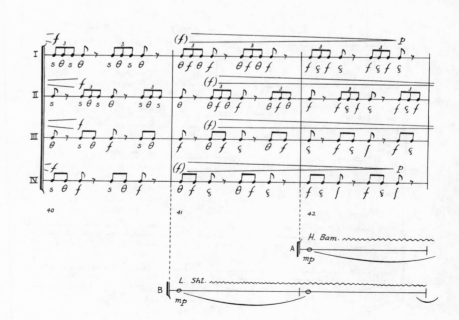

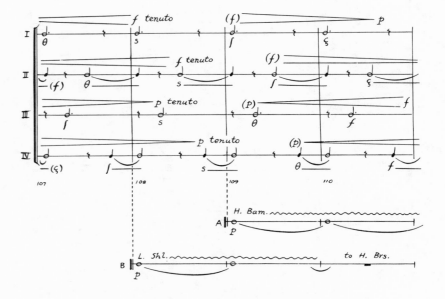

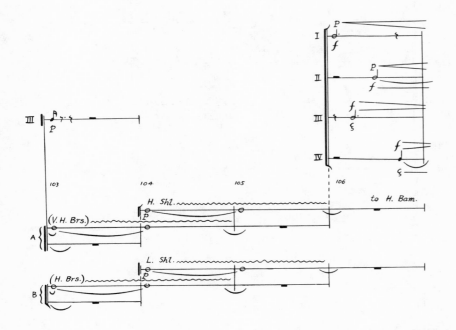

238

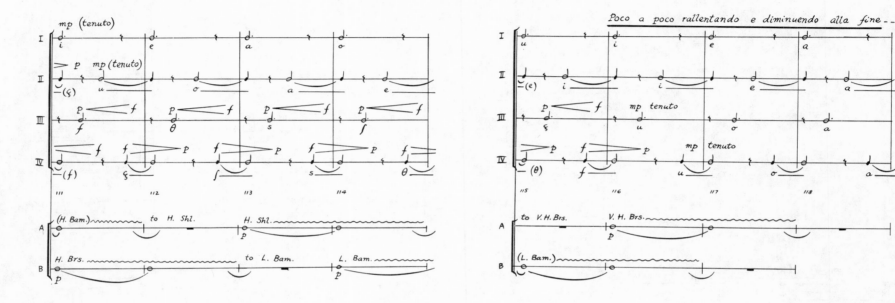

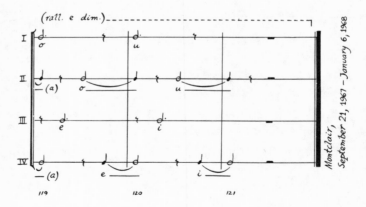

Plastic Containers

Carmine Pepe

Basic Symbols

The performer is urged to use his imagination in interpreting individual and combined symbols, keeping in mind that (breathing) sound increases in tension and volume with line weight, and rises and falls with line direction . . . The shape, weight and direction of the symbols should essentially create a sound feeling. The sight-sign-sound relationship should not be thought of as three separate acts, but one.

Breathing Symbols

↑ = inhale

↓ = exhale

∞ = nose

○ = mouth

— = a popping of the lips

↙ = a short, abruptly terminated pronunciation

Foundation and Control Symbols

——————— (thin line) = a light, thin breath

▬▬▬ (heavy line or band) = a heavy, full, somewhat tense breath

extremely tense, full breath

(expanding line or band) = a breath increasing in tension and volume

All breathing, whether constant, rising, or falling, is understood to commence on a median pitch, unless otherwise indicated.

= a thin light breath rising in pitch but not increasing in volume.

= a thin light breath increasing smoothly in volume and tension and dropping in pitch.

= a thin light breath increasing in volume and tension and rising in pitch to an even plateau with the two portions of the continuous sound sharply articulated.

 = an even and constant breath (according to the above) increasing in speed and oscillating in pitch, attained through an accelerating quivering of the chin.

 = (group of small dots) stopping the breath quickly and repeatedly with the hand upon the hose or mouth as indicated.

 = a quick opening and closing of the mouth without a popping of the lips, with the size of the dot indicating the aperture of the mouth

Examples

↑○ = inhale with mouth

○↓ = exhale with mouth

↑∞ = inhale with nose

∞↓ = exhale with nose

↑○— = inhale with mouth and with popping of lips

—○↓ = exhale with mouth and with popping of lips

General Description of Score

Each page of the score is divided into an upper and lower portion, showing respectively the voice and instrumental parts.

Between these parts is located a time graph, which approximates a natural breathing rhythm. This is not intended as an absolute measure of time, but rather as a relative, human measure of time flow and to form a "gestalt" over longer rhythmic units.

The entire score falls into four divisions:

First: a movement, pp. 1-3, employing normal breathing in unison, which in its final portion leaves this unison and enters into rhythmic voice groupings, rising and falling according to the positioning of the appropriate symbols in flexible high, median, and low pitch areas;

Second: a movement involving a shaping of the breath in units of greater duration as indicated by the extension, weight, and the rise and fall of lines (and other symbols);

Third: a movement interpreting William Blake's words: "Do what you will, this world's a fiction and is made up of contradiction," and employing the same breathing symbols. Each letter is pronounced continuously in the context of the word, and each of its sounds integrated into the whole;

Fourth: a final movement turning upon the articulation of the word: *STOP*, in which each sound is given full value: "s" is produced with the tip of the tongue touching the area just back of the front teeth with the air issuing laterally; "t" is produced with the tongue in a similar position a little further back with the air escaping suddenly; "o" is the sound between the "a" in *father*, and the "o" in *cope*; and the final "p" sound is the unvoiced, bilabial plosive, pronounced powerfully just short of becoming a "b".

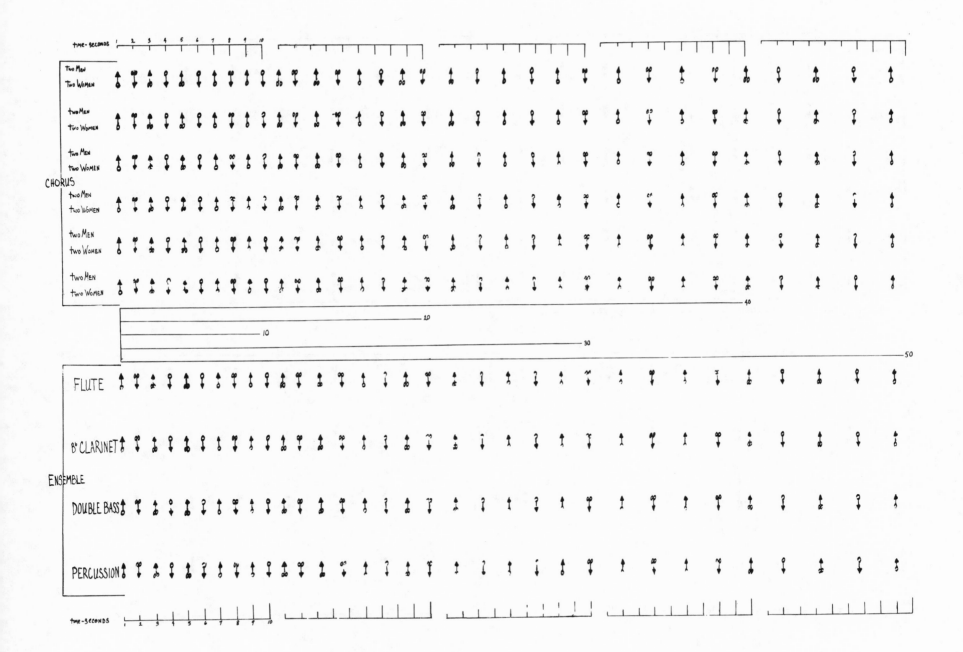

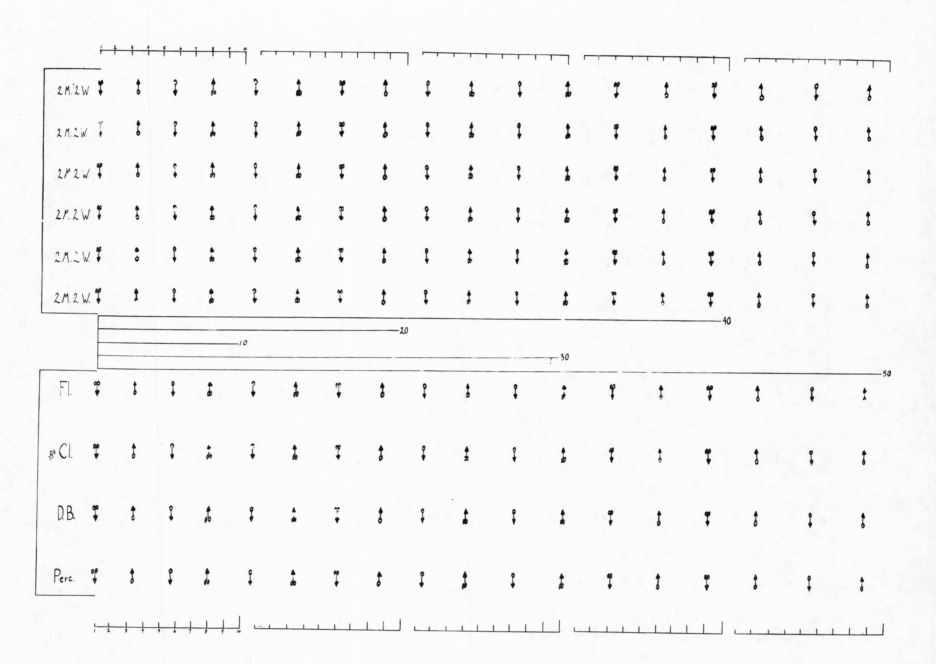

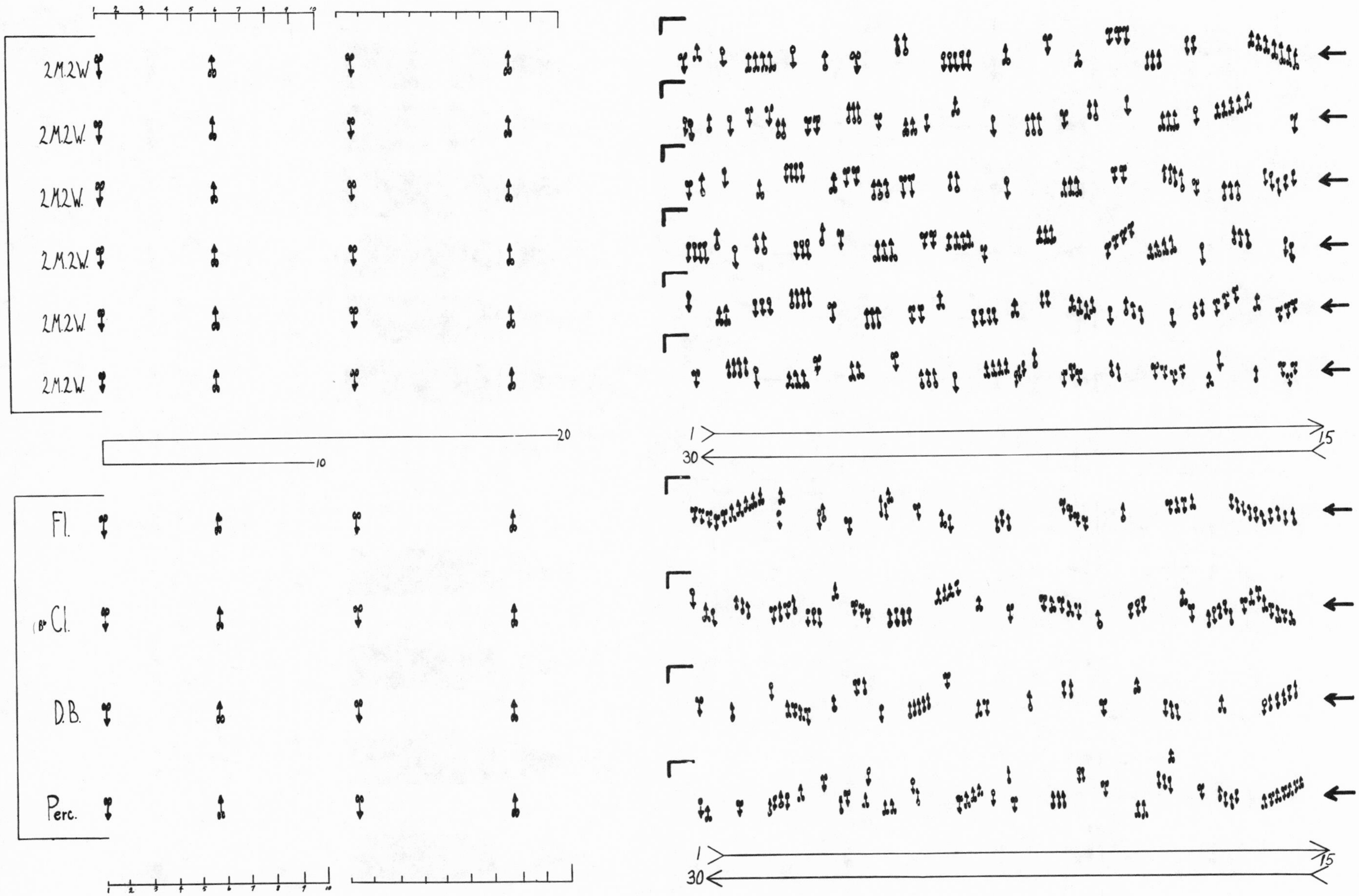
2M.2W.
2M.2W.
2M.2W.
2M.2W.
2M.2W.
2M.2W.
20
10
1
15
30
Fl.
(B♭) Cl.
D.B.
Perc.
1
15
30

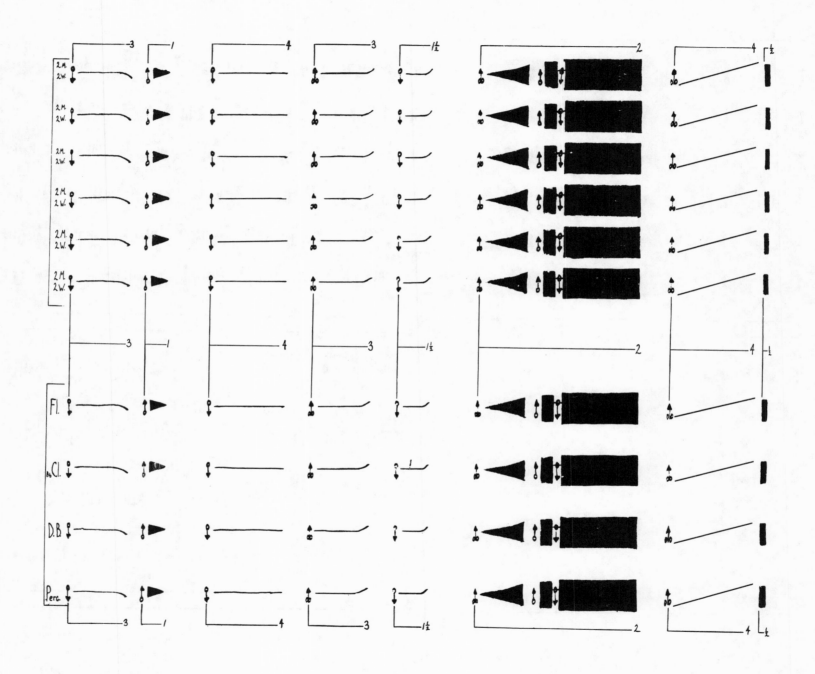

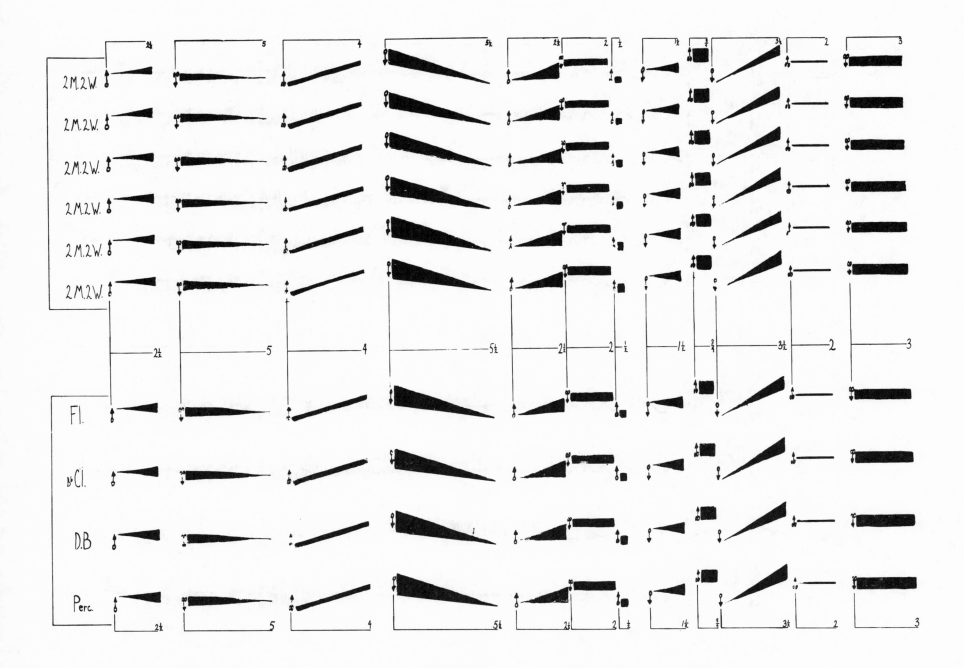

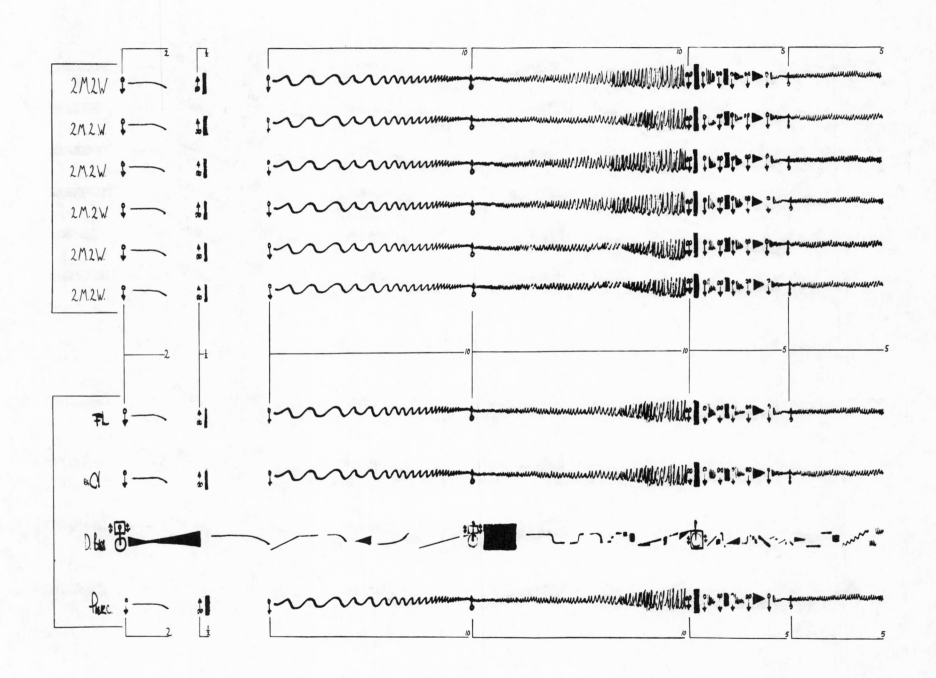

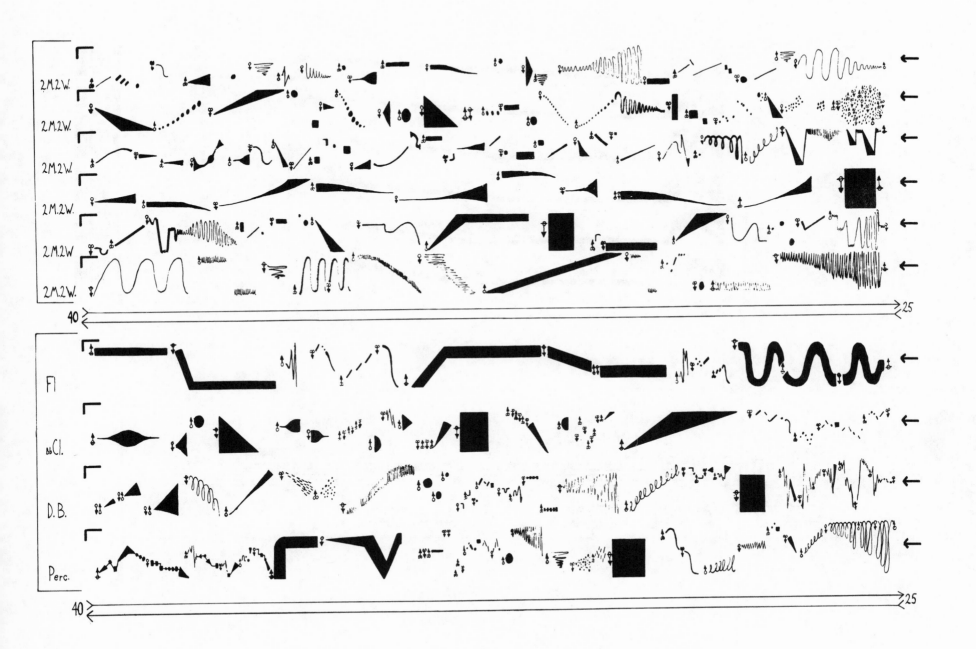

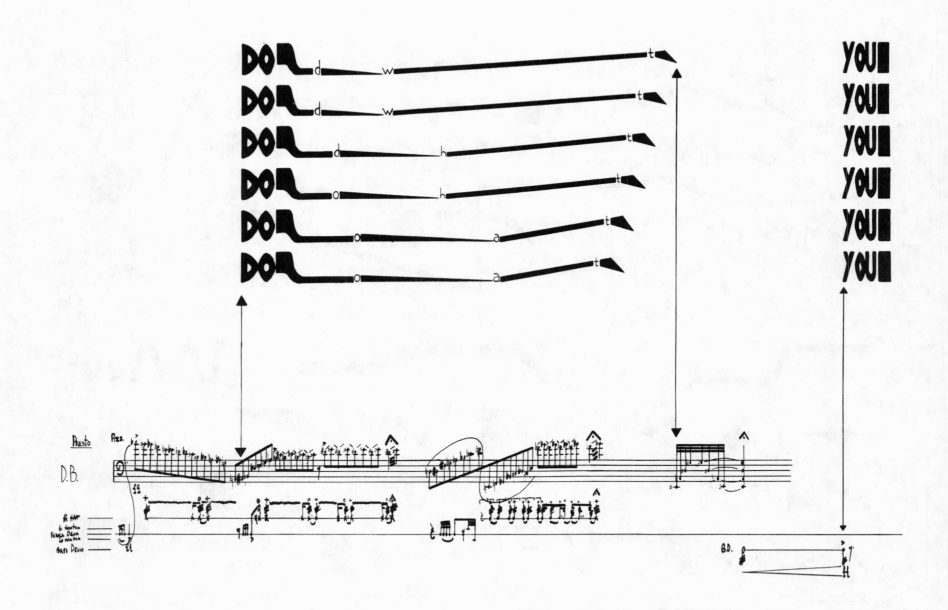

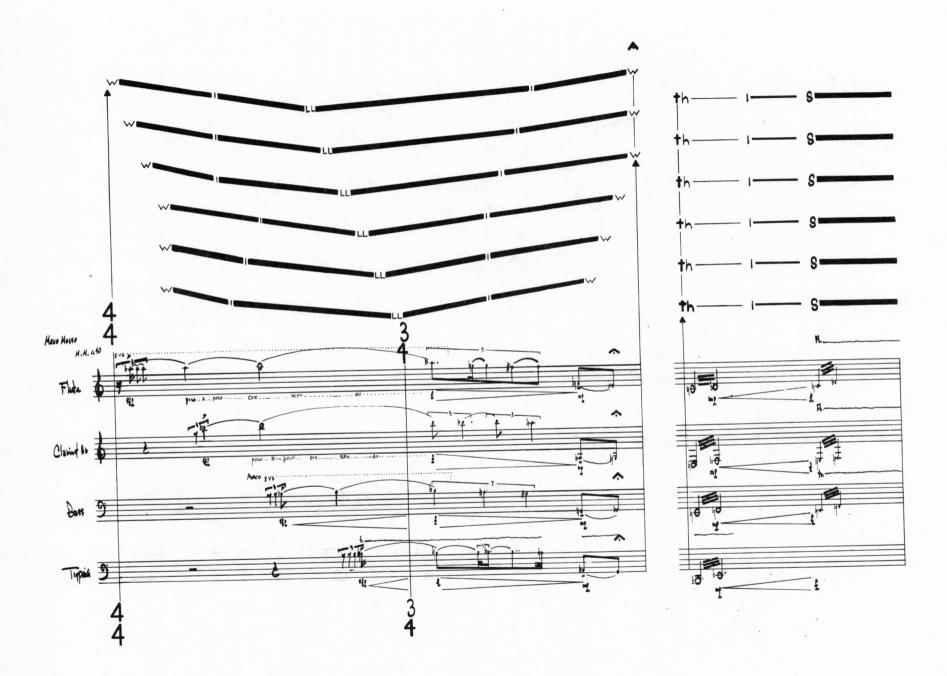

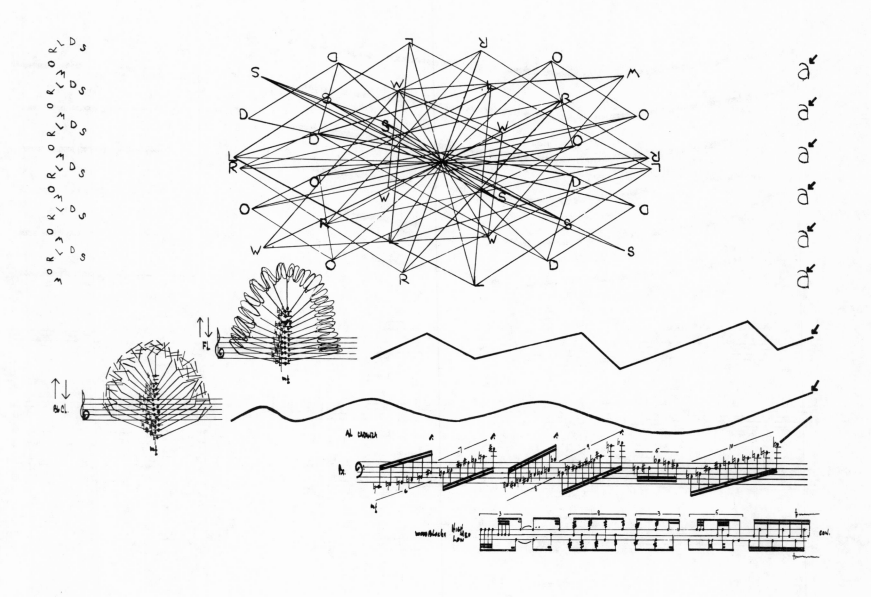

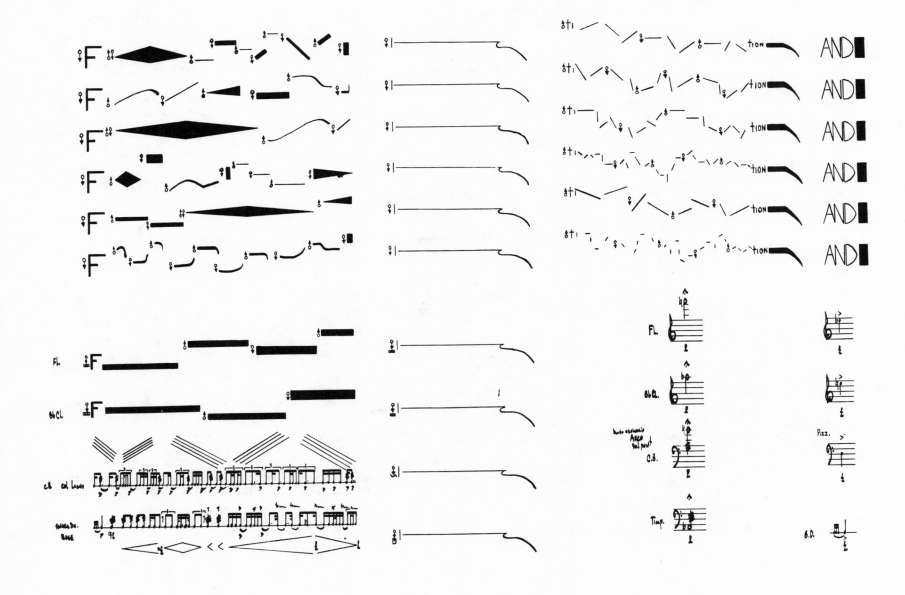

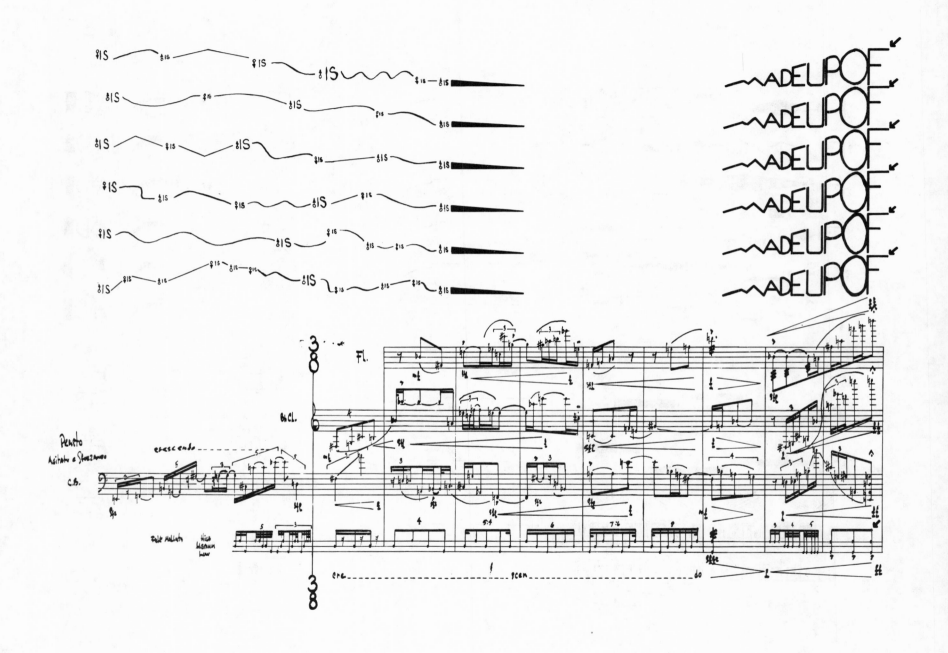

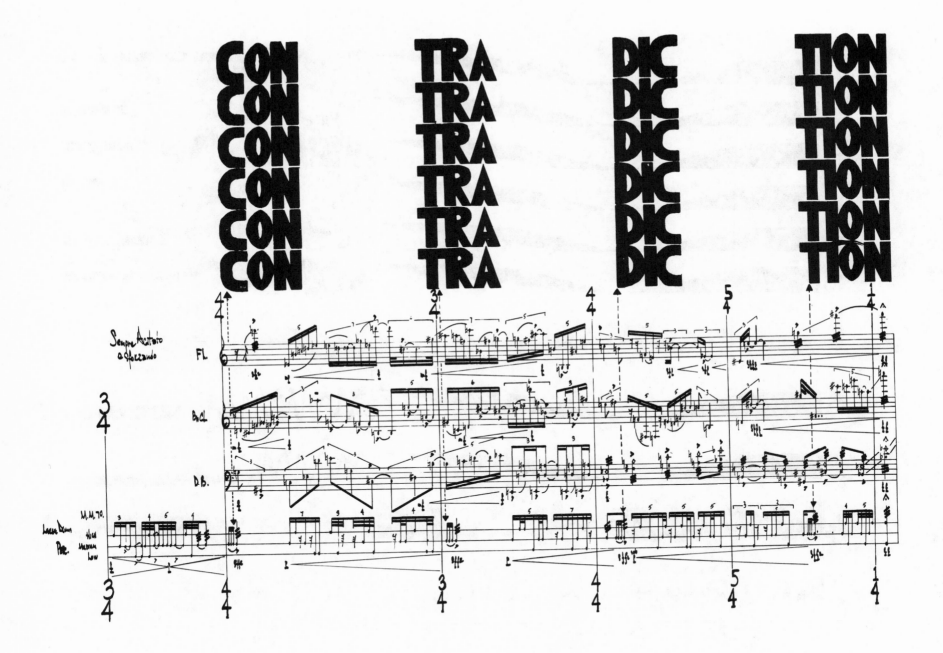

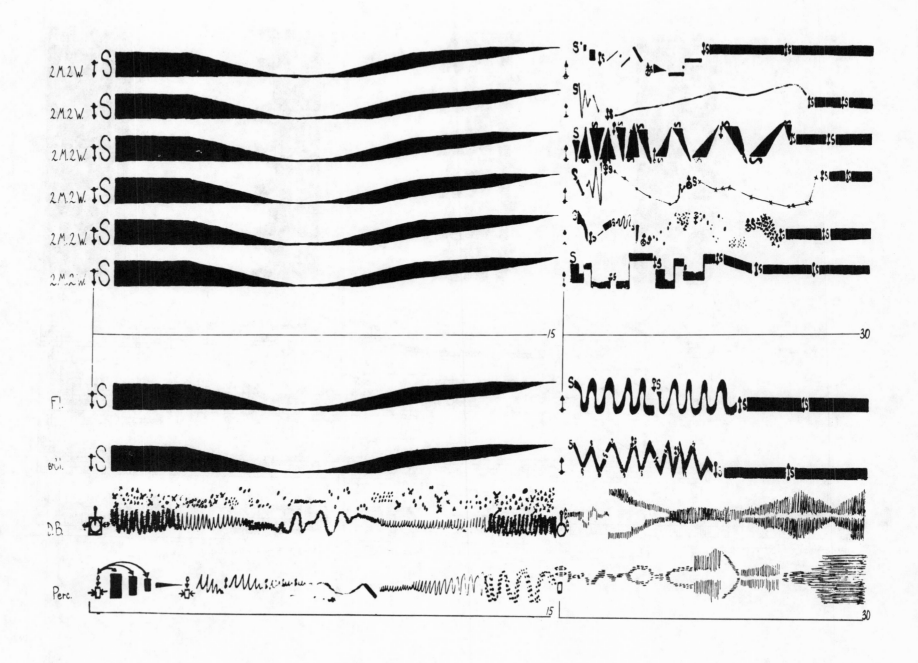

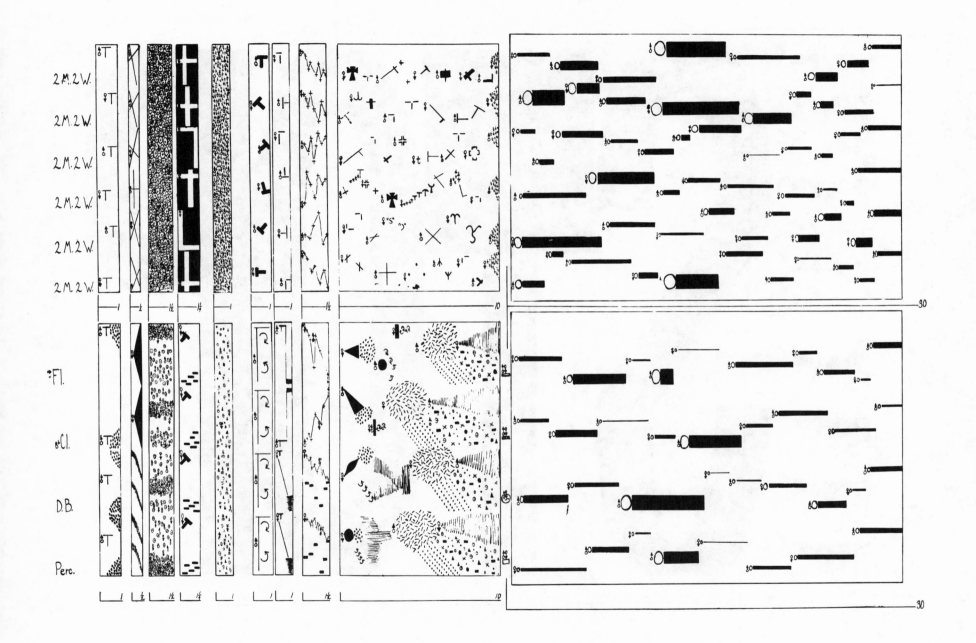

Time Goes By
for any voices and instruments

Karl H. Berger

The above melody is sung by the voices over and over.

Playing the scale of the song from F downwards, as bass and chord root, use one note per bar of the song and continue as the song repeats. Note that, while there are seven bars to the song, there are ten bass notes so that on each repeat of the song there is a different bas and cord.

After a number of repeats introduce also improvisations.

Bass + Chords

Resulting combination:

The Smile That You Send Out
for any voices and instruments

Karl H. Berger

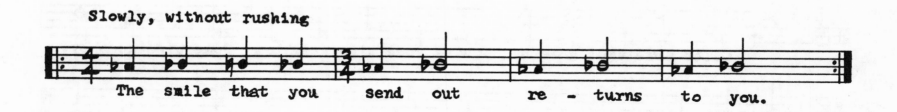

1. Sing or play in treble clef.
2. Add the version using bass clef.
3. Keep repeating the bass clef version while the treble part proceeds from A. to H.

4. Repeat full cycle three times:

5. Repeat 3. (A to H) introducing solo improvisations.

6. Repeat 3, 4 and/or 5 ad lib. introducing transportations.

Fairy Song
from
Music for "A Midsummer Night's Dream"
For Soprano and Tenor Soli and Mixed Chorus (SATB)
with Guitar*, Double Bass or Bass Guitar, and Percussion.

Richard Peaslee
Text by William Shakespeare

* A zither or autoharp tuned to the same basic chord will sound better than a guitar.
** Finger Cymbals, Gong, Tabla or Bongos, Serrated Gourd [at least two players – may be chorus members].

Fine

Repeat mm. 18-29

Tom Thumb

Stephen Mayer

for Tui St. George Tucker

Tom Thumb is an improvisatory work in ABA form. It should be approached with freedom:

- instrumentation can be determined by the resources available.
- improvisations by instrumentalists and vocalists are possible.

Further suggestions are noted below by rehearsal letter.

A. Vamp any number of bars. Flute or any instruments in the range can be used.
B. The same.
C. Duration and interpretation up to the Tenor.
D. Texture and dynamic changes will evolve from the entrances.
E. Simile C.
F. At the end a quick Molto Dim. to Letter G.
G. Duration approximate.
x. Last bar cue (finger raised to Piano and cut Chorus).
H. May be very short, either two or a few voices.
I. African Drums &/or Bongos ad libitum can be added to the Percussion part which is indicated. This is a rythmic vamp and therefore, the number of bars is variable.
K. Horns and Bassoons double Piano.
L. Is repeated 4 times. Trumpets may double voices.
M. The fourth time, use this ending.
N. Begin the Ostinato with Flutes.
O. As before.
P. This Chorus should be the largest.
Q. As before.
R. This Chorus can be very small, featuring a few of the best singers or a solo Chorus member.
S. As before.
T. Soloist and Chorus together – Morendo.
x. As before: last bar cue to Piano; let Chorus die out to the last voices.

At all choral entrances, instruments, e.g. horns, basoons and trombones on low F♯ and A, oboe and trumpet on F♯ and A above middle C, baritone horn below middle C, may augment the choral texture.

If a large chorus is used, it should be divided into several groups widely spaced in the hall.

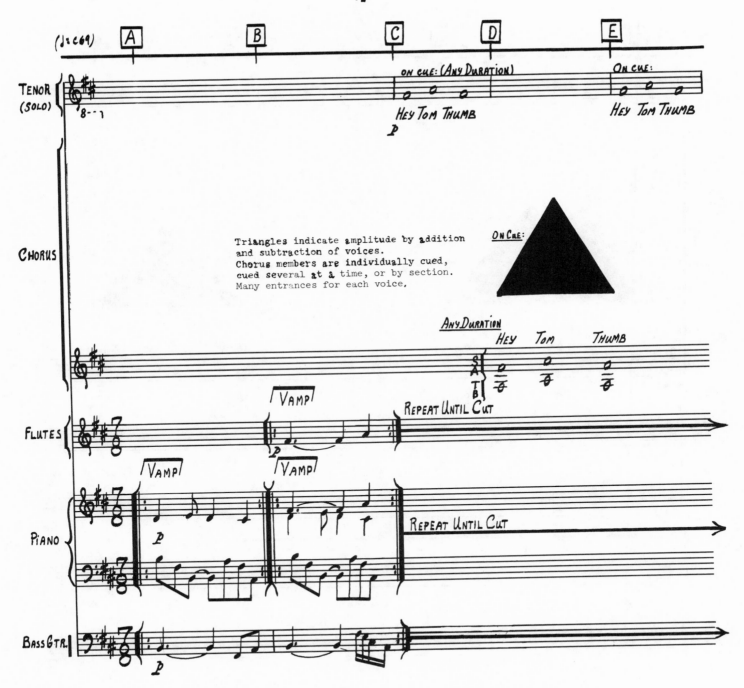

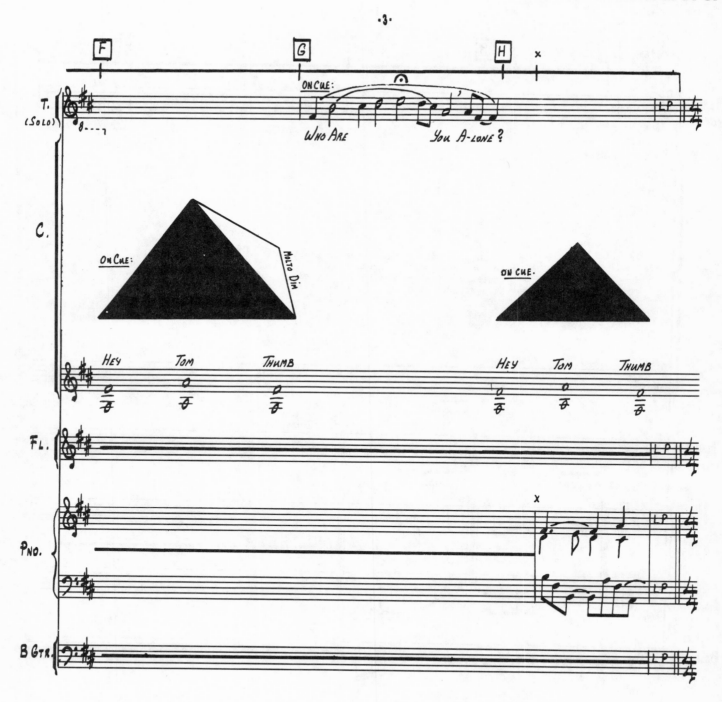

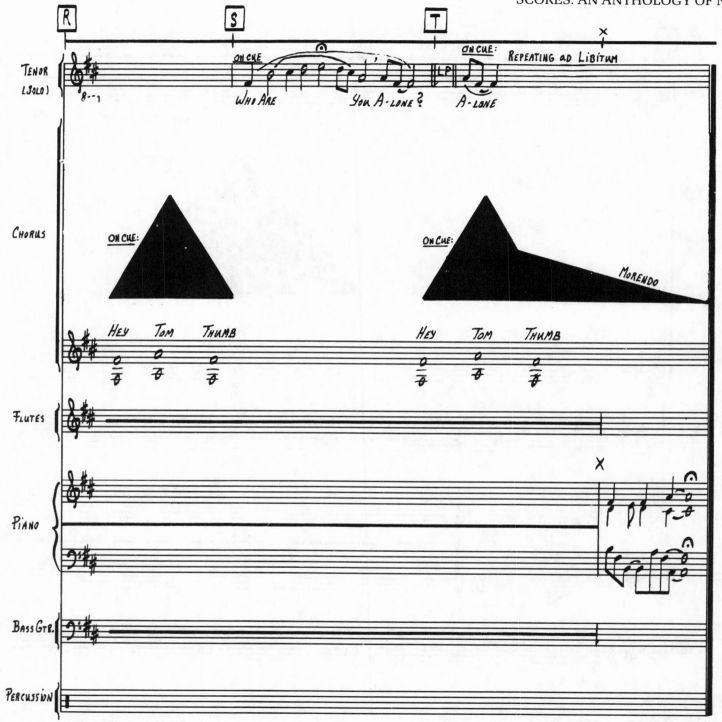

Pavali
to Carol

D.B. Rama

(1)

Directions =

☐ the melody only is notated fully, both in Indian and Western notation (the Western notation is to be considered loosely & imprecise or approximate). melody may be performed by any number of instruments (or one) doubled in any octaves. though notated in "F" (tonic) both melody and drone may be transposed to any pitch (or tonic). if voice is used, sing on "ah." In veena use "Ma sruti."

☐ Indian notation is similar to solfa, the syllables standing for scale steps 1-7 (not for fixed pitches) as follows = 1) s = sa, 2) r = rī, 3) g = ga, 4) m = ma, 5) p = pa, 6) d = da, 7) n = nī.

☐ Raga is the expressive mode and includes its scale (and characteristic musical phrases). Pavali is a ragamalika ("garland of ragas") = 1 + 1' Senjuruti raga, 2 + 2' Neelambari raga, 3 + 3' Sindhubhairavi raga, and 4 Hamsanandi raga.

☐ Tala is a time cycle. two South Indian talas are here combined (Adi tala = 4 + 2 + 2 = 8 beats in slow tempo; and Khanda Chapu tala = 2 + 3 = 5 beats in fast doubletime). In Pavali the bells and finger cymbals mark the cycles =

(2)

☐ a drone should be used (tambura, harmonium, voices, whatever) tuned to tonic, fifth, & upper octave (sa-pa-sā).

☐ drums (mridangam, tabla, or similar in sound or style) should be used.

☐ begin as shown (drone - cymbals/bells - drums - melody) or simultaneously or invent a way. end similarly.

☐ structure the sections of the melody as shown here, or invent other arrangements. 2 possibilities =

(A) 1 - 1 - 1' - 1' ▭ 2 - 2 - 2' - 2' ▭ 1 or 1' ▭ 3 - 3 - 3' - 3' ▭ 2' ▭ 1' ▭ 4 - 4 ▭ 3' ▭ 2' ▭ 1' ‖ (end)

(B) 1 - 1 - 1' - 1' ▭ 2 - 2 - 2' - 2' ▭ 1 or 1' ▭ 3 - 3 - 3' - 3' ▭ 1 ▭ 4 - 4 ▭ 1' ▭ 2' ▭ 1 ‖ (end)

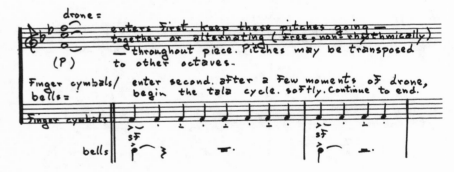

(4)

(5)   (6)

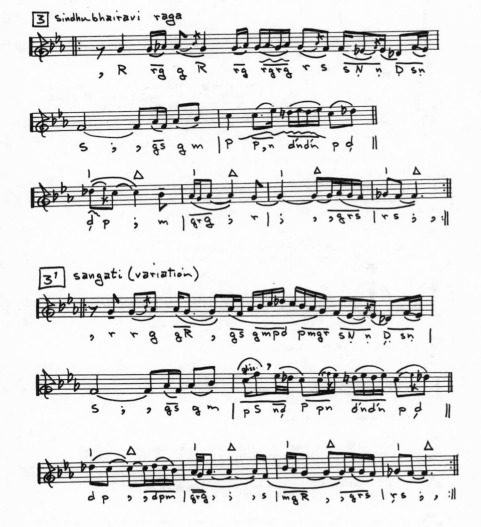

□ a tape recording of <u>Pavali</u> on cassette is available
to aid in performance. For information write:

> David Reck
> Music Department
> Amherst College
> Amherst, Mass.
> USA 01002

□ the original performance was by David Reck, veena;
Douglas Knight, mridangam; Lauren Paul, thalam;
Carol Reck, tambura. Quebec, Spring, 1976.

Here and There

Stuart Smith

GENERAL DIRECTIONS

HERE AND THERE is not a collage. It is not a static object. It is a process to unify the energies around us --- an exploration through inner-outer space. This piece is a way of being. It was composed as a process in which the players receive and transform themselves, others, and the environment, into a unified landscape.

HERE AND THERE must be played at night for proper short wave sounds.

The length of the piece is 10 to 30 minutes. Each box of the charts is played 1/10' to 15". An empty box is a mandatory rest of 1/10" to 15".

The symbols indicate the parameters of either one sound or the components of a musical event. For example, ↑ indicates one high sound or a phrase of high sounds.

Vocal sounds, such as whispering, laughing, whistling, or singing, may be used by all the players at their own discretion.

When parameters are given, such as register or duration, then all the remaining parameters are improvised, and should be made to fit the musical situation.

The players must begin at one of the four corner boxes of the charts and proceed in one of the following systems:

    a. In horizontal rows across the chart.
    b. In horizontal rows across the chart and back.
    c. In vertical rows up or down the chart.
    d. In vertical rows up and down the chart.

For example, if the upper left box is chosen, the player has the following four choices:

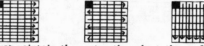

The player must maintain the system throughout the performance.

PIANO

Most of the part should be played on the piano interior with a wide assortment of mallets. The piano part contains mostly imitative events and therefore the part serves as a unifier. Special care should be taken to make all the sounds blend.

SHORT WAVE RADIO

Treat the radio as a musical instrument. The ensemble should balance with the volume capabilities of the radio. Tuning the radio between chart boxes is considered part of the piece, so it should be done musically.

ANY MELODY INSTRUMENT OR VOCALIST

As well as standard sounds, the instrumentalist should use many "non-traditional" sounds in realizing the score, i.e. multiphonics, tapping, key clicks, singing through the instrument, etc. The player should take care to blend with the other instruments.

HERE AND THERE, VERSION II

A radio telescope and short wave radio play the short wave part.

VERSION IIa.

The performance with a radio telescope is immediately broadcast to other groups performing the piece. The broadcast performance is then used as the short wave radio part.

VERSION III

A performance of HERE AND THERE is translated into light energy in direct analog to the pattern of sound energy and broadcast into deep space.

EXPLANATION OF SYMBOLS

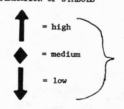

= high

= medium

= low

These symbols apply to register and/or dynamics.

L = long

M = medium

S = short

These symbols apply to the duration of one sound or of notes or sounds within a musical phrase. They do not apply to the length of the realization of the box, but to the components of the event.

= imitate any sound or event that you hear, after you hear it.

= imitate or blend with an event as it happens.

 or = imitate or blend with an event after you hear it, higher or lower (depending on the direction of the arrow.)

 or = imitate or blend with an event as it happens, higher or lower (depending on the direction of the arrow.)

= imitate an event in diminution.

= imitate an event in augmentation.

= all parameters are free.

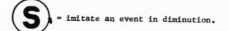 = repeat an event or sound from 8" to 15". In the case of ANY MELODY INSTRUMENT, play one of the melodies 1 - 7. Repeat it, continually transforming it in some way.

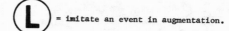 = "real sound events" (applies only to short wave radio) Examples --- music, people talking, news, etc.

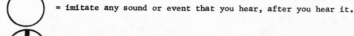 = applies only to ANY MELODY INSTRUMENT. The numbers refer to melodies 1 - 7. The performer may play any melody listed under the appropriate number. Rests may be inserted freely to fragment the melodies. When you reach a box containing two symbols, choose to play either symbol. However, on two out of three such occasions, choose the number.

PIANO

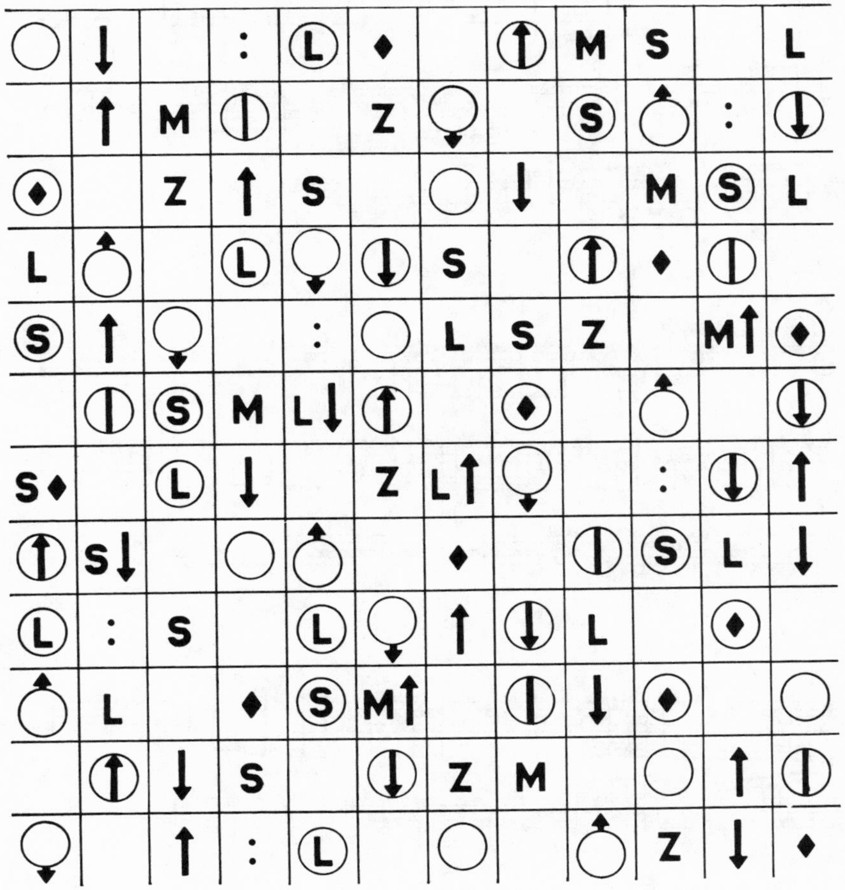

SHORT WAVE RADIO

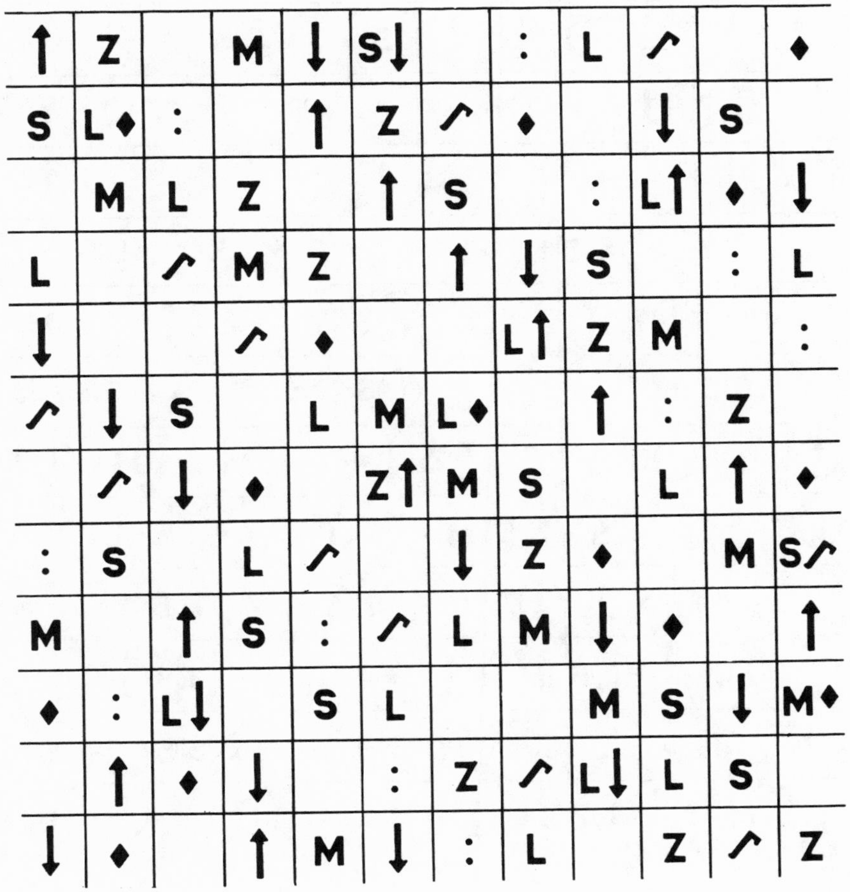

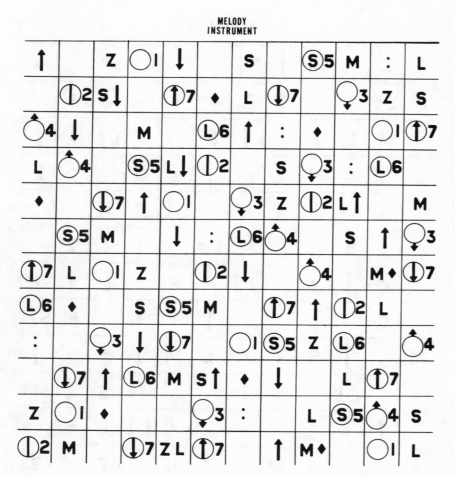

MELODY
INSTRUMENT

MELODIES

4.

5.

6.

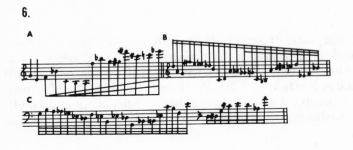

7.

towards the capacity of a room
for metal instruments of percussion
with amplification, tape sources and lights.

david jones

"towards the capacity of a room" is a companion piece to and a more intimate version of "towards the capacity of an auditorium". performance is limited to halls seating less than 250 people, or if within the 300 range still retain an intimate chamber music type of atmosphere and accoustic—for halls above this size the score and conditions for "towards the capacity of an auditorium" must be substituted.

from two separate stations within the performance space, two players create long durational sound events exploiting the beat and pulse potentialities of sound instruments, predominately gongs and cymbals together with a small selection of related instruments with long decay; each player having from two to four cymbals of various diameters together with two or more gongs one of which is suspended and portable for performance within the hall or room.

gong players concentrate on the possibilities obtainable from the rim of the instrument where pulses are more evident, try to avoid the ear detecting the moment of attack, the total area of the instrument is also to be used to exploit vibration ratios; cymbal players concentrate on long rolls exploiting beats, vibration ratios, etc., extended crescendi of a single intensity; freely alternate instruments and entries as the sound situation develops: from the opening of the piece slowly evolve a sound continium at low intensity phrasing in and out in sympathy with the other player, progress towards a changing of sound events in which players and listener share a new sense experiences in an evolving situation of ritual sonic exploration.

at a selected point in time one player using glockenspeil or vibraphone introduces a static chordal event of repetative yet evolving material—this can if the situation suggests be even of a banal nature—eventually this event evolves into silence and new constructive areas—the other player does not react to this situation; pitched percussion (excluding gongs and cymbals) must be used with discretion and only to contribute to an ensemble situation of timbres, never as melodic decoration—the total situation alone will indicate the necessity for pitch material.

move towards a single section of high intensity which may last any duration, after exploiting possibilities end the performance abruptly. during earlier mobile sections within the performance space share the sound experience with the audience—communicate an atmosphere of peace and togetherness through the sharing of new sonic sound experiences.

pre-recorded material should be used during the performance or live recorded material through time delay systems—distribute sound systems where applicable to the architectural accoustic. lights reduced to semi-darkness using amber, green, violet and during the final section of the performance slowly introduce purple to full lighting.

8 Music/Theater/Dance Pieces

This final selection reflects an increasingly strong trend in new music toward pieces that combine music with the other performing arts, particularly theater and dance. All the pieces here use theatrical or visual elements as very important aspects of performance. Eric Salzman's "Notes on Music Theater" and his two compositions are very interesting and relevant to the other works in this chapter. *Phrase* is a particularly good exercise for less experienced performers, since it integrates sound and movement, using one to draw out the other directly and simply. *Signalling* presents a more complex situation; it should be very exciting for those with a little more experience. (It should be remembered that Kirk Nurock's "Natural Sound" exercises from Chapter 2 and others developed by dance and theater people are very useful—really, essential—to all of the work in this section.)

While not theater in the usual sense, Trevor Wishart's *Bicycle Music* does present a particularly attractive and very simple performing piece for people riding through a city or town. Barney Childs's *The Roachville Project* and David Cope's *Dragoon* are more directly theatrical pieces that have a humorous quality and are also very easy to organize and perform. The works by Elliott Schwartz and Larry Austin are large-scale theater pieces involving quite a range of activities and use of space. Alison Knowles's *Proposition IV (Squid)* is similar to J. George Cisneros's *Continental Drift* in that performers form themselves into groups and then arrange their activities. The works by Laura Dean, Randolph Coleman, Phil Winsor, and Daniel Lentz all involve movement or dance of various sorts. Dean's *Jumping Dance* is, strictly speaking, a dance rather than musical piece, but is one in which the dancers create pulse patterns through their jumping and their voices. It is very attractive visually. Winsor's *Gloria Patri* is for a solo dancer and several percussionists, along with slides and an electronic tape, (both made by the performers). Coleman's *Format 5,* is an abstract graphic score interpreted by dancers and musicians. A very specific time chart—but no description of actual content—is used. Lentz's *North American Eclipse* is a beautiful setting of a text based on American Indian ritual; it is for moving singers and instrumentalists. Finally, Pauline Oliveros's *Bonn Feier* and *Aeolian Partitions* are both extraordinary extensions of the normal parameters of the performing arts by this most imaginative composer.

Finally, it is interesting and exciting to think about an entire concert or other performance event as a "theater" piece in which all of the individual pieces themselves as well as the placement, transitions, movement, costume, and character of the performers, staging, lighting, etc. are treated as one integrated piece. In this way many of the pieces in this book can become theater pieces or parts of larger scale theater pieces.

Notes on Music Theatre by Eric Salzman

A music-theater ensemble differs from contemporary dance and theater groups in several ways. Dance and theater companies are made up of people who essentially do the same thing; a music-theater ensemble is, by contrast, a heterogeneous group made up of specialists. One of the first problems in creating an ensemble is to discover common ground. The human body and voice are the essential common denominators and the connections between the two the starting point for the work. Everyone must vocalize and everyone must move; only later are instruments and language introduced.

Using vocal sound as a springboard gives the work a very special character. Vocalization is a faculty that lies very close to the seat of the emotions. Without the usual conventional releasers, opening one's mouth to make a sound can be a highly charged experience and a source of energy which can propel the performer into movement. Establishing the need to move through the direct physicalization of sound is an important way of attacking the problem of movement in music-theater. This kind of movement, which has little to do with dance, is closer to a kind of stylized, rhythmicized theater movement-stylized because the movement itself is as much a metaphoric language as the sound that comes with it. Movement does not follow the rhythmic dynamic of the music but is, ideally, entirely of a piece with it-sound and movement as a single, organic whole.

At this early stage, most of the work is based on establishing continua between polar extremes: breathing to vocalization, vowels to consonants, feeling to thinking, singing to physical rhythms, language to music, voices to instruments, individual expression to group awareness; in short, ensemble study based on connections and continuity. Later the emphasis shifts to the interaction between individuals based on dialectical principles of conflict. This provides a bridge between exercises (largely group work), improvisations (individual interaction), and set pieces.

Phrase explores the connections between individuality and invention on the one hand and a sense of ensemble on the other. It poses the problem of group work in the most difficult manner, defining individuality in terms of invention and isolation and forcing the performers to work through those conditions to reach each other. It also studies the relationship between sound and physical movement and makes the performer define his or her individuality through a highly focused invention. The phrase becomes a metaphor for one's sense of oneself; one's individuality must, for the moment, flow through a simple, repeated sound-and-movement endowing it with some kind of richness and assurance. Often, the invention will at first seem foolish, absurd, and unsustainable; it is essential to push past this and keep working towards a complete identification with one's idea. At that point, one begins to relate to other people. The surer one is with one's own phrase, the easier it is to relate to what other people are doing—as in life itself. This is first of all an essentially musical task. No matter how great one's isolation, it is always possible to connect by listening. The first area of relationship will be an awareness of a series of overlapping rhythmic cycles. Other relationships come later: interaction of physical rhythms, of meaning, of tones, of actions, and even of personalities, but always defined in terms of the limitations set forth by the character of the original inventions.

Signalling illustrates the structure of a more complex form of work based on the idea of dialectical choice. The starting point is actually a mirror exercise, akin to the traditional acting exercise but with a defined thrust into the area of sound making. The second phase involves a dialectical reversal which itself sets up complex relationships. In the mirror-imitation it is never defined who is leading whom; similarly, in the reversal phase a special tension arises from the fact that either individual may attempt to reverse or return to imitation at any time, while his or her partner may agree to go along with this shift or may in fact attempt to continue with the previous phase of imitation or opposition. So, in addition to agreed-upon imitation and agreed-upon opposition, there are also the phases of imitation opposed by opposition and opposition opposed by imitation. Furthermore, over the pure structure of sound other grids of mood, relationship, and physical movement may be opposed as indicated.

There are more structures here than can be indicated by conventionalized notations. For example, there is an interplay between intuition and conceptualization which parallels the notions of imitation and opposition. Imitation, as such, is essentially a non-intellecutal activity dependent largely on a high level of concentration: the ability to loose one's sense of self in the activity and personality of the other person. But the switch to opposition requires a sudden mental reversal; the intellectual faculties come into play. What is the other person doing? What is my reaction to it? How can I focus intention as a clear sound-and-movement that can be clearly read by the other person? The importance of developing the skills of thinking as well as feeling cannot be overemphasized. In *Signalling* the signals must always be conveyed in such a manner that the thinking-feeling nexus is maintained with no loss of tension between the individuals.

After familiarity and skill in this kind of work has been achieved, experiments can be made with larger groupings of voices and instruments, always organized in pairs. Further, more directed developments are also possible through the use of hand signals, a device for integrating larger forces on similar principles.

Phrase

Eric Salzman

Invent a phrase

A phrase may be a sound or a collection of sounds organized in a sentence or phrase. It may be an actual word or sentence. It may be a musical note or melodic sequence, invented or remembered. It may be an expressive noise or collection of noises. Or it may be some combination of the above. It can be vocal, percussive, instrumental or some combination of the above. It can be as short or as long as a single breath.

A phrase is also a physical movement as closely identified with the sound as possible. It is better to let the movement flow from the sound rather than the other way around; however, ideally, sound and movement should be a total unity.

The phrase—sound and movement as a totality—should be something that the performer can identify closely with and that he or she can repeat, indefinitely if necessary. The rate of repetition (in musical terms, the tempo) and the amount of space between repetitions must be part of the invention itself. Similarly, the amount of actual movement from one place to another and the extent to which the phrase is directed inward or outward must be part of the invention itself.

At the beginning of the exercise, the performers should look for a space in the room within which they can work and begin to conceptualize their sound and movement before actually doing it. There is no set order of entry and it is highly desirable that the performers take their time in focusing on their section. Every attempt should be made to come in—whether or not anyone else has already begun—with a phrase that is as fully conceived and as uninfluenced by what others are doing as possible. The aim is to articulate and settle into one's phrase as totally as possible.

When as complete an identification as possible has been achieved with one's invented phrase, one may become aware of others and begin to relate to them. However one must relate through one's chosen phrase only. A sense of individual relationships may or may not be succeeded by some sense of the relationship of everyone participating.

Spaces between repetitions—however long or short—may be marked by neutral activity or no activity at all. Anyone at any time may drop out by extending the period of no activity idefinitely or breaking the tension and leaving the area of the exercise. It is possible to re-enter the exercise but only with the same phrase and at the same level of tension as it was left.

The exercise ends when everyone has achieved some kind of relationship with everyone else—sequentially or collectively—or when further relationships become impossible.

Signalling

Eric Salzman

Signalling is an exercise for two individuals or pairs of performers. It is recommended that, at the start, pairings be made on the basis of similarities: i.e. two singers, two horn players, two actors, etc.

This exercise is based on a pattern of seven types of sound making as shown in Example 1. Performers have the choice of imitation-in unison or in response-or opposition as represented by a choice of one or other of the two sound types placed opposite on the grid.

The two performers should face each other seated or standing. Chairs are often helpful, particularly for instrumentalists, and they define a kind of arena; however performers need not be limited by them. The starting point is a concentration ritual in the form of a spiral. Performers are asked to focus inward, observing their own mind without thinking of anything in particular. They are to focus visually on the tip of their nose and aurally on some sound, heard or unheard. The ritual takes the form of a slow spiral from the tip of the nose (the most inward visible point), to one's own physical body, to the space that separates the two people, to the physical presence of the other person (no engagement yet), to the space around the person, to the wall behind and the ceiling above and all the way back as far as possible. At this point, the performer must return to the partner and look for his or her glance. If the other person has not yet finished the ritual, wait. At the point that the glances meet, the exercise begins.

The first phrase is a mirror, akin to the traditional aacting mirror exercise but consciously extended into the domain of sound. Sound must be part of the opening ritual so that it is as much a part of the opening of the exercise as the physical presence of the two parties. The usual starting point will be held tones or murmurs, but this is not necessarily the case. Each person has the task of imitating thoroughly what the other person is doing, or mirroring the physical totality as far as possible: sound, movement, facial expression, mood. There is no leader and no call for imposed change.

When the mirror has been clearly defined and a good state of inter-active concentration has been reached, each person may choose to react by switching to one of the two opposing sound types indicated on the top of Example 2. The first performer must then make an instantaneous choice: continue to imitate or switch to opposition. If opposition, there is the choice of simply continuing whatever he or she was doing or switching to the other opposite mode as shown on the grid. The first person must, of course, react to this decision by continuing to react-with one or the other of the indicated modes of opposition—or by switching back to imitation. Either party then always has the choice of imitation or one of two modes of opposition with the possibility of switching up and back between them.

Important as this freedom of choice is, it will not be meaningful unless the performers define clearly for themselves the various relationships of imitation and opposition, congruence and disagreement, interaction and reaction, "consonance and dissonance." Therefore no switch should be made until the existing situation is perfectly clarified. Once an extended interactive or dialectic situation has been established, a return to imitation should be postponed until it can no longer be avoided. If, however, the necessity to react becomes too great a strain at any time, it is always possible to return to imitation to relieve the tension. At least one major return to a state of opposition should follow a second shase of imitation. The exercise may end with a third phase of imitation or any agreed upon number of such returns.

The sound types in Example 1 must be learned in conjunction with the musical qualities suggested by the grid in Example 2. Note that various qualities are combined here in a single grid so that a high, loud sound may be opposed by a low, disjunct sound, a soft, low sound or even a soft, smooth sound. This grid, unlike the other, must be used in groups of two or three adjacent qualities applied to the sound types of Example 1. Additionally, a related pattern of tempo-suggested by the grid at the bottom of Example 3—should be used.

In addition to the purely musical-sonic character of this exercise, other important dimensions must be added. These are illustrated in Examples 3 and 4 and give a structure to three important areas: individual mood, physical movement and relationship between the performers. Each of these may be studied separately and then, one by one, superimposed. For example, a situation may arise in which loud, high-pitched murmuring sounds are opposed by smooth soft verbalizations. The murmuring sounds might however be expressed through a mood of sadness, a physical movement forward and with the intent of rejecting the other person whose verbalized responses might convey excitement, a physical movement back or down and the expression, however ironic, of liking or loving. The possible combinations are many.

After similar pairs of individuals have gained a certain confidence with this material, experiments can be made with enlarging the number of people involved. One simple method is to pair an instrument with each singer or actor. Each pair must then act as a unit with either voices or instruments "in the lead." Larger ensembles can be built up in this way always using the same basic dialectic principles. With larger groups, associated had signals may be used; in this case, two conductors may be used working alone or supporting a pair of "soloists" (singers, actors, dancers, instrumentalists). In one form of this exercise, Signs and Signals, a single conductor may create his own dialectic, dividing and sub-dividing the performers through the use of hand signals and, under certain circumstances, involving the audience as well.

A much more difficult form of Signaling involves unequal pairings; for example, a singer and a horn player. Literal imitation is impossible and mock imitation is limiting and of dubious value. Interaction must be conceptual with a constant process of translation taking place even in a purely imitative, mirror phases. Where there are gross inequities of one kind or another, the reaction may be responsive. This is a difficult, largely untapped but promising area for experimentation.

EXAMPLE 1

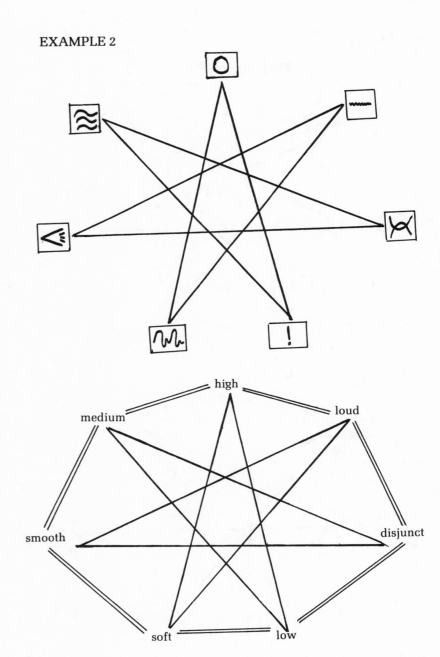

O	sustained sounds, pitches
!	short, staccato, consonants, percussive sounds
≈	flowing, legato, melodic, simple phrases
✕	rhythmic, repeated patterns
—	murmurs (extended sounds, tremolos, flutter-tongue)
⌇	patter, up-end- down, on a sliding continuum, touching extremes
◁	speech, phonemic, any language, language fragments or simulation

These areas should be as clearly differentiated as possible. The aim is to convey clearly to your opposite number what area you are working in through clarity and focus of invention. Do not hesitate to work an idea untill its essential clarity has been established.

EXAMPLE 3

Physical movement

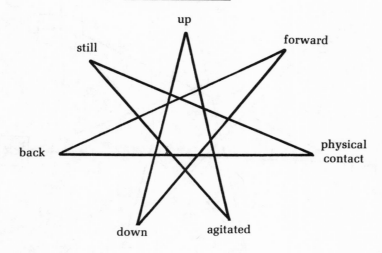

EXAMPLE 4

Mood

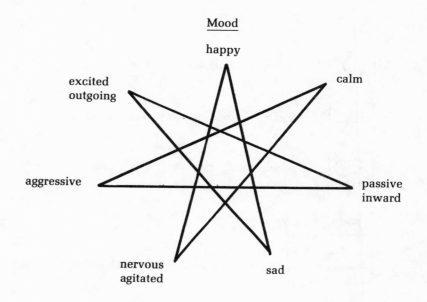

Tempo

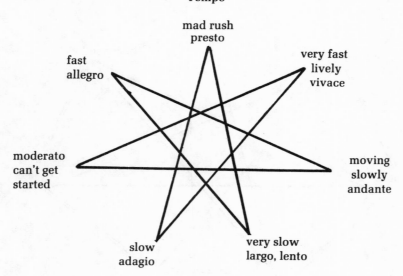

Relationship

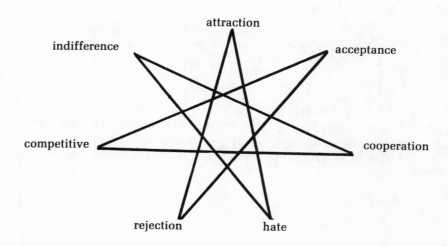

The Roachville Project*

Barney Childs

Commissioned by, and dedicated to, Joseph Byrd

4 to 10 performers, minimum duration 30 minutes.

Provide a great deal of material, most of which should be capable of soundproduction, either immediately (wires, pipes, blocks, tubes, containers, bits and pieces of musical instruments, junk, etc.) or potentially (material which when assembled or altered or worked with can be made, maybe, to produce sound in some fashion).

The piece begins with the arrival of the performers at the material. They begin to assemble the material, as they please, any way they wish, into a "musical instrument" of sorts. The complete construction is to be a unit—that is, separate people may work for a while on separate sub-units, but these must eventually be built into the complete construction. All that is necessary for assembly, finally, is ingenuity: the *means* of assembly (nails, staples, glue, string, sticky tape, leather straps, baling wire, rivets, etc.) are up to the performers. Performers may converse together concerning problems of assembly and sound potential, but this must be done very quietly, and other conversation is to be avoided; performers may test parts they are working on for sound as they are assembling (i.e. test string tension by plucking, test resonances by tapping, etc.) but this must also be done very quietly. At a stipulated time, or when all agree that the instrument is completed, the performers improvise music on it, for any length of time. The composition is finished with the completion, at a pre-arranged time or by agreement among the performers, of this "piece-within-a-piece." All material provided need not, or perhaps will not, be used. If passing members of the audience wish to become performers they may, as long as the total working number of participants never exceeds 10.

* Roachville and White Mountain City were "settlements just over the White Mountain summit from Owens Valley . . . A writer visiting there in 1864 tells all that we know of those would-be mining centers. The 'city' from which he wrote was on Wyman Creek, on the Deep Spring slope; its rival, Roachville, was on Cottonwood Creek, and was named by its proprietor, William Roach. . . . "

W.A. Chalfant, *The Story of Inyo*

Bicycle Music

Trevor Wishart

PROCEED FROM
VENUE TO
VENUE
IN THIS WAY
BRINGING
MUSIC
TO THE ENTIRE
CITY

e- -mer -ging from the city in all directions dismount at your meetingplace

invert your bicycles to form a neat group

sit down behind the back-wheel & holding it firmly to your body

play delicate harp music on the spokes, with the style and manner of a harpist

having concluded remount your bicycles and dissolve into the city in different direc- -tion- -s

while you move your future music is unpredictable while you play your future venue is unpredictable

DISCOVER ALL THE SOUNDS WHICH YOUR BICYCLE WILL MAKE: Use them

From *Sun: Creativity and Environment* by Treavor Wishart and Friends. Copyright© 1974 by Universal Edition (London) Ltd. Used by permission.

Dragoon

David Cope

(a theatre work for 4–9 players)

Dragoon is the 4th in a series of theatre works designed for concert situations (*BTRB, The Deadliest Angel Revision* and *Towers* being the first three). For those who must 'cubbyhole' music separate from theatre and the other arts, these works are indeed separate from this composer's main musical output and should be considered more theatre than music *per se*. For those who enjoy all arts and any combinations thereof, it is hoped that *Dragoon* will work and be effective whatever be its definition. *Dragoon* is dedicated to my four children and to all the children of the world whatever their age.

Dragoon is a multimedia beast whose shortlived (8 to 12 minutes) lifespan should be as immediate and colorful as is possible. The 4 to 10 players need not be able to perform well on their instruments (of their choice excepting the upright piano and the trombone) excepting that they be able to make as diverse a number of sounds and effects as possible. The instruments chosen (aside from piano and trombone) may include traditional as well as non-traditional instruments and indeed there are no limitations in this regard at all except in size (as will be shown later). It is quite possible that this piece be performed by willing persons with no immediate background on their chosen instrument and/or by children capable of following the directions given here.

The following are needed for constructing Dragoon:
one large platform on wheels capable of carrying the ensemble and the piano if necessary
one upright piano (with the front open to provide inside sounds for performance; use keys rarely).
one trombone (large ripping glissandi work well both aurally and visually)
one very large translucent tarp in which are evenly spaced 1/4 to 1/2 inch holes; make more than one for performer to provide air for breathing as well as spray cans.
Various paints; the more translucent the better so that the lights from within can penetrate using the paint as gel.
various lighting objects (flashlights, etc.): these should be battery operated if possible but can be attached to a multiple AC cord if more power is needed; line out the rear
various cans of spray-can perfume (the same number as performers); cans should be able to be placed next to holes in tarp to visually give impression of escaping gas.
various instruments as wanted or needed (these can be any sound producer provided they make short bursts of sound)

two larger lights for piano (these should be small but powerful and as work progresses they should blink on together)
one rather dim neon light or the like for Dragoon (this is optional as dim stage lighting can be used instead) so that the performers can see each other and watch for timing.
the necessary performers (as creative as possible).

Dragoon is constructed by first placing the upright piano either on the platform or (if the piano has usable wheels) attaching the platform to the piano with the keyboard 'inward' such that the keyboard is accessible to a performer on the platform and the backsides of the piano are directly away from *Dragoon*. The two large lights should be placed on the rear of the piano in such a way as to give the impression of eyes. Each performer is given his spraycan, instrument and light and placed on the platform. The large translucent tarp with holes is then placed over the entire ensemble attached to the top of the piano at one end (the head) such that the eyes are still visible to the audience and around the sides of the platform such that the performers cannot be seen. A larger hole should be cut in the rear of *Dragoon* (opposite of the head) for the trombone slide to protrude as the tail. The tarp should have already been prepared with splashes of paint done in such a way as to add color but not destroy the translucent nature of the material (so that the lights from within can shine through).

It may be necessary for the performers to hold up the tarp with their backs. If necessary it is quite possible to have small poles inside to help hold the tarp to full position. (N.B. at beginning and end the tarp should be completely collapsed over the performers.) If the neon light is used it should be very dim and be at center platform. At no point should any more than just the outlines of the performers be visible to the audience (like organs in translucent fish).

Dragoon should be placed at stage left. If wall current need be used it can become the umbilical cord to *Dragoon* and should be centered out the rear just below the trombone opening. The work should begin and end in complete darkness and silence. No hint of *Dragoon's* presence should exist to the audience therefore it would seem best that a curtain be closed before the performance and raised silently in the dark. The effect of *Dragoon* should be that of a beast slowly coming to life (a multimedia beast no less), moving slowly across the stage (with the aid from the behind of a non-visible stagehand), gaining momentum and intensity (both with faster and faster sounds and lights), impaling itself against stage right at which point all the gas (spray cans directed out from the holes) goes out of it and its collapsing death throes into darkness. The score reveals the general timings and activities required of the performers but the general effect of ONE BEAST is most important. At no time should there be any direct relationship between the lights from within and the sounds from the same. This is an un-coordinated multimedia beast from beginning to end. The score directions and timings should be followed fairly closely for a successful performance.

sffz

DRAGOON IMPALES ITSELF AT STAGE RIGHT ON WALL OR SIMILAR OBJECT

ALL SPRAY-CANS SPRAYED THROUGH HOLES AS TARP COLLAPSES OVER PERFORMER!

SILENCE AND DARKNESS.

short bursts of light and sounds at least 10" apart. DRAGOON tarp collapsed and in the dark at stage left.

sounds and lights become faster.

continue faster DRAGOON begins to move.

As fast as is possible all lights and sounds.

one last burst or flurry of light and sound.

ONE LONG EVEN CRESCENDO FROM BEGINNING UNTIL THE DESTRUCTION ON THE WALL! tarp collapsed....slowly rise to fullest size...........

2' - 3'   2'   2'   1'   1' - 2'

N.B. All sounds and lights should be as colorful and diverse as possible. *All performers should use their fullest imaginations in creating the beast and performing its senseless suicide. No sound or light should be considered outside the realm of usability for this work. Dragoon must grow slowly and die quickly. All else should be sudden* (i.e., the impaling and spraying should be immediate).

Elevator Music

Elliott Schwartz

A theater piece for twelve groups of performers arranged in the vestibules or lobbies outside the elevator doors of a tall building and an audience which is taken for rides in groups by the conductor/elevator operator among the floors.

The piece was originally conceived for the 15 floor Senior Center at Bowdoin College. Here the ground floor was used as an entrance/exit for the audience and there were fourteen vestibules for use by the performers. Of these only twelve were put to use. The number twelve suggested obvious possibilities for vertical arrangements of pitches in tone-rows, and the two empty floors (not adjacent ones) created "vessels" into which sonorities above and below could flow and mix. Instrumentation is not specified, although someone on each floor must produce specific pitches when asked to, at other times produce percussive noises.

The piece was performed for an audience of roughly 200, divided into groups of 10. Each group was taken into the elevator on the ground floor and moved vertically at random for 3 minutes, exiting at the ground floor at the end of this period. 20 such trips were made, so that the performance lasted one hour (although only 3 minutes for any individual member of the audience).

The conductor selected the floors to be visited, avoiding any conscious pattern in favor of a more random selection such as, perhaps, (1)-7-3-14-5-4-8-2-10-15-6-9-3-(1). At any floor visited, the elevator doors would open as long as desired; the result was a succession of visual experiences (there were lighting effects, costuming. optical illusions with mirrors, etc.) as well as a sudden increase in volume at each step, i.e. the sounds made on that particular floor acting as a solo or cadenza. One could, of course, also choose to stop at an empty floor—"empty" only in the sense that no live activity was going on, for those areas were certainly filled with sound.

This second task of the conductor, within the elevator, was the timing of cues within 5 minute intervals, each cue inaugurating a new stage of the piece (see score). This was simply done by pressing the emergency button within the elevator, thus activating a loud bell alarm clearly audible in each vestibule. Each performer, reacting to the cue, moved smoothly into the next stage of the piece. (All performers were playing at all times, of course, whether their elevator doors opened or not. They functioned as members of an ensemble in a total performance, and the visits by the audience were irrelevant to their own performing tasks. The most exciting sonorities of the piece, in fact, occured while the elevator was in transit, moving between floors and "passing" through great cloud banks of audible fabric.)

It should be noted that the 3 minute duration of each individual ride and the 5 minute duration of each stage in the performance of the piece were designed to overlap, so that most individuals in the audience were exposed to two different textures falling within their own ride.

In the score, non-pitched noise-oriented effects were termed "auxiliary," and written AUX; those effects included the striking of one's instrument or any part (floor, walls, etc.) of the performance area, playing on the drums or other non-pitched percussion, recitation by the narrator, and use of distorted "electronic-sounding" material on the phonograph and tape deck. Handclaps, finger-snapping, stamping of feet, etc. were also permissible.

In stages 4 and 11 of the piece, each floor is assigned a single pitch of a twelve-note series, that pitch hand-written into the blank box provided on the score sheet. In the original Bowdoin performance an all-interval set (for example: C,C#,B,D,B b,E ,A,E,A b,F,G,F#—ed.) was used in stage 4, the retrograde of that set ascending and the retrograde inversion descending in stage 11.

Elevator Music: Performers' Score

For any number of players, grouped on 12 floors of a tall building, outside the doors of an elevator.

Do not begin until you hear the emergency bell (or other signal). This is the signal to begin Stage 1. *Each* stage is cued by the sound of the *emergency bell*. Drop what you are doing and move into this new stage four seconds after the bell stops ringing.

STAGE 1: Gradual *building up* from the lowest to highest floor. Lowest begins in dignified martial tempo. 4/4 meter, etc. Next floor waits at least 4 beats and then enters one *synchronized* beat and *same* tempo. Keep piling up until all floors are in, listening to the floor below you for your entrance. About one minute of this. NO AUX. SOUNDS! Then free, with much silence between stabs of sound, vary sounds between fff and ppp. No "beat" in your part, no coordination with other parts.

STAGE 2: FREE, as *rapidly* as you can play . . . make silences brief and occurring at irregular points. fff throughout, cover entire range of your instrument. AUX sounds O.K. *if rapid.*

STAGE 3: Free, *very* quiet, ppp, repeated notes *only,* with great silences between events (but repeated patterns themselves may be slow, fast, any tempo, etc.). Choose no more than four notes to repeat, and no synchronization with other floors.

STAGE 4: Sudden *building down* from the highest to lowest floor (12 tone series). Your note is written in the box given below. Play your note as soon as the floor above has sounded its, then hold or repeat note, continuing for two minutes. Vary dynamics, NO AUX SOUNDS. Then free, anything you choose.

STAGE 5: AUX SOUNDS *ONLY* for two minutes or so. Then instruments added, very brief and loud at irregular intervals.

STAGE 6: *Wavering pitch,* glissandos of all kinds, very slow, dynamics varied, for about three minutes. Then AUX SOUNDS may be added, but only very softly.

STAGE 7: FREE, anything you choose.

STAGE 8: Single notes, played at random with much silence between; any notes in any register. Eventually you *all* reach the note C (middle C if possible). and play *only* that note; this must take place not later than four minutes into the stage.

STAGE 9: FREE, anything you choose, but *all* events are to be very soft, almost inaudible.

STAGE 10: Play familiar phrases from well-known songs, varying the tunes and the keys if possible. Throughout this stage all is very loud.

STAGE 11: Sudden *building up* from the lowest to highest floor (12 note series). Your note is written in the box below. Hold or repeat your note for at least one minute, and then *all out off except the highest floor.* When it is alone on a solo note, the next floor below begins a sudden *building down* of another 12 note series (your note is given in the third box below). TAKE NOTE: You *do not* have the same note to play for the upward and downward series. Hold this new pile-up for at least one minute. NO AUX SOUNDS. Then FREE, with AUX SOUNDS if you wish, for remaining time in this stage.

STAGE 12: AUX SOUNDS only for first two minutes, growing gradually from pp to mf. At moment of their choice, the lowest floor begins dignified martial music (as in stage 1, although not necessarily identical music), each floor adding to it while maintaining tempo. AUX SOUNDS continue through all this. The entire amalgam grows louder and louder, reaching fff before final emergency bell.

AFTER FINAL EMERGENCY BELL RINGS . . . count five seconds after bell stops, and play *one sharp, shrill, piercing* concluding sound, as loud as possible.
FINIS

PITCH for STAGE 4

PITCH for STAGE 11 up

STAGE 11 down

NOTE: duration of each stage above is five minutes; total duration is one hour.

Roma

Larry Austin

A Theater Piece in Open Style for Improvisation Ensemble* and Tape**

Duration: 16 minutes (the length of the tape)

Performance Instructions

Roma is an abstract theater piece. Within the explicit context described below the piece asks the improvisers for interpretive movement as well as interpretive sound. The attitude of the "movement improvisation" is suggested by the reaction—before, during and after the event—of the player to the lighting, the stage properties, the movements of other players, the audience and the nature of the hall; similarly, the reaction to the tape and/or the group's improvisations determines the attitude of the "sound improvisation".

Movement improvisation

1) Movement is to be concerned mainly with getting from one point to another on the stage. For large stages actual movement by each player should be limited to the equivalent distance of three complete crossings of the width of the stage. For small stages one or two of the players may also make one foray into the audience area to increase the visual scope of the movement.

2) All players, excepting cellists, must stand. Players may, however, sit on one of three stools found on stage.

3) Players must be completely visible in a beam of light on four separately articulated occasions during the piece. Conversely, players must be invisible on two occasions; e.g., behind a flat or off stage.

4) All movements should be subtly stylized and mostly unhurried. Associational and/or provocative motion should be limited. The players can, for example, imagine themselves part of a large mobile. Though all movements should be spontaneous and no specific sequences pre-arranged, vis-a-vis "blocking" procedures, a director and/or dancing coach could suggest refinements of the players' improvisations.

5) When stationary on stage players should strike a stylized pose, moving only those parts of the body necessary to perform their instruments.

6) Players may choose to sit on a stood, stand next to it, or place his instrument on it and then to walk away. Until such an "abandoned" instrument is recovered by the owner, other players may not approach or congregate about the area of such an "occupied" stool. However, any number of players may congregate about an "unoccupied" stool.

7) Players must not make inappropriately casual movements. Even while playing, conventional movements should be kept to a minimum. In other words the "playing movement" should compliment, through association, contrast or a mixture of the two, the attitude of the sound.

Sound improvisation

1) Play. However, each improviser must, on five separately articulated occasions (not necessarily coinciding with the movement articulations), silent for a significant span of time.

2) Pianists will stand while playing. In addition to a visible piano on stage, there should also be an unvisible piano off-stage or behind a flat.

3) Percussionists are to arrange their instruments at random on and off stage, but in cooperation with the director. In addition to a limited number of conventional instruments there should be unconventional

instruments such as bottles, tin cans, noise makers, etc. If a vibraphone is used, the player may only use hard rubber mallets and/or plastic knitting needles to play the instrument and may never engage the sustaining pedal. Snare drums may not be used. Tenor drums, dumbegs and other deep membranic instruments may only be played with the following: a 3-inch horse hair paint brush; a toy, plastic mallet; two large, soft lambswool bass drum beaters. Temple blocks are to be played with hard rubber mallets or wooden sticks. Xylophones, marimbas, and cowbells are to be played with hard, felt mallets and/or knitting needles. Other instruments may be played with any type beater.

4) Individual improvisers are free to invent sounding schemes. It is best, however, to invent spontaneously during the progress of the piece and, ideally, as a result of the intellectual/emotional catharsis taking place.

5) Players should be cognizant of and responsible for the dynamic balance between the tape and the improvisers.

6) It is hoped that the tape appears to react to the attitudes of the players rather than always the converse.

Lighting, properties, dress and makeup

Except for the last 2'20", the stage will be lighted with only three narrow and stationary beams of light projected at different angles from overhead directly onto three tall stools placed about the stage. Two or three flats may also be used. The beams of light will change intensity and color through the piece according to the following scheme:

a) 0"____2'16": three red beams come up very slowly.

Elements Quadrant

b) 2'16"____; two of the red beams suddenly change to white and remain unchanged until 5'38".

c) 5'38"____8': one of the red beams gradually changes to green.

d) 8'____: the remaining red beam changes to yellow and remains unchanged until 11' 13".

e) 11' 13"____13' 40": the white beam changes to blue, but not suddenly.

f) 13' 40"____ 16': all colors shift at any speed and at any intensity abruptly returning to darkness at the end of the piece.

The players should dress in black and wear black rubber soled shoes. Mime faces are appropriate.

*The Improvisation Ensemble is any grouping of from three to nine instruments and/or voices. The performers should be relatively experienced improvisers.

**The two-track tape is available from the composer (School of Music, North Texas State University Denton 76203). Readers are encouraged to write for it.

A practice tape, which should *not* be used in public performance, can be made as follows:

1. Record an environment, preferably of people talking at a distance, not knowing you are making the recording. Ideally it should be in the Italian language, but this is not absolutely necessary.
2. Record an event.
3. Record random sounds from radios and any musics you like.
4. Mix them, using any other material or process that pleases you.
5. The final tape should be at least 16 minutes.

Proposition IV (Squid)

Alison Knowles

Four or five people gather to study the score and elect a leader. The leader coordinates things and begins and ends the performance. There is no rehersal. Each performer (you) make your own score card by selecting from the quadrant sections that follow and writing them on your score card. For example, your card might read: +7, +10, + +14, + +8, +water, +west/blue, silence. You plan what activity you will be doing in each quadrant and what tools/objects you will need. The leader begins the performance by drawing a circle on the floor with chalk; or if outdoors, with a stick on the ground. The circle should be about 10 feet across. The leader then divides the circle into quadrants, labels them (numbers/elements/compass-color/silence). The leader also places a compass in the compass/color quadrant. You and the other performers enter, chose a quadrant and begin. Your activities may extend beyond the circle into the audience or the environment but the quadrants should be respected even if extended when you enter, set your various tools for performance in the quadrant they apply to and will be used in. Perform your prepared activity with directness and composure and according to the energy dynamic provided on your score card. The energy level is indicated by the plus signs in front of the word or number. + means very soft and slow, + + + + means the opposite. The categories are abstract leaving you full freedom in planning what you will do. For +water, should you carefully and slowly wash your leg, you must come prepared with the water, basin and soap. If you plan to activate the direction + + + +North/green by running in a northerly direction with a green banner, those tools must be placed beforehand in the compass/color quadrant. In the numbers section do not speak the number but sound it/them somehow. You might choose to read fourteen lines of a poem according to the dynamic +14, in that case, whispered. The elements section is self explanatory. You might use your own breath for + + + +air. In sounding the numbers section you may use musical instruments. The silent quadrant is just that . . . to be quiet there should you stop in it. Your performance is single; it does not relate to what anyone else is doing. Your concerns are invention and enjoyment in the atmosphere of self-perusal that takes place. The attitude of the piece is matter-of-fact as opposed to theatrical. The leader concludes the piece when he wishes. Performances of *Proposition IV* have lasted twenty to forty-five minutes; when the leader decides the performance is over, he/she leaves the circle. Finish up what you are doing before you follow. You may move clock-wise or counter-clockwise in the circle, not across the center.

The elements in *Proposition IV* were randomly programmed and run at Bennington College by Andrew Schloss.

Numbers Quadrant

```
+ + +20    +11    +17    +5    +14    +13    +19    +7
+5    +3    +11    +7
+10    + +14    + +8    +9    +14    + + +20    +14
+5    +4    +4    + + +16
+4    +16    +16    +7    + +3    +11    + + +0    +11
+ +18    +15    + +18
+ +4    +0    +0    +17    + +13    +5    +16    + +9
+2    +3    +19    + + +17
+ +9    +12    +7    +18    + +17    +2    + +10    +7
+14    +6    + + +17
+ + +1    +14    + +20    +15    +7    + +9    +5
+ + +3    +17    + + +16    +4
```

Elements Quadrant

+ +water	+water	+ + + +air
+water	+paper	+ + + +water
+air	+fire	+ +fire
+air	+ + + +air	+air
+water	+fire	+ + +water
+ + + +paper	+water	+fire

Silent Quadrant

Compass Color Quadrant

+east/red	+east/red	+ + +south/green
+ + + +east/blue	+ + +west/red	+ + +north/yellow
+north/red	+ + + +west/yellow	+south/blue
+ +east/blue	+east/yellow	+ + + +west/green
	+ +north/blue	+ +east/blue

Jumping Dance

Laura Dean

Jumping on a steady pulse

Jumping Dance is formed on a grid of twelve squares, with one person in each square, *each facing the same direction* and standing close together. The step is to jump up and down on two feet. Everyone keeps a steady pulse together throughout the dance. Every time the feet hit the ground a "ha" vocal sound is released. The tone of this "ha" sound is individual and *remains the same for the individual* throughout the dance. The dancer/singer should choose a comfortable sound for him/her self. The sound happens from the impact of the feet hitting the ground and only at that time. *The dancer jumps for as long as he/she wants,* rests until he/she feels another surge of energy, jumps for as long as he/she can, rests, then begins again, etc,. This continues until all of the dancers have exhausted their jumping energy. During the rest, the dancer should remain *very* stilled, with focus forward and arms easy by the sides. The dance ends when there are 2 seconds of silence. This dance should not be pre-set in any way; i.e., who jumps when and for how long; what tone each dancer should make (the dancer chooses this). One important thing to watch is that the steady pulse the dance starts out with has a tendency to drop. One person should be picked to maintain the pulse in the dance. To start the dance, this person will give four jumps and then the other dancer/singers join in.

JUMPING DANCE

Gloria Patri

Phil Winsor

Requirements:

2 dancers (need not be highly trained, but should be able to assume and project a variety of postures of worship.): They may be male or female, but should both wear black body stockings.

2 percussionists (anyone will do): #1 plays tubular chime, #2 plays large gong. Both should be dressed in choir robes, or something similar.

2-35mm slide projectors with one slide each (made according to the instructions) project from the front left and front right stage corners on the dancers throughout the duration of the piece. Multiple shadows will be thrown on the rear stage wall which, preferably, should be covered by a white skrim or curtain.

Stereo tape playback system: Loudspeakers should be placed at the extreme right and left stage front facing the audience.

Instructions for performance

Dancers and percussionists are in stage position when the piece begins. (Dancers should assume a worship posture facing each other and hold it for the first minute of the tape.) The projectors are turned on simultaneously with the tape, which should fade in over 30 seconds.

The percussionists begin playing after one minute of the tape and slowly stroke their instruments with soft mallets. Long preparation is required with exaggerated stroking gestures—no sudden or abrupt motions. Produce an undercurrent to the tape and a feeling of time suspended.

The dancers work with frozen images. Throughout the piece they should slowly flow from one position to the next. Any position of worship or variation may be used, and the dancers may relate or not

relate to each other as they choose. After they have held the opening position for one minute they should imperceptibly begin to change.

Gloria Patri should be felt as one extended moment in time. No attempt for variety should be made on the part of the percussionists. If a good effect can be achieved the last two minutes of the tape may be accompanied by long, long, soft chant-like moans and utterances from the percussionists. Fade the percussion out 30 seconds before the end of the tape, at which point the dancers assume one last fixed position. Wait for the end, shut off projectors or dim stage lights and close the curtain.

Instructions for Tape Preparation

1. Use as a source any continuous sound which is timbrally active enough to be interesting, yet gives the effect of a dorne. Either record the sound for enough time to make a tape loop of workable length or simply record nine minutes of the sound.
2. Two tape recorders (1/2 or 1/4 track stereo) are required for completion of the tape.
3. Make two stereo tapes using the above sound in normal, half or double speeds in accordance with the stereo tape plan.
4. To make a half speed recording set the playback deck at half its normal speed and dub onto the record deck set at its normal speed. To make a recording at double speed set the playback deck at normal speed and the record deck at half speed.
5. Care will have to be taken with record volume controls to avoid adding a click to the tape when the machine is started and stopped while recording on any given channel. An alternate method is to record four separate tapes, then edit out any extraneous noises using blank tape for silences. This necessitates additional dubbing steps in producing the final stereo master and is less preferable.

Stereo Tape Plan

(elapsed time in minutes)	0	1'	2'	3'	4'	5'	6'	7'	8'	9'

TAPE I

Channel A:
- half speed (0-2')
- normal speed (2'45"-4'20")
- double speed (5'20"-7'10")
- half speed (7'45-9')

Channel B:
- half speed (1'30"-3'30")
- normal speed (3'45"-5')
- normal speed (5'30"-6'45")
- double speed 7'20"-8'40")

TAPE II

Channel A:
- normal speed (45"-1'15")
- double speed (2'50"-4'50")
- half speed (5'15"-6'45")
- normal speed (7'15"-9')

Channel B:
- double speed (2'-3'30)
- half speed (4'10"-5'40")
- normal speed (6'10"-7'30")
- half speed (8'-9')

The starting and ending times for each segment of the four channels is given together with approximate relative positions of each. Each of the four segments per channel starts at a very low volume level, rises to the maximum half way through and drops back gradually to the low level at the end. It is followed by blank or silent tape until time for the next segment to begin. These two stereo tapes are finally mixed down to one stereo tape.

Instructions for slide preparation

Buy a package of two inch by two inch slide cover glass at a camera store. Make two abstract color slides of similar character by the following method.

1. Use a variety of colors of transparent india ink.
2. Use the droppers in the bottles to apply the colors to a single glass plate; try for a colorful, amorphous quality allowing one color to dry before applying the next. Do not try to "paint" recognizable objects. Suggest stained glass windows.
3. Repeat step two using a second glass plate.
4. Sandwich the two plates and tape the edges so they cannot come apart.
5. Repeat steps 1 to 4 for a second slide.

Format 5
For 4 or more performers
(musicians, dancers, actors)

Randolph Coleman

- assume a time interval between one and five minutes, this will constitute the duration of one version of the piece; one complete performance consists of three versions (discussed later)

- call this interval X; performer #1 develops an event (movement or sound) which takes X time to complete; the other five performers execute the same event but at varying speeds (depending upon their assigned time interval) and commencing at different times (according to the pre-selected structure)

STRUCTURE A (all performers conclude simultaneously):

assume X = one minute
assign time intervals to each performer according to the following scheme:　#1 = 60"　　#4 = 30"
　　　　　　　　　　　　　　　　　#2 = 50"　　#5 = 20"
　　　　　　　　　　　　　　　　　#3 = 40"　　#6 = 10"

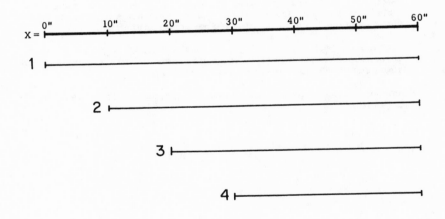

STRUCTURE B (all performers commence simultaneously):
assume X = one minute
use same time interval assignments as the preceeding example

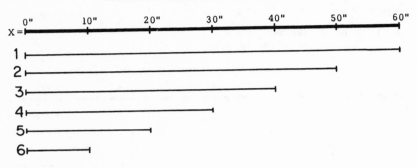

STRUCTURE C (pyramid around a point, in this example the mid-point)
use same assumptions as above

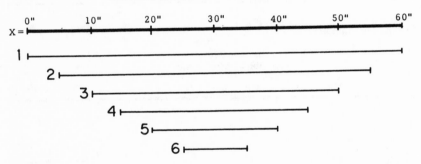

STRUCTURE D (non-symmetrical)
use same assumptions as above

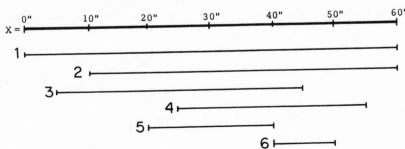

Using a different method of assigning time intervals:

S T R U C T U R E   A: assume X = 130"

use Fibonacci series x 10   #1 = 10"   #4 = 50"
                              #2 = 20"   #5 = 80"
                              #3 = 30"   #6 = 130"

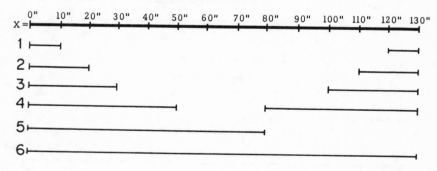

Using a variant:

S T R U C T U R E   A & B: assume X = 130"

use Fibonacci as above

- there are, therefore, two main variables, (1) the time interval and (2) the structure which includes the durations of each performer's event and the entrance and exit points for each performer; the assignment of the durations may be done on any basis but there must be a clear rationale for this assignment (linear, exponential, Fibonacci, stochastic model, etc.)

- the event must always be executed as strictly as possible

- any predetermined or historic series of movements may provide the basis for the event (e.g. Tai Chi Chuan or other martial arts)

- any time-keeping device may be employed (counting out loud, clocks, music, etc.) but the time units must be rigorously maintained

- one performance variable which is not determined here but which must be carefully considered is the placement of the performers in the space; a possible performance could consist of the precise repetition twice of one version but at each repetition re-position the performers in the space

- normally one performance of Format 5 consists of three successive versions of the piece; the event itself must remain consistant but the lengths and the structures should normally vary with each version

- another variable is to have the second half of the event be the retrograde of the first half

North American Eclipse
A 12-Part Ballad for In-Motion
Performers, Bone Rasps, and Drums

Music—Daniel Lentz
Text—Kit Tremaine

NORTH AMERICAN ECLIPSE is based (ritualistically) on the *O-ke-wa*, the Seneca Indian dance for the dead.

The piece should be performed in a very resonant environment. Also, it should be performed in near darkness (One candle in an otherwise pitch-black space should allow enough light). Because of this and other factors, it should be memorized by the performers.

Each of the twelve "in-motion" performers is assigned a number which he or she retains for the duration of the piece. The number assigned will depend upon the singing (and whistling) range of each individual. In the ideal configuration of six male and six female performers numbers 3,4,7,8,10, and 12 would be males and numbers 1, 2,5,6,9, and 11 would be females.

Each "in-motion" performer must carry two strings of bells which he or she keeps in constant motion through-out the performance. Each string should contain at least twenty very small, high-pitched bells. Optionally, ankle bells would be used in addition.

The twelve performers should enter the performance arena according to the numbers assigned with number 1 entering first, followed four to six drumbeats later by number 2, and so on. After all twelve are within the performance space and have established a complete circle around the listeners, the whistling "Introduction" begins. This Introduction (the first two pages of the score) must be peaceful almost to the point of being "eerie". The first cycle begins immediately after the completion of the chord which ends the second page.

The twelve performers establishing the circle around the listeners remain in motion through-out the performance. The distance between each individual should remain constant. This is done by means of a slow shuffle, never varying in time or space, and always independent of the drum(s) pulse.

The Tempo (44 to 60) will depend upon the size of the performance space with a larger space necessitating a slightly quicker tempo.

Drum = Tom Tom. If one drummer is used, he should be situated in the center of the performance space. If two are used, they should be situated at separate ends of the space with their alternating pulses traversing the space.

The dynamics should be as follows:

Rasps mp p	Drums p mf
Whistling p	Humming $p < mf$ (always performed closed-mouthed)
Singing $mp < f$ (expressively, but without exaggeration)	

Humming and singing are always in the octave as written.
All sustained notes, whether sung or hummed, should be taken to silence before breathing
The piece should be performed in a highly legato manner. There should be no pause between cycles.

When a consonant is placed within parentheses it should not be sounded, only implied. When a consonant is underlined it should be elided with another consonant (usually the same consonant belonging to another word) in a different line (also underlined).

Symbols:
▲ = hum the individual note
▲ = hum the entire line (or, to next symbol used)
△ = whistle the individual note
△ = whistle the entire line

When a tie in the whistling parts is notated with a connective triangle (——⌃——) it should be considered as a phrasing symbol. These are intended as opportunities for the performer to sustain a note without a break in its sound. Like the up and down bowing of a string instrument, these markings represent the suspension of a note of a line through the use of two types of techniques. The performer simply begins each line in the normal manner of whistling ("out") and changes at a point where the note is tied with the above-mentioned symbol by whistling while breathing "in". In this way no break in the note should be noticeable to the listener. Also, it is not necessary that this change takes place at each point where this symbol occurs in the score. In fact, the longer a note can be sustained without any type of change, the better.

The whistling and humming should be clear and without vibrato.

At least one of the twelve performers should have "perfect pitch." This will aid in preventing any pitch fluctuation between (and within) cycles. Ideally, this person would be assigned the first number in the score.

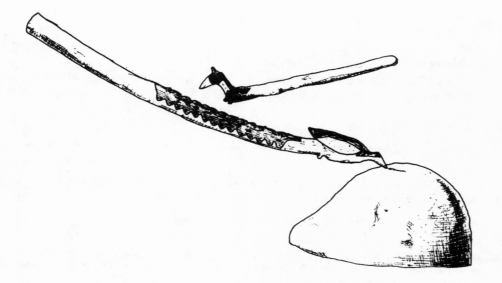

The Bone Rasps (or Notched Resonators) consist of a resonator (a drum, a half-gourd, or even an inverted basket) and two bone or wooden sticks with notches cut in one of them (see drawing). The notched bone or stick is placed against the resonator and the second one is rubbed over it. Enough of these instruments should be used so as to produce a full and continuous (non-rhythmic) sound. The use of four would be ideal although two would suffice. These are available from the composer or, if necessary, can be easily built using either wood or bone. If bone is used, the notched bone should be the metatarsal bone of a deer (about one inch in diameter and twenty to twenty-six inches in length) and the other a deer's scapula (about twelve inches in length). If bone is not available and wood is used, it is suggested that cedar be the material.

The Rasp players should be situated in the center of the performance space.

The lay-out of the text as printed on the following page should be copied and distributed to all potential listeners before any performance of the piece. Also, it should be explained that the texts unfold in order (from 1 through 12) successively as well as additively and that the printed example is but one of many textual configurations and/or combinations used in the course of the piece.

```
1                    Stirring                    in      soft            murmuring                                                                                        air
2                Life stirring                            songs of                                                           summer
3    Whispering                          souls                   of dark murmuring Indians
4                    Ripening                            murmuring    dreams          of                                                                                  dawn
5                                               Vanishing  flights of     wild                                                              geese scattering    light
6    Whispering              ripening                                murmuring                                                             fields of                          grain
7    Whispering                      the    soft history    of dark murmuring Indians                                           echoes                          [over]
8    Whispering                                                 vanishing         herds in summer[s]  echoes               of                                   wispy hidden graves
9                    Stirring                        songs    murmuring            in                      vast     and silky fields of              light
10      Streams of  stirring                  wind                                                                                                          scattering    grain over    wispy       graves
11                  Far away             soft    songs               vanishing in                          echoes            of              light      thunder
12                  Ripening earth    in                          dust heavy      summer                                                          light
```

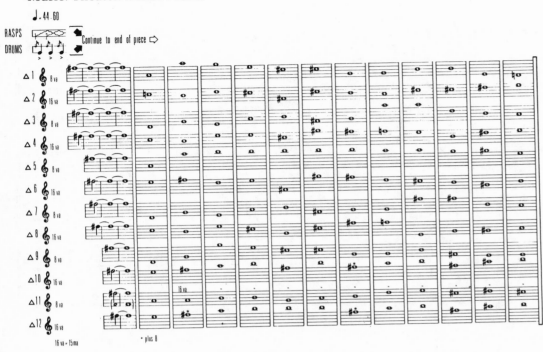

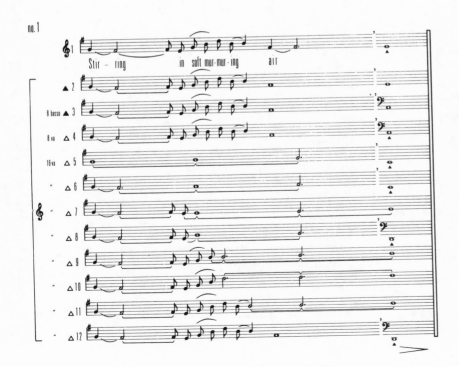

no. 1

no. 2

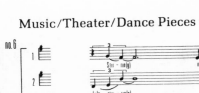

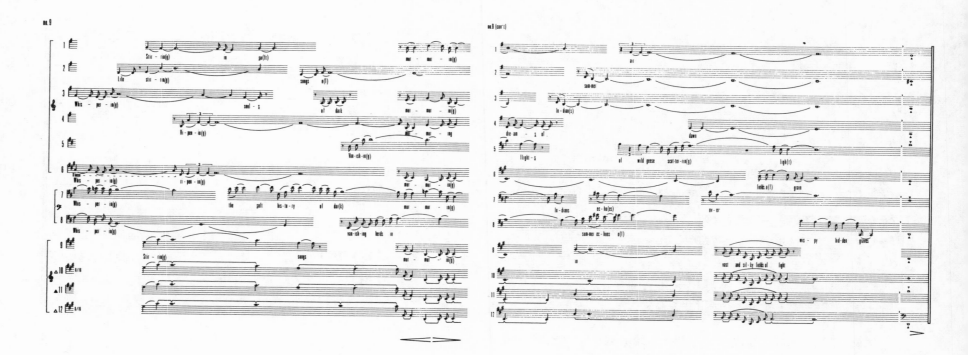

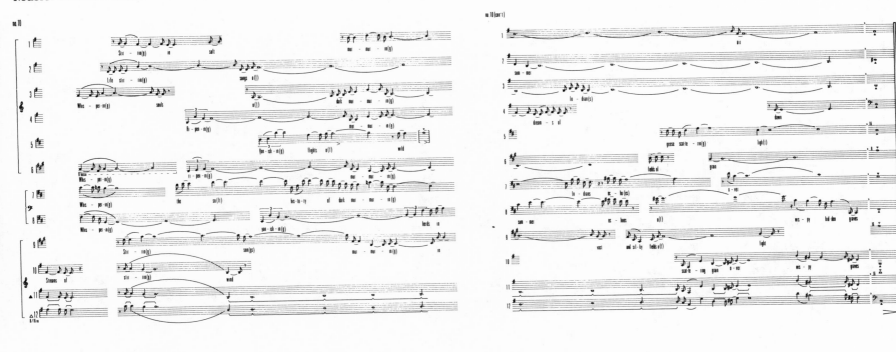

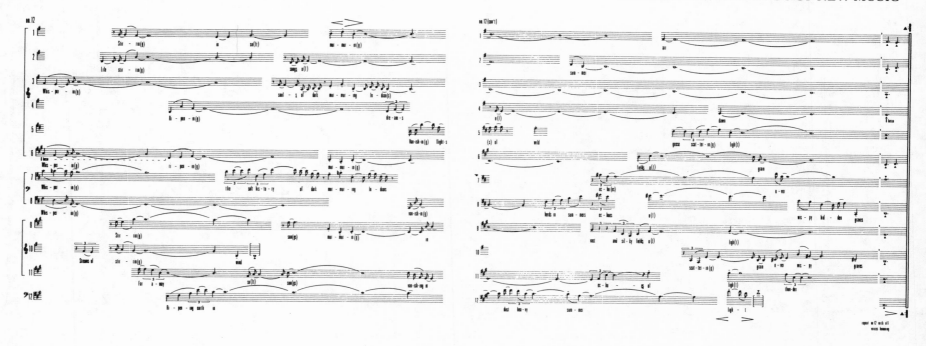

ENDING / EXITING

Hum these chords (pp)
while gradually exiting
the performance space.

Each measure should
be from 4 to 8 beats
in duration.

Bonn Feier (excerpts)

Pauline Oliveros

Bonn Feier is intended for performance in a city, college or university environment. All normal city or campus activity, as well as specially arranged activity, is a part of *Bonn Feier*. Anyone who enters the city or campus during the designated but unannounced time of the performance is a knowing or unknowing participant in *Bonn Feier*. Special rituals, activities, and sights, described below, are to be blended smoothly with normal city or campus activity all during the normal working day and evening. The intention of *Bonn Feier* is to gradually and subtly, subvert perception so that normal activity seems as strange or displaced as any of the special activities. Thus the whole city or campus becomes a theater, and all of its inhabitants, players.

. . .

Bonn Feier is intended to be continuous over a long period of time. A minimum performance time is fifteen hours of a normal working day. An optimum performance time might be a week, or a month, or as much as a year.

. . .

Participants must agree to perform during all or any specific part, or parts, of the designated time length. *Bonn Feier* should grow gradually through the day (week, month, year) from events which are hard to distinguish from normal activities of the city or campus, but have been displaced or modified in some way, to very unusual events which culminate in a ritualistic ceremony . . .

The most crucial instruction for any knowing participant in *Bonn Feier* is to always remain focused on the particular activity he or she has chosen, and to *blend in with the environment* no matter what happens or what social demands arise. *Normal city or campus activity must continue undisturbed.*

Aeolian Partitions

Pauline Oliveros

Commissioned by Bowdoin College
Conditioned by the Aeolian Players
for
Flute   Clarinet   Violin   Cello   Piano

Aeolian Partitions is composed for a proscenium stage with wings. Performers must be able to enter and exit from stage right and left during the performance and to get on to the stage from the house. In lieu of a proscenium stage, effectively equivalent entrances and exits must be arranged.

A total house and stage blackout is necessary. If these conditions cannot be met, abandon the performance entirely.

The stage is clear except for one chair placed slightly off center stagq left. A music stand is not necessary unless performers do not know their cadenzas.

Prop list
Cellist—broom
Pianist—newspaper
flashlight (6 volt lantern with a white beam and red blinker)
Extra - transistor radio (battery operated)
Page turner - megaphone
Violinist - large gong on stand bow, suction cup arrows, and quiver
Stage crew - 7 six volt flasher lamps (amber color)
1 slide projector
1 slide of Star of David

Performers
Violin, Viola
Cello
Clarinet, Bass Clarinet
Flute, Piccolo, Alto Flute
Piano
Formal attire for above
Page turner (if absolutely necessary, Clarinetist can double as page turner)
Two extras, preferably familiar to the audience, i.e. Dean of the College, Department Chairman, Mayor of Town, etc., who walk across performance area on cue.

Two stage hands - to move piano and gong and to set out flashers
Stage manager - for lights and projector
All performers are expected to maintain an attitude of serious concentration during the theatrical parts.

Flasher positions on stage for
Telepathic Improvisation

X = volt flasher lamps

Projection Surface for Star of David*

Viola			**Alto Flute**
X			
			X
	Piano		
	X	X	X
Bass Clarinet			**Cello**
X			X

*A slide screen should not be used. The Star of David should appear on the back wall above the players, even if the wall or backdrop is not very reflective.

Sequence

Red spotlight shines down on the chair.

Enter Violinist and Cellist. As they enter red spotlight fades.

Acknowledge audience.

Cellist be seated,

Violinist remain standing.

Clarinetist and Flutist take places behind audience unobtrusively, facing stage, Clarinetist to the left and Flutist to the right, as far apart as possible.

Pianist and piano remain off stage right.

1

Violinist gives down-beat to Cellist.

Violinist turns back to audience, begins to draw bow soundlessly across string (fingering A 880 on the E string), and begins to walk slowly to the back wall, pacing himself for one minute.

On downbeat Cellist begins to draw bow soundlessly across string (fingering A 880 on the D string). Appears to play PPP.

30 seconds after Violinist gives down-beat, Clarinetist begins to play barely audible A 880.

Flutist begins to play whistle tones on A.

Both continue until Cellist begins cadenza.

After approximately one minute and thirty seconds Cellist looks to see where Violinist is,

2

then launches into a virtuoso cadenza from the existing literature (double stops, fast passages, etc.), stops abruptly before the resolution, exits to his left briskly, returns with a broom, sweeps around chair then exits again.

Violinist turns left and exits when Cellist begins cadenza.

3

When Cellist stops cadenza, Clarinetist and Flutist appear on the apron at stage right and left respectively.

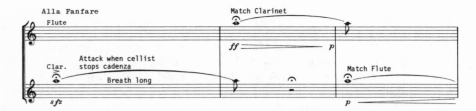

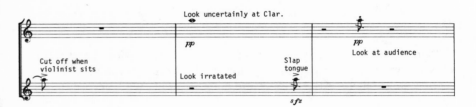

Stop on cue from Violinist.

When Cellist sweeps around chair, Violinist re-enters with violin in case, sits in chair, takes out violin, rosins bow and prepares to play. In an irritated manner he cues Flutist and Clarinetist to stop. He plays A 880 espressivo with extremely wide vibrato, one bow only. Puts violin in case and exits.

4

As Violinist plays A 880, Stage Hands begin to roll piano into view. As Violinist exits, piano should be in place, the keyboard about one half the distance to center stage. Stage Hands place bench, open lid and keyboard, then exit.
Pianist enters and acknowledges audience.
Sits down, adjusts bench, prepares to play.
Reaches inside piano, whips out newspaper and begins to read.

5

When Pianist begins to read newspaper, Cellist brings out hard cello case, stands it upright, upstage about one half the distance from center stage (stage left). He exits and cues Extra I to walk across stage.

6

Clarinetist enters from stage right as Extra enters from stage left. He carries his clarinet in a viola case. He acknowledges the audience, sits in the chair, takes out his clarinet and plays a virtuoso cadenza from the existing literature. When Clarinetist begins to play, the Pianist gradually looks up from the newspaper, looks at Clarinetist, folds up newspaper and exits (stage right). Clarinetist stops cadenza abruptly before resolution, puts clarinet in viola case and exits (stage right). Cellist takes broom across stage to Clarinetist in wings. Clarinetist re-enters, sweeps around chair and exits.

7

Pianist re-enters and acknowledges audience. He sits down and prepares to play. As his fingers start to touch the keys, he begins slowly and intensely to raise both hands (as if to play a tremendous crashing chord) until both arms are straight overhead. At this point he stretches and yawns.
Extra II is cued by Cellist when Pianist yawns to walk from stage right to stage left, carrying transistor radio which is playing. Pianist exits when Extra passes him (stage right).

8

When Extra reaches wings (stage left), blackout occurs, radio off. Pianist is ready to re-enter with flashlight. Both beam and blinker are on. He searches in and around piano with flashlight. While Pianist is searching piano, Violinist enters in the dark and plays virtuoso cadenza from existing literature. After Violinist begins to play (upstage right) Pianist begins to search the stage, finally illuminating Violinist from the feet up, then audience, then Pianist exits.
Violinist stops cadenza abruptly before the resolution and exits in the darkness.
Lights come on and broom is seen disappearing into the wings.

9

Pianist re-enters with Page Turner and acknowledges audience. Page Turner places large thick score on piano and prepares to turn pages. Pianist plays lowest A, sfz, with sustaining pedal, and freezes in attentive pose. Page Turner turns page in middle of decay. Both continue to listen until decay is complete. Pianist continues to hold pedal down. When decay is complete, Page Turner takes megaphone, aims into bass strings, and shouts "BEETHOVEN" into piano. They freeze and listen to the reverberation. While reverberation continues, Stage Hands bring out large gong and face it toward stage left.
Violinist enters with bow and quiver of suction cup arrows. He aims carefully and hits gong with arrow, then exits (stage left). Stage Hands immediately remove gong but allow it to continue vibrating.

10

When Beethoven reverberation stops, Page Turner exits. When all have exited, Pianist gets Stage Hands and directs them to move piano to a new location (center stage). When he is satisfied with new location, Stage Hands exit and Pianist sits down and plays virtuoso cadenza from existing literature. When Pianist is close to resolution Violinist, Cellist, and Clarinetist come slowly on stage and take places like pall bearers by cello case. Pianist stops cadenza abruptly before resolution and joins them as pall bearer. Piccolo begins to play wake music from center of auditorium:

Pall bearers carry off cello case like a coffin, head first, (stage left to right). Stagelights dim as they reach the wings and go out as Stage Hands bring on lit flasher lights and place them on stage. All players come on stage in the darkness and begin telepathic improvisation. (Change piccolo to alto flute, violin to viola, and clarinet to bass clarinet.)

11

Each performer concentrates on another single performer. When he hears an interval or a chord mentally, he plays one of the pitches and assumes that he is sending the other pitch or pitches to the other performer by mental telepathy. Each performer plays only long tones, but varies dynamics, vibrato, and timbre. He tries to influence different performers and to make silences by becoming mentally blank.

After about 10 minutes when the Star of David appears, start to introduce vocal long tones and gradually eliminate instrumental sounds. Prepare to end telepathic improvisation. Begin to carry flashers off stage. When all performers and flashers are off stage, lights come on, performers bow together.

The audience may be invited to join in the telepathic improvisation with the following instruction:
Concentrate on a single performer, try to hear a pitch mentally. See if you can influence the performer to play your pitch by mental telepathy. If you cannot hear a pitch mentally try to influence the performer to play higher or lower, louder or softer or to be silent. Think only of long pitches.

When you are able to hear pitches mentally try to join the performers by singing your pitches.

Composer Biographies

WILLIAM ALBRIGHT (b. 1944, Gary, Indiana)

Composer, pianist, organist.

Study with Ross Lee Finney, Olivier Messiaen, and George Rochberg.

Widely known interpreter of new music for piano and organ as well as classic ragtime and the early jazz styles swing and stride. Composer of works in almost every medium, several of which involve electronic, visual, or theatrical elements; also composed many concert rags.

Many major awards and fellowships, including Queen Marie-jose Prize, Fulbright and Koussevitzky Awards, National Endowment Composers Grant, and Guggenheim.

Associate Professor of Composition and Associate Director of the Electronic Music Studio at University of Michigan.

Many works published by Jobert, Elkan-Vogel, Bowdoin College Music Press, and Dorn Productions.

Recordings:

Brass Knuckles (Nonesuch 71257)
Grand Sonata in Rag (Grenadilla 1020)
Organbook (CRI S-277)
Organbook II (Nonesuch 71260)
Take That (Opus One 22)

School of Music
University of Michigan
Ann Arbor, Mich.

BETH ANDERSON (b. 1950, Kentucky)

Composer, pianist-organist, singer, performance artist, writer, editor, astrologer.

Study at University of Kentucky, University of California at Davis, and Mills College. Composition study with John Cage, Robert Ashley, Larry Austin, and Terry Riley.

Wide background as a traditional and experimental performer. Special interest in text-sound pieces and in vocal music. Composer of an opera, an oratorio, a wide variety of instrumental music, tape music, and environments.

Active as a concert organizer, dance accompanist and editor of *Ear* magazine. Her own work is a combination of formalist elements and numerology with romantic, dramatic, personal, emotional, and confessional material.

Publications of her music and text-sound pieces are found in *Report from the Front* (The Kitchen, 1979), *Text-Sound Texts* (Richard Kostelanetz, ed.), *Break Glass in Case of Emergency* (Mills College, 1979), and in such periodicals as *Dramatika, Heute Kunst, Flash Art, Ear,* and *Poetry Mailing List.* A variety of musical compositions are available from American Composers' Alliance.

She has received grants and awards from National Endowment for the Arts, B.M.I., and several others. She is currently teaching at College of New Rochelle and writing criticism for *Soho Weekly News* and *Ear.*

Recordings:

Torero Piece (1750 Arch Records 1752)
If I Were a Poet (Watershed Foundation, Breathing Space/77)
Sugar, Alcohol and Meat (Giorno Poetry Systems Records)

26 Second Ave.
New York, N.Y. 10003

DENNIS ANDERSON (b. 1951)

Composer, percussionist.

Study at California State University (Fullerton) and at University of Michigan with George Cacioppo.

Performed with New Music Co. Founder of Direct Image Ensemble and group called Impro Vision. Fullbright grant for work in Poland in 1978 and Stockholm in 1979 for performance and electronic music. Active in designing and building new percussion instruments.

Works available from composer include several for percussion ensemble and for piano, and others which use live electronic processes and multi-media.

3289 Minnesota Ave.
Costa Mesa, Calif. 92626

LAURIE ANDERSON (b. 1947, Chicago)

Performer, visual artist, film maker, composer, violinist.

Study at Barnard College and Columbia University; influenced by "films of

Godard, work of Screamin' Jay Hawkins, Balinese monkey chants, and performances of fellow artists in downtown Manhattan."

She has performed widely at Museum of Modern Arts, Whitney Museum, Akademie der Kunst (Berlin), Louisiana Museum (Copenhagen), Museum of Contemporary Art (Chicago), La Jolla Museum, Samangallerie (Genoa), and many other galleries, universities, and festivals in the United States and Europe. Her work has been shown in a variety of solo and group exhibitions New York, Seattle, Hartford, Berkley, and other cities.

Her work has been reviewed in *Artforum, The Village Voice, Soho Weekley News, New York Times, Los Angeles Times, October,* and many other publications. Examples of her work are included in such books as *The Package* (New York: Bobbs-Merrill, 1971) and *Individuals* (Alan Sondheim, ed.; New York: Dutton, 1977).

Recordings:

Airwaves (110 Records)
Big Ego (Giorno Poetry Systems Records 012-013)
It's Not the Bullet That Kills You-It's the Hole (Holly Solomon Gallery)
New Music for Electronic and Recorded Media (1750 Arch Records, 1765)

530 Canal Street
New York, N.Y. 10013

T.J. ANDERSON (b. August 17, 1928, Coatesville, Pa.)

Composer, educator.

Study at West Virginia State College, Pennsylvania State University, and University of Iowa (Ph.D., 1958). Additional study with T. Scott Huston and Darius Milhaud.

As co-director of the Afro-American Music Workshop at Morehouse College, he orchestrated, edited (with William Bolcom), and presented the first performance of Scott Joplin's *Treemonisha,* sponsored by grants from National Endowment for the Arts and Rockefeller Foundation. The work was subsequently presented in New York on Broadway.

Special interest in writing for orchestra; many major compositions, commissions, awards, publications, and recordings. Several teaching positions; Composer-in-Residence with Atlanta Symphony. Presently Chairman of Music Department at Tufts University.

Music is available through American Composers' Alliance and on the following recordings:

Chamber Symphony (CRI S-258)
Squares (Columbia M-33434)
Variations on a Theme by M.B. Tolson (Nonesuch 71303)
Conducted *Classic Rags and Ragtime Songs* (Smithsonian Institution Recording N 001)

Department of Music
Tufts University
Medford, Mass. 02155

ROBERT ASHLEY (b. March 28, 1930, Ann Arbor, Mich.)

Experimental composer–performer.

Study at University of Michigan and Manhattan School of Music.

From 1958 to 1966 operated the Cooperative Studio for Electronic Music in Ann Arbor with Gordon Mumma. Co-founder of "Once" festivals and "Once" group. Founded the Sonic Arts Union in 1966 with David Behrman, Alvin Lucier, and Gordon Mumma.

Collaborated with painter–sculptor Milton Cohen on the design and performance of his Space Theater productions and produced soundtracks for several prize-winning films of George Manupelli. Recent work involves a project of composer interviews and a new style of "portrait" performance in various media.

Co-director of the Center for Contemporary Music and director of the Electronic Music Studios at Mills College. Presently living in New York.

His music is included in *Source* and *Pieces* and an interview, with a piece, is found in *Desert Plants.*

Recordings:

Automatic Writing (Lovely Music UR-1002)
Christopher Columbus (Lovely music VR 1062)
Interiors with Flash (Giorno Poetry Systems Records 012-013)
In Memoriam . . . Crazy Horse (Advance FGR 5)
Music for Voice and Tape (ESP 1009)
Private Parts (Lovely Music LML-1001)
Purposeful Lady Slow Afternoon (Mainstream MS 5010)
She Was a Visitor (Odyssey 32160158)
The Wolfman (Source Record 4)

Videotapes available from Artservices.

Artservices
463 West St.
New York, N.Y. 10014

LARRY AUSTIN (b. September 12, 1930, Duncan, Okla.)

Composer, performer, jazz musician, writer.

Study at San Antonio College, North Texas State University, Mills College, and Univ. of California (Berkeley).

Extensive experience as a jazz trumpet and bass player; early composition worked with a synthesis of jazz and concert elements, particularly his *Improvisations for Orchestra and Jazz Soloist.* Very involved with improvisation ensembles using an "open style"; gradually has used more visual and theatrical elements.

Co-founder and editor of *Source,* an early and still major publication of a wide range of experimental music. Many writings on music in *Source,* the *New York Times* and other publications.

Taught at University of California (Davis) and in a new inter-arts program at University of South Florida.

His music is published by Composer/Performer Editions; many pieces use tapes which are available directly from the composer.

Recordings include:

Improvisations for Orchestra and Jazz Soloist (Columbia)
Current (Advance FGR-95)
Piano Music (Advance FGR-105)

Department of Music
North Texas State University
Denton, Texas

BONNIE MARA BARNETT (b. May 2, 1947, Chicago)

Composer, singer.
　　Study at Universities of Illinois and California (San Diego). Special research on vocal multiphonics.
　　Active as a singer–performer with several new music groups in California, including New Music Choral Ensemble (dir. Kenneth Gaburo) 1966–72, directed Experimental Chorus in Richmond, Calif., member of Ensemble with Pauline Oliveros 1969–73, and leader of own Sonic Meditation Group in San Francisco.
　　In Europe, 1975–76, teaching Vocal Resonance and African Rhythms in Rotterdam and Amsterdam. Collaboration with dancer Pauline de Groot, contributing music for several dancers in June 1976. Also formed a Women's Sonic Meditation Group in Amsterdam. Presently living in San Francisco.

Recordings as a performer include:

Music for Voices, Instruments and Electronic Sound (Nonesuch 71199)
20th Century Choral Music (Ars Nova/Ars Antiqua)
Maledetto for 7 Virtuoso Speakers (CRI S-316)
703 Cole St.
San francisco, Calif. 94117

BILL BECKLEY (b. February 11, 1946, Redding, Pa.)

Visual/photographic artist.
　　Study of art at Temple University with Steven Green and Italo Scanza. Study of music (trumpet and voice) in early years, but not professionally.
　　His art work has been called "Narrative Art" or that which combines visual, verbal, and (in his case) musical materials in close relation to each other. Many of the *Songs* resulted from gallery shows in which they were associated with objects or visual images, although they were also performed.
　　His work has been widely shown and reviewed in the U.S. and Europe. Recent shows at John Gibson Gallery (N.Y.); in Milan, Brussels, and Cologne; at the Venice Biennale, San Francisco Art Museum, among many others. Reviews and features in

Flash Art and *Data* (Italy) and in *Art in America*. Several grants from New York State Arts Council (CAPS). Faculty at School of Visual Arts in New York.

Work, shows, lectures, and performances through:
John Gibson Gallery
392 West Broadway
New York, N.Y.

BARBARA BENARY (b. 1946)

String player, singer, composer, ethnomusicologist.
　　Study of World Music at Wesleyan University.
　　Performer of Karnatic music of South India on violin. Wide experience performing new music with Philip Glass, Jon Gibson, Richard Teitlebaum, Daniel Goode, and Philip Corner.
　　Currently teaching world music at Livingston College where she constructed and now directs the Gamelan Son of Lion.
　　Earlier compositions were for theater, the best known being *The Only Jealousy of Emer* which was performed for several seasons in New York by the E.T.C. Company of Cafe La Mama. "My own composing is centered at this time on procedural music, or scored music which allows for improvisation on the part of the performers. I like the idea of the performers having a free hand, and the piece reincarnating itself differently every time."

Call Hollow Road
Stonypoint, N.Y. 10980

KARL BERGER (b. March 30, 1935, Heidelberg, Germany)

Composer, pianist, vibraphonist.
　　Study at Heidelberg Conservatory and at Freie Universit, Berlin (Ph.D., 1963)
　　Many performances and recordings with improvisational groups conducted by Don Cherry and Steve Lacy, and with his own groups since 1965.
　　Grants from National Endowment for the Arts; won *Downbeat* critics' polls as vibraphonist (1968 and 1971). Guest fellowships at several American universities, faculty of New School for Social Research (1969–73) and director of Creative Music Studio.

Recordings:

From Now On (ESP 1041)
Peach Church Concerts (2 disks—Creative Music Studio 00101)
With Silence (Enja 2022)
Just Play (Quark 9996)

Creative Music Studio
P.O. Box 671
Woodstock, N.Y. 12498

ELLIOT BORISHANSKY

Composer, specialist in theater pieces.

Study at Queens College, Juilliard, Columbia, Hochschule für Musik (Hamburg), and University of Michigan.

Awards include George Gershwin Memorial Award, two Fulbrights, MacDowell Colony residencies, and Ford and DURF grants.

Head of theory and composition at Denison University.

Compositions include a wide variety of instrumental, vocal, and theater pieces.

Published compositions:

Music for Orchestra (Chappell and Co.)
Pieces for Solo Clarinet (Media Press)
Silent Movie (solo Clarinet; Media Press)
Other pieces are available from the composer.

Recording:

Music for Clarinet (Advance FGR-155)

Music Department
Denison University
Granville, Ohio 43023

EARLE BROWN (b. December 26, 1926, Luneburg, Mass.)

Composer, conductor, lecturer, recording engineer, and editor.

Study of mathematics and engineering at Northeastern University; study of Schillinger system and traditional music history.

Early association with John Cage and David Tudor through the Project for Music for Magnetic Tape. Also pioneer in graphic scores, "time notation," and various other forms of open scores. His work has been widely performed throughout the world and has been highly influential.

Recording engineer for Capital Records (1955–60); Artistic Director of Time-Mainstream Records' "Contemporary Sound Series" since 1960.

Many major awards and commissions (Guggenheim, National Institute, Koussevitzky, etc.). Professorships and composer residencies at Peabody, Rotterdam, and Basel Conservatories; currently associated with California Institute of the Arts during parts of the year.

Early work was published by Associated Music Publishers; recent music with Universal Edition.

Recordings:

Corroboree (Mainstream 5000)
Four Systems (Columbia MS 7139)
Music for Violin, Cello and Piano, Hodograph (Mainstream 5007)
Quartet (3 Vox SVBX 5306)
Times Five: Octet 1 December 1952; Novara (CRI S-330)

Additional European recordings on Wergo, D.G.G., and La Boite à Musique.

Broadcast Music, Inc.
320 West 57th Street
New York, N.Y. 10019

MARION BROWN (b. 1935, Atlanta)

Jazz saxophonist, composer, ethonomusicologist.

Studied at Clark College, Atlanta.

Noted contemporary jazz musician; performed and recorded as a leader and sideman with many major musicians, the best known being John Coltrane *Ascension*. Many European festivals and tours.

Director of Afro Roots group through which he is involved with lectures and performances combining traditional American music with fife-and-drum music and Afro-American rhythms. Special study of the origins and music of the bamboo flute.

Taught at Bowdoin, Brandeis, Colby, and Amherst. Artist-in-Residence at University of California (Santa Barbara), Crighton University, and Cité Internationale des Artistes (Paris).

Many recordings made in U.S. and Europe, the most readily available being:

Marion Brown Quartet (ESP S-1022)
Why Not? (ESP S-1040)
Three for Shepp (Impulse S-9139)
Geechee Recollections (Impulse 9252)
Sweet Earth Flying (Impulse 9275)
Vista (Impulse 9304)
Soundways (with Elliott Schwartz; Bowdoin College Press)
Reeds 'N (IAI 373855)
Duets (Arista/Freedom 1904)
Porto Novo (Arista/Freedom 1001)
Solo Saxophone (Sweet Earth SER-1001)
NIA Music
184 Main St.
Northampton, Mass. 01060

RICHMOND BROWNE (b. 1934, Flint, Mich.)

Composer, pianist, theorist.

Study at Michigan State University (with H. Owen Reed) and Yale (with Richard Donovan). Fulbright for study in Austria 1958–59. BMI awards in 1957 and 1958.

Taught at Yale from 1960–68 and at University of Michigan since. Work is now mainly concentrated in theory with special attention to the work of Forte and Schenker, and to linguistics.

Founding member and executive board member since 1962 of the American Society of University Composers; secretary and archivist of the Society for Music Theory.

School of Music
University of Michigan
Ann Arbor, Mich.

HAROLD BUDD (b. May 24, 1936, Los Angeles)

Composer, performer.

Study at L.A. City College, San Fernando State College with Aurilio de la Vega, and University of Southern California with Dahl.

His music is influenced by jazz; Cage and Feldman; and by the visual arts, particularly Rothko and "minimal" art. Very involved with a sensuous, quiet sound and with simple materials and structures. Another project was his *California 99* in which eight composers wrote thirty-six events which were then "choreographed" into a piece.

Taught at California Institute of the Arts; very well regarded and influential, particularly on West Coast.

His *Mangus Colorado* has been published in *Source*, several works are included in *Pieces*, and his *November* in *Esquire* (May 1970).

Recordings:

New Work #1 (Advance FGR-95)
Oak of Golden Dreams, Coeur D'Orr (Advance FGR-165)
". . . only three clouds . . ." (Avant 1006)
The Plateaux of Mirror, Ambient 2, with Brian Eno (Editions EG, EGAMB 002)

23149 Oakbridge Ln.
Newhall, Calif. 91321

GEORGE CACIOPPO (b. September 24, 1926, Monroe, Mich.)

Composer, pianist.

Study at University of Michigan with Ross Lee Finney, Roberto Gerhard, and Leon Kirchner. Extensive study of mathematics, physics, and acoustics.

Co-founder and organizer of the Once Festivals and Once Group in Ann Arbor from 1960–68. Broadcast engineer with WUOM since 1960.

Wide range of compositions including the series of *Cassiopeia* pieces for various combinations of pianos and electronics; several works for organ, electric organ, and/or electronic instruments; other pieces for orchestra or strings; and *Advance of the Fungi* for winds, percussion, and male chorus.

Most works are published by Berandol Ltd. (Toronto).

Recordings:

Time on Time and *Cassiopeia* (Advance FGR 5)

School of Music
University of Michigan
Ann Arbor, Mich.

JOHN CAGE (b. September 5, 1912, Los Angeles)

Composer, performer, lecturer, writer.

Study at Pomoma College; composition with Henry Cowell and Arnold Schoenberg.

Major figure in contemporary and experimental music since the 1930s. Important as an "inventor" and philosopher; impact on all the performing and visual arts. Early experiments with sound (percussion, prepared piano, electronics) were followed by exploration of intedeterminacy (chance methods of composition, improvisation, and open form). Greatly influenced by Asian thought (Zen, I Ching, etc.) and by the writings of Thoreau.

Early association with dancer/choreographer Merce Cunningham as composer. Performance throughout the world with many other musicians and artists. Several important books and many articles, including *Silence* (M.I.T. Press), *A Year From Monday* (Wesleyan University Press), *Notations* (Something Else Press), *Empty Words* (Wesleyan).

Recordings:

Amores for Prepared Piano and Percussion (Opus One 22)
Aria with Fontana Mix (Mainstream 5005)
A Book of Music (Tomato 1001)
Cartridge Music (Maintream 5015)
Concerto for Prepared Piano and Orchestra (Nonesuch 71202)
Dances for Two Prepared Pianos (Angel S-36059)
Double Music (Mainstream 5011)
Dream (Finnadar 9007)
Fontana Mix (Columbia MS-7139)
H P S C H D (Nonesuch 71224)
Indeterminacy (Folkways 3704)
Music for Keyboard (Columbia Special Products CM2S-819)
Perilous Night (Avant 1008)
The Seasons (CRI 410)
Solo for Voice 2 (Odyssey 32160156)
Sonatas and Interludes (New World 203 and CRI 199)
Song Books I–II, EMPTY WORDS III (Wergo 60074)
Songs and instrumental music (3-Avakian S-1)
String Quartet (3-Vox SVBX 5306)
Variations IV (Everest 3132, 3230)
Winter Music (Finnadar 9006)
26'1.1499" for a String Player (Nonesuch 71237)

All music is published by C. F. Peters Corp.

Artservices
463 West St.
New York, N.Y. 10014

CHARLES CAPRO (b. February 19, 1954, Newark, N.J.)

Composer, pianist, synthesizer player.

Study at Montclair State College, Ramapo College, and Manhattan School of Music.

Active as a composer and performer of live electronic music. Compositions include *The Bulletin, Garage Sale, Weather Report,* a setting of E.E. Cummings' *Maggie, Millie, Molly and May,* and several "New Wave" songs such as *Science Fair* and *Subway Police* performed by the group Angry Young Salesmen.

Tapes and scores are available from the composer.

418 Cranford Ave.
Cranford, N.J. 07016

CORNELIUS CARDEW (b. May 7, 1936, Winchcombe, England)

Composer, performer.

Study at Canterbury Cathedral (1943–50), Royal Academy of Music, London (1953–57); studied electronic music and was assistant to Stockhausen in Cologne.

Earlier works, mostly piano, were in the serial/avant-garde idiom; move in early 1960s toward graphic scores and indeterminacy culminating in *Treatise,* a large graphic score without instructions. Recent work has been performable by nonmusicians and has been strongly influenced by political thought of modern China.

Active in concerts and lectures in England, Europe, and U.S. Co-founder with Parsons and Skempton of the Scratch Orchestra and published the *Scratch Orchestra Draft Constitution* in *Musical Times,* London (June, 1969), as well as a book, *Scratch Music.* Very involved then and since with collective and group improvisation; concept of performer as a member of a "society" rather than an individual ego. Very influential composer, particularly in England.

Work is published by *Experimental Music Catalogue* and Universal Edition.

Recordings:

Improvised Electronic Music (Mainstream 5002)
Treatise (Two Realizations) (Advance FGR-215)

BARNEY CHILDS (b. 1926, Spokane, Wash.)

Composer, writer.

Self-taught as composer until late twenties when he studied with Leonard Ratner, Carlos Chávez, Aaron Copland, and Elliott Carter.

Academic work in English literature included a Rhodes Scholarship and doctorate from Stanford University on the setting of poetry in the Elizabethan madrigal.

A broad range of compositions, some very specifically notated and intended for professional performers, others experimental, graphic, or open in other respects. Some forty pieces have been published.

Co-editor with Elliott Schwartz of *Contemporary Composers on Contemporary Music* (Holt, Rinehart and Winston) and author of many articles in various musical journals.

Professor of Composition and Director of the New Music Ensemble at University of Redlands.

Many compositions published by several noted publishers.

Recordings:

Barnard I (Advance FGR-17S)
Music for Two Flutes, Duo for Flute and Bassoon (CRI S-253)
37 Songs (Avant 1008)
Sonata for Solo Trombone (Avant 1006)
Trio for Clarinet, Cello, and Piano (ABC 9005)
Variations sur une chanson de conotier (Advance 2)

School of Music
University of Redlands
Redlands, Calif. 92373

J. GEORGE CISNEROS (b. 1951, San Antonio, Texas)

Composer, performer.
(Biographical information unavailable)

1407 Fannin
Houston, Texas 77002

RANDOLPH COLEMAN (b. 1937, Charlottesville, Va.)

Composer, theorist.

Studied at Northwestern (Ph.D.)

Many commissions and awards including Fromm Foundation, Oberlin Research Award. Currently teaching theory and directing Inter-Arts Program at Oberlin College.

The Format series of compositions is a continuing collection of pieces in which "overall structures are highly controlled while many of the details of performance are left open to the interpretive capabilities of the players." Some involve performers other than musicians. The series is published by Smith Publications.

Conservatory of Music
Oberlin College
Oberlin, Ohio

DAVID COPE (b. May 17, 1941, San Francisco)

Composer, writer, editor.

Study at Arizona State University and University of Southern California.

Large catalogue of works, widely performed in U.S. and Europe (Pittsburg and

Vermont Philharmonics, Nueva Musica Ensemble in Lima, Autumn Festival in Como, Italy, Ensemble MW 2 of Poland; had a complete program in Carnegie Recital Hall).

Author of three books: *Notes in Discontinuum* (Dicant Music, 2250½ Bentley, Los Angeles), *New Directions in Music* (Wm. C. Brown, Dubuque, Iowa), and *New Music Composition* (Schirmer Books, New York). Editor of *Composer* magazine and founder of Composers' Autograph Publications, which has now been absorbed by Seesaw Music Corporation.

The majority of music is published by Seesaw Music and a few pieces by Discant Music, Media Press, and Dorn Productions.

Recordings include:

Bright Angel (Redwood ES-5)
Cycles for Flute and Double Bass (Opus One 14)
Iceberg Meadow (Capra 1201)
Margins and Arena (Orion 75169)
Navajo Dedications (Folkways 33869)
Piano Sonata (Capra 1204)
Re-birth (Cornell University 16)
Threshold and Visions (Folkways FTS 33452)
Triplum, Three Pieces for Clarinet (Capra 1203)
Variations for Piano and Wind Orchestra (Cornell University 13)

Music Department
University of California
Santa Cruz, Calif. 95064

PHILLIP CORNER (b. 1933, Bronx, N.Y.)

Composer, pianist, writer, calligrapher, concert organizer.

Study at City University and Columbia. Study of "musical philosophy" with Olivier Messiaen and piano with Dorothy Taubman.

Co-founder of the group "Tone Roads" and closely associated with the "happenings" movement of the early 1960s. Composed and performed music for the Judson Dance Theater and founded the collaborative ritual sound exploration group "Sounds out of Silent Spaces." Also interested in calligraphy and notations as well as the art and ritual aspects of Tibetan Buddhism.

Works such as *Ear Journeys: Water, Metal Meditations, The Muse . . . From Lines and Curves, Popular Entertainments, Identical Lunch*, and other writings and calligraphy are available from Printed Editions. *Gong!, Sprouting,* and *Seven Joyous Flashes* are available from C.F. Peters Corp. and *The Four Suits* from Backworks. Other music and writings have been published by a wide variety of journals, periodicals, and publishers, including *Soundings* and *Pieces*. An interview with him is included in *Desert Plants.*

Currently teaching at Livingston College of Rutgers University.

Recordings:

Breath Chants and *Metal Meditations* (New Wilderness Audiographics 7701 A-B)

75 Leonard St.
New York, N.Y. 10013

GEORGE CRUMB (b. 1929, Charleston, W.Va.)

Composer.

Study at Mason College of Music, University of Illinois, and University of Michigan.

Internationally noted composer, recipient of virtually every major award in music, including Pulitzer prize, Guggenheim, Fromm, Koussevitzky, Rockefeller Foundation. Works have a very personal sound, strong sense of drama, delicate and coloristic quality; special involvement with the poetry of Garcia Lorca.

Six years teaching at University of Colorado; currently Composer-in-Residence at University of Pennsylvania.

Most works are published by C. F. Peters Corp.

Recordings:

Ancient Voices of Children (Nonesuch 71255)
Black Angels for String Quartet (Vox SVBX-5306, Turnabout 34610, Phillips 6500881, CRI S.283)
Dream Sequences, Four Nocturnes, Lux Aeterna (Odyssey Y 35201)
Echoes of Time and the River (Louisville S-711)
Eleven Echoes of Autumn, 1965 (CRI S-233)
Five Pieces for Piano (Advance FGR 3)
Madrigals (Turnabout 34523)
Makrokosmos, Vol. 1 (Nonesuch 71293)
Makrokosmos, Vol. 2 (Odyssey Y 34135)
Music for a Summer Evening (Nonesuch 71311)
Night Music I (Candide 31113, CRI S218)
Night of the Four Moons, Voice of the Whale (Columbia M32739)
Sonata for Solo Violoncello (Desto 7155)
Songs, Drones & Refrains of Death (Desto 7155)

Music Department
University of Pennsylvania
Philadelphia, Pa.

ALVIN CURRAN (b. 1938, Providence, R.I.)

Composer, performer.

Study at Brown University with Ron Nelson and Yale with Elliott Carter. Further study with Carter in Berlin on Ford Foundation grant; Bearns and BMI prizes in 1963.

Settled in Rome in 1965; founded Musica Elettronica Viva with Frederic Rzewski and Richard Teitelbaum; much performance of live–electronic and collective music with them. Active since then with solo music and work for film and theater. Founded Ananda label for recording of new music with composers Roberto Laneri and Giacinte Scelsi. At present teaching at National Academy of Dramatic Arts in Rome.

His music consists of several tape pieces, works for voice(s) and instruments, and collections of music for nonmusicians.

Music for Every Occasion, collection of 48 monophonic pieces, is published by New Music Catalogue (London) and work is included in *Pieces;* several recordings with MEV on Polydor, Mainstream, and BYG; *Songs and Views From the Magnetic Garden* (Ananda No. 1, No. 4) and *Fiori Chiari Fiori Oscuri* (Vista, RCA Italiana)

via dell'Orso, 28
Rome 00186
Italy

NOEL DA COSTA (b. December 24, 1929, Lagos, Nigeria)

Composer.

Early study with poet Countee Cullen; later work at Queens College and Columbia; two years with Dallapiccola in Italy on a Fulbright.

Teaching positions at Hampton Institute, Queens and Hunter Colleges; at present Associate Professor of Music at Rutgers.

Extensive catalogue of compositions; several theater pieces for children and other works of a dramatic nature for voices and instruments. Many songs and choral pieces (some with a strong Afro-American content) and a wide variety of instrumental works. Music is available from Atsoc Music, P.O. Box 270, Radio City Station, New York, N.Y.

250 W. 94 St.
New York 10025

LAURA DEAN (b. December 3, 1945, Staten Island, N.Y.)

Dancer and choreographer.

Study with Lucas Hoving, American School of Ballet; work with Paul Sanasardo, Martha Graham, and Merce Cunningham. Member of Paul Taylor Dance Co.

Many solo and ensemble works choreographed and performed by Laura Dean Dance Co. throughout the country and Europe. Collaboration with Composer Steve Reich to whose music she developed *Square Dance* (to *Phase Patterns*), *Walking Dance* (to *Clapping Music*), and *Drumming.* Recent works include *Song, Dance, Spiral,* and *Music.* The Walker Art Center and the Joffrey Ballet have both commissioned new pieces for the fall of 1980.

American Dance Festival commissioned her *Changing* in 1974, and she has received a Guggenheim Fellowship and many other grants and awards. She has published articles in the *Drama Review, Dancescope,* and *Performance.*

Dean Dance & Music Foundation, Inc.
15 West 17th St.
New York, N.Y. 10011

AURELIO DE LA VEGA (b. November 28, 1925, Havana)

Composer, critic.

Study of humanities at De La Salle College, law at university of Havana (Ph. D., 1946) and music at Instituto Musical Ada Iglesias (Ph. D., 1955). Private study with Ernst Toch and Frederick Kramer.

Director of Music Department, University of Oriente, president of Cuban ISCM, music advisor to National Institute of Culture. Active as a music critic and author of numerous articles for Latin American and U.S. periodicals. Since 1959 Professor of Composition and Director of the Electronic Music Studio at California State University at Northridge.

Large catalogue of music from mid-1940s to present, recent works being involved with electronics, graphic and aleatoric procedures, and instrumental color. His *Adio's* was premiered in 1977 by Zubin Mehta and was awarded a Kennedy Center Friedheim Award. Most music is published by Facsimile Editions (Northridge, Calif.) and Private Editions (Sherman Oaks, Calif.).

Recordings:
Inflorescencia (Orion 78302)
Sound Clouds (Klavier KS 565)
Levenda del Ariel Criollo (Panart 4001)
Tangents, Vn. and Tape (Orion 73128)
Para-Tangents, Tpt. and Tape (Avant 1009)
Exospheres and *Interpolation* (Orion 76239)

Department of Music
California State University
Northridge, Calif. 91324

JIM FOX (b. April 9, 1953, Indianapolis)

Composer.

Study at Butler, De Paul and Redlands Universities, studying with Russell Peck, Phil Winsor, and Barney Childs.

Active as a Composer of instrumental chamber music for a wide variety of combinations and of tape pieces. Works are often formed from various small "gestures of motions." Founder of *Improvisers' Orchestra.*

Presently instructor of electronic music and director of Redlands University Improvisation Ensemble. Several pieces have been included in a recent Soundings and in a new anthology of clarinet music.

Recording:
Music for Clarinet and Piano (Grenadilla 1046)

1813 Orchid Ave.
Los Angeles, Calif. 90068

JON GIBSON (b. March 11,1940, Los Angeles)

Composer, saxophone and flute player.
    Study at San Francisco State University.
    Jazz performer and founding member of New Music Ensemble (Davis, Calif. 1962–65). Intense performing activities with Steve Reich, Terry Riley, La Monte Young, and Philip Glass (1968–present). Also work with Rzewski, Wolff, and the dancer Nancy Topf. Active as a composer–performer.
    His music has been published by *New Music Catalogue* (London) and by other journals.

Recordings:
    Visitations (Chatam Square 12)
    Two Solo Pieces (Chatam Square 24)
    Performer on recordings of Philip Glass and Steve Reich

17 Thompson St.
New York, N.Y. 10013

PHILIP GLASS (b. 1937, Baltimore)

Composer, keyboard player.
    Study at University of Chicago and Juilliard, composition with Bergsma, Persichetti; private study with Milhaud and Boulanger on a Fulbright.
    Ford Foundation Composer-in-Residence with Pittsburgh schools from 1962–64. Work in Paris with Ravi Shankar notating and conducting a film of his began active interest and study of music of India which eventually "radicalized his way of composing." Several trips through Asia and India since.
    Formed ensemble of amplified keyboard and wind instruments in 1968 which has since made eight tours of Europe and played extensively in the New York area and on the West Coast. Frequent collaboration with experimental theater company, Mabou Mines, and lately with Robert Wilson (*Einstein on the Beach*) and dancer Lucinda Childs.
    Several early works are published by Novello (London) and Elkan-Vogel, and an interesting interview is included in *Desert Plants*.

Recordings:

    Einstein on the Beach (Tomato 101)
    Music in Fifths, Music in Similar Motion (Chatam Square 1003)

Music with Changing Parts (Chatam Square 1001/2)
North Star (Virgin P2-34669)
A Secret Solo (Giorno Poetry Systems Records 012-013)
Strung Out (CP2 Records CP2/6)
Two Pages (Folkways 33902)

Artservices
463 West St.
New York, N.Y. 1001

MALCOLM GOLDSTEIN

Composer, violinist, conductor.
    Study at Columbia University.
    Composer–performer with Judson Dance Theater and co-director (with Philip Corner) of Tone Roads. Performed with Merce Cunningham and directed New Music at the Bridge and New Roots of Music and Dance. Performed a wide repertory of violin music, particularly of the twentieth century, and has done much work in improvisation. Active in workshops.
    Taught at Columbia, New England Conservatory, New School of Social Research, and Dickinson, Goddard, and Dartmouth Colleges. Currently teaching at Bowdoin College.

Publications include:

    From Wheelock Mountain (Pieces Press)
    Sirens for Edgard Varèse and *Majority–1974* (Soundings)
    Death Act or Fact of Dying, recorders, and *Illuminations from Fantastic Gardens*, 3-5 singers (Dramatika)
    Recent work is included in *Text-Sound Texts* and *Scenarios*,both edited by Richard Kostelanetz

Recordings:
    A Summoning of Focus (Organic Oboe O.Q. #1)
    Soundings for Solo Violin (MG Records, from composer)

P.O. Box 134
Sheffield, Vt. 05866

DANIEL GOODE (b. 1936, New York)

Composer, clarinetist.
    Studied at High School of Music and Art (N.Y.), Columbia University with Henry Cowell and Otto Luening, and in California with Kenneth Gaburo, Robert Erickson, and Pauline Oliveros. Dance workshops with Elaine Summers, Meredith Monk, and Simone Forti.

Taught at Universities of North Dakota and Minnesota; at present with Livingston College of Rutges University. Music Director of Walker Art Center (Minneapolis) and performed with New Choral Music Ensemble under Kenneth Gaburo. Recent performances at Whitney Museum, The Kitchen, La Mama ETC, Real Art Ways, London Musicians Collective, and others. Active as a clarinetist and member of Gamelan Son of Lion.

His music ranges from works for solo clarinet, particularly *Circular Thoughts* (published by Theodore Presser), to pieces for orchestra, chamber ensembles, gamelan, electronic music, sound sculptures,pieces involving moving performers, and several using fiddle tunes. Other pieces are published by Lingua Press, Pieces Press, Will Parsons, and *Painted Bride Quarterly*. Articles have appeared in *Perspectives of New Music, Interval*, and *Writings* (Lingua Press).

Recording:
   Circular Thoughts for Gamelan Ensemble (Folkways 31313)

Box 268 A, Main Road
Neshanic, N.J. 08853

JANA HAIMSOHN (b. 1952, New York City)

Primary study was of classical ballet and modern dance technique; more recent study of voice.

Her solo performances have been presented at Akademie der Künste (Berlin), De Appel Gallerie (Amsterdam), Louisiana Museum (Denmark), the Whitney Museum, and at various events organized by Jean DuPuy in New York; recent concerts with Don Cherry. She received a CAPS Grant in Mixed Media, 1976.

In addition to reviews she has rcently been featured in *Flash Art*.

Recording:
   Airwaves (One Ten Records)

530 Canal St.
New York, N.Y. 10013

RICHARD HAYMAN (b. July 29, 1951, Sandia, N.M.)

Composer, performer.
   Study at Columbia University and privately with Philip Corner, John Cage, Ravi Shankar, and Grete Sultan.
   Active as experimental composer/performer in California, Colorado, New York, and other places. Performed with "Sounds of Silent Spaces" Group and an organizer of other events. His recent *Dreamsound*, an event for sleeping audience, was performed at the Kitchen in New York.
   Editor, With Beth Anderson, of *Ear* magazine and has published articles in

Hudson River Anthology, New York magazine and *Colorado Daily*. Worked as a mastering engineer, organ renovator, sleep lab experimenter, and ear-plug peddler.

326 Spring St.
New York, N.Y. 10013

WILLIAM HELLERMANN (b. July 5, 1939, Milwaukee)

Composer, guitarist, concert director, talker, drawer.
   Study at Columbia with Otto Luening and Chou Wen-chung. Further work with Stefan Wolpe.
   Director of Composers' Forum, presenting music of younger composers in New York. Frequent solo and ensemble performances on guitar of new music.
   Past work involved tape and instruments; more recent music is of the "meditative–participative or–reflective" form. Increasingly involved with visual material with several gallery performance–installation pieces.
   Many grants and fellowships, such as CAPS, National Endowment, Rome Prize, and Gaudeamus. Music is published by ACE Publications of Theodore Presser and *Pieces*.

Recordings:
   ariel (Turnabout TV 34301)
   ek-stasis ii (CRI SD 299)
   passages 13-the fire (Nonesuch H-71275)
   on the edge of a node (CRI S-336)

Composers' Forum
Box 501
New York, N.Y. 10013

DICK HIGGINS (b. March 15, 1938, Jesus Pieces, England)

Composer, poet, writer, performer, artist, publisher, translator.
   Study at Yale and Columbia Universities; musical work with John Cage and Henry Cowell.
   Active in the early happenings (from 1958) and in the group Fluxus (from 1961). Developed and named the concept of intermedia (fall, 1965). Writer of concrete and visual poetry, theatre, criticism, satire, music, and performance pieces.
   Founded Something Else Press in 1964 through which he published many important books in the arts. Founded and currently directing Printed Editions. Also taught at California Institute of the Arts (1970–71) and received a DAAD Fellowship for Berlin in 1975.
   Publications include *some recent snowflakes (and other things), Classic Plays, A Dialectic of Centuries: Notes Towards a Theory of the New Arts, Everyone Has Sher Favorite (His or Hers), foew&ombwhnu, Legends and Fishnets, Modular Poems, Some Poetry Intermedia, The Ladder to the Moon, The Epickall Quest of*

the *Brothers Dictung and Other Outrages*, and *Piano Album*, among many other shorter works and translations. Most of his work is available from Printed Editions of from Bookslinger.

Printed Editions
P.O. Box 26
West Glover, Vt. 05675

ROGER JOHNSON (b. November 12, 1941, San Mateo, Calif.)

Composer, teacher.

Study at University of Washington, Yale, and Columbia; composition with Powell, Luening, Chou Wen-chung. Work at Columbia/Princeton Electronic Music Center.

Active in college teaching since 1966 and at present at Ramapo College (N.J.). (Structure and content of present book developed through classes.) Also worked as a horn and cornetto player, editor/copyist.

Compositions are mostly instrumental chamber music with some vocal, choral, orchestral, and electronic music. Performances in U.S. and Europe at many universities and by such groups as Dorian Quintet, N.Y. Trio da Camera, Delaware Quartet. Awards include BMI,and L.A. Horn Club Prize.

Scores are published by Carl Fisher and Shawnee Press.

Recordings include:
Quintet (CRI S-293)
Suite for Six Horns (Angel S-36036)

38 West 106th St.
New York, N.Y. 10025

TOM JOHNSON (b. 1939,Greeley, Colo.)

Composer, pianist, writer, music critic.

Study at Yale University and privately with Morton Feldman.

Composer of several widely performed music-theater pieces, the best known being his *The Four Note Opera*, which has received over 40 productions including ones in New York, Japan, and on national television. Other theatrical works include *The Masque of the Clouds* and *Five Shaggy Dog Operas*.He has also been quite involved with music for dance and has done a number of pieces with Kathy Duncan.

Most of his music reflects a minimalist attitude and has explored visual and verbal as well as musical media. Works such as *Lectures with Audience Participation*, *Secret Songs*, *Risks for Unrehearsed Performers*, and *Nine Bells* have all been performed on various tours and guest appearances by Mr. Johnson.

Since 1971 he has been a regular music critic for the *The Village Voice* in New York and contributed numerous articles to other publications.

His *Imaginary Music*, a book of 104 drawings using musical symbols, *Private Pieces: Piano Music for Self-Entertainment*, and many of his other scores are available from Two-Eighteen Press and Associated Music Publishers.

Recording:

An Hour for Piano (Lovely Music LMV/VR-1091)

Two-Eighteen Press
Box. 218, Village Station
New York, N.Y. 10014

BEN JOHNSTON (b. 1926, Macon, Georgia)

Studies at William and Mary College, Cincinnati Conservatory, and Mills College.

Large and diverse catalogue of compositions: traditional ensembles, a range of experimental pieces, environments, tape pieces, a series of works exploring microtones, several speech–sound pieces, and a "rock" opera. Many important commissions and performances (La Salle Quartet, St. Louis Symphony, Swingle Singers, and such noted solo performers of new music as Bert Turetzky, Stuart Dempster, Jack McKenzie, and John Cage).

Professor of Composition and Theory at University of Illinois since 1951.

Main publishers of his work are Composer–Performer Editions and Smith Publications; some pieces also with Media Press and Josef Marx.

Recordings:

Carmilla (Vanguard VSD 79322)
Casta Bertram (Nonesuch H-71237)
Ci-Git Satie (Ars Nova/Ars Antiqua Records, AN-1005)
Duo fo Flute and Bass (Advance FGR-1, CRI S-405)
Sonata for Microtonal Piano (New World Records 203)
String Quartet No. 2 (Nonesuch H-71224)

School of Music
University of Illinois
Urbana, Ill. 61820

DAVID JONES (b. 1929, Twickenham, England)

Composer, percussionist.

Study with Christian Darnton, Marc Wilkinson, and Stefan Wolpe. Seminars with Luigi Nono and Bruno Maderna at Dartington Summer School.

Compostitions include chamber instrumental and media works and a series of prose pieces, the latter being representative of a concern with "creative activies for professional and nonprofessional musicians that explore the intuitive world, beyond improvisation, of sense perception."

Active as composer–performer, member of the English ensemble Twenty-Three and a percussion duo with Keith Potter. Current works include instrumental and percussion pieces, and environmental tape projects without electronics associated with the basic elements: earth, fire, and water.

29 Kings Ave.
Sunbury-on-Thames
Middlesex, England

ALISON KNOWLES (b. April 29, 1933, New York)

Visual artist, writer, performer.

Study at Pratt Institute–painting with Lindner, Gottlieb, and Albers; graphics and photography at Manhattan School of Printing.

Many one-woman and group shows since 1958. Active in producing and showing various environments and events such as *The Big Book, Identical Lunch, House of Dust and Bean Garden.* Active in the early happenings movement and with Fluxus in the early 1960s. Regular contributor to the New York Avant-garde Festival and many other performance activities in the U.S. and Europe.

Guggenheim Fellowship in 1968; director of Graphics Laboratory at California Institue of the Arts (1970–72).

Editor of *Women's Work* with Annea Lockwood. Publications include several computer poems and performance pieces, of which *Proposition IV (Squid)* is one, and even an Alison Knowles Tee Shirt. Additional visual art, writing, and performance pieces are available from Printed Editions.

122 Spring St.
New York, N.Y. 10012

DAVID KOBLITZ (b. 1948, Cleveland)

Composer, performer.

Study at Universities of Pennsylvania and Michigan, principal teachers being George Crumb, Ross Lee Finney, and George Cacioppo.

Resident composer–performer with Michigan Contemporary Directions Ensemble, Crofts Fellow at Tanglewood; taught at Emerson College.

In 1975 and 1979 awarded grants from the National Endowment for the Arts, Massachusetts Arts and Humanities Foundation, and the Charles E. Ives Scholarship from the National Institute of Arts and Letters. CAPS grant, 1978, and Guggenheim Fellowship, 1979–80.

Nomos for unaccompanied double-bass is published by Yorke Editions

(London, 1974). Other works for solo instruments, small ensembles, orchestra, and tape are available from Margun Music and the composer.

241 E. 76th St.
New York, N.Y. 10021

JOAN LA BARBARA (b. June 8, 1947, Philadelphia)

Composer, singer, experimental vocalist.

Study at Syracuse and New York Universities.

Wide range of experience as a singer from classical, jazz, rock, commercials, and theater to her present work with new music. Past activity with such composers as Philip Glass, Steve Reich, John Cage, Alvin Lucier, Robert Ashley, and others.

Her own solo work is involved with "extending the sound spectrum associated with the vocal instrument, exploring its vast and relatively unexplored possibilities." Her "Voice is the Original Instrument" concerts have been performed throughout the United States and at several important European festivals. She also does other solo performance, workshops, and sound installations.

She has written articles in *Data-Arte* (Milan) and *Solo Weekly News* and been featured in *Kunst, Flash Art, The Village Voice, Avalanche, Painted Bride Quarterly,* and *Soundings.* An interview with her, and *Voice Piece,* is included in *Desert Plants.*

She has received grants in music, visual art, and multi-media from the National Endowment for the Arts, CAPS, DAAD, ASCAP, and others. She also writes regular concert and record reviews as New Music Editor for *Musical America.* Currently preparing a book on new vocal techniques for Theodore Presser Co. for release in 1981.

Recordings:

Tapesongs (Chiaroscuro 196)
The Voice Is the Original Instrument (Wizard 2266)
Reluctant Gypsy (Wizard 227)

Wizard Records are available from the composer and from New Music Distribution Service.

P.O. Box II
Old Chelsea Station
New York, N.Y. 10011

DANIEL LENTZ (b. 1942, Latrobe, Pa.)

Composer, performer.

Study at St. Vincent College, Ohio University, Brandeis, and on a Fulbright at Stockholm Univesity and Swedish Radio–TV.

Early work was very involved with live electronic music and briefly with political and "anti-" music. Now working to "develop an aesthetic composed of two things: sensous sonic beauty and new structural or formal approaches."

Formerly director of California Time Machine, now directing San Andreas Fault (a group of fifteen percussionists) and co-director of Syncantics: The Pacific Coast Center for a New Musical Language (a new organization involved with research and performance).

Taught at University of California, Santa Barbara (1968–70) and Antioch (1973). Many lectures and workshops; numerous prizes, awards, and grants.

Compositions are available from Syncantics and include *Missa Umbrarum* for eight amplified voices, amplified crystal glasses, and 263 "sonic shadows" (1973): several works for voices used in a somewhat similar way; taped and live electronic music; and a series of conceptual performance pieces. A recording, *Song(s) of the Sirens* (MCA 67013; 5306-67013H) is available, and a color video tape of *King Speech Song* has been produced.

Syncatics
67 La Vuelta Rd.
Santa Barbara, Calif. 93108

JEFFREY LEVINE (b. 1942, Brooklyn, N.Y.)

Composer, bass player.

Study at Brown and Yale with Mel Powell, Gunther Schuller, and Franco Donatoni. Further study in Rome on a Fulbright.

Active as a performer of new music (double bass) with such groups as Contemporary Chamber Ensemble and Gruppo Sperimentale Chigiano (Italy). Taught at Rutgers, Berkeley, and Hayward (Calif.) State University. Currently with the San Francisco Ballet and and free-lancing in California Bay Area.

Several important commissions (Berkshire Music Center, Oakland Ballet, etc.) and performances of his music in U.S. and Europe; National Endowment for the Arts grant in 1978. Mostly instrumental chamber music, though several piano and orchestral pieces.

Music is published by Edizione Suvini-Zerboni in Milan and available through MCA Music in this country.

6425 Colby
Oakland, Calif. 94618

ANNEA LOCKWOOD (b. 1939, New Zealand)

Composer, performer.

Study at University of Canterbury, Royal College of Music (London). Musikhochschule (Köln), CEM studio (Bilthoven), Darmstadt, and EMS studio course in computer programing.

Awards and scholarships from Deutsche Academische Austauschdienst, Arts Council of Great Britain, Gulbenkian Foundation, CAPS, and N.E.A.

Particularly known for tape and live electronic music, some tapes being in the form of extended environments. Works widely performed in Europe and U.S. in such places as ISCM Austria, Paris Biennale, Queen Elizabeth Hall and BBC in England, and Composers' Forum, The Kitchen, and with Merce Cunningham Dance Co. Co-editor, with Allison Knowles, of *Women's Work*. Other pieces published in *Source, Ear*, and British Music Publishers.

Recordings:
    End (Swedish Radio Records)
    Glass World of Annea Lockwood (Tangent Records, London)
    Annea Lockwood (New Wilderness Audiographics 7704 A-B)
    Tiger Baum (Source Records)
    World Rhythms (1750 Arch Records 1765)

Baron de Hirsch Rd.
Crompond, N.Y. 10517

EDWIN LONDON (b. March 16, 1929, Philadelphia)

Composer, conductor, horn player, arranger.

Studied at Oberlin and University of Iowa with Clapp and Bezanson; horn at Manhattan School of Music with Schuller. Further study with Dallapiccola in New York and Milhaud at Aspen.

Free-lance horn player in New York and elsewhere; directed music for Toledo Shakespeare Co.; taught at Smith College and University of Illinois and conducted Smith–Amherst Symphony (1962–68).

His music is published by MJQ Music, Alexander Broude, and Joseph Boonin.

Recordings include:

    Choral Music (UBRES 302)
    Psalm of These Days III (CRI S-405)
    Sonatina (Advance FGR-7)
    Trio (UBRES 301)

Music Department
Cleveland State University
Cleveland, Ohio

ALVIN LUCIER (b. May 14, 1931, Nashua, N.H.)

Composer, performer, conductor.

Study at Yale and Brandeis; two years in Rome on a Fulbright.

Co-founder, with Ashley, Mumma, and Behrman, of the Sonic Arts Union, through which he has performed widely in the U.S. and Europe.

Formerly Director of the Brandeis University Chamber Chorus, which devoted much of its time to new music. Since 1969 teaching at Wesleyan University and music director for Viola Farber Dance Company.

Pioneer in gestural notation (performers' actions described, rather than sound) in *Action Music for Piano* (1962) first use of brain waves in musical performance (*Music for Solo Performer*, 1965), articulation of resonant frequencies (*I am sitting in a Room*), and considerable involvement with visual imagery and movement of "sound geographies in space" (*Still and Moving Lines of Silence in Families of Hyperbolas*, 1974). Active as a composer–performer.

His work is included in *Source* and in various other more recent periodicals; an interview with him is found in *Desert Plants*. A new book *Chambers* is published by Wesleyan University Press.

Recording:

North American Time Capsule (Odyssey 32160156)

Artservices
463 West St.
New York, N.Y. 10014

OTTO LUENING (b. June 15, 1900, Madison, Wis.)

Composer, flute player, conductor, electronic music pioneer.

Study at Munich Academy and Zurich Conservatory (Germany) with Busoni, Jarnach, and Andreae.

Active in new music in New York and Europe in the 1920s and 1930s where he knew and worked closely with Varese, Cowell, Ives, Rudhyar, Ruggles, and many others. Conductor for theater and opera; music director with James Joyce among others.

In the early 1950s, with Ussachevsky, was one of the major pioneers of electronic music and creator of some of the first pieces for tape and tape with live instruments. His *Fantasy in Space* remains one of the most interesting early electronic pieces. Many articles on electronic music.

Very influential as a teacher of many major composers through his positions at Bennington and particularly Columbia University. Many major grants, commissions, and performances; particularly active in chamber music, orchestral, and educational music.

His music is published by many of the major publishers, including C. F. Peters and Galaxy. A long article on the history of electronic music is included in *The Development and Practice of Electronic Music* (Jon Appleton and Ronald Perera, eds.; Englewood Cliffs, N.J.: Prentice-Hall, 1974).

Recordings:

Concerted Piece for Tape Recorder and Orchestra (CRI S-227)
Fantasy in Space and other electronic music (Desto 6466, Folkways 6160)

Gargoyles (Columbia MS-6566)
Poem in Cycles and Bells (CRI 112)
Short Suite (Golden Crest 4140 Q)
Solo Sonata No. 3, String Quartets, Trio (CRI S-303)
Sonata for Piano, other music for organ and tape (CRI S-334)
Suites 3, 4 and 5 (CRI S-400)
Symphonic Fantasy, Kentucky Rondo (CRI 103)
Symphonic Interlude (Desto 6429 E)
Synthesis for Orchestra and Electronic Sound (CRI S-219)

American Composers' Alliance
170 West 74th Street
New York, N.Y. 10023

KENNETH MAUE (b. 1947, New York State)

Composer, performer, health professional.

Study at Wesleyan University (piano, Western and avant-garde music, World Music) with Barlow, Winslow, and Lucier; Ph.D. in 1973 in composition. Greatly influenced by Ives, Cage, and the I Ching.

Most composition is in a continuing series called "Info-Flow," or structured activity as musical process. Interested in "the inner essence or quality called 'music' without getting involved in instruments" and elaborate sound notation, and in the "musical sense which can be brought to virtually any activity."

Active as a teacher through the use of Info-Flow concept in the classroom. Taught at Teacher Center in New Haven, at Wesleyan, and lectures elsewhere. At present involved professionally in the holistic health field and "growth movement" centered in California's Bay Area, particularly the Bates Method of vision improvement at Wellness Resource Center in Mill Valley.

Two Info-Flow pieces, *Info-Matrix #1* and *Three Days of Red*, have been published in *Source 7/8*, edited by John Cage. Maue's book, *Water in the Lake*, was published by Harper & Row in 1979.

40 Monterey Ave.
San Anselmo, Calif. 94960

STEPHEN MAYER (b. September 9, 1943)

Composer, pianist, conductor.

Study at Brooklyn College, particularly Greek with Vera Lachmann. Piano study with Grete Sultan.

Nine years teaching and conducting at Camp Catawba in North Carolina. Presently Composer-in-Residence at John Dewey High school in Brooklyn, and Hewlett High School in Long Island, N.Y.

Active in New York area as pianist, conductor, and teacher. Carnegie Recital Hall debut in 1976.

Published by Harold Branch Publishing, Inc.

126 East 57th St.
New York, N.Y. 10022

FRANK McCARTY (b. November 1941, Pamona, Calif.)

Composer, percussionist, live electronic performer.

Study at San Diego State College with Ward-Steinman, University of S. California with Dahl, and University of California (San Diego) with Erickson, Gaburo, and Oliveros (Ph.D.).

Active as a percussionist, particularly with San Diego Symphony, and National Chairman of Percussive Arts Society. His most recent performing and compositional activity is in live electronics with group Biom (Allen and Patricia Strange). Interested in instrumental extensions and designing–building electronic music equipment.

Also involved in notation through Percussive Arts Society and the Ghent Conference on New Notation.

Works are published by HaMaR Press (Huntington, N.Y.), Media Press, Artisan Music, and J. Boonin. A recording of *Saxim* and *Tactus Tempus* is available on Composers' Cassettes.

Department of Music
University of North Carolina
Greensboro, N.C. 27412

CARL MICHAELSON (b. 1959, New Zork)

Composer, electronic music specialist, publisher.

Study at Clark University and Queens College. Private study with J. Edward Mueller.

Since 1968 he has been working almost exclusively with electronic music; he is particularly interested in music for the theater. Several tapes for Irene Dowd (*Subway and Nyarlathotep*) performed at Juilliard and Columbia University.

Musical Director for the Wetzig Dance Company, for whom he has composed seven tape pieces which have been performed many times. The *Pining Wind* was commissioned by the Centrifugal Theater and performed at the Clark Center in New York in May of 1973. Active as a designer and builder of electronic music equipment. Founder of Greene Street Music, which specializes in electronic music.

354 Van Duzer Ave.
Staten Island, N.Y.

MEREDITH MONK

Composer, choreographer, director, singer, actress.

Study at Sarah Lawrence College, 1960–64.

Since 1964 she has been active as a solo dance performer–choreographer and working to develop vocal techniques to fulfill her notion of the "dancing voice; the voice as an instrument as flexible as a foot or a spine; an aural manifestation of waves of energy." In 1966 she presented *16 Millimeter Earrings*, the first of her dance–theater pieces using her original vocal music. This was followed by *Juice*, for eighty-five voices; *Vessel*, an opera epic; and, recently, *Quarry* (all presented by her performing group, The House). Recent pieces include *Dolmen Music, The Plateau Series, Recent Ruins*, and *Specimen Days*.

In 1970 she presented the first of several solo concerts which have been widely performed in this country and Europe; they include *Raw Recital No. 1, Our Lady of Late*, and others.

She has received many awards and fellowships and much critical acclaim ("Obie" awards for *Vessel* and Quarry, Guggenheim Fellowship, Brandeis Creative Arts Award, and several ASCAP awards).

Three recordings of her work are available through New Music Distribution Service:

Anthology
Key: An Album of Invisible Theatre
Our Lady of Late

Recordings from other sources:

"Biography" from Educaton of the Girlchild (Giorno Poetry Systems Records 012-013)
Songs from the Hill/Tablet (Wergo)

KLS Management
250 West 14th St.
New York, N.Y. 10011

GORDON MUMMA (b. March 30, 1935, Framingham, Mass.)

Composer, performer, writer, specialist in live electronic music.

Study at University of Michigan where he also organized and co-founded, with Robert Ashley, the Cooperative Studio for Electronic Music and the annual Once Festival.

Since 1966 a musician and composer with Merce Cunningham Dance Co. and the Sonic Arts Union, and has made extensive tours throughout the world.

Designer of electronic equipment for Expo 70 in Osaka, and for various electronic music studios. Articles on contemporary performance and electronic technology have been widely published, particularly *The Development and Practice of Electronic Music* (Prentice-Hall) and *Merce Cunningham* (Dutton).

Taught and lectured at many universities; currently teaching at University of California, Santa Cruz.

Music published by Berandol and Universal Edition.

Recordings:

Cybersonic Cantilevers (Folkways 33904)
Hornpipe (Mainstream 5010)
Megation for Wm. Burroughs (Lovely Music LML/vr 1091)
Mesa for Cybersonic Bandoneon (Odyssey 32160158)
Music from the Venezia Space Theater (Advance FGR-5)

Department of Music
University of California
Santa Cruz, Calif.

NEW VERBAL WORKSHOP

An ensemble of poets and musicians who use their voices as instruments to explore the musical possibilities in verbal and nonverbal combinations. The pieces they do are based on "hard improvisation," that is, improvisation which is developed collectively through rehearsal and performed with a definite structure.

Formed in 1970 under a grant from the University of Illinois Research Board, the group performs in the Midwest and has attended conferences and appeared on concerts in other parts of the U.S. and Europe. In addition to their own work they have done music with composer Ben Johnston. Members are Janet Gilbert, Joan Korb, Herbert Marder, Norma Marder, and Fred Simon. Tapes are available and publication is pending.

Herbert Marder
Department of English
University of Illinois
Urbana, Ill. 61801

KIRK NUROCK

Composer, pianist, conductor, arranger.
Study at Juilliard with Vincent Persichetti and Roger Sessions.
Jazz prodigy at fifteen; performed with Dizzy Gilespie, Phil Woods, Lee Konitz, Donald Byrd, Chet Baker, and others. Active as a studio musician, conductor, arranger, and solo jazz pianist.
Conductor of Broadway productions of *Two Gentlemen of Verona* and *Shelter*, the national touring company of *Hair*, and off-Broadway production of *Salvation*. Composed for many other New York theater productions and dance companies such as Louis Falco, Daniel Nagrin, and Kathryn Posin. He recently did orchestrations for the Broadway production of *Working* and an electronic score for *G.R. Point*.
Founded Natural Sound Workshop in 1971, through which he has explored the sonic range of the voice and body. From this work he has composed music for a number of varied smaller ensembles and worked with singers, particularly Jay Clayton. He is currently collaborating with Tom O'Horgan on a musical adaptation of Kipling's *Jungle Books*.
Many lectures, workshops, and articles in *Performance Magazine* and other publications.

Recordings:

A solo jazz piano recording *Nurock* (Adamo ADS 9504)
A Natural Sound recording *Induced Meditation* (Environments Series, Syntonic Research SD 66007)
Working, orchestrations (Columbia Masterworks 35411)

For Natural Sound:
Sheldon Soffer
130 West 66th Street
New York, N.Y. 10023

For Jazz:
Universal Jazz Coalition
156 Fifth Ave.
New York, N.Y. 10010

MICHAEL NYMAN (b. 1944, London)

Composer, musicologist, critic, writer.
Studied at Royal Academy of Music with Alan Bush; research at King's College, under Thurston Dart; collected folk music in Rumania.
Music critic since (1969, currently with Studio International. Co-editor of *Experimental Music Catalogue*. Performed with Scratch Orchestra, Portsmouth Sinfonia, Foster's Social Orchestra, Gavin Bryars, Steve Reich, and others. Recently completed soundtrack for film *Keep It Up Downstairs*. Currently teaching in Fine Arts Department of Goldsmith's College (London) and Trent Polytechnic (Nottingham).
Publications include editions of Handel and Purcell for Bentham and Hooker and *Experimental Music* (Schirmer Books, 1974).

200 Ladbroke Grove
London W 10

PAULINE OLIVEROS (May 30, 1932, Houston)

Composer, performer.
Study with Robert Erickson in San Francisco.
Work at San Francisco Tape Music Center from 1961 to 1966, taught at Mills College and U. of California (San Diego) since 1967.
Since the late 1950s her work has been very involved with group improvisation and has moved toward mixed media, dance, film, and electronics. Early involvement with live and performed electronic music. Work with David Tudor, dancer–choreographer Elizabeth Harris and many others. Developed "sonic meditation" and worked with her ♀ Ensemble and women's and feminist groups.
The primary source for her music is Smith Publications with additional scores from Boudoin College Music Press, Media Press, *Source*, and European American Music. Books such as *Pauline's Proverbs*, *The Initiation*, and *Software for People* are available from Printed Editions. an interview and her *Crow Two* are included in *Desert Plants*.

Recordings:

Bye, Bye Butterfly (1750 Arch Records 1765)
I of IV (Odyssey 32160160)
Outline for Flute, Percussion and Bass (Nonesuch 71237)
Sound Patterns (Odyssey 32160156)
Trio for Flute, Piano and Pageturner (Advance FGR-95)

Music Department
University of California
La Jolla, Calif.

CHARLEMAGNE PALESTINE (b. 1945, New York)

Composer, pianist, visual and video artist.

Study at High School of Music and Art, Julliard, Mannes College, and New School in New York.

Composer-in-Residence at NYU Intermedia Center (1968–69), carilloner at St. Thomas' Church, New York (1964–70), and taught multimedia at California Institute of the Arts (1970–72).

Works have performed mostly as an extension of the art rather than music world. Pieces for chorus, carillon, piano, organ, synthesizer, strings, video tape, and body performer; many visual works and visual scores called *Books of Continuity*.

Active as a performer throughout the U.S., Canada, and Europe, such as at Festival d'Automne (Paris), and in Cologne, Bremen, Rome, Brussells, and elsewhere. An interview is included in *Desert Plants*.

Books, records, video tapes, and drawings available through:

Castelli-Sonnabend Gallery
420 West Broadway
New York, N.Y. 10012

MICHAEL PARSONS (b. December 12, 1938, England)

Composer–performer.

Studied at Oxford and Royal College of Music. Study of experimental music with Cornelius Cardew at Morley College, London.

Co-founder, with Cardew and Howard Skempton, of the Scratch Orchestra, an experimental group of thirty to fifty members who worked with improvisation, random juxtaposition of multiple events, and relatively strict composition; very active from 1969 until disbanded in 1972.

Recent music is fully composed and often uses various rhythmic systems that determine small-scale events and larger forms. Particularly interested in ways in which jazz and many non-Western musics use a regular, driving pulse, and polyrhythms. Also fascinated by the "very slow pulse which hovers on the edge of timelessness."

Presently teaching in the Fine Arts Department of Portmouth Polytechnic.

Most music is published by *Experimental Music Catalogue* and includes several pieces each for piano(s) and percussion.

148 Fellows Road
London, N.W. 3

RICHARD PEASLEE

Composer, arranger, performer.

Study at Yale, Julliard, and privately with Nadia Boulanger in Paris.

Particularly noted for music for the theater, including *Marat/Sade, A Midsummer Night's Dream, Us, The Screens,* and *The Theater of Cruelty,* all with Peter Brook and the Royal Shakespeare Co. Composed five musicals: *Boccaccio, The King of the United States, Songs of Love and War, Legends of King Arthur,* and *Flying Sunflower.* Music for many other major plays and productions: *Indians, Cry*

of Players, *Troilus and Cressida, The Serpent, Terminal,* (with Open Theater), *The Fable,* and many more.

Two years composing–arranging for Bill Russo's London Jazz Orchestra (*Stonehenge, A London Anthology,* and others) and *Chicago Concerto* for Gerry Mulligan. Several film scores, including *Marat/Sade, Tell Me Lies,* and *Where Time Is a River,* plus shorter works with Ralph Steiner. *October Piece* for rock group and symphony has been widely played (Philadelphia, Detroit, Milwaukee, Buffalo, etc.)

Presently involved with a live electronic music performance group Linera B with Ken Bichel and Mike Redding.

Marat/Sade music is published by Highgate Press (2121 Broadway, New York); most of the remaining music is with J. Boonin (theater scores, jazz scores, and chamber music).

Recordings:

Marat/Sade (Caedmon TRS S-312 and United Artists 5153)
Passage (Linera B Records)

90 Riverside Dr.
New York, N.Y. 10024

Booking manager:
Christine Estes
159 Mackenzie St.
Brooklyn, N.Y. 11235

CARMINE PEPE (b. October 10, 1929, Newark, N.J.)

Composer, percussionist.

Study at New York University, University of Indiana, and privately with Nadia Boulanger, Bernhard Heiden, and Juan Orrego-Salas.

Awards include Fontainebleau Scholarship, Fulbright to Rome, Bennington Composers Conference, and MacDowell Colony Fellowship.

Several works for strings; *Silver Screen* and *New Ark* for brass and percussion; the symphonic work *Thyrsus* and several others pieces for voice and/or instruments. Completing an opera, *Garofulous,* and a work for chorus, soloists, brass, and percussion *Mind-Forged Manacles,* in which he develops and explores a system of gestural notation.

Recordings:

Rue de la Tombe Issoire (Opus One 32)
Sonata for Violin and Piano (Opus One 18)

116 East 92nd St.
New York, N.Y. 10028

D.B. RAMA/DAVID RECK (b, 1935 [Capricorn], Rising Star, Texas)

Composer, ethnomusicologist, veena player.

Study at University of Texas with Pisk and Phillips; Pennsylvania with Rochberg. Ethnomusicology with specialization in Indian music at Wesleyan. Further study at College of Carnatic Music in Madras, India, and with the great veena master Thirugokarnam Ramachandra Iyer.

Worked as a country and jazz musician in Texas. Concertized widely on the veena in India and U.S.

Widely performed composer in this country and Europe. Commissions from Fromm Foundation, Ars Nova Trio, American Brass Quintet; Guggenheim Grant in 1970 plus several others.

Author of book *Music of the Whole Earth* (Charles Scribner's Sons) in collaboration with wife Carol Reck, photographer.

Published music is available through C. F. Peters, Composer–Performer Editions, Tu Fu Music Co, and included in *Source* and *Pieces*.

Music Department
Amherst College
Amherst, Mass.

STEVE REICH (b. October 3, 1936, New York)

Composer, performer.

Study of philosophy at Cornell; music at Juilliard and Mills College with Berio and Milhaud. Further study of African and Balinese music.

Early work was in electronic music at San Francisco Tape Music Center (*It's Gonna Rain* and *Come Out*) in which he first evolved his idea of music as gradual process. Final electronic work was with his "Phase-Shifting Pulse," built by the composer with help from engineer Larry Owens.

Since the late 1960s all of his music has been for live performance by his ensemble; this has culminated in several widely performed works (*Drumming, Four Organs, Six Pianos, Music for Mallet Instruments, Voices and Organ*, etc.). Collaboration with dancer–choreographer Laura Dean on several pieces. Most recent work has been for large, almost orchestral, ensembles.

Concepts of music well discussed in recent book *Steve Reich: Writings about Music* (co-published by Press of Nova Scotia College of Art and Design, Halifax, and New York University Press). His early music is published by Universal Edition, London.

Recordings include:

Come Out (Odyssey 32160160)
It's Gonna Rain and *Violin Phase* (Columbia MS-7265)
Four Organs and *Phase Patterns* (Disques Shandar 10005, Paris)
Four Organs (Angel S-36059)
Drumming, Six Pianos, Music for Mallet Instruments, Voices and Organ (Deutsche Grammophon DG 2740-106)
Music for 18 Musicians (ECM/Warner Brothers 1129)
Octet, Music for Large Ensemble, and *Violin Phase* (ECM/Warner Brothers)

Lynn Garon Management
1199 Park Ave.
New York, N.Y. 10028

DENNIS RILEY (b. May 10, 1943, Los Angeles)

Composer, pianist.

Study at Universities of Colorado, Illinois, and Iowa (Ph.D.) Composition with Crumb, Effinger, Frederickson, and Hervig.

His work has received many performances and awards, including Bearns and BMI Prizes; Ford Foundation, MENC, and Guggenheim Fellowships.

Recording:

Variations II: Trio (CRI S-324)

Broadcast Music Inc.
320 West 57th St.
New York, N.Y. 10019

TERRY RILEY (b. June 24, 1935, Colfax, Calif.)

Composer, performer, soprano saxophone player.

Studied at San Francisco State University with Robert Erickson and at University of California, Berkely.

Considerable experience as a jazz musician his work is still based on improvisation and spontaneity. Along with La Monte Young he was one of the first composers in the early 1960s to explore long-term repetition, regularity, and singularity. This culminated in his very well-known *In C*. Most of his music is for himself as soloist with various tape loops, delay and multi-track systems (*Dorian Reeds, Keyboard Studies, Rainbow in Curved Air*).

He has performed widely throughout the world. Special guest of Swedish Radio and Academy of Music; with Creative Associates at State University of New York Buffalo. At present teaching at Mills College.

Recordings include:

Dorian Reeds (Massart)
In C (Columbia MS-7178)
Rainbow in Curved Air (Columbia MS-7315)

Department of Music
Mills College
Oakland, Calif.

JIM ROSENBERG (b. 1947, Denver)

Poet, reader, mathematician.

Study at Pomona College and University of California (Berkeley) in mathematical logic.

Primarily a poet whose work ranges from the use of techniques closely related to music—such as compositions for tape and scored performances for several readers—to traditional poetry and work closely related to the visual arts—such as word environments.

His work has been performed at Les Salons Vides in San Francisco and the Kitchen in New York, among others.

Current work is "centered on an ongoing project entitled *Permanent & Temporary Poetry*, in which words and word constructions are accumulated in reservoirs as elements kept autonomously for free conbination with other elements, in either temporary or permanent works."

Publications include *Notes for the Foundations of A Theory of Meter* (Grabhorn-Hoyem, 1970) and appearances in magazines *Open Reading, Toothpick, Vort,* and *Buttons* and in the anthology *Episodes in Five Poetic Traditions,* ed. R. G. Barnes (Chandler, 1972).

Box. 42
Merrittstown, Pa. 15463

NICOLAS ROUSSAKIS (b. June 14, 1934, Athens, Greece)

Composer, clarinetist.

Study at Columbia University with Luening, Beeson, Cowell, and Weber; Hochschule für Musik in Hamburg and Darmstadt with Boulez, Berio, Ligeti, Pousseur, and Stockhausen. Additional study with Shapey and Jarnach.

Active as composer, performer, and administrator with Group for Contemproray Music, American Composers' Alliance, American Society of University Composers, and Composers' Recordings. Work also as a free-lance clarinetist and conductor for a variety of groups, particularly new music and avant-garde dance companies, the Living Theater, and others. Now teaching at Rutgers University.

Music is available from Alexander Broude and ACA; *Night Speech* and *Sonata for Harpsichord* are available on CRI S-255 and other music is on Nonesuch.

Department of Music
Rutgers University
New Brunswick, N. J.

FREDERIC RZEWSKI (b. April 13, 1938, Westfield, Mass.)

Composer, pianist.

Study at Harvard with Thompson and Spies and at Princeton with Sessions and Babbitt.

Early association and collaboration with Christian Wolff and David Behrman. Lived from 1960–70 in Europe, where he was closely associated with Boulez and Stockhausen. Founded Musica Elettronica Viva (MEV) with Alvin Curran and Richard Teitelbaum in Rome in 1966, and has played well over 200 concerts of experimental live electronic music with them throughout the world.

Highly regarded as a pianist and interpreter of a wide range of new music (Boulez, Cage, Stockhausen, etc.). Active as an improvising musician with MEV and with Karl Berger, Anthony Braxton, and others.

His early music was highly influenced by serialism; from the mid-1969s he moved toward experimental, live electronic, theater, and improvisatory music. His most recent work combines vernacular elements and political texts. An interview and several pieces are included in *Desert Plants.*

Recordings:

Attica, Les Moutons de Panurge, Coming Together (Opus One 20)
Musica Elettronica Viva (Mainstream 5002)
The People United will never be defeated (Vanguard 71248)
Song and Dance (Nonesuch 71366)
3 Songs (Folkways 33903)
Variation on "No place to go but around" (Finnadar 9011)

Linda Goodman Concert Management
142 West End Ave.
New York, N.Y. 10023

ERIC SALZMAN (b. September 8, 1933, New York)

Composer, music–theater director, writer, critic.

Study at Columbia with Luening, Ussachevsky, and Beeson; at Princeton with Sessions and Babbitt. European study in Rome and Darmstadt.

Particularly known for his music–theater and dance works; several others of a multi-media, environmental nature. Work with dancer–choreographer Daniel Nagrin and director of his own music-theater company, Quog. Recent productions include *Lazarus* and the opera *The Conjurer* (written with Michael Sahl, and produced at Joseph Papp's Public Theater in New York, directed by Tom O'Horgan) and *Stauf.*

Five years as music critic for New York Times and New York Herald Tribune. Many critical writings: *Twentieth-Century Music* (Prentice-Hall) and a book on vernacular harmony, *Making Changes* (McGraw-Hill) with Michael Sahl.

Music Director for Pacifica's WBAI and founder of its Free Music Store; also directed New Image of Sound Series at Hunter College and The Electric Ear at The Electric Circus.

Recordings include:

Larynx Music, Queens Collage, Wiretap (Atlantic-Finnadar 9005Q)
Nude Paper Sermon (Nonesuch 71231)

29 Middagh St.
Brooklyn Heights, N.Y. 11201

R. MURRAY SCHAFER (b. 1933, Sarina, Ontario)

Composer, writer.

Study at Royal Conservatory in Toronto and in Vienna and England.

Active as concert organizer and founder of Ten Centuries Concerts in Toronto. Faculty positions at Memorial University (Newfoundland) and Simon Fraser University (Vancouver).

Compositions widely performed in Canada, U.S., and Europe. Opera *Loving* on CBC national television; many commissions since. Recent work reflects a strong interest in Eastern culture (*From the Tibetan Book of the Dead, Lustro, Bita, Arcana,* and others).

Founder of World Soundscape Studies involving detailed study of sound environment (noise pollution, acoustic design, aesthetics) and Sonic Research Studio at Simon Fraser University (studies available from A.R.C. Publications). A journal, *Music of the Environment,* has been published by Universal Edition; *Tuning the World,* a major study of the soundscape project, has been published by Knopf.

Innovative series of booklets on music education have been very influential and are now collected together into the book *Creative Music Education* (Schirmer Books). His music is published by Universal Edition, Canadian Music Centre, and Berandol, Ltd.

Recordings include:

Minnelieder, Son of Heldenleben, String Quartet (RCI Canadian Collection)
Requiems for the Party Girl (CRI S-245)
Threnody, Epitaph for Moonlight, Statement in Blue, and a talk on soundscape studies (Melbourne)

R.R. 5
Bancroft, Ont. KOL 1 Co
Canada

ELLIOTT SCHWARTZ (b. January 19, 1936, Brooklyn, N.Y.)

Composer, performer, writer.

Study at Columbia with Luening, Beeson, Creston; additional work with Brant, Goeb, Aitkin, Chou Wen-chung, Shapey, Varese, Wolpe, Feldman, and others.

Many compositions for orchestra, chamber groups, tape, theater, and mixed media. Performances by major orchestras and leading chamber music groups (Cincinnati Symphony, Minnesota Orchestra, New York Chamber Soloists, Aeolian Chamber Players, California Time Machine, etc.) Many awards and fellowships (ASCAP, Ford, MacDowell, Gaudeamus, National Endowment, etc.)

Professor of Music and Chairman at Bowdoin College; guest positions and lecturer at many other universities.

Author of three books: *The Symphonies of Ralph Vaughan Williams* (Univ. of Mass. Press), *Contemporary Composers on Contemporary Music,* co-edited with Barney Childs (Holt, Rinehart & Winston), and *Electronic Music: A Listener's Guide* (Praeger).

Compositions are published by Carl Fischer, Alexander Broude, General Music, Media Press, Bowdoin College Press, M.M. Cole, E.C. Schirmer, Smith Publications, Hinshaw Music.

Recordings include:

Arias 1, 2, 3, 4; Essays (Advance, FGR-7)
Chamber Orchestra Music (Opus One 23)
Four Studies for Two Clarinets (Advance FGR-15)
Interruptions (Advance FGR 11)
Signals (DGG-2543005)
Soundways, duo-improvisation with Marion Brown (Freedom-Arista AL-1904)
New Recrodings due on Folkways and Orion labels in 1981.

Music Department
Bowdoin College
Brunswick, Maine

MARK SIBLEY (b. December 13, 1947, Hornell, N.Y.)

Mathematician, computer programmer.

Study at George School and Wesleyan and Alfred universities. Graduate study at Wesleyan in mathematics. At present living in New York City working as freelance computer programmer and systems analyst.

STUART SMITH (1948, Portland, Maine)

Composer, percussionist, conductor.

Study of jazz arranging and composition at Berklee School of Music, further study at Hartt College and University of Illinois; composition with Brun, Diemente, and Johnston.

Experienced in jazz and classical music as a percussionist having performed in a variety of situations.

Most work is instrumental, much of it using percussion, and is involved with various improvisational systems. A recent piece, *Return and Recall,* is for "any temporal artform, dance, music, film, etc." Currently involved in inventing "transmedia" notational structures.

His music is published by Belwin-Mills, Media Press, See Saw Music Corp., and Smith Publications.

Recordings:

Faces ("American Society of University Composers Recording Series" Advance FGR-255)
A Gift for Bessie (Advance 255)
Gifts (UBRES Records 301)

Music Department
University of Maryland–Baltimore County
Baltimore, Md.

TIMOTHY SULLIVAN (b. September 1, 1939, Clifton Spring, N.Y.)

Composer, lecturer.

Study at University of Buffalo with Ned Rorem and Virgil Thomson and at Yale with Yehudi Wyner, Hall Overton, and Bulent Arel.

Considerable involvement with electronic music through tape, sound environments, and live electronics. A taped "lip-sync." lecture–performance with John LoPresti has been performed widely throughout the Northeast (Hampshire College, Toronto, many secondary schools, etc.). Also has done music for dance and multimedia performance and composed a series of pieces for single instruments and tape.

Teaching at Nazareth College in Rochester since 1966.

Cadenza for alto saxophone and piano is available in *American Society of University Composers Journal of Music Scores* (Joseph Boonin).

Music Department
Nazareth College
4245 East Ave
Rochester, N.Y. 14610

BRIAN TAYLOR

Composer, classical guitarist.

Study at Stanford and New England Conservatory (guitar with Stanley Buetens and Robert Sullivan). Graduate study in composition at Goddard College.

Works for solo guitar, other solo instruments, and small ensembles; other pieces using open structures and graphic notation. Active in teaching guitar and performing new and traditional music.

Recently working with theatre pieces, one of them being *Transfiguration for Organ, Recorder, Voices and Movement.* Currently studying for the priesthood in Episcopal Church and working with plainchant and shape-note music.

1298 Bay Laurel Dr.
Menlo Park, California 94025

JAMES TENNEY (b. August 10, 1934, Silver City, N.M.)

Composer, pianist, writer.

Study of engineering at University of Denver; Piano with Steuermann at Juilliard; at Bennington with Nowak and Brant and University of Illinois with Gaburo and Hiller. Further piano study with Yi-an Chou and informal composition with Ruggles, Varese, and Cage.

Sound and computer research at Bell Labs (1961–64); research at Yale 1964–66). Teaching at Brooklyn Polytechnic, New School, California Institute of the Arts, University of California, Santa Cruz, and currently York University.

Wide experience as performer of new music; particularly noted for playing of Ives and Ruggles. Co-founder of Tone Roads.

A number of articles on music and acoustics in such journals as *Journal of Acoustical Society of America* and *Journal of Music Theory, Book Meta + Hodos* (Tulane University Press, New Orleans).

Music Department
York University
Downsview, Toronto
Ontario, Canada

CARTER THOMAS (b. January 2, 1950)

Composer, guitarist, electronic designer and builder.

Study at Mt. Senario College and California Institute of the Arts. Composition with Morton Subotnick, Harold Budd, James Tenney, and Leonard Stein.

Particularly involved with tape and live electronic music. Composer of many film and video sound scores; work with video synthesizer. Designed and built custom electronic music systems with Serge Tcherepnin and collaborated on several animated films with Dennis Pies.

An article on the twenty-second–microtone system of South Indian scales (with L. Subramaniam is published by Indian Music House. *To Dawn* is published by Media Press; other pieces published by Rasheva Music (Newall, Calif.). Received a grant from National Endowment for the Arts for his *Illuminations* for acoustic instruments and live electronics.

Currently teaching at the State University of New York at Fredonia and doing concerts and work shops of live electronic music.

American International Artists
275 Madison Ave.
New York, N.Y. 10016

KIT (KATHERINE) TREMAINE

Poet.

Grew up in New Orleans and was educated in New York state. Raised and raced thoroughbred horses in Ireland with husband. Presently living on Mendocino coast and in Santa Barbara, California. Member of Nixon Administration Enemies List.

Poetry published in *Modern Haiku, Soundings, Pieces,* and by Unicorn Press and Basheva Music. Currently writing memoirs.

Syncantics
P.O. Box 5598
Santa Barbara, Calif., 93108

JERRY TROXEL (b. 1936, Maryville, Mo.)

Composer, conductor.

Study at University of Michigan with Albright, Bassett, and Wilson and at University of Iowa with Bezanson and Hervig.

Primary activity has been in teaching and conducting; recent activity in composition has been toward pieces for inexperienced as well as professional musicians. Increasingly interested in "visual processes and imagery and how these can relate to things musical." Particularly interested in percussion.

At present teaching in an interdisciplinary arts program at Sangamon State University.

Creative Arts Program
Sangamon State University
Springfield, Ill. 62708

TUI ST. GEORGE TUCKER (b. 1924, Sagittarius, Los Angeles)

Composer, recorder virtuoso, conductor, broadcaster, teacher.

Particular involvement since the mid-1950s with quarter tones and the timbral and technical resources of recorders, including a complete quarter-tone fingering chart.

For many years director of music at Camp Catawba in North Carolina and active with Catawba Composers in New York. Work is widely played in New York and has been represented on a special series devoted to women composers at the New School. Her String Quartet has been performed and recorded by the Kohon Quartet.

She has been active in presenting programs of new music on radio stations WBAI, WNYC, and National Public Radio. Her work is published by The American Recorder Society (141 West 20th St., New York), *Eikon, Win, Iconograph,* and *Ear* magazines, and Harold Branch Publishing. Several recorder works and *Quarter-Tone Fingering Chart for Recorders* are available from Anfor Press (1619 East 3rd St., Brooklyn, N.Y. 11230). Several pieces are included in *Catawba Assembly* by Charles Miller (Trackaday, New Market, Va. 22844).

Recording:

Tui St. George Tucker and Spencer Holst (New Wilderness Audiographics 7703 C)

47 Barrow St.
New York, N.Y. 10014

CAROLE WEBER (b. Rochester, N.Y.)

Composer, flutist, performer, dancer, artist.

Studied art, education, and dance accompaniment at Berkeley and U.C.L.A. Further study of music and art at California State University.

Member of Aman Folk Ensemble specializing in music and dance of Middle East; collected and orchestrated folk music, played jazz and Afro-Cuban music. Taught elementary school for eight years and coordinated a special art and music workshop in Watts, L.A. Musical director for educational documentary and other films.

Musical Director for Long Beach City College dance concerts; staff dancer-musician at California Institute of the Arts. Worked with many noted dancer-choreographers (Sanasardo, Nagrin, Falco, Elaine Summers, Marilyn Wood, etc.).

Member of New Wilderness Preservation Band for two years with Charlie Morrow and Sounds Out of Silent Spaces with Philip Corner and "new music for home-made instruments and home-made music for traditional instruments" with Skip La Plant.

PHIL WINSOR

Composer, performer, lecturer.

Composition study with Luigi Nono, Robert Erickson, Salvatore Martirano, and Wilber Ogdon. Further study in Europe on a Fulbright and Prix de Rome.

Wide range of compositions for voice and/or instruments, many of which include tape or live electronics. Active in multimedia works for dancers, visual projections, and electronic and live instruments for Chicago Contemporary Dance Theatre.

Active in lectures and workshops with the Contemporary Forum in Chicago. Chairman of Composition at De Paul University.

Works are published by Carl Fischer.

Recordings:

Melted Ears (Advance S-14)

Music Department
De Paul University
Chicago, Ill. 60604

TREVOR WISHART (b. 1946, Leeds, England)

Composer, performer, writer, organizer of concerts and events.

Active with improvisations, tape pieces, and environmental events. Founder of YES (York Electronic Studio) and committee to set up National Musicians' Collective in U.K. Visiting composer at New South Wales Conservatorium of Music, (Sydney, Australia).

Works include environments, works for particular settings (towns, shopping centers, many-roomed buildings), and assemblages using tape and other means to collect sounds. His *Son et Lumiere/Domestic* is for tape, chest of drawers, visual effects, live mice, smoke, bombs, aerial plant pots, etc.

The book *Sun* (Universal Edition) goes into these areas in depth through pieces and commentary and a paticular involvement with children.

Music Department
University of York
Heslington
York Y01 5AX
England

CHRISTIAN WOLFF (b. March 8, 1934, Nice, France)

Composer, performer, classicist.

Study of Classics at Harvard (Ph.D.). Though closely associated with John Cage, Morton Feldman, and David Tudor, self-taught as a composer.

Widely known as an experimental composer particularly involved with various modes of freedom, indeterminacy, and cooperative musical activity. Recent music has been somewhat related to that of Cardew, Rzewski, and others with a strong political element. An interview on this and other subjects is included in *Desert Plants*.

Taught at Harvard, Mills, Darmstadt; currently Associate Professor of Classics, Comparative Literature, and Music at Dartmouth College.

His work is published by C. F. Peters and available on the following recordings:

Duo, Duet, Summer (Mainstream 5015)
For 1,2 or 3 People (Odyssey 32160158)
Lines, for Quartet and *Accompaniments* (CRI 5-357)
Summer (Vox SVBX 5306)

Department of Music
Dartmouth College
Hanover, N.H.

Publishers, Distributors, and Agents for New Music

The following list includes small and large publishers involved with new music that each represent at least one of the composers in this anthology. They all have interesting catalogues of new music and are the major sources for additional material. A number of these publishers are also dealers that distribute new music by other publishers. Included also are several who deal in recordings—particularly CRI and New Music Distribution Service—several periodicals and a number of agents for new music performers.

Aesthetic Research Centre of Canada
A.R.C. Publications
P. O. Box 3044
Vancouver, B.C. Canada, V6B 3X5
*Journal of Experimental Aesthetics
and a number of interesting
publications and recordings.*

American Composers' Alliance (ACA)
Composers' Facsimile Edition
Composers' Recordings, Inc. (CRI)
170 West 74th St.
New York, N.Y. 10023
*CRI has a large catalogue of recordings
of new music.*

American Music Center
American Society of University Composers
250 West 57th St.
New York, N.Y. 10019
*AMC is the major center for information
American music.*

Artservices
463 West St.
New York, N.Y. 10014
*Represents a number of major performing
artists and ensembles.*

Associated Music Publishers
866 Third Ave.
New York, N.Y. 10022
Important catalogue of new music.

Backworks
488 Greenwich St.
New York, N.Y. 10013
Documents of experimental arts.

Berandol Music, Ltd.
11 St. Joseph St.
Toronto, Ontario, M4Y 1J8, Canada
Leading Canadian publisher.

Bookslinger
2163 Ford Parkway
St. Paul, Minn. 55116
*Distributor of Printed Editions,
Something Else Press, etc.*

Boosey & Hawkes
30 West 57th St.
New York, N.Y. 10020

Bowdoin College Music Press
Brunswick, Maine 04011
*Their catalogue of new music is particularly
interesting.*

Harold Branch Publishing, Inc.
95 Eads St.
West Babylon, N.Y. 11704

Alexander Broude, Inc.
225 West 57th St
New York, N.Y. 10019

Centre for Experimental Art and Communication
15 Duncan St.
Toronto, Ont. Canada M5H 3H1
Art books, manuscripts, tapes, newsletter.

Composer/Performer Edition
Source Magazine
2101 22nd St.
Sacramento, Calif. 95818
An important journal on experimental music in the 1960s and early 1970s.

Composer's Cassettes
c/o Allen Strange
Music Department
California State University
San Jose, Calif. 95114

Composers' Facsimile Edition
see American Composers' Alliance

Composers' Forum
Box 501 Canal St. Station
New York, N.Y. 10013
A calendar of new music events and articles of interest.

Composers' Recordings, Inc. (CRI)
see American Composers' Alliance

Criss-Cross Art Communications
P.O. Box 2022
Boulder, Colorado 80306
An art magazine.

Dial-A-Poem Records
Giorno Poetry Systems
222 Bowery
New York, N.Y. 10012
An interesting series of spoken art records which include John Cage, Philip Glass, Laurie Anderson, Meredith Monk, and others.

Ear Magazine
99 Prince St.
New York, N.Y. 10012
A periodical devoted to experimental arts.

Edizioni Suvini Zerboni
c/o MCA Music
445 Park Ave.
New York, N.Y. 10022

Elkan-Vogel/Theodore Presser Co.
Bryan Mawr, Pa. 19010

European American Music
195 Allwood Road
Clifton, N.J. 07012
A major American distributor of both European and American publications and recordings.

Experimental Intermedia Foundation
224 Centre St.
New York, N.Y. 10013
Presenting performances of experimental work in the arts.

Experimental Music Catalogue
c/o Gavin Bryars
208 Ladbroke Grove
London, W-10 England
Many interesting anthologies of British experimental music.

Carl Fischer, Inc.
62 Cooper Square
New York, N.Y. 10003

Harold Flammer
Delaware Water Gap, Pa. 18327

Franklin Furnace
112 Franklin St.
New York, N.Y. 10013
Performances, exhibitions, publications.

Gàlaxy Music Corp.
2121 Broadway
New York, N.Y. 10023

John Gibson Gallery
392 West Broadway
New York, N.Y. 10012
Represents several performance artists.

Linda Goldman Concert Management
142 West End Ave.
New York, N.Y. 10023

Greene Street Music Co.
354 Van Duzer Ave.
Staten Island, N.Y.
Electronic music and devices.

Interval
P.O. Box 2087
La Jolla, Calif. 92102
Newsletter on microtonal music.

Journal of Experimental Aesthetics
see Aesthetic Research Centre of Canada

The Kitchen
484 Broome St.
New York, N.Y. 10013
Presents many performances of new music.

KLS Management
250 West 14th St.
New York, N.Y. 10011

Lingua Press
P.O. Box 1192
La Jolla, Calif. 92038
  *Music of Kenneth Gaburo, Harley Gaber,
  and others. Very interesting catalogue.*

Lovely Music
463 West St.
New York, N.Y. 10014
  *Interesting series of recordings of new
  music.*

Margun Music, Inc.
167 Dudley Rd.
Newton Centre, Mass. 02159
  Publisher of new music.

Media Press
Box 895
Champaign, Ill. 61820
  *Very broad and diverse catalogue of new
  music.*

Natural Sound Workshop, Inc.
c/o Sheldon Soffer Management
130 West 56th St.
New York, N.Y. 10019

New Music Distribution Service
500 Broadway
New York, N.Y. 10012
  *One of the best sources of recordings
  of experimental music and contemporary
  jazz.*

New Music News
see Composers' Forum

New Wilderness Foundation
365 West End Ave.
New York, N.Y. 10024
  Many good publications and recordings.

One Ten Records
110 Chambers St.
New York, N.Y. 10007
  *International Catalogue and distribution
  of audio art.*

Open Loop Records
P.O. Box 704
Islington, Mass. 02090
  Distributor of new music records.

Will Parsons
P.O. Box 2655
La Jolla, Calif.
  *Publisher of Music for Citizens Band,
  other music, and records.*

Performance Art Magazine
P.O. Box 858
Peter Stuyvesant Station
New York, N.Y. 10009

Perspectives of New Music
Bard College
Annandale-on-Hudson, N.Y. 12504
  *Back issues contain some important
  articles on new music.*

C. F. Peters Corp.
373 Park Ave South
New York, N.Y. 10016
  Very large catalogue of new music.

Pieces Press
Michael Byron
75 Leonard St.
New York, N.Y. 10013
  Several good anthologies of new music.

Theodore Presser Co.
Bryan Mawr, Pa. 19010

Printed Editions
P.O. Box 26
West Glover, Vt. 05875
  *Writings and music by John Cage,
  Philip Corner, Dick Higgins,
  Allison Knowles, Pauline Oliveros,
  and others.*

Public Access Synthesizer Studio
16 West 22nd St.
New York, N.Y. 10011

Jaap Rietman Art Books
157 Spring St.
New York, N.Y. 10012
  *A good source of journals, books,
  and out-of-print material in
  the arts.*

RK Editions
P.O. Box 73
Canal St. Station
New York, N.Y. 10013

Editions Salabert
see G. Schirmer

Samaya Foundation
75 Leonard St.
New York, N.Y. 10013
  *Center for the arts and ritual
  aspects of Tibetan Buddhism.
  Seminars with such musicians as
  Philip Corner, Pauline Oliveros,
  Alison Knowles, and others.*

G. Schirmer, Inc.
866 Third Ave.
New York, N.Y. 10022

Seesaw Music Corp.
1966 Broadway
New York, N.Y. 10023
  *Publisher of younger and less
  established composers.*

Shawnee Press
Delaware Water Gap, Pa. 18327

Smith Publications
1012 Wilmington Ave.
Baltimore, Md. 21223
  *Small and attractive catalogue
  of new music.*

Something Else Press
see Bookslinger

Sonnabend Gallery
420 West Broadway
New York, N.Y. 10012
  *Representative of several
  performance artists.*

Soundings
Apt. 216E
4202 Cathedral N.W.
Washington, D.C. 20016

Source Magazine
see Composer/Performer Edition

Studio International
14 West Central St.
London WC1A 1Jh
  *A good English art magazine that
  also deals with experimental music.*

Two Eighteen Press
Box 218
Village Station
New York, N.Y. 10014
  Tom Johnson's music.

Universal Edition, Ltd.
2/3 Farnham Street, Dean St.
London W1V 4DU, England
(Order music from European
American Music)
  Major catalogue of contemporary music.

Unpublished Editions
see Printed Editions

Vital Records
see Lovely Music

Wergo Records
see European American Music
  *German recording company with
  a very interesting catalogue.*

Women's Work
c/o Annea Lockwood
Music Department
Hunter College
New York, N.Y. 10021
  *A periodical devoted to experimental
  work by women artists.*

Selected Bibliography

APPLETON, Jon, and PERERA, Ronald, eds. *The Development and Practice of Electronic Music.* Englewood Cliffs, N.J.: Prentice-Hall, 1974.

BRECHT, George. *Chance Imagery.* New York: Something Else Press, 1966.

BUSONI, Ferruccio; DEBUSSY, Claude; IVES, Charles. *Three Classics in the Aesthetic of Music.* New York: Dover Publications, 1962.

BYRON, Michael, ed. *Pieces: An Anthology.* Vancouver, B.C.: Aesthetic Research Centre, 1976.

CAGE, John. *Silence.* Cambridge, Mass.: M.I.T. Press, 1961

_____. *A Year from Monday.* Middletown, Conn.: Wesleyan University Press, 1967.

_____. *M: Writings '67-'72.* Middletown, Conn.: Wesleyan University Press, 1973.

_____. *Empty Words: Writings '73-'78.* Middletown, Conn: Wesleyan University Press, 1979.

_____. *Writings Through Finnegans Wake.* Tulsa, Okla.: University of Tulsa Press, 1978.

CARDEW, Cornelius. *Scratch Music.* Cambridge, Mass.: M.I.T. Press, 1974.

_____. *Stockhausen Serves Imperialism.* London: Latimer New Directions, 1974.

CHASE, Gilbert. *America's Music.* New York: McGraw-Hill, 1966.

COPE, David. *New Directions in Music.* 2nd Ed. Dubuque, Iowa: Wm. C. Brown, 1976.

_____. *New Music Composition.* New York: Schirmer Books, 1977.

Ernst, David. *The Evolution of Electronic Music.* New York: Schirmer Books, 1977.

FULLER, R. Buckminster. *Operating Manual for Spaceship Earth.* Carbondale, Ill.: Southern Illinois University Press, 1970.

GRAYSON, John, ed. *Sound Sculpture.* Vancouver, B.C.: Aesthetic Research Centre, 1975.

_____. *Environments of Musical Sculpture You Can Build.* Vancouver, B.C.: Aesthetic Research Centre, 1976.

HALPRIN, Lawrence. *The RSVP Cycles: Creative Processes in the Human Environment.* New York: George Braziller, 1969.

HAMEL, Peter Michael. *Through Music to the Self.* Berkeley, Calif.: Shambhala, 1979.

HENDRICKS, Geoffrey. *Between Two Points.* West Glover, Vt.: Printed Editions, 1976.

HIGGINS, Dick. *Foew&ombwhnw.* New York: Something Else Press, 1969.

_____. *A Dialectic of Centuries: Notes Towards a Theory of the New Arts,* 2nd ed. West Glover, Vt.: Printed Editions, 1979.

JOHNSON, Tom. *Private Pieces: Piano Music for Self-Entertainment.* New York: Two-Eighteen Press, 1967.

_____. *Imaginary Music.* New York: Two-Eighteen Press, 1974.

KAPROW, Allan. *Assemblage, Environments and Happenings.* New York: Abrams, 1966.

KNOWLES, Alison. *By Alison Knowles.* New York: Something Else Press, 1965.

_____. *More By Alison Knowles.* New York: Unpublished Editions, 1976.

KOSTELANETZ, Richard. *The Theatre of Mixed Means.* New York: Dail Press, 1968.

_____, ed. *John Cage.* New York: RK Editions, 1970.

_____, ed. *Esthetics Contemporary.* Buffalo, N.Y.: Prometheus Books, 1978.

_____, ed. *Text-Sound Text: North America.* New York: William Morrow, 1980.

_____, ed. *Scenarios: Scripts to Perform.* New York: Assembling Press, 1981.

LUCIER, Alvin, and SIMON, Douglass. *Chambers: Scores by Alvin Lucier.* Middletown, Conn.: Wesleyan University Press, 1980.

MAC LOW, Jackson. *The Pronouns—A Collection of 40 Dances—For the Dancers,* 3rd ed. West Glover, Vt.: Printed Editions, n.d.

MAUE, Kenneth. *Water in the Lake.* New York: Harper & Row, 1979.

MONTANO, Linda, ed. *Pauline's Proverbs.* West Glover, Vt.: Printed Editions, 1977.

NYMAN, Michael. *Experimental Music.* New York: Schimer Books, 1974.

OLIVEROS, Pauline. *Software for People* (To be published by Printed Editions in 1980).

PARTCH, Harry. *Genesis of a Music.* New York: Da Capo Press, 1973.

RECK, David. *Music of the Whole Earth.* New York: Charles Scribner's Sons, 1977.

REICH, Steve. *Writings about Music.* New York: New York University Press, 1975.

ROSENBOOM, David, ed. *Biofeedback and the Arts: Results of Early Experiments.* Vancouver, B.C.: Aesthetic Research Centre, 1976.

SALZMAN, Eric. *Twentieth-Century Music: An Introduction.* Englewood Cliffs, N.J.: Prentice-Hall, 1967.

SCHAFER, R. Murray. *Creative Music Education*. New York: Schirmer Books, 1976.

———. *Tuning the World*. New York: Alfred A. Knopf, 1977.

SCHECHNER Richard. *Essays on Performance Theory 1970–76*. New York: Dramabook Specialists, 1977.

SCHWARTZ, Elliott, and CHILDS, Barney, eds. *Contemporary Composers on Contemporary Music*. New York: Holt, Rinehart and Winston, 1967.

SCHWARTZ, Elliott. *Electronic Music: a Listener's Guide*. New York: Praeger, 1975.

TOMPKINS, Calvin. *The Bride and the Bachelors*. New York: Viking Press. 1965.

VINTON, John, ed. *Dictionary of Contemporary Music*. New York: E.P. Dutton, 1974.

WELLS, Thomas. *The Technique of Electronic Music*. New York: Schirmer Books, 1980.

YOUNG, LaMonte, ed. *An Anthology of Chance Operations*. Munich: Heiner Friedrich, 1970.

YOUNG, LaMonte, and ZAZEELA, Marian. *Selected Writings*. Munich: Heiner Friedrich, 1969.

ZIMMERMANN, Walter, ed. *Desert Plants: Conversations with 23 American Musicians*. Vancouver, B.C.: Aesthetic Research Centre, 1976.

See also back issues of such periodicals as *Source, Soundings, Numus-West, die Reihe, Studio International* (particularly November, 1976), *Ear, Village Voice, Prespectives of New Music, The Composer*, and *Proceedings: American Society of University Composers* for interesting articles, reviews, and interviews by and about composers in this book and new music in general.

Index of Scores and Composers